DIVISIONS

1ST DIVISION

2D DIVISION

3D DIVISION

4TH DIVISION

5TH DIVISION

6TH DIVISION

7TH DIVISION

8TH DIVISION

26TH DIVISION

27TH DIVISION

28TH DIVISION

29TH DIVISION

30TH DIVISION

31ST DIVISION

32D DIVISION

33D DIVISION

34TH DIVISION

THE DOUGHBOYS

Also by Laurence Stallings

THE FIRST WORLD WAR: A Photographic History

WHAT PRICE GLORY? (with Maxwell Anderson)

The Doughboys

THE STORY OF

THE AEF, 1917-1918

By Laurence Stallings

MAPS BY HARRY SCOTT

HARPER & ROW, PUBLISHERS
NEW YORK,
EVANSTON,
AND LONDON

Greet Them Ever With Grateful Hearts

FIRST EDITION

D-N

LIBRARY OF CONGRESS CATALOG CARD NUMBER: 62-14547

CONTENTS

A 32-page section of illustrations follows page 214.

DIVISIONS

86TH DIVISION

87TH DIVISION

88TH DIVISION

89TH DIVISION

90TH DIVISION

91ST DIVISION

92D DIVISION

93D DIVISION

SPECIAL UNITS

SERVICES
OF SUPPLY

ADVANCE SECTION
S. O. S.

CHEMICAL
WARFARE SERVICE

DISTRICT
OF PARIS

AMBULANCE
SERVICE

RESERVE
MALLET

TANK
CORPS

RAILHEAD

A. E. F.
NORTH
RUSSIA

REGULATING STATION

DISTINCTIVE INSIGNIA
AMERICAN EXPEDITIONARY FORCES

GENERAL HEADQUARTERS

ARMIES

FIRST ARMY

SECOND ARMY

THIRD ARMY

CORPS

I CORPS

II CORPS

III CORPS

IV CORPS

V CORPS

VI CORPS

VII CORPS

VIII CORPS

IX CORPS

DIVISIONS

1ST DIVISION

2D DIVISION

3D DIVISION

4TH DIVISION

5TH DIVISION

6TH DIVISION

7TH DIVISION

8TH DIVISION

26TH DIVISION

27TH DIVISION

28TH DIVISION

29TH DIVISION

30TH DIVISION

31ST DIVISION

32D DIVISION

33D DIVISION

34TH DIVISION

DIVISIONS

35TH DIVISION

36TH DIVISION

37TH DIVISION

38TH DIVISION

40TH DIVISION

41ST DIVISION

42D DIVISION

76TH DIVISION

77TH DIVISION

78TH DIVISION

79TH DIVISION

80TH DIVISION

81ST DIVISION

82D DIVISION

83D DIVISION

84TH DIVISION

85TH DIVISION

MAPS

ACKNOWLEDGMENTS

My first obligation in writing this history is to M. S. Wyeth, Jr., of Harper & Row, who for a period of more than three years has been my guide, torturer, and friend. Another obligation is due Donald Elder for an independent reading of the text. Then there are the librarians: Mrs. Arlene Paul, Research Head, the Hoover Institution for War, Revolution, and Peace, at Stanford University; Mrs. Helen Keene, History Procurement for the Los Angeles County Library; Colonel Willard Webb, Chief of Stack and Reader Division, The Library of Congress; and Miss Margaret Fulmer, Whittier City Librarian.

I owe thanks to Oliver Jensen, editor, *American Heritage* magazine, for permission to use material from an earlier contribution on "The War to End War;" to Leo J. Bailey of Homer, New York, whose single typescript has given me much insight into the heart of the man in the ranks; and to Paul Shaffer of Whittier, California, for permission to use one of his rousing stories of life among the Doughboys.

I want also to express my special appreciation to Arthur Krock, dean of Washington correspondents, who can move bureaucratic mountains; to Colonel Arthur A. McCrary, Chief, Army Pictorial Division, Signal Corps, U.S.A.; and to Miss Norma Sherris, Chief, Photographic Branch, Office, Chief of Military History, Department of the Army.

There are thousands of others who have provided me with information over a lifetime and two wars. Chief among these is the late Colonel John W. Thomason, Jr., USMC, a graduate of both the Naval War College at Newport and the Army War College at Washington as well as an ardent student at l'Ecole de Guerre Supérieure. Then there are some great public servants I have had the privilege of serving under, such as Robert Lovett,

Air Secretary in the late Henry L. Stimson's War Secretariat; and the greatest war horse of them all, Brigadier General Merian C. Cooper, USAFR, whose letters to his father and his stories of captivity have never been published. Lastly, I wish to thank Mrs. Hope Scrogan of Whittier, copyist and critic; Larry Stallings, Stanford student, who made the preliminary sketches for the cartographer; Sally Stallings, who helped with the proofs; and Louise Stallings, bibliographer, mail orderly, and company cook.

Note

Interesting facts and general information about American divisions sent to Europe, their dates of arrival, localities from which originally raised, nicknames, casualties, commanding officers, etc., will be found in an appendix beginning on page 375. This information is based on *American Armies and Battles in Europe,* prepared by American Battle Monuments Commission (U.S. Government Printing Office, 1927 and 1938).

PROLOGUE

Why write of them at this hour? Why open the door of a room sealed off in my mind for many years? I chose to walk among these buddies of the past so that they may be remembered. There was never an official history written of them. No anthologist has brought back the full savor of their ignorance or their valor, of their ultimate skill. The gulf between the Doughboys and their sons who fought in a far more complex war is simply unfathomable. Woodrow Wilson himself seems to have set the tone for an historical limbo by his conduct when he reached Paris and the Peace Conference. Only an hour away was Château-Thierry, where a West Point lieutenant with his army of fourteen Doughboys carrying two Hotchkiss guns had dashed across the wagon bridge to begin the last-ditch defense of Paris. A right turn and a five-mile spin could have brought the President to the railroad embankment at Mézy, where Ulysses Grant McAlexander's 38th Infantry slaughtered a brigade of Prussian Grenadiers. A left turn for the same distance and Mr. Wilson would have stood by the hunting lodge in Belleau Wood. Or, proceeding north by west to Picardy, he might have been in the village square where the 1st Division opened the ball at Cantigny. Or by lunching at Verdun he could have stood on Whittlesey's bench with The Lost Battalion. But he seemed reluctant to face any of the scenes of the battles his acts had brought about, however noble his motives must have been. It was as if some camper had left a careless fire, and was loath to view the blackened stumps of a once verdant wood.

He did see some of the Doughboys. Sergeant York recalled that he was bidden to Mr. Wilson's Paris residence, arriving about the time of day when Tennessee cabin folk pull back their sweet potato from where it shoots

1

smoke through the ashes. The sergeant may have expected to be asked to pull up a chair and mind his own 'tater; but after a few minutes of condescension an aide informed him that he must be moving on, as the Wilsons were expecting guests for dinner. And so the sergeant walked back to his Paris lodgings supperless. Theodore Roosevelt would have been in the courtyard with him shooting at beer bottles. Abraham Lincoln would have invited him to share his bed, as he did that captain of the Pennsylvania Bucktails. Andrew Jackson would have made Sergeant York postmaster at Nashville on the spot, throwing some stay-at-home rascal out of office. But Mr. Wilson visited no battlefields.

The tales of the Doughboys were told by correspondents of the Richard Harding Davis tradition, Davis himself a dashing fellow with a storyteller's flair who would have been hooted out of camp by the sons of the Doughboys accustomed to reading Ernie Pyle, to seeing themselves in muddy Bill Mauldin's great cartoons. So curbed were the bits of war correspondents that Sir Philip Gibbs, ace of the English, would sprint uncurbed into print after the Armistice with a book he called *Now It Can Be Told,* which was tantamount to confessing that he had been a liar for four bloody years. It was Ernest Hemingway's contention that all the good American writers who went to war were killed before they could write anything about it, and only when the youths who survived had learned to write did the truths begin to be set down about it. But truth still seems buried in the past; it seems almost absurd now to say that the Doughboy reached for the throat of the enemy with Caesarean celerity. Yet such was the case, and Colonel Paul Malone of the 23rd U.S. Infantry, like Caesar at Pharsalus, when a Doughboy battalion broke over to the east of Belleau Wood to get at a Grenadier division where Marines were fighting for their lives, refused to discipline the battalion, saying it was unwise to check the fine spirit of fight in such troops. The Doughboy had this alacrity; and it never deserted him; though he had no heavy tanks, the premier tactical weapon of 1918. He went along with what he had, like the Chicago sergeant who made his solo entrance into a twenty-three-man concrete pillbox with a sawed-off shotgun, or the Jersey City noncom who toted a mortar shell like a log of wood as a hand grenade.

There were dozens of correspondents around the Château-Thierry bridgehead, but who among them ever described such a tent as I recall somewhere around Coulommiers, where some of us there suffered from gangrene? Valor they wrote of, yes—but never the cost of it. A lieutenant I loved would alternately emerge from his delirium to apologize for the noise he knew he must have been making; what prayerful thanks we gave when the green of his groin mercifully reached the valves of his heart and the gravediggers came for him. Seeing the backwash of the Korean War a generation later, I marvelled at the fine condition of men flown into the Naval Hospital at Oakland six days after receiving wounds which, at Coulommiers, would have meant months of agony. There were no miracle drugs, no sulpha, or antibiotics, to quiet the canvas air at Coulommiers. There was only morphine sulphate; yet such was the fellowship of those who survived that tent, I know of none who failed to rid himself of morphine's toxic baggage when he reached the solid wards. You could tell who was quitting the drug by watching the cigarettes glowing among the night lights, where some lad stretched his left arm aloft and bared a bicep nostalgic for the poison he had willed from his veins forever, as he began his withdrawal from narcotics and his acceptance of pain. "Tough, eh?" "Yeah, I think I'll ask the nurse for a goddam aspirin." The Doughboy was a humorist throughout his ordeals—a trait by which soldiers everywhere make war bearable.

My own favorite jest is the one about the carrier pigeon which arrived back at the Argonne wagons with the following message: "I'm tired carrying this damned bird!" Perhaps the writer was kinsman to the private in the 20th Vermont, which had held the line the first day at Gettysburg, who, when asked by his West Point colonel why he was chewing hardtack in ranks, could reply, "For the juice, sir. I'm very fond of the juice"; or to the Confederate prisoner at Spottsylvania Courthouse who, led back among Grant's profusion of guns, could say, "You fellers got almost as many of them guns marked U.S. as we have." The U.S. 6th Division, virtually without transport, animals and trucks, tried to reach the Argonne front before November 11, jesting as they hitched themselves to wagons in lattices like Eskimo dogs, barking and yapping, gunners serving as army mules, heehawing and kicking from time to time.

Mainly I have avoided the stories of those whose loss hurt me the most: of such as Tom Ashley of Amherst who saw only a few minutes of war; of Al Simons of Berkeley who saw a great deal more than that; of Private Capehart, who was awkward, and with whom I worked long at rifle and bayonet. But I write of young corporals and sage sergeants; of captains and majors; of pastors and rabbis and priests; of the buck privates who, without benefit of grenades, trench mortars, or tanks, plunged into machine-gun thickets to fight the War to End War and, frequently advancing beyond their own line, fell beneath the flash screens of the Maxims and the Spandaus. There are others, too—blond boys from beyond the Rhine—those who, the young Brigadier General Douglas MacArthur warned the Rainbow Division on the Ourcq River, would fight on with consummate skill if permitted to withdraw by the first wave. What was the Ourcq River? A little stream beside which the poet Joyce Kilmer died. A favorite jest in his regiment was the story of the Doughboy, wounded nearby and offered a sip of water from a field medic's scarce canteen, who could reply, "Give it to the Ourcq River; it needs it more than I do." Who was the German boy who stood in his gun pit, the only one left alive, when I got to him with the brutal Colt 45? He would have come from somewhere around Breslau and the bauxite mines, and know nothing but victories over the Russian, when the fortunes of war found him on the north bank of the Marne eager to send home the loot of Paris after the Royal Navy's blockade had given his mother a potato winter. How cruel and clever and violent he was, though he was only second-class. "Days of soldierly comradeship on the Marne," his division commander would write to some of us later on. Comradeship? Yes, in a way—a European way, ever since the Neanderthaler swarmed from Asia across the great plain of the Pleistocene past, improved his war weapons, and unaccountably turned himself into ourselves, into Homo sapiens. I suppose we are sapiens, for, as Professor Einstein said, the greatest miracle of the universe is that man is able to comprehend it; though at times it seems that Homo sapiens must soon attend a still greater miracle—when he learns to comprehend himself.

America's participation in World War I began, as the history books tell us, on April 2, 1917. Before a joint session of the Senate and the House of Representatives, attended by the justices of the Supreme Court and a gallery of distinguished spectators, President Woodrow Wilson asked the Congress of the United States for a declaration of war against Germany and her allies. Congress, composed largely of men who had little idea of what a large-scale war was like, eagerly granted his request, and the United States, after 134 years of studious disengagement from the affairs of Europe, committed itself to its first military adventure in the hemisphere which its founding fathers had left partly to avoid just such holocausts.

Goaded by greed and suspicion, the great powers of Europe had been girding for war and choosing up sides for years before it began. Yet when war came, it was a complete surprise to most Americans, and a shock to many a European as well. Both sides of the Atlantic had adjusted to an era of optimism and promise, thanks to the lunacies of such prophets as Sir Norman Angell. (Higher commanders knew that war was inevitable—two big dogs on the same street will always fight—but the politicians had retired to a collective farm—an ostrich farm.) The spark that "ignited the timbers of a rotting world" was a Bosnian assassin's bullets that killed the Archduke Francis Ferdinand, heir to the Austrian throne, with a pistol presented to him by a Serbian G-2. In the two and one-half years of slaughter that followed, the United States under Woodrow Wilson's guidance had maintained a precarious neutrality that had split asunder German-American communities and families, and created a breach in public sentiment that could be resolved only in the general enthusiasm with which the declaration was received. For a decade, the advocates of total unpreparedness had kept the country armed to the bare minimum necessary to preserve civil order and peace in neighboring Latin-American nations. The Regular Army was hardly large enough to have plugged a gap in the Western Front in Europe, the General Staff was unorganized for active warfare, there were not enough rifles to arm half the proposed army, and there were scarcely any plans on paper for providing any more. Yet Congressional leaders and an uninformed public thought that six weeks of American action would suffice to defeat the most formidable military machine ever created, and the American troops would be back home by Christmas. It took six weeks for the Draft Act to become law, and it was June before the first American soldiers set foot on French soil.

The raw American recruits who were rushed to Europe were called the Doughboys. There can be little dispute as to the derivation of the name. In Texas, U.S. Infantry along the Rio Grande were powdered white with the dust of adobe soil, and hence were called "adobes" by mounted troops. It was a short step to "dobies" and then, by metathesis, the word was Doughboys. The weight of their masses, the Allies hoped, would turn the scales, making anything less than a looter's victory implausible. The Doughboys entered the tragedy at the beginning of the fifth act, with millions of men already dead, like off-stage soldiers in a play; and they entered singing. Woodrow Wilson had given them their simple theme: Kaiser Bill was a villain and they marched to make the world safe for democracy.

The Doughboys' battlefields ranged as far as Archangel in North Russia and the Italian Piave, but they centered in France from the Swiss border to the North Sea. To treat of their endeavors in detail, it is necessary to pass over briefly the great tragedies of the Allies and their enemies that preceded them. In 1916 alone, a million men were casualties at Verdun, another million in Flanders, still another million in Brusilov's break-through on the Eastern Front. The Doughboy losses in 1918 were a sacrificial pittance by comparison with these figures, and with 1917's murders as well. Yet he held the line at the critical Marne in 1918, broke the back of Ludendorff's offensive spirit at Soissons, wiped out the four-year torment of the Saint-Mihiel salient, cracked the Saint-Quentin Canal complex of the main Hindenburg Line, destroyed the great German bastion of Blanc Mont behind Reims, fought across the rain-swollen Scheldt to give the Belgians bridgeheads to Brussels, and most notably plunged into the maze of the

Meuse-Argonne front to cut the broad highway of the Sedan-Mézières railroad network, forestalling any German hope of a last ditch at the Rhine.

The strategy of the Doughboy was never dictated by his own high commanders—who were good—but by Allied generals who had never been conspicuously successful in any offensive operations over a three-year period. It would be a gross libel to say that none of these Allied generals understood the art of war; once they were freed of the politician's stalemate on the Western Front, soldiers like Allenby at Damascus and Franchet d'Esperey in the Balkans showed themselves capable of conducting war with great strategic skill. However, the Doughboy strategy—a word coined by the Greeks to denote "the art of the general"—to seize Metz astride the Moselle, and to capture the Briey iron fields and the Saar coal basin, was vetoed by Marshal Foch at Field Marshal Haig's insistence. For reasons of European *Weltpolitik* that are not a part of this narrative, the only war the Doughboy was permitted to wage was tactical—the science of killing your enemy without getting killed yourself. Two million Doughboys reached France, most of them deficient in the basic school of the rifleman. But in the savage clinics conducted by the veteran Germans, the Doughboy progressed and by the war's end he and his generals had become superior fighters. This chronicle is mainly a delineation of the Doughboy: what he was, how he looked, and with what arms and over what fields he fought.

I sing not so much of arms, which the Doughboy mainly borrowed, as of the man himself, conscious of being unable to summon him back in entirety, and heartsick of enduring the melancholy of trying to recover long-buried remembrances of things past, of those who, in the phrase of Captain Cyril Falls, "were denied long life." I have avoided, too, as much as possible, the traits of the professional historians, who would instantly recognize me for an armchair impostor; but I must occasionally sketch the big picture, and can only hope that readers will find my chronicle designed to be read and remembered, and not studied. I was not long enough among the combat Doughboys—two attacks and two counterattacks, some breathless patrols, a slight wound or two before the big one when the surgeons in the sewer lifted the blanket and Colonel Neville cried, "Oh, Laurence, your fighting days are over!" I have my Idaho willow foot to remind me now, but at the time I could not share my colonel's anguish over the loss of another of his few remaining young officers. I was thinking of the blood that dripped upon my face from the boy above me in the Tin Lizzie on the jolting ride from Lucy-le-Bocage to Coulommiers. "I'm going to be blind for life, sir," he said. "But I'm glad you threw me into the shell hole and shouted, '*Stay there!*' " I still do not know who he was, with his face an arabesque of crimson torment in the split second I had time to look at it as the first wave swept on. . . .

But, unlike Frederick the Great's mule, who had attended as many battles as the king and had yet learned nothing of war, I must have learned a great deal one way or another; notably learned field intelligence from a limping Major Lucas of the Black Watch; machine guns from a First Lieutenant Gates present at the Canadians' immortal Vimy Ridge, where he breathed out much lung tissue; barbed wire and digging from a pukka-sahib Lieutenant Dimmock of the English; open warfare from West Point instructors in the Anniston maneuvers of boyhood days in the National Guard; above all, learned war from the senior Marine officers and Leatherneck rifle coaches and artillerymen who thought of war in entirely different terms— even though all of these men, from the then Colonel Lejeune to Major Lucas, held to the same basic principles, as did the veteran Germans who completed our education. The Doughboy's War, like all others, was a matter for laughter and tears, and of thoughts sometimes too deep for tears. . . . The antique Roman of his great Republic signed off his letters with *"Cura ut valeas!"* O America, see to it that you too are strong!

PART I ★ JUNE, 1917—JUNE, 1918

Build-up

Chapter 1

THE FIRST ARRIVALS

Nous voilà, Lafayette!

Few great moments in American history have been as inconspicuous as the arrival of the first of the Americans in France. They came ashore at ten o'clock on the sunny morning of June 13, 1917, at Boulogne-sur-Mer, a pleasant resort on the English Channel, to break forever with the tradition of George Washington's Farewell Address. There was no fanfare about their arrival. They had crossed from England by Channel steamer, heavily escorted against German submarines. The group numbered 177 generals, colonels, majors, captains, sergeants, and included few riflemen. They were led by Major General John J. Pershing.

Paris was some 175 miles away to the east, the Germans about seventy miles northeast of Paris behind the Aisne River above Soissons. The big brass hats were awaiting Pershing and his handful of men at Paris, and had sent their emissaries to meet the Doughboys. Marshal Joseph Jacques Césaire Joffre, the washed-up hero of the 1914 resistance to the German drive for Paris, had sent along a Major Thouzellier because he was one of three officers he now commanded, having honors galore, but no authority. General Henri Philippe Pétain, hero of Verdun, where the French had lost 550,000 men in 1916, and now field commander, was represented by a feisty Brigadier General Pierre-Georges Duport. Major General Dumas, commanding the French Army to the north, intent with the British upon keeping the Germans away from Calais and its sister seaport, Boulogne, was present as a courtesy. The President of the Republic sent Under Secre-

11

tary of War Bénard. The British, who were presently to vie with the French for the services of the Doughboys, saw to it that Major General Pershing would be greeted by an old China friend, Lieutenant General Fowke, Adjutant General of the British Expeditionary Forces. The French Navy was represented by Admiral Ronarc'h, who had led a doomed naval division of French Marines in the slaughter at Mons in 1914. France had added a gracious personal touch: Colonel Jacques Adelbert de Chambrun, lineal descendant of Lafayette, and himself and all his tribe in perpetuity American citizens by Act of the United States Congress, presented himself to be Pershing's personal aide for the duration. The welcoming committee was completed by the French liaison officer, an old boy with a breast emblazoned with ribbons; and proving that these were not all honorary, Brigadier General Peltier had an empty sleeve tucked into the Sam Browne belt above his sword knot. This was the tally on the pier at Boulogne-sur-Mer, together with the mayor, a wide sash about his frock coat, and some town worthies who foresaw a swelling business in shops, brothels, and saloons.

Some heels were clicked, hands touched to visors, and the party set out to tour the city. Boulogne-sur-Mer had an old fort on the heights above the lower town. Then there was a bell tower to admire, and an *hôtel de ville,* where some light refreshments were served around noon. One historical monument had been carefully skirted: it was a column to Napoleon, who a century before at Boulogne fondly gazed across the Channel toward the white cliffs of Dover.

After the rounds were finished, the party boarded the train for Paris. As the locomotive cheeped its way through some of the loveliest countryside in the world, the Doughboys, being heavy with wine, unbuttoned the torturous collar of the 1917 blouse and, loosening their shoes, promptly went to sleep. Pershing had been provided with a compartment. Being a practical man, he pulled off his boots, shucked his fashion-plate uniform, and went to bed. All ranks and grades were aroused in time to alight at Paris in full uniform, where the populace had also been alerted, by newspaper extras, exactly at the let-out hour. The first man in the welcoming committee was M. Paul Painlevé, Minister of War, soon to become Prime Minister and, soon after that, to be thrown out of office by a man the French called *Le Tigre,* Georges Clemenceau, a formidable old pirate indeed. Marshal Joffre was there on the station platform, a robust mustachioed old figurehead, immensely sympathetic to Pershing and, with equal immensity, unable to comprehend what the First of the Doughboys had in mind. There was a celebrated War College professor of strategy—something of an eccentric—on the platform: Major General Ferdinand Foch, Chief of the General Staff, who would presently, when similar disasters finally drove the British and the French together, become a Marshal of France and Generalissimo of the Allied Forces.

Paris had long since lost its gaiety. Three years of grinding sacrifices, every house wet with a mother's tears, dark with a widow's weeds, aching with a sweetheart's eternity of loneliness, had left the city as insipid to the French as a tale without love, or a ham without truffles. Yet the people gathered to see the long-awaited Yanks. With difficulty the automobile carrying Pershing and M. Painlevé made its way through the crowds to the Place de la Concorde and the great façade of the Hotel Crillon. Those who had not been able to touch the automobiles of the cavalcade, who had been unable to glimpse the Americans, filled the Place de la Concorde to the point where, like sardines in a can, there could be no more shoving. Pershing again and again had to make an appearance upon a balcony, perhaps as no other man in history feeling his own inadequacy, his own helplessness in delivering, immediately, what the French people had led themselves to expect, a mighty army with American banners hurling the Germans back to the Rhine.

Two weeks later, June 28, 1917, fourteen thousand American fighting men came ashore at Saint-Nazaire. They were thirteen thousand combat troops of the Regular Army—the Doughboys destined for the 1st Division —and a detached battalion of the 5th Marine Regiment. The "Regulars" stood at attention in campaign hats, neck-choking collars that permitted no rolls of fat, breeches tailored for a gymnast's knees, leggings pipe-clayed and fitted to the calf, blouses with patch pockets that would hardly accommodate a pack of cigarettes. (Whatever talents the West Pointers who designed this smart uniform may have had, consideration of comfort or serviceability was not among them.)

Pershing, on the docks to greet them, observed that two-thirds of the infantry hastily formed into battalions were raw recruits. "They are sturdy rookies," he said after running a practiced eye over them where they stood stiff-legged and blinking after having bunked in shifts aboard overcrowded transports, sleepless through the submarine zone. "We shall make great soldiers of them," he told his friend and roving observer, Major Frederick Palmer, war correspondent turned soldier for the duration.

As they stood that first morning on the docks at Saint-Nazaire they looked exactly what they were: boys from all over America who had volunteered, enlisting in the Regular Army the instant war was declared, shipping overseas before learning to wear, or even physically fill out, their constraining uniforms. The slight leavening of seasoned troops among the infantry battalions—even these ill-spared from the vast task of training millions of civilian soldiers at home—would have their hands full working the rookies up to parade-ground decorum before showing the flag to the French. It was Pershing's wish to hold these battalions in the obscurity of a training area until they were ready. Instead, the French began making demands that the Doughboys show the flag at once to the citizens of Paris. Pershing, through a long military life always known as a well-nigh intractable man, could not refuse it. Six days later, on July 4, in the 141st year of our independence, not yet recovered from their ocean passage, a battalion of the 16th U.S. Infantry, two-thirds "sturdy rookies," stood in the courtyard of the Invalides at Paris, facing a battalion of French poilus who had been fighting a war for thirty-two months.

The French soldier was bearded and warlike in a coat of horizon blue, with swept-back skirts revealing baggy breeches and spiral gaiters. His trench helmet, with a *chic* traditionally French, was also horizon blue, of light steel, curving from forehead to nape of neck in a graceful arc. On the left sleeve he wore short horizontal stripes, one for every six months he had spent in the zone of fire. Many Doughboys of the 16th's Battalion, staring across at the poilus in the courtyard that July 4, would encounter such men later on lying face to the sky, the life drained from them.

On this day M. Raymond Poincaré, President of the French Republic, was thinking of the exhilarating effect these Americans would have upon the weary people of France when they marched from the Invalides to Picpus Cemetery, where their commanding general would lay a wreath upon the grave of Lafayette. Joffre and Foch, their war dogs about them, were thinking nothing of the sort, and Pershing realized it; if these were American Regulars, what in God's name would their new civilian armies look like? They had seen how the British, after losing the flower of their Regular Army in Flanders in 1914, had needed two long years to build up the civilian army they lost in 1916 on the Somme. The very day the Doughboys arrived at Saint-Nazaire the British had lost three thousand seasoned men. Pétain, after seeing these big Yanks, now wanted a half-million of them in battalions led by French officers, fighting alongside the poilus until they too showed that indefinable quality of battleworthy veterans who had managed to stay alive. But these problems plagued only the minds of the professional soldiers, and while Pershing would long suffer their consequences in his relations with his Allied colleagues this day belonged to the Doughboys and the citizens of Paris.

Before the Doughboys began their five-mile march, Pershing entered the Invalides and looked down upon the sarcophagus of Napoleon; he was offered Napoleon's sword to kiss; he strode silently around the glories of the past, tortured by the prospect of the future. His embarrassment over the raw rookies was soon relieved; they began their parade, after suitable ruffles and flourishes by trumpeters of the French *clique,* the blare of their own regiment's brass band, and were immediately engulfed in a sea of ecstasy. It mattered little whether a buck private tried to hold his unfamiliar Springfield at the proper dress for right-shoulder-arms; whether he had two left feet; whether he permitted his eyes to wander. The men of the 16th U.S. Infantry were a spawn of campaign hats garlanded with wreaths, bobbing in a sea of French crowds, flower-pelted, lipstick-smeared, cologne-drenched. Here were the Doughboys; they were big, they were young, and there were millions more of them coming over from the richest nation on earth. At this moment it mattered little that Pétain and his practiced captains knew that the nation these men represented was wholly unprepared for any war whatsoever, possessing no ships to ferry such raw millions through three thousand miles of an ocean infested with German submarines threatening their British allies with starvation. "The column as it moved forward," said Pershing, "looked like a moving flower garden."

There were as many things to see in the parade as there were marchers and onlookers. The regimental chaplain of the 16th Infantry saw many women in black weeping as the moving garden passed on. They came out to the Doughboys with fine handkerchiefs and, as the men moved along, wiped the sweat from foreheads burdened by garlanded campaign hats. The chaplain thought of Veronica, who, some nineteen centuries before, had broken ranks at Jerusalem to wipe the blood from a brow crowned with thorns, when her Savior moved forward, His face set toward the distant Hill of Skulls.

At the cemetery, standing before the chaste marble tomb of Marie Joseph Paul Yves Roch Gilbert du Motier Marquis de Lafayette, Pershing, a man of few words, determined to say none. Instead, he delegated an old friend, Colonel (then Captain) C. E. Stanton, who was "good on his feet," to say a few well-chosen words. While mounted men of the Garde Mobile and French gendarmes struggled to hold the crowd beyond the iron gates, Captain Stanton stepped forward and saluted and cried: *"Nous voilà, Lafayette!"* The French brass, sticklers for military protocol, insisted that the commanding general say something. He could well have said, *"Où est le lavabo?"* for all it mattered in the weeping, shouting, laughing maelstrom.

Thirteen years later, when Pershing wrote his memoirs, he could not recall what he had said, but believed it had been appropriate; but he knew at tombside that Stanton had created a slogan which could not be improved upon. It would be repeated by thirty-five million French and at home bring tens of thousands of "sturdy rookies" into recruiting stations where doctors held stethoscopes over young hearts beating to the rhythm of "Lafayette, we are here!" Many months later, that battalion of the 16th U.S. Infantry, shredded after severe fighting, would sing out to the upcoming Doughboys relieving them: "We've paid our debt to Lafayette; who the hell do we owe now?"

But on this magnificent note the parade ended. The glorious day was over. The men were marched back to the battalion collecting area at the Caserne de Reuilly, and were given leave to see the historic sights of Paris until evening. That night they entrained for Lorraine and the serious business of training, and Paris went back to its widow's weeds but with new hope. It would be some time before the world would know if the hope was justified.

The American Army staff officers, lodged in the Crillon to be briefed on the Allies' situation, knew of the Great War only by indirect means; for Mr. Wilson's tacit injunction against Army interest in the conflict left them far less posted on these military matters than, say, a backwoods doctor patching cuts in a lumber camp might know of medical progress in the great clinics of Christendom. At least the village sawbones had his medical journals and monographs dedicated to truth. The men in the Crillon knew only what was published in the newspapers. No one who believes in a free press wants to say that front-page war bulletins of 1915-16-17 were mainly a tissue of lies, but such was the censorship in Europe that they were all tinged with mendacity. A correspondent had to sugar-coat the bitter medicine of colossal blunders, coloring his dispatches with falsehoods, if he wished to witness the horrors of the Western Front. The men in the Crillon knew that all Europe had soon gone to war following the murder of an Austrian archduke in July, 1914. They had followed as best they could the instant surge of Germans through neutral Belgium in an effort to seize Paris between pincers and capture it from the south.

There had been five great progressions in the Battle of France—in August, September, October, and November of 1914. The Germans had tried to swing a two-million-man gate on Paris, the hinge around the fortified area at Metz, the latchstrings at the Belgian gatepost of Liège. The first movement was the Battle of the Frontiers, when an obscure general named Gérard Mathieu Leman, who held the Liège forts at enormous cost, checked the Germans who were rushing toward the plains of Flanders until an equally obscure major general named Erich Ludendorff brought up Mörser 42 cm. siege guns and destroyed him. The prime mover in this surge was General Alexander von Kluck; among the shocks he received was the great stand by the British Army and French elements including Admiral

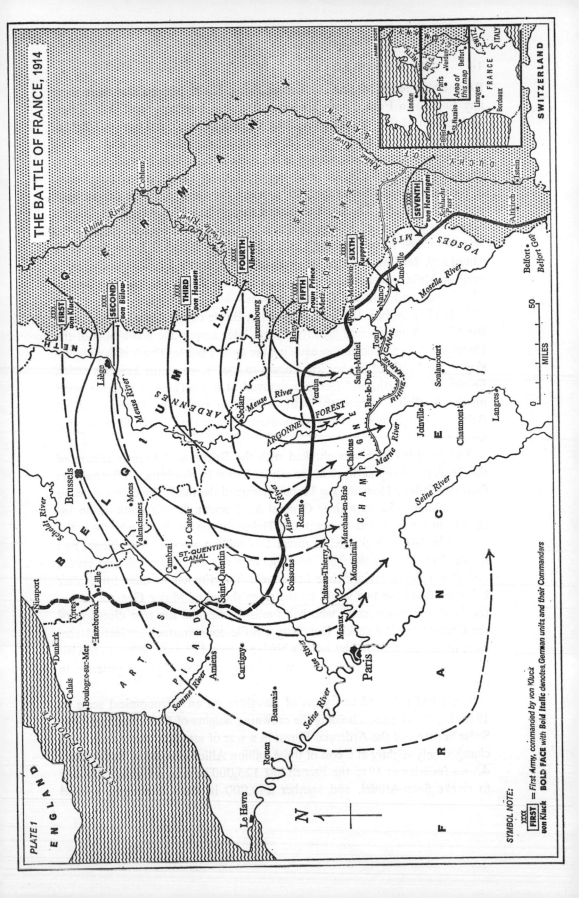

THE BATTLE OF FRANCE, 1914

PLATE 1

SYMBOL NOTE:

XXX
FIRST = First Army, commanded by von Klučí
von Klučí   BOLD FACE with Bold Italic denotes German units and their Commanders

Ronarc'h's French Marine Division at Mons. Kluck had no idea there were any English in France until his forward troops ran into them. His Kaiser had spoken of the "contemptible little English Army," and the four British divisions he faced set the tone for British courage for four years.

The second movement, known as the First Battle of the Marne, one of the greatest of European fights, involving upwards of three million men, came to a climax in early September, 1914, when the Germans were driven back just north of Paris. The tide was turned there when Major General Joseph-Simon Galiéni rushed a corps by Paris taxicabs into a breach, creating the first motorized force in history, and when Major General Louis Ernest de Maud'huy, leading a corps in Franchet d'Esperey's French Army, by a perilous night attack seized some high ground above the rail junction of Montmirail and split the German masses.

In late September, 1914, came the First Battle of the Aisne, where, as on the Marne, Yanks would fight four years later among the chalk hills of the Champagne on a scale almost equaling the earlier battle. The fourth progression in the Battle of France was known as the "Race to the Sea," in which French and British, and Germans, moved at a snail's pace to seize ports on the English Channel, the battle ending in early October with all of Belgium's coast save a narrow strip above French Dunkirk in German possession.

The great invasion was checked with the British and French seizure of the Belgian railway network at the city of Ypres in November. Why had the Germans failed? How had the French stemmed the tide? The Germans were stopped mainly because their General Staff under the direction of an insignificant nephew and namesake of Helmuth von Moltke—who beat the French in 1870—had tried to direct two million men from Coblenz, two hundred miles from the fight. And this in a day when wireless was crude, and staff officers mainly rode horseback. The French in their turn, after being confused for two weeks by the sluggishness of Major General Joffre, their over-all commander, who had foolishly misread the true direction of the German tactical shock, launching a futile counterattack against Alsace, were finally coordinated by Joffre's bovine intrepidity once he began to visit his combat units, where he unceremoniously sacked fifty-two generals in ten days.

There had followed two years of slaughter on an astronomical scale in 1915-16, the Germans holding the crowning heights of France between the Swiss border and the Ardennes Forest in a war of attrition where lines were changed only slightly at a cost of three million Allied casualties. In the murderous futilities of 1915 the French lost 125,000 men in a fruitless attempt to retake Saint-Mihiel, and another 240,000 in the Champagne around

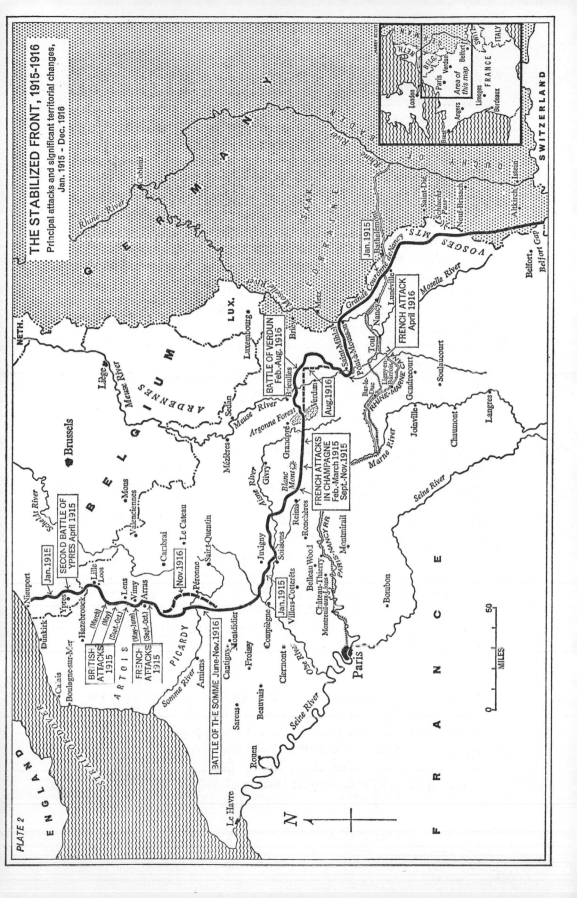

PLATE 2

THE STABILIZED FRONT, 1915-1916
Principal attacks and significant territorial changes,
Jan. 1915 – Dec. 1916

N

ENGLAND

Le Havre

Rouen

Beauvais

Sareus

Amiens

PICARDY

Somme River

ARTOIS

Boulogne-sur-Mer

Calais

Dunkirk

Nieuport

Jan. 1915

SECOND BATTLE OF
YPRES April 1915

Ypres

Lille

Loos

(March)

(May)

BRITISH
ATTACKS
1915

(Sept.-Oct.)

Hazebrouck

Lens

Vimy

Arras

(May-June)

(Sept.-Oct.)

FRENCH
ATTACKS
1915

BATTLE OF THE SOMME June-Nov.1916

Péronne

Nov.1916

Saint-Quentin

Cambrai

Le Cateau

Valenciennes

Mons

Liège

BELGIUM

Brussels

Schelt River

Meuse River

Mézières

Sedan

ARDENNES

LUX.

Luxembourg

Montdidier

Clermont

Froissy

Ose Rive

Compiègne

Juvigny

Soissons

Aisne River

Givry

Blanc
Mont

Grandpré

Argonne Forest

Meuse River

Reims

Roncières

Villers-Cotterêts

Belleau Wood

Château-Thierry

Montreuil-aux-Lions

PARIS-NANCY R.R

Montmirail

Bombon

Paris

Seine River

Seine River

Marne River

FRENCH ATTACKS
IN CHAMPAGNE
Feb.-March 1915
Sept.-Nov.1915

Jan.1915

BATTLE OF VERDUN
Feb.-Aug. 1916

Brieulles

Verdun

Aug.1916

Saint-Mihiel

Pont-à-Mousson

Briey

Metz

SAAR

Moselle River

Toul

Nancy

Lunéville

Bar-le-
Duc

Ligny-en-
Barrois

RHINE–MARNE CA

Gondrecourt

Soulaucourt

Joinville

Chaumont

Langres

FRENCH ATTACK
April 1916

Grande Couronne de Nancy

Jan. 1915

Bathelémont

Saint-Dié

Schlucht
Pass

Neuf-Brisach

Altkirch

Thann

Belfort

Belfort Gap

VOSGES MTS

FRANCE

GERMANY

Rhine River

Coblenz

Moselle River

Meuse River

NETH.

SWITZERLAND

MILES

0   50

HARRY SCOTT

NETH.

BEL.

London

Paris

Verdun

Area of
this map

FRANCE

Angers

Limoges

Bordeaux

Brest

GER.

LUX.

SWITZ.

ITALY

Belfort

Reims. The British in their turn sent men forward bare of armor in three attacks that year around Vimy Ridge and Loos in Flanders, destroying what was left of their trained fabric and most of the new volunteers.

The American Army staff officers knew all this. They also knew that, in 1916, the two great battles had been at Verdun in Lorraine—February 21 to July 11—and on the Somme in Picardy—July 1 to November 13. At Verdun, in a German effort to break through the forts there and destroy all French will to fight, the forces of the Kaiser had lost 434,000 men, the French 542,000 resisting them. On the Somme, the British threw away their new armies, the flower of their youth, sustaining 420,000 casualties. In their turn, the British caused the Germans to lose 650,000 men, among them the most practiced captains and sergeants in Europe.

On any map smaller than a billiard table, the changes effected in the battle line from Switzerland to the North Sea would show as no more than two blotches made by a cartographer's nicked ruler, and it was to remain substantially the same until the next great German offensive in the spring of 1918. At the moment when the American staff officers were being briefed in the Crillon, that line ran, roughly, from Nieuport on the English Channel some twenty miles above Dunkirk, south to Ypres, down through Artois and Picardy in France, across the Somme, to a point some seventy miles northeast of Paris. Then it swerved southeast to Reims in Champagne, running east through the Argonne Forest to a point just above Verdun, where the French forts still held. Here it turned almost at a right angle to run south through Lorraine for a distance of about thirty miles. This was the eastern face of the Saint-Mihiel salient, which the Germans had held effortlessly for almost three years. South of Saint-Mihiel, the line ran almost due east again for thirty miles, above the town of Toul; then it curved south through the Vosges Mountains to Switzerland, the key sectors east of Nancy being Lunéville and Belfort. Along the front were innumerable bulges and salients, and it was honeycombed on both sides with trenches, in villages that would never have appeared on a map if they had not become battlegrounds and graveyards for hundreds and thousands of fallen soldiers.

Since the American Congress had declared war on the Central Powers, April 6, 1917, the British and French, acting for the first time in concert, had launched an offensive to break through German lines and win the war. Russia had collapsed the month before and the Allies envisioned hordes of German divisions, freed from the Eastern Front, pouring into France. Their April operation was known as the Nivelle offensive. General Robert Nivelle, a great leader at Verdun, where he was field commander under Pétain, was an apostle of the flamboyant offensive, a surprise burst into the enemy lines with little artillery preparation. In the jargon of the trade it was known as the "Brusilov break-through" after its Russian originator under whom, the year before, the Slavs had lost a million men and their last hope of victory. Nivelle proposed to strike his blow in the plain of Juvincourt, north of the Aisne River in western France. Son of an English mother, Nivelle could spellbind both British and French politicians, and he persuaded Sir Douglas Haig to follow his plan, although Haig reserved the right, if the attack failed, to save his army without regard to the French. Haig was to attack with great force at Arras in Artois, to draw German divisions away from the French; Nivelle would then fling open the door a week later.

Nivelle circularized his battalion commanders, and even company captains, apprising them of secret details; and the British, always horsemen at heart, polished their boots and readied their nearly useless cavalry for a dash into open warfare. The Germans knew of Nivelle's Paris and London talks, and by raids they acquired the plans of various French battalions. They shortened their own lines, echeloned artillery and machine guns for crossfire, briefed shock brigades for counterattacks. The British lost 177,000 men in the tragic enterprise, and kept bulldogging on through the next winter until their casualties on that front totaled about half a million. Nivelle, with great *élan* and no surprise whatever, lost 180,000 men, 80,000 of them in two days. The Germans' supposed "weak point," Hurtebise Farm, became a cemetery. The gratified Germans for once gave little heed to events taking place behind French lines. Had they done so, Paris might have been theirs.

Pershing and his skeleton staff learned, bit by bit, the shocking facts of life on the Western Front. What they did not know yet was that mutiny— the ugliest word in the military vocabulary—had broken out in the French Army, infecting approximately 100,000 men in fifty-two divisions two months before the Americans stepped ashore at Boulogne. Many of the divisions were still unfit to enter an active line. Throughout sixteen army corps—three-quarters of a million men—it had been a matter of hive activity, of the humming bees might make when the queen signals her decision to take flight. There had been no wholesale slaughter of officers. A few were beaten and killed. "We will not harm you," said the French poilu, who had survived thirty-two months of war, to his lieutenant. "You have been abused as much as we have. But we will not obey you. The war must end." The mutiny had been so quietly effected that even the British did not know of it. . . . Pétain, succeeding Nivelle, had quelled it by judicious hearings, privileges, sympathy. In the end 23,385 soldiers were tried before court-martial and found guilty of "grave collective indiscipline." Of these, 412

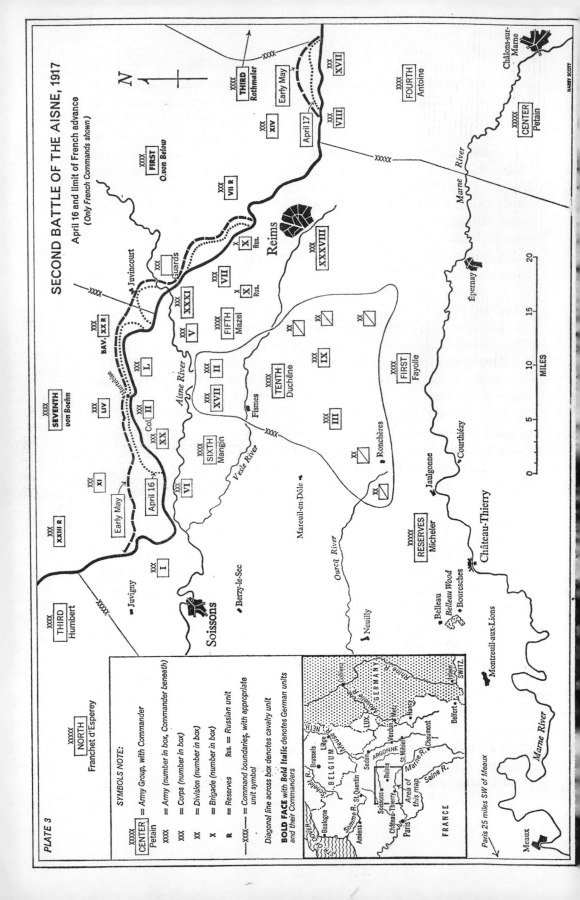

PLATE 3

SECOND BATTLE OF THE AISNE, 1917

April 16 and limit of French advance
(Only French Commands shown)

SYMBOLS NOTE:

XXXXX CENTER Petain	= Army Group, with Commander
XXXX	= Army (number in box, Commander beneath)
XXX	= Corps (number in box)
XX	= Division (number in box)
X	= Brigade (number in box)
R.	= Reserves Rus. = Russian unit
————	= Command boundaries, with appropriate unit symbol

Diagonal line across box denotes cavalry unit

BOLD FACE with **Bold Italic** denotes German units and their Commanders

HARRY SCOTT

Paris 25 miles SW of Meaux

MILES
0   5   10   15   20

were condemned to death, but only 23 are known to have been executed. (This figure does not include soldiers shot out of hand in the act of mutiny.) Among the privileges accorded were vacations; one-third of the French Army was on leave, while the British still slogged away in the desolate mud baths of Flanders. This was the situation that faced Pershing and his staff.

When the French launched their Nivelle offensive, their mission in Washington, headed by Marshal Joffre, had asked for no American troops. They did not think Americans would be trained in time to affect a situation which would find dozens of German divisions returning from the Russian front. The French only asked for all the money in the world. The British mission, with a memorandum signed by Sir William Robertson, Chief of the Imperial General Staff, and Field Marshal Sir Douglas Haig, commanding the Western Front, was more pragmatic in its requests. It formally asked that America ship to England 500,000 boys in their shirt tails, where they would be issued British uniforms and Enfield rifles and given seven weeks' training in trench warfare. They would then be given seven days' orientation in France before being sent into battle as riflemen. The request was not as lunatic as it might sound. Superiority in rifles was the only way to save the Allied war. The proposed period of training was the same the British gave their own sons before shipping them off to death or mutilation in France.

Mr. Wilson had notified the Allies his troops would fight only as an independent army, just as the King of France served notice on George Washington that French troops departing for Yorktown could not be piecemealed among the buckskin brigades. The British paid a token respect to Wilson's wishes: they promised that Yanks who survived would be formed into native battalions, and then into regiments, brigades, divisions; and eventually into an independent American Army, all ranks presumably having acquired a taste for tea as strong as battery acid, suet pudding, and beef boiled to the consistency of blotting paper. The French meanwhile had changed their minds since the mutiny. They saw no time to form an independent American Army at all. They knew that Ludendorff and Hindenburg, having destroyed the Russians, would have far better than a gambler's chance of destroying them. So the French under Major General Ferdinand Foch wanted some—not too many—token American platoons of around fifty men to revive French spirits. These would enter French lines to follow lieutenants in horizon blue, after learning about fifty words of command. The situation was desperate, the notion of an American Army a tragic delusion.

Americans can be thankful that eighteen months of entreaties from all

the great Allied figures of the day—until the last weeks when victory was assured—changed the course of the Yanks in the Crillon by not one military stride. Pershing was resolved not to send American troops into action until they were ready for it; he wanted a properly trained and equipped army of one million men, the smallest force capable of forming an effective army. He sent his request for a million Doughboys to the Secretary of War on July 6, 1917, only two days after his first battalion had received a tumultuous welcome from the people of Paris.

Chapter 2

THE EDUCATION OF PRIVATE BAILEY

We were woefully ignorant . . .

No Paris welcome awaited Private Leo J. Bailey, M Company, 9th Infantry, en route to form up the 2nd Division, when he debarked early in September. He recalled that his company of "Regulars" contained not a single man who had ever fired a Springfield rifle, and few who had ever discharged a firearm of any kind. Not many of the 250 men in his outfit possessed scabbards; and Private Bailey, wearing thin barracks shoes and canvas leggings, arrived in the village of Soulaucourt with his bayonet wrapped in a newspaper, ten rounds of live ammunition in his belt, ready to beat the German to his knees. "To have sent us to the front at that time," Bailey wrote, "would have been murder; but we were all willing to go. We were woefully ignorant of the basic principles of the soldier." Bailey was a fair example of the state of American preparedness when Pershing asked the War Department for a million men. There were 285,000 Springfield rifles on hand, about 400 clumsy field guns, and fewer than 1,500 machine guns, of four noninterchangeable types. There was enough American ammunition to support what Sir Douglas Haig would call an exploratory regimental attack for about nine hours. The aviation section of the Signal Corps possessed a few backyard airplanes—for fifty aviators, of whom five were ready for combat.

Transport and supply to the interior of France were almost nonexistent, and the French ports, jammed with troops, were a turmoil of disputes

25

between petty officials of the French National Railways and Yank majors almost rabid over red tape and delays in sending the Doughboys who had already got to training camps the scant necessities of life. Yet long before the transportation bottlenecks were broken, four divisions had taken up billets under the red-tiled roofs of villages beside small rivers and creeks that fed the Marne River. By the end of July, 1917, all the elements that were to make up the 1st Division had begun their training in villages lying around Gondrecourt and the fortress town of Langres in the rolling country-side of Lorraine south of the Saint-Mihiel salient, quiet since 1915. Every village of sad old men and women had its monument erected to the memory of sons fallen since 1914; there were no young women in the clusters of small houses attached to big barns—they were away in barracks beside the great munitions factories. But the villages swarmed with grandchildren in black smocks and wooden sabots. The Doughboys drove an entering wedge into the block of French provincialism. After they had passed out candies and chewing gum for a month, there were few unfriendly gaffers. The wineshops began a boom-town business and wartime inflation reared its head.

Following the 1st Division came the 26th Division, New Englanders of the National Guard, arriving early in September. By the end of the month a brigade of Marines had arrived and, along with an infantry brigade of the Regular Army, three artillery regiments, one of engineers, and a field signal battalion, were organized into the 2nd Division. They were followed late in October by the 42nd Division—the Rainbow—National Guards-men from twenty-six states plus a battalion of clerks from the District of Columbia. All of them were to train along the pattern laid down for the 1st Division. Being arrant individualists, not one of the other three gave a damn about the pioneer Big Red One.

Soulaucourt, on a tributary of the Marne north of Chaumont, was a vil-lage of 250 souls clustered about a granite shaft commemorating seventeen of its sons dead on the Field of Honor. Six more of its lads lay wounded in hospitals and one other, home from the wars for good, hobbled about on two sticks in the uniform of the Chasseurs Alpins, the "Blue Devils" of dark berets and circus muscles. Private Bailey's squad buddies astounded the villagers in the chill frost of the Lorraine dawn when they streamed from boxcars, stripped to the waist, and sluiced themselves at the horse trough. If this was not an indication of madness to a French villager, the sight of all hands brushing teeth with the horse-trough water, and spitting foam on the cobbles must have convinced him.

Half of Europe was represented in Bailey's company. His own squad included, besides Irishman Bailey, a corporal, American born of Jewish parents, and a Dutch immigrant named Louis van Eisel who was later to win the Medal of Honor and live to attend another great war. Then there was a boy of New England stock who got the Distinguished Service Cross for an outstanding caper at Soissons in Foch's great counterattack; a New York Italian lad from the pushcart district; a boy of English blood who had immigrated from the West Indies; and another Jewish boy, who had spent his first night in America on Ellis Island. The company was commanded by a Regular Army captain who was an immigrant from Bohemia and who must have shuddered when his company of "Regulars" was first presented to him. Three of the platoon leaders were second lieutenants, college boys with little more knowledge than Bailey, who confessed he knew nothing at all. Only the fourth platoon leader, who had been a Regular Army sergeant, knew something about soldiering, and with his captain he set about the business of training immediately.

The training was twofold and relentless. A Doughboy had to learn the formal trench warfare of the French, with emphasis upon Chauchat and Hotchkiss guns, bayonet and grenade, barbed wire and the shovel—and little attention to the rifle. Frenchmen pursued Germans in a clash of patrols by throwing grenades at them, as if the Lebel rifle possessed no trigger assembly.

But the Doughboy was never allowed to neglect the school of the rifle in open warfare, and learned marksmanship against any hillside butte that was handy. Neither the British nor the French wanted to revive an art lost when the Old Contemptibles perished; they thought exercises in minor tactics, where a rifleman did not feel isolated if he had no convenient trench to jump into, were a waste of precious time. But Pershing was unswerving and villagers saw Doughboys moving as skirmishers in condemned turnip patches and fallow fields as the rains came early to Lorraine and the Vosges Mountains, followed by early snows in the worst winter in village memories. An army had to be made, not born, in the sodden fields of France.

For weeks Bailey drilled in thin-soled shoes on plowed earth, soaked by the incessant, bone-chilling rain. For breakfast, he received a strip of bacon, two hardtack crackers, and a cup of weak coffee. At noon, after five hours of drill, the ration was repeated, with the addition of a potato boiled in its jacket. For supper, after a hard afternoon, he was given a few spoonfuls of rice and another canteen cup of weak coffee. Over these scant supplies, prepared by miserable cooks, the men merely jested—they were still too enthusiastic and green to begin griping.

Pershing would soon want a million more men, then a third and fourth million whenever it pleased the Secretary of War. The Congress that had joyously acceded to Woodrow Wilson's plea for a declaration of war had believed that America would send token forces across the sea, show the colors in a few minor *dégringolades,* then stage a spectacular victory march. Washington thought Pershing's request as mad as William Tecumseh Sherman's in 1861, when he regarded a call of 300,000 men to the Yankee colors a mere nest egg for the hatching of an eagle's brood that could restore luster to the American shield. In Europe, seasoned soldiers like Foch and Haig inclined to the belief that the American general was living in a dream, that the whole notion of a trained American Army would lead to tragic defeat; the French could never hold out while the Americans got ready, and the outflanked British would be driven into the sea. But at Soulaucourt, Private Bailey thought things would go according to Pershing's plan.

Few of the Doughboys training in French fields ever got to know John J. Pershing, though hundreds of thousands of them were lashed by those hard eyes above the set thin lips as the Iron Commander inspected them. Many went forward cursing him, but they went forward, which was what he demanded.

"U. S. Grant," says the historian Bruce Catton, "usually went about camp in a short blue coat and an old slouch hat, wearing nothing that indicated his rank, nothing indeed that even proved he was in the Army." This puzzled people because "greatness, somewhere along the line, should look like greatness." And he also says, "Grant had the Regular Army way of doing things at his finger tips, but he was always aware that the volunteer soldier was not the Regular, and he never treated Volunteers as Regular recruits were treated."

Pershing was the exact opposite. He demanded that the standards of the American Expeditionary Forces in France be those of the Corps of Cadets at West Point. He was possibly more savage to a West Pointer who failed him than he was to a Reserve officer, but he could draw blood from either without distinction. He himself was the very portrait of a soldier, and he never excused anyone from maintaining a similar standard. Doctors at an Army hospital never forgave him when they lined up at the front door, as if expecting a visit from the chairman of the board on Founder's Day: "This is an inspection, gentlemen. Go back to your posts and stand at attention."

He had three words to compliment a subordinate, and they were all the same word. When he said of a man, "He is a fine officer," it meant that he still withheld judgment. When he said, "He is a fighter," it meant that the fellow, if he stayed alive, might someday win a command. When he said, "He is a fighter . . . a fighter!" that chicken colonel was getting a little closer to brigadier. But when the accolade was "He is a fighter . . . a fighter . . . a fighter!" it was then time to go out and buy the stars.

Secretary Baker said repeatedly that he did not see how a man who had his mind so much on buttons could still have time to think about how to win a war. But for Pershing the only common meeting ground among all the soldiers he ever respected was that they would all fight. After he had gained command of two million men he retained the services of some who were slow-witted and far from the model of the soldier he himself presented because they were fighters. The man he came to admire most among the Doughboys was Acting Captain Samuel Woodfill, an ex-sergeant of the Regular Army, who wiped out five nests of German gunners singlehanded, finishing off the fifth, when he ran short of ammunition, with a pickax. To Pershing he was the outstanding figure in the A.E.F.

Pershing proposed to hammer the Doughboys into a creation after his own image and send them against the enemy in open warfare in the spring of 1919 in his own, typically American tradition.

He himself had been a Missouri plowboy and a country schoolteacher who hoped to become a circuit judge. He was the oldest of the nine children of a Missouri railroad section foreman whose grandfather had immigrated to a Pennsylvania farm from Alsace about the time when young Virginians such as George Washington were opening up routes to the prairie country beyond the Alleghenies. When Pershing was thirteen, his father was ruined when the bubble of the Missouri land boom of the seventies burst. At eighteen he was a country schoolteacher who could break a colt, plow a straight furrow, bark a squirrel with a long rifle, and put down the exuberant schoolyard bullies who had been reared in the ferment of Bleeding Kansas and the border feuds of the frontier *banditi* of Missouri.

At twenty-two he was working in a cornfield when his younger brother came out to tell him that there was to be a competition for an appointment to West Point. Despairing of ever saving enough money to read for the bar, he dropped his plow handles, and resolved to win it. Four years later he was a cavalry shavetail fighting the Apaches of the Tonto Rim, and after that chief of scouts for General Nelson A. Miles in the suppression of an uprising among the North Dakota Sioux. Still a second lieutenant at thirty-two, he arrived at the University of Nebraska to become commandant of a corps of university cadets who were little better than a shambling bunch of hay-shaking tramps. Three years later he was graduated with honors from law school, having found time to volunteer to teach a class in calculus, and turn out a corps of cadets which Army inspectors cited as second only to the Corps at West Point.

If he ever debated leaving the Army there is no record of it. (With reasonable luck a second lieutenant might hope to be retired at the age of sixty-five at three-quarters of a major's pay.) Possibly his cloud of destiny could first be observed a year later, in 1897, at Madison Square Garden in New York City, where the Indian fighter found himself sitting next to the police commissioner of the city, himself an ardent lover of the Old West. The commissioner was Theodore Roosevelt, a magnetic man who was to spend many hours in the company of the middle-aged lieutenant of cavalry who had no personal magnetism at all. Shortly thereafter, Roosevelt heard that Pershing, who was also on San Juan Hill with his Negro troop of the 10th U.S. Cavalry, was "the coolest man under fire I ever saw"—in the words of Major General F. M. B. Young, a veteran of many Civil War battles in which coolness under fire had become a staple commodity.

Frederick Palmer, the war correspondent who was Pershing's friend for years, notes, in the memorabilia he published (according to a long-standing promise) only after the general's death in 1948, that Pershing was changeless. In August, 1915, when Pershing, stationed in El Paso, received word that his wife and three little daughters had burned to death in the fire which razed the family quarters in the Presidio in San Francisco, it did not change his manner or deportment. Palmer says the only change he observed was that "Pershing no longer looked notably younger than his years. . . ."

Roosevelt followed Pershing's career through his years in the Philippines, as administrator of the Mindanao Province of fanatical Moros, a diplomat-soldier who would always negotiate with the fierce tribal chiefs but was ready to fight at the drop of a hat. As President, Roosevelt was furious that Captain Pershing, under Army rules, could not be advanced to major or colonel. He requested the Congress to make him a brigadier general, and Pershing was jumped over 882 senior officers. There was some cackling over the fact that Pershing, at the age of thirty-nine, had taken for a wife the daughter of a powerful Republican senator. But Pershing wore no man's label. In 1917, when Teddy Roosevelt beseeched Woodrow Wilson to allow him to raise a Rough Rider Division, as he had raised a regiment in the Spanish-American War, Pershing went on record against it. He had read his Civil War history and knew the abominable results of mixing politics with the military, and he wanted no such cadres among the Doughboys. The Secretary of War, Newton D. Baker, had also read his history and, unlike Lincoln's Stanton, did not engage in the usual Washington practice of keeping both front feet in the political trough.

Wilson and Baker were of a single mind in their choice of the First of the Doughboys. They wanted Teddy Roosevelt's brigadier—even after he had led a hopeless 1916 expedition into Mexico to break up the bands of Pancho Villa, who had crossed into Columbus, New Mexico, one marauding night, to slaughter the inhabitants. It was a poor task for a fighter. Pershing knew that his expedition was more diplomatic than martial and that for him it would be a face-losing chore. Two years before, Wilson had inflamed the Latin-American world with a punitive assault on the city of Vera Cruz. It would have been awkward to capture Pancho Villa, candidate for the presidency of the Republic of Mexico. Pershing knew he was supposed to fight as little as possible.

Now in 1917 he had been given the task of defeating the greatest military power in the world. Before a war begins, Rebecca West says somewhere, the plans read like astronomy, afterward, like astrology. Pershing already knew this when he came to France: a state of war was, in a word not yet invented, a state of snafu. He had stated his views on it years before as a lieutenant of cavalry in Cuba. A brother officer had been griping because the commanding general, Major General William R. Shafter, weighed 250 pounds and fought his war seated in an oversized folding chair. Pershing's friend called him "that fat old slob."

"Why did you come to this war if you can't stand the gaff?" the Missouri plowboy asked him. "War has always been this way. Did you expect to see the Old Man standing out here with a book in his hand, telling these mule skinners how to handle their outfits? The fat old man you talk about is going to win this campaign. When he does, these things will be forgotten. It's the objective that counts, not the incidents."

Newton D. Baker had said to Pershing, "I shall give you only two orders, one to go and one to return." Of the thousands of orders he was urged to cable overseas, Baker forwarded only a few suggestions. The illustrious mining engineer, Herbert Hoover, himself a birthright Quaker, had, under the auspices of the Society of Friends, fed the starving Belgians in German-occupied territory despite spirited interference from the German High Command. He had been named food administrator and his high reputation insured that his orders to conserve food need be little more than suggestions which people would willingly follow. Mr. Hoover sent his suggestions via Baker to Pershing. In effect, the Doughboys would henceforth "Hooverize"; there would be sentries on the chow lines to see that nothing was wasted. The Iron Commander read this communication and invited comment from his staff. A young officer said that he wouldn't give a damn for a Yank who couldn't have seconds if he wanted them. The hard man at the desk, who almost never smiled at the staff officers who sat stiffly on flimsy French chairs, smiled now, and threw Mr. Hoover's suggestion into the file-and-forget basket. No Doughboy ever Hooverized, though there would be days when not even cold food could reach him and he would welcome a piece of black bread from the pocket of his prisoner.

Wearing the three hats of diplomat, administrator, and fighting general, Pershing had come to France determined to forge an army in the tradition of Grant—who had no personal magnetism either—who had forged a shield for the Republic. He also had in mind that the Doughboys would leave a great General Staff and a Reserve Officers Corps as a legacy to their sons that would endure forever. Long before he could build such an army he would have to make the agonizing decision to throw green troops against the Germans.

Pershing chose Chaumont as General Headquarters for the A.E.F., a provincial town on the Marne about 150 miles east by southeast of Paris, with strategic railways from French Atlantic and Mediterranean ports unclogged by British and French logistics. Its huge quadrangle of cantonments came alive with typewriters and switchboards, some of its tenants dedicated to the yet unpromulgated "Parkinson's Law" that the more subordinates you control, the less work you get done and the swifter your promotion.

Railway transport was Pershing's first crash program. He began to work on it when he brought William W. Atterbury, General Manager of the Pennsylvania Railroad, to France, and that lifelong railroad man raided the United States for subordinates—from roundhouse hostlers to division superintendents. Washington proposed sending several army engineers to France to take over this new empire. Pershing refused to entertain the idea of some lieutenant colonel of the Corps of Engineers saying to Atterbury, "But this isn't the way we run a railroad in the Army." Instead he made Atterbury a brigadier general. If in those days there was one phrase paramount in Pershing's brimstone thesaurus, it was "To hell with the War Department." And he did not seem to regard Newton Baker, Secretary of War, as a member of the department at all. Baker seemed more the generous patron of a struggling artist of great promise than a bureaucrat; the correspondence between these two men is unlike any in the annals of American wars.

While Atterbury haggled with French officials and Regular Army men over problems of transport, a training program for all ranks was organized, a task of enormous complexity because of the size and structure of American divisions, the lack of experienced officers and specialists, and the demands of a kind of warfare Americans had never waged.

A U.S. division was immense in 1917. Where a French division was now reduced to five thousand rifles, and a British one soon shrunk to little more, a Yank outfit possessed about three times that many. From the primary group to high command, the division consisted of eight men to

a squad, seven squads to a platoon, with a platoon sergeant and a lieutenant making fifty-eight men. An infantry company was composed of
four platoons, commanded by a captain (with a headquarters detachment), numbering 250 men. Four companies made up a battalion commanded by a major. The regiment held three battalions of infantry and
one machine-gun company, commanded by a colonel. Two regiments of
infantry and one machine-gun battalion made up a brigade, and two
infantry brigades plus a third machine-gun battalion were the rifles of a
division. Thus an infantry brigadier general commanded about 250 officers
and 8,200 men. A major general of division, with his supporting elements,
controlled the lives of two infantry brigades and one artillery brigade—
two regiments of French 75s and one of 155s—plus a regiment of engineers and his own machine-gun battalion. His division also included
a field signal battalion, with sanitary and supply trains. On paper he had
at his disposal 17,666 rifles, 72 guns, 260 machine guns, 979 officers—
for a total of 27,082 human beings, over whom he held the power of life
and death on the field of battle. But due to sickness, and the absence
of officers and men detached to schools, or to special training programs,
a major general usually found himself commanding around 25,500 men.
No two-star officer had ever commanded more than a brigade, and this
in peacetime maneuvers, usually an imaginary brigade in the wheatfields
of Kansas around the staff school at Leavenworth. As the divisions poured
into France to begin their twofold training, less than 5 percent of their
officers were Regulars. Less than one percent of the captains commanding
250 men had more than a year's service.

Brigadier General Robert Lee Bullard set up infantry schools in the
Gondrecourt area, Brigadier General Peyton C. March—later Newton
Baker's hatchet man and Chief of Washington Staff—set up artillery
schools at the old French grounds at La Valdahon in the Vosges Mountains. There was a school for General Staff officers at Langres, set up
admirably by Major General James W. McAndrew, who on Pershing's
advice borrowed liberally from French and British systems. There were
schools for line officers, for noncoms, for machine gunners, for engineers,
for aviators, for caisson postilions. There was a scarcity of trained men
everywhere.

All of M Company's officers in the 9th Infantry were soon sent to
school, and Private Bailey reported that a new lieutenant was given temporary command. He was a martinet at first, but Bailey's buddies were
patient with him until he settled down. Headquarters sent up an agent,
in enlisted man's uniform, to ferret out any German sympathizers. Sergeants spotted him and saw to it that he spent most of his tour peeling

potatoes. "Would you like your spuds German-fried?" a grinning mess sergeant would ask him.

The Gondrecourt training area was in the sector of the French Armies Group of the Center, commanded by Major General Pétain. More than any other soldier, he was responsible for the French influence on trench-warfare training for the Doughboys. Each U.S. division was nominally under the direction of a French major general commanding a French corps in rear areas—whose pleas to suspend training for open warfare were disregarded. The French combat leaders—captains and sergeants—knowing that only a great army of Doughboys could save their war, went at the task with great devotion. Major General Maud'huy, when Pershing inspected the 26th Division in training, said that the troops were excellent stuff, their younger officers alert, but only one of their brigadiers, Peter Traub, ready for combat. The general, who had seized Marchais-en-Brie, crossing a river in the dead of night to split the Germans in 1914, apologized to Pershing for intruding into the division's kitchens. Frenchman Maud'huy had, understandably, a Gallic horror of the New England boiled dinner. French sergeants were now teaching Down-Easters the art of thin, delicately flavored sauces to relieve the tedium of this—to them—swill. And so Pershing ordered a school for cooks; though in the interest of accuracy, it must be said few of its graduates would win a *cordon bleu* rating in the *guide culinaire* of Escoffier.

Wherever the Iron Commander, ceaseless in touring villages, climbing ladders into barn lofts, tasting the miserable slum in the cook's kettles, saw men dispirited and slack, then some battalion or regimental commander was on his way to the rear. From Chaumont back to Bordeaux, locomotive engineers and master bakers from America were sometimes being told by Regulars that "this isn't the way we do it in the Army." For refusing to change a skill that needed a lifetime to learn, some were returned to Chaumont under charges of insubordination. It became a stock phrase in Pershing's office: "You tell that narrow-minded Regular for me to leave you alone." And around the training areas, there was another phrase: "Your men are listless and dispirited, and that is your fault. I never give an officer a second warning." Or, more often: "I don't see how you did it, Major. But your battalion shows that you have done it. My compliments to you."

In the villages, troops returning from open fields sat drenched and shivering in stables and barns on floors they had broomed until they pleased the Iron Commander's observant eye. To light a cigarette in one of these highly inflammable structures could mean long hours of tidying manure piles. One Marine major imposed a standard penalty in his battalion—an offender, with his mess-kit spoon, to the consternation of the villagers, removed a century of horse manure deposits from cobblestone crevices in the village square, and the back-breaking business of manicuring and polishing five square yards made the Leatherneck unlikely to smoke in his barn again. And there were no campfires; men simply removed their tattered garrison shoes and rubbed numb feet with a blanket's corner. Many barns bore such signs as: WELCOME TO VALLEY FORGE. BRING YOUR OWN POTATO.

Sanitary conditions drove such Medical Corps officers as Colonel Paul Mabee of the Regulars into a state bordering on manic depression; and the Parris Island drill instructor could be heard in villages two miles away from his anger. One sergeant major noted that elderly farmers on their way to work in the fields always relieved themselves against the last wall of the village—which was committing a nuisance on what the sergeant major now regarded as U.S. Government property. He set up urinals of iron pipes crowned with tin funnels, inside each a black-and-white drawing of Kaiser Wilhelm II, mustaches fluted above the spout hole. It became a fad with French grandsons. "I swear this little Marcel's got a ten-gallon tank in him." Sanitary conditions improved somewhat as shower facilities began to appear. Doughboys remodeled hundreds of washhouses where kneeling women for centuries had beaten linen white with wood battens.

The training in open warfare tactics was relentless; thin lines of skirmishers soon looked like snowmen in the fields as they alternately charged and sprawled, numb fingers working the beautifully templed bolt of the Springfield rifle. Drill settled down to eight hours a day, five days a week; but a good battalion commander wanted a platoon leader so far away from the cook shack that he could not hear the bugles blowing Recall. An experienced major might rein his horse and call a lieutenant to him as a weary platoon began its two-mile hike to supper. "Why do you stick with your men, Lieutenant? Keep two hundred yards back of them and let 'em call you the bastard I hope you've been to 'em today. Let 'em blow off steam. Then when they are rated the best platoon in their company they'll be affectionate when they start sonsabitching you. I can't make you into a brave leader, but I can teach you the art of command."

By October 21, after three months in France, the 1st Division, according to Major General de Pouydraguin, its French tutor, was ready to defend quiet trenches in the Lunéville sector. Between Lunéville and Nancy was the hilly Grande Couronne de Nancy, where Foch's (Iron) XX Corps had blunted the German drive in 1914. Pershing, on the way to inspect the division, enjoyed a gourmet's luncheon with Major General Franchet d'Esperey in one of Verdun's unconquerable forts. Franchet d'Esperey had just given the Germans a local beating in the vicinity of Verdun, as if to prove that the Italian disaster at Caporetto in the preceding month, where they had lost 250,000 prisoners and barely prevented the Austro-German team from seizing Venice and the Adriatic, was not indicative of Allied will to cease fighting. There was no shop talk by the French Army Group commander. Instead, this future marshal of France, his royalist father a godson of a French king, described at length a tour he had once made across the state of Iowa when the corn belt had been experimenting with Prohibition. The throat of Louis Félix Marie François Franchet d'Esperey became parched at the memory of his forty-eight hours without a glass of wine.

Greatly helpful to Yank commanders learning the intricacies of the French Staff, he is shown in photographs as strongly resembling Yogi Berra in face and configuration—and like that great athlete, Franchet d'Esperey could hit any pitch an opponent threw. Like Foch, he was a devout Roman Catholic and had suffered from counterpersecution after the Dreyfus Affair. French Army politics would greatly affect the lives of the Dough-boys.

The Big Red One took over a quiet sector from two of Franchet d'Es-perey's divisions. French soldiers around the long-quiet Lorraine area, how-ever much they welcomed American manpower, loathed the arrival of these eager beavers into their trenches for training. The battle lines on the right of the French front, stretching from the Vosges Mountains to Switzer-land, had been regarded as a rest sector, until all elements of the Big Red One began streaming in to learn their trade of trench war. (It was not an art.) The poilu had long since zoned in his artillery, marked the fields of enemy fire; and he was now content to smoke his pipe in the quiet evenings of the pleasant countryside, washing his underwear on sunny days. He would, if he ascended some small eminence, have little fear of snipers. Indeed, he could see the vile Boches also hanging out their washing. Each side had lost about 500,000 men the year before, around Verdun. *"C'est suffisant, Monsieur."*

In the evening it was customary to send over a few rounds of shrapnel from French 75s, with a similar compliment from German 77s, all shells aimed precisely at open fields. Few high explosives from howitzers and heavy guns shattered the peace of the evening, or the red-tile roofs of the village houses on either side of the lines. No one dreamed of hurl-ing mortar shells into comfortable, well-drained trenches. An occasional machine gun chattered in the distance, sending tracers above the heads of contented men who understood that some inspector might be visiting the other side. If Intelligence desired a raid, with a prisoner brought back for interrogation, it was understandable but deplorable. Some friend might be killed by grenade or bayonet, and a wounded enemy dragged back through gaps in barbed wire.

The arrival of *les américains* was like a sudden burst of noisy roisterers into the truce of the family fireside. Every man in the 1st Division wanted to go on a patrol, and then a raid; each wanted to kill a German, to capture one, to be the first. If not the first in the A.E.F., then he wanted to be the first in the whole damn division, or brigade, regiment, battalion, company, platoon, squad. C Battery of the 6th U.S. Field Artillery fired the first round into the Germans near the town of Xanrey in the Lunéville sector of the Lorraine front at five minutes past six o'clock of a cloudy morning, October 23, 1917. The gun was a French 75 and Sergeant Alex L. Arch pulled the lanyard, aiming at nothing in particular—just in the direction of Kaiser Wilhelm II, Emperor of the Germans. The first Doughboy wounded, as was fitting to the occasion, was a second lieutenant, D. H. Harden of the 26th U.S. Infantry Regiment; and, equally befitting, the second man on the casualty list was a buck private, one Ashburn of the 18th Infantry, wounded the following day. The first prisoner dragged back was a mail orderly, Leonard Hoffman, of the 3rd Machine Gun Company, 7th Regiment, 1st Landwehr Division, III Bavarian Army Corps. Badly wounded, he died the next day.

The French, always courteous, tutored ignorance with polite resignation, disliking these minor exercises in the barbarous curriculum of war. The Germans loathed the disturbances with great intensity. Private Hoffman's Landwehr outfit knew that Americans would not arrive in time to weight the scales of victory against them. The Landwehr were merely holding troops, sedentary lads and gaffers inured to trench warfare, while Ludendorff gave postgraduate seminars with live ammunition to 1,500,000 shock troops in rear areas to win his war in the summer of 1918. Raids were standard operating procedures to veteran troops, and raids by ignorant, pigheaded Americans had to be borne.

It was beautiful country, rolling hills and clumps of larches and poplars screening the small villages with their wisps of smoke from chimney pots —quiet, serene, unscarred by heavy warfare. The 1st Division entered deep trenches, wickered and sandbagged, with bays cut in long traverses to localize shell burst and mortar fire. All elements moved in—the four infantry regiments of the two brigades—18th on the right, then the 16th and 26th, with the 28th positioned on the left. Courtesies were exchanged in this delicate business of the night, and the 1st Battalions of all four

Doughboy regiments entered the first line. They were backed up by their own artillery, engineers, signalers. Field Hospital No. 13 staked out its gear in the rear, awaiting the few expected casualties, Ambulance Company No. 13 joining it. It was a quiet tour that late October, with leaves turning to gold and red on trees, few being shaken down by occasional cannon fire.

Across from them the Germans became curious. They brought up an Assault Company of a hundred men to study the terrain, the convolutions of wire and the fall of the ground before the village of Bathélemont, which lay along the rim of a bald hill beetling above the Rhine-Marne canal. The Assault Company was less interested in the beauty of the late autumn scene than in signals from the village of Bathélemont. These could have been in code, by some familiar device such as spacing of colored garments on washlines, the lowering or raising of a window shade, the sporadic bursts of smoke from some chimney pot where small twigs kept a pot of lentils boiling. The Assault Company, swaggering among the holding troops, awaited its hour. Some among them took out pocket whetstones and sharpened trench knives, others looked to their Bangalore torpedoes for blasting barbed wire, or blew sand from the stringed triggers of potato-masher grenades. Luger pistols were repeatedly cleaned and oiled, bayonet studs looked to.

When night fell on November 2, the Assault Company was brought into the German front line and sent to the deepest dugouts to await its hour. Someone in Bathélemont had signaled that the 1st Battalions of the Big Red One were being relieved by the 2nd Battalions. The Assault Company found itself facing the battalion which had marched to Lafayette's grave. The battalion had moved in stealthily, silently, through deep communication trenches to the fire steps of the first line. The trenches were deep, with muddied bottoms from the constant rains. The Doughboys wore the long overcoats of the peacetime army, dripping skirts and soggy shoulders. Behind them, artillery battalions changed places, engineers and signalers also in relief. By midnight the exchange had been made. It was a quiet affair, with city boys trying to become accustomed to the faint sound of the dark, country boys sleepy after the long traverse. Platoon leaders earnestly inspected lines, surveyed fields of fire. Listening posts were manned. It was all new, all exciting, all strange, despite the many practices in dummy trenches behind the lines. The division was now undergoing the first real exercise in trying to stay alive.

Exactly at three o'clock in the morning all hell broke loose. Enemy guns spoke in chorus, tons of metal descended heavily along the Yank front, communicating trenches were plastered with mortar fire, machine guns sent their whispering streams of nickeled steel over the heads of the Doughboys in the line. After a strident overture, with men for the first time knowing the bone-shaking, head-rocking effect of eight-inch mortar shells breaking nearby, the fire was concentrated, isolating in a box barrage F Company, 2nd Battalion, 16th U.S. Infantry. The box soon closed in on one platoon front. There was nothing now, on the face of the earth, which could reach this chosen platoon. The Assault Company, facing it, leaped from their trenches and started across the two hundred meters that separated Americans from Germans. Bangalore torpedoes blasted a path through the wire. The side of the box barrage nearest the Germans now vanished, the other three sides roaring with breaking shells. The platoon first knew of the Germans' presence when grenades burst among them.

It was a formal exercise along established principles, as clever and as dull as a number from a corny ballet. It was over in three dark minutes —pistols, bayonets, knives. The platoon did not blench. It fought in the dark. There was no mad rush for a communicating trench or a deep dugout. The Assault Company left on a precise time schedule, taking their own wounded, together with a Doughboy sergeant and ten men, some of them wounded, too, and all of them stunned; dragging them back through the gaps in the wire as the open side of the box barrage again was closed with forbidding shell bursts. Another three minutes, and all guns ceased. Again there were only the faint noises of the dark, the sickly sweet smell of picric acid fumes, the smoke of high explosive rolling into trenches with the cold brume of autumn dawn in Lorraine.

The platoon leader of F Company took stock now. Eleven men were missing, forty-four men still miraculously on their feet. Three men lay dead in the muddy bottom of the trench: Corporal James B. Gresham, Private Thomas F. Enright, and Private Merle D. Hay. They were buried that afternoon near Bathélemont on a little rise of pasturage. A French general of division came to the funeral, bringing with him a detachment of French gunners to raise their *fusils* for an unaccustomed volley—the French setting no great store by riflemanship—along with a detail from the battalion which had marched to Lafayette's grave.

The Big Red One was relieved from front-line duty on the night of November 20, everything having gone according to plan, with thirty-six men killed or dead of wounds, one officer and thirty-five men wounded, and the bleeding sergeant and his ten men missing from F Company of the 16th Infantry. The division had been blooded at a bargain price.

The 2nd, 26th, and 42nd Divisions, knowing they would soon undertake such exercises with live ammunition, redoubled efforts to make themselves into bodies of first-class fighting men. In the States, tens of thousands of new Doughboys were drilling with wooden guns, backed up by artillerymen who used sawed-off telegraph poles to simulate artillery. With basic training often less than half completed, they were being carried by Pullman sleepers to Atlantic ports whilst folks along the railway tracks waved and cheered themselves hoarse. Aboard a transport, they saw no more luxury. Crowded into hastily commandeered transports, or ferried in British ships—convoyed by a fast-growing American Navy of cruisers and destroyers—they came ashore to ride the boxcars—*hommes 40, cheveaux 8* —toward the peaceful villages of Lorraine, or toward Flanders, where the British in front of them were beginning to weary of their sequence to Nivelle's offensive. "I got all my forty artillerymen in the boxcar, Lieutenant. But if you try to put eight of our horses in, somebody's gonna be trampled to death."

In Soulaucourt by Thanksgiving Day, Private Bailey and his buddies knew everything was going according to plan. Did not every ten men of M Company have a roast turkey among them? Specialists who would never hear a grenade's angry burst were coming ashore, timber-toppers from the Northwest flocking to Alpine forests to cut telegraph poles, sawyers moving south to the Pyrenees to fashion duckboards and bridge planks. Everything American was moving to France, but no Doughboys were beefing up the dwindling French and British brigades. There was deep pessimism everywhere save in the training areas of the innocent Americans. Official German hopes were high.

Just before Christmas came, Major General Bullard was summoned to Chaumont and given command of the 1st Division. In his diary he set down his opinion that Pershing was the wrong choice for a commanding general. Bullard said the cadet he (probably) had hazed at West Point was known as a soldier who would rather negotiate than fight. Pershing twice detained Bullard, when the latter attempted to leave the room. He was concerned about the pessimism and defeatism of the French, which he feared was infecting some of his Yank commanders. He wanted Bullard to combat it strongly, and when the Big Red One's new general left Chaumont he felt that Pershing was sparring for time, in hopes of seeing a peace made before he had to fight. Years later, Bullard penciled into his diary the exclamation: "I was wrong!"

Certainly Pershing was not concerned about the morale of the Doughboys in village billets and along the lines of supply. By Christmas, there were a quarter-million of them in France, most of whom had never spent this day away from home before. They set about making the best of it: Christmas had meant children since the Day of the Nativity at Bethlehem; at home it also meant widows and orphans, stockings filled with toys, trees, colored lights, needy families, Salvation Army dinners. The four divisions devoted that first Christmas to children. Few Christmas packages arrived before the year was out, but all companies and battalions passed the tambourine and delegated purchasing agents—Doughboys with an established reputation as nondrinkers and nonwenchers—to proceed with the money to the nearest market town and buy out the shops.

Floyd Gibbons of the Chicago *Tribune* cabled home a description of the big day as enjoyed by the members of a field artillery battalion. The curé gave them the village church for the celebration, and the regiment's band, in its swing around the battalions, scheduled them for an afternoon parade. Engineers and signalers provided a tree with lights, and French children who had known few instances of a *Joyeux Noël* were in an ecstasy of anticipation. They were not disappointed. There was a fat Santa Claus wearing red flannel bloomers purloined from a washline, and the colonel's best boots, temporarily on unauthorized loan. He rode a sled pulled by Hindenburg, the wagon train's gentlest mule, now caparisoned in a bright robe. The band led the way playing "Dixie," the battalion in column of squads. Once in the church, the barbershop quartet from B Battery rendered "Down in the Coal Hole," and then the presents were bestowed— the colonel having warned Saint Nick not to try any Chicago French on the children. Either his breath, which was fruity, or his accent, which was atrocious, might frighten the little kids. There were capes, cloaks, mittens, real leather shoes, tin soldiers, toy battleships, dolls, fruits, candies, and nuts. Afterward the colonel, despite West Point breeding, expropriated government property for personal use in a manner frowned on by the Judge Advocate General. He was mellow by twilight and gave a fireworks display, expending flares and rockets of great beauty as he called for a barrage, signaled that enemy airplanes were overhead, asked for a counterattack, demanded reinforcements, said his guns were overrun, and informed the surrounding countryside that his outfit was in a hell of a fix. Actually, the colonel and his command would only be in a bad way the morning after.

It was not all hilarity. Sergeant Joyce Kilmer, poet of the 42nd Division's Rainbows, spent his Christmas Eve aglow in a fine village house with some members of New York's old "Fighting Sixty-Ninth" Irish, along with village grandchildren who marveled that Kilmer and his buddies could sing the same Psalms, in the same church Latin, that they used. The children gladly "rushed the growler" to the corner *estaminet,* returning not with beer, but with red wine. Some Marines in the 2nd Division said their "Toys for Tots" were more generous than those of the infantry brigade's, while others said the Marine Christmas was cheapskate in comparison. The New Englanders of the 26th Division, from families of careful providers, had most of *their* Christmas packages on time, though a plum pudding turned up after a perilous passage from Boston as flat as an opera hat. In Soulaucourt, Private Bailey and his buddies translated a billet-doux from a French lass in a distant village for a semiliterate buddy, and then composed a reply in French which must have taxed the intelligence of the French lass and her grandmother. It was a grand Christmas, with few lost buddies to mourn.

Across the lines, Germans in dugouts sang songs not unlike those of the Doughboys, "Silent Night" and "Tannenbaum," and received packages—knitted sweaters and such comforts made from unraveled woolens—and enjoyed the *Lebensmittel* of chocolates and confections. The troops were not despairing; they had knocked Russia out of the war, and they would drive the British into the sea and reach Paris long before the Dough-boys arrived in any force. In Berlin, the Hohenzollern Crown Prince noted that the situation was becoming serious. Widows and orphans sat in darkness at four in the afternoon, in cold rooms with few amenities. Coffee was made of roasted acorns unless someone had a last brooch to pawn to a profiteer. Potatoes were the staple article of diet; any schnapps left had been sent to some son or husband at the front. German economy, beginning to be geared by Ludendorff to all-out attacks, gave city dwellers little to live on. Contrasts were violent. War contractors and the gaudy tarts they always attract in any wartime nation crowded the cabarets, and sullen resentment could only be stifled by the great victories that were expected in the spring.

Chapter **3**

LUDENDORFF'S GLORIOUS SPRING; DIVERTISSEMENT AT SEICHEPREY

All that I have . . .

By March, 1918, there were about 325,000 Doughboys in France, some in new outfits not yet ready to go forward to be murdered in the methods of siege warfare long practiced by the French and British commanders. Most advanced in training were the 1st Regulars, the 26th National Guard, the 2nd with Regulars and Marines, and the 42nd National Guard Rainbows. The 32nd Division, National Guardsmen from Michigan and Wisconsin, was ashore by late February, scattered all the way across France, one infantry brigade slaving as railroad coolies. Elements of the 77th Division, draftees from New York City, were also in Flanders.

On March 21, Pershing knew that his resolve to withhold the Doughboys from active theaters of warfare until he trained an army of one million men was now past fulfilling. That morning Ludendorff jumped the British Fifth Army at Saint-Quentin, on the Picardy front, almost destroying it, and broke through into open warfare, pushing westward forty miles in four days to Montdidier and its spearhead village of Cantigny, fifty-five miles northeast of Paris.

The German offensive began along a fifty-mile front between La Fère and Arras; it was aimed at the British Armies between the Oise and the Scarpe rivers, and Ludendorff's objective was to separate the British and the French forces, crack the British front and push their armies back to

43

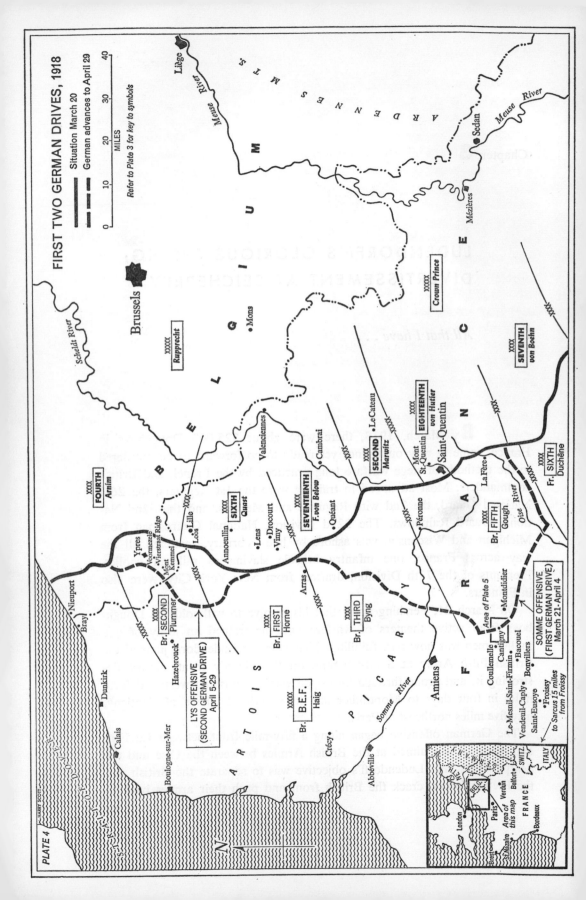

PLATE 4

FIRST TWO GERMAN DRIVES, 1918

Situation March 20
German advances to April 29

Refer to Plate 3 for key to symbols

MILES
0   10   20   30   40

HARRY SCOTT

N

A R D E N N E S   M t s.

Meuse River

Liège

Sedan

Mézières

Meuse River

B E L G I U M

Scheldt River

Brussels

Mons

XXXXX
Rupprecht

F R A N C E

XXXX
Crown Prince

XXXX
SEVENTH
von Boehn

XXXX
EIGHTEENTH
von Hutier

Le Cateau

Cambrai

Valenciennes

XXXX
SECOND
Marwitz

Mont
St.-Quentin
Saint-Quentin

La Fère

Oise River

XXXX
Fr. SIXTH
Duchêne

XXXX
FOURTH
Arnim

B E L G I U M

XXXX
SIXTH
Quast

Lille
Loos

Annœullin

Lens
Vimy
Drocourt

XXXX
SEVENTEENTH
F. von Below

Quéant

Péronne

XXXX
FIFTH
Gough

Br.

A R T O I S

Nieuport
Bray

Ypres
Voormezele
Vierstraat Ridge
Mont
Kemmel

XXXX
SECOND
Plummer
Br.

Hazebrouck

LYS OFFENSIVE
(SECOND GERMAN DRIVE)
April 5-29

Dunkirk

Calais

Boulogne-sur-Mer

XXXX
FIRST
Horne
Br.

Arras

XXXX
THIRD
Byng
Br.

XXXXX
B.E.F.
Haig
Br.

Crécy

Somme River

Abbéville

Amiens

P I C A R D Y

Montdidier

Coullemelle
Cantigny

Area of Plate 5

Le-Mesnil-Saint-Firmin
Vendeuil-Caply
Saint-Eusoye

Bacouel
Bonvillers

Froissy
to Sarcus 15 miles
from Froissy

SOMME OFFENSIVE
(FIRST GERMAN DRIVE)
March 21-April 4

London
NETH.
Brussels
Paris
Area of
this map
Brest
St. Nazaire
F R A N C E
Verdun
Belfort
SWITZ.
Bordeaux
ITALY

the North Sea. The French Armies would fall back to cover Paris. Once separated, the armies faced total destruction.

Pershing had left headquarters at Chaumont to learn of the British situation, and was stopping at the Ogden Mills house in Paris, his for the duration by a gracious gesture. He set out along the roads leading northward, every artery choked with transport, to find Major General Ferdinand Foch, Chief of Staff of the French Army. He located the headquarters of the French Third Army, but no one there knew where Foch was. Somewhere to the west, before the vital rail junction of Amiens, Sir Douglas Haig was fighting for his life, but there was no Allied unity anywhere— and this was forty-four months after the German hordes had poured through the Liège gate in Belgium. The American commander found the French general—who, after ten months of bitter wrangling still had no authority over Pershing's troops—in a farmhouse near the little town of Clermont-sur-Oise, a place near enough to Paris to have some *chic* about it, the surrounding orchards carpeted with the violets of spring beneath a canopy of cherry blossoms.

Foch was in the kitchen with Pétain and Clemenceau, bent over a map, debating Ludendorff's probable next move. If the Iron Commander, wellnigh intractable, deserved no other ticket to immortality, he earned one with the gesture he made that day. He wanted no wrangling with the Tiger of France, nor any of the cautious Pétain's timidity. So he offended Clemenceau for the hundredth time by asking Foch to suggest that they leave the room, thus snubbing the Premier of France.

Once alone, he told Foch he would not fight on less than a division front, but he would fight with "all that I have" wherever Foch wanted him to take on the veteran Germans, and he told him so in French. Pershing spoke atrocious French. (He confessed he once tried his French upon a little porcelain child of six, daughter of a French general, and seeing her uncomprehending stare had bent low to ask, *"Comprenez vous?"* The child, still staring, said, *"Non."*) Whatever he said, the frenetic, unconquerable bantam from the Pyrenees immediately issued a press release for his flagging armies, paraphrasing Pershing into a Gallic orator. General Tasker H. Bliss, beloved of the innocent intellectuals of the time—a man like Pershing was rarely understood by them—called upon Foch the next day. He was Wilson's High Commissioner to the Supreme Allied Council; he was a wit, a philosopher, and also a man of great soul. Bliss could have made the speech that Foch attributed to Pershing. Instead, Bliss said, "Well, we came over here to get killed. Where do you want to use us?"

"All that I have" meant four divisions of troops which Pershing believed to be of assault quality. He gave the preference to Foch according to their time in training: the 1st, the 26th, the 2nd, and the 42nd. This combat force seemed so small that Foch, at Pétain's suggestion, made no mention of it a week later when the British and French finally were driven to naming Foch Supreme Allied Commander. The Order of the Day ignored Pershing, who immediately saw in this another ruse to piecemeal his troops into French and British replacements. Pétain informed him that there was no American Army in existence in France. When Black Jack Pershing was angry, which was not infrequently, he could pound the table and shout oaths strong enough to turn a team of Missouri mules around. The order was amended: Foch was now master of British, French, and American Armies in France, the four American divisions being equal to eight or nine in other armies, or about two corps.

Pétain, the French Field Commander, still persisted. Within a month he was to ask Pershing to strengthen twenty-five French divisions with two battalions each of Doughboy infantry: about fifty thousand men. To Pershing's astonishment Haig asked for ten thousand artillerymen. It was all incredible to the Iron Commander, who, after a Paris conference with the Chief of the Imperial General Staff, Sir William Robertson, told his friend Frederick Palmer that "I did not swear this time." The rugged, politician-baiting old British battle-ax had come up the hard way from the ranks. How was it possible, Pershing wondered, that an ex-enlisted man would expect men to fight well in foreign ranks, so much cannon fodder under foreign brigadiers? The British had to keep their own cadres—wonderful ones, too—as national entities; the Scottish battalions, the Canadian, Australian–New Zealand, Irish could not have been brigaded into English regiments—though these latter actually bore the brunt of the fighting.

At no time was Pershing ever free from attempts to break up the Doughboys. Clemenceau, Lloyd George, Foch, Haig, Pétain, Orlando, Díaz—the list was endless and the figures illustrious—never once conceded that the Doughboys had a national psychology of their own. (The first to perceive it, and appraise it for all its vital force, was a German Intelligence officer, Lieutenant von Buy, after a week of questioning Doughboys and Marines amidst the horrors of Belleau Wood.)

Early in April, Foch pulled the 1st Division out of its trenches in the quiet Toul sector of the Saint-Mihiel salient in Lorraine, to prepare for action. By April 5, the German offensive in Picardy had been stopped, and the Second Battle of the Somme had dwindled to a holding action, with reserves replacing exhausted British and French outfits. Foch wanted to take up the slack at Montdidier, the sector for which the Big Red One was destined. As the 1st Division left the Toul sector to move northwest, the 26th Division moved foot, horse, and gun to replace it in badly positioned, four-year-old trenches just east of Saint-Mihiel around the village of Seicheprey.

England still grieved over its new civilian armies massacred in 1916 along the Somme, the flower of the British nation buried there in the mud; youths who had volunteered en masse from their local cricket clubs, from soccer fields, from friendly communities. The Doughboys of the 26th Division resembled these armies in their complexions and their village origins, but not in lack of military experience. The sergeants among them had seen service for months along the Mexican border in 1916, and battalion commanders had fought in the Spanish-American War. Many of the companies represented the center of social life of a New England town, these cadres dating back in history to pre-Revolutionary times—the train bands of Colonial militia, the First Corps of Cadets of the Massachusetts Bay Company, New Hampshire men with memories of Burgoyne's defeat by their forefathers, Vermonters whose forebears had been with the Green Mountain Boys, had held the line Gettysburg's first day when Winfield Scott Hancock rode the hill with a groin wound bloodying his saddle. There was a father-son continuity in many platoons, companies, and battalions, and among brothers and cousins. These Yankees had an independence, a dignity about them. When replacements began to be drafted, and a Vermonter received the White House greetings, the local weekly might say that "Mr. Obadiah Littlejohn has accepted the position of Private in the United States Army."

But the rank-and-file was not confined to old stock. Many of its best men were fresh volunteers whose first memories were of setting lobster pots with Portugal-born fathers; from families where the breadwinner came home from a Polish-manned shoe factory or an Italian fruit stand; from Irish lace-curtained windows on the Quincy side of Boston. There was diversity among them, yet somehow they were made homogeneous by the strongest of all American influences, the New England town meeting. Captain Miles Standish would have signed them all on—Top Sergeant Benny Shapiro, who won a Distinguished Service Cross; a remarkable field medic named Rudolph Foster of Chicopee Falls who carried a purloined stock of morphine, and gave hypos to the badly wounded in defiance of all Army regulations; a simple buck private named Abraham Cohen who wore the red-and-white-bordered blue ribbon of the D.S.C.

These guardsmen did not care a damn about the Regular Army; they held themselves better men than the catch-all Regulars of the peacetime Army. Officers knew all their men; knew where they lived, had talked with their mothers. They had a fierce loyalty, and when they were elected to an officer's rank, even the many who had stooped to the chicanery of militia politics to gain a commission, set about, conscience-stricken, to make officers of themselves; to shine when the West Pointers came around to give them tactical problems with blank ammunition. When they came ashore in France in September, 1917, their infantry were the best-coached riflemen the American Army sent over. They were commanded by a West Pointer, Major General Clarence Edwards, himself frowned upon by many of his fellow Leavenworth graduates for his effusive magnetism and charm. One of their brigades had another West Pointer for a leader, Brigadier General Peter E. Traub. Aside from Traub, most commands were held by individuals who through all their adult years had been soldiers for the fun of it, and they were always seeking special privileges for the New Englanders, small things in themselves, but taboo in the regimentation decreed by the Iron Commander as he set about massing an armed host. The division carried its own special correspondent, having secured after some wrangling a civilian Boston newspaperman who was privileged to live at Division Headquarters and share secrets until the inevitable happened: there was a staggering change of command in the Argonne, and he was booted out.

Among the curiosities of the outfit was a second lieutenant who was awarded the Croix de Guerre by the French, not because he was an excellent interpreter and liaison officer capable of leaping from shell hole to shell hole in times of urgency, but simply because Mr. Richard F. Peters was sixty-seven years old. There was an Irish wagon master for the 101st Infantry who was the only nonexpendable second lieutenant in France. In civil life he was a court clerk in the South Boston Police Court, and it was impossible for red tape to tear him away from the division, though he was presumably left at home as unfit when the outfit sailed from Boston. This invalid was repeatedly sent back to hospital in France to be surveyed out of the service, but inevitably at the next push he could be seen expertly shepherding his wagons at the tail end of the regiment.

A man of indeterminate age, Second Lieutenant Bill Drohan was officially diagnosed as having cirrhosis of the liver, hardening of the arteries, coronary thrombosis, a set of false teeth, and weak lungs. (He fell dead while recounting his exploits, six months after the Armistice.)

His regimental surgeon was an old friend, Major Fred Bogan, of Boston's City Hospital, which may have explained Drohan's unexpendable status. His colonel was Edmund L. Logan, the judge of the South Boston Police Court, who enlisted in the Guard in the Gay Nineties, and had commanded the 9th Massachusetts on the Mexican border. His lieutenant colonel was John H. Dunn, who saw service in the Spanish-American War and who, when he sailed for France, resigned as Boston's street commissioner. Major William T. Cusey, 2nd Battalion, had to resign as superintendent of the city's printing plant. Like Dunn, he had been in the Guard for twenty-nine years. When the Northeast Command was organized, General Edwards was assigned to it, and immediately made a study of the New England Guard and its many characters. He promised grandmothers he would "look after" their forty-year-old sons.

The division's choice of chaplains was the accepted thing: there were numbers of priests and ministers, with a rabbi or two; but Catholic priests and Unitarian ministers and Jewish rabbis in great numbers wished to go along. They did so, too, as civilian servants of the Y.M.C.A., the Knights of Columbus, and the Jewish Welfare Board, vying with one another as to the number of wounded they personally carried back from No-Man's Land in all the division's engagements.

The Yankee Division moved into the trenches around Seicheprey in wretched confusion as the Big Red One pulled out. French Corps G-3s had written obscure orders on the change-over, in which two divisions —half of "all that I have"—passed to widely separated French Armies. The Boston judge, seeking his regiment's position, had to make his own reconnaissance to discover his lines, as the 1st Division hastily scurried out, following orders equally obscure. Nothing went right about the relief, and the recriminations were so bitter that staff studies soon appeared citing it as a prime example of what not to do when one division relieves another. It was characteristic that 26th Headquarters instantly complained of the disorder that Major General Bullard's men left behind, even though Beaumont Buck, Bullard's brigadier who remained behind to supervise the relief, officially commended them for their bearing. (Bullard later had to answer the criticism while under stress at Cantigny and it infuriated him: Clarence Edwards had gone National Guard! Later when Hunter Liggett, his corps commander, was told that Edwards was criticizing him, he shrugged and said, "Oh, nobody could ever stop Clarence from talking. . . .")

The Yankee Division was in place on a front of eighteen thousand meters by April 3, 1918. One regiment got there without any knowledge of its destination; the men were simply dumped out of French camions in the dead of night by a poilu shavetail who said that this was as far as he was told to go. *"Bon secteur, M'sieu. Au 'voir, M'sieu."* And with a sidewinder salute to the side of his helmet he was gone.

The *bon secteur*—known as Toul—was on the south flank of the Saint-Mihiel salient which the Germans had held since 1914, content to immobilize the French there, posing a constant threat to their flank east of

Verdun and pinning down poilus who might have been used elsewhere. Not since early in 1915, when the French had sustained shocking losses in Joffre's attempt to improve an impossible position, had there been any excitement. But company commanders of the 1st Division regiments headed for Cantigny told the captains from Connecticut not to be deceived into thinking it a quiet sector. The Germans held the high ground of an east-west ridge dominated by the hill before the town of Montsec, north of the miserable trenches enfiladed on both ends of the lines at Seicheprey, and from their watchtowers observers would order a salvo from 77s thrown at a Doughboy putting arnica salve on the mangy patches of a machine-gun mule. From time to time they raided the vulnerable, poorly drained trenches around the towns of Apremont and Seicheprey, or the woods thereabouts; they had recently exchanged training raids with the 2nd Division's Marines and Regulars, and with a brigade of the Big Red One, but these exercises meant nothing much to them. Watching the arrival of the New Englanders in the Saint-Mihiel salient, the Germans wanted to talk to some of them. After forty-two months of occupancy, their field intelligence was faultless; agents, traitors with flashlight blinkers, infiltrating patrols tapping telephone wires had developed a perfect system.

Now they wanted especially to talk to some of the officers and men of the 104th Infantry, learn their origins and the name of their commander, who was Lieutenant Colonel George H. Shelton. When General Edwards went to examine his position, he found Shelton in an "awful hole" about six hundred yards from an enemy battery of sixteen mortars. The general ordered him out of the forward trenches. French liaison demurred, saying the Germans would capture the entire regiment. Edwards retorted that he hoped the Germans would occupy the hole, in which case Shelton would then "lick the hell out of them." Shelton withdrew, the Germans came over after shelling empty positions, and Shelton promptly licked hell out of them with rifle and bayonet, killing about fifty of them, seizing prisoners, and driving the rest of the Landwehr troops back to their own lines.

This was the first of a series of hand-to-hand battles in which the Germans were to engage the New Englanders, even bringing up *Stosstruppen* of *Sturmbataillone,* the cream of Ludendorff's assault teams, to mix it with them in something like saloon brawls where all the belligerents were armed with rifles, pistols, and bayonets, no holds barred, and no police to interfere. The Yankees went into the business as if to a clambake.

The Germans were roused now and very anxious to talk to some lad with a Down East twang, an Irish brogue, or a Yiddish accent. The outpost skirmishes became sanguinary around the town of Apremont, sometimes lasting five days and nights.

"How many Heinies you think came at us this morning, Sergeant?"

"Oh, not too many this morning. I'd say about three saloonfuls."

Nettled at being bested in so many stand-up-and-fight encounters, the Germans changed to formal warfare the morning of April 10 and came over behind a barrage with a front some eight hundred men strong. They fought all night and through the next day and night around the crazy-quilt trenches, and there were many feats of reckless bravery on both sides. The French decorated more than one hundred Yankees, citing small units such as Sergeant John A. Dickerson's squad of Headquarters Company, Stokes mortars. (He had just two.) On the foggy morning of April 12, Dickerson was to open fire as a preliminary to a countercharge from the second line, retiring after three minutes when the field artillery would begin its rolling barrage. The artillery never saw the flares and signal rockets, so the sergeant remained in position to send over little trench mortar bombs from his two Stokes guns. It was not much of a barrage, but it was all the sergeant and his buddies had to give. Privates Alston, Knudson, and Cole were killed. Private Howland, though wounded, assisted the corporal of the outfit, Henry Mack, who was unharmed. Sergeant Dickerson, who had an eye shot out and a leg shot off, could only give advice.

The Germans on Montsec were growing angry. Three regiments brought in for these assaults on the 26th had suffered three-to-one casualties, leaving forty prisoners in New England hands and taking only one Dough-boy back to their lines. Now *Stosstruppen* were seen marching through Montsec's village streets, strangers with the hauteur of roving troops dedicated to assault situations, newly uniformed, booted and armed. The observers in the watchtowers began to study the Yankee dispositions around Seicheprey and Remières Wood. They intended to capture the village and take permanent possession of it to show the brash New Englanders who were the masters of No-Man's Land. The old professionals rehearsed their raid until the very morning of the appointed day, April 20. The Doughboys of the 26th had impressed them by their carriage and physique, and the joyous ferocity they demonstrated in small encounters. Intelligence officers estimated them as not yet having the qualities of assault troops, still green in staff work and communications, but capable of rounding into formidable fighters worthy of premier assignments if released to an active sector.

German Intelligence as usual left nothing to chance. Later, talking genially to captured officers from New Haven and Hartford, they wanted little information; they already knew everything about the 26th Division. They jested about having shelled Brigadier General Traub from his headquarters. They asked about the health of various company cooks, calling them by their first names, explaining that they often infiltrated their scouts into rear units dressed in Doughboy uniforms, and they produced Germans with a working knowledge of New England geography who spoke excellent English. In ten days of raids before the *Stosstruppen* came over, the German had sometimes infiltrated a half-mile behind the patchwork front lines, killed the mules pulling a ration wagon, carried away its driver and a sack of company mail. German officers considered themselves, and not the French, the true teachers of the Americans. (Wonderful old French General Noël Joseph Édouard de Curières de Castelnau, whose three sons had been killed in action, had said the same thing.) They intended soon to give the Doughboys across the way a lesson in minor tactics: how to capture a town by flanking its environs to overwhelm its garrison from the rear. The crazy-quilt pattern of the wretched trenches around Seicheprey was ideal for the lesson.

Around three in the morning of April 20, Montsec opened with hundreds of guns, even sending the Doughboys some shells from railroad artillery. The morning was foggy, the haze still upon the ground when at five o'clock the *Stosstruppen* battalion, six hundred strong in the center and lightly encumbered, stepped out to follow the first rolling barrage. On either end of the line, salted with other storm troopers, came some thousand troops wearing heavy packs; these expected to remain in Seicheprey, in the woods to the Doughboy right, in other villages along the line. With various specialists—engineers, signalers, machine gunners, contact-mine layers—the force numbered 3,200 Germans. They were first intent upon annihilating the four hundred New Englanders who, in sacrificial dedication, held the American right. A Scottish soldier would have said, "Mon, the barrage was that fine ye could ha' lighted a pipe at it," as Ludendorff's polished killers plunged into the wooded ravine that gave access to the slate-roofed houses of Seicheprey. Above them Fokker pilots held absolute mastery of the air.

The *Stosstruppen* raid was a smashing success. One column pinched the west of Seicheprey's narrow little salient, a second flanked the buffering Remières Wood to the east, and a third drove straight at Seicheprey. The four hundred Doughboys in Seicheprey appeared to be doomed. The two claws of the flanking columns closed on the town from the rear, while the center outfit moved into the streets to clean out cellars and gun pits. The Yankee lines here had been badly mangled in the horrendous bombardment, one platoon reduced from fifty to eight men before attackers ever reached them. The surgeon and his first-aid personnel at the battalion's advanced dressing station were picked up as prisoners, and survivors of outposts and machine-gun positions went down fighting with clubbed rifles.

A box barrage now enclosed a Connecticut battalion fighting for its life. Regimental Headquarters was out of touch, battalion runners killed as soon as they leaped into the open for a run through the gantlet of bursting shells. In the village, the field-gray troops unslung their heavy packs and began consolidating the newly won positions. They were in touch by buzzer wires with Montsec before the last defender had been killed or captured or driven out.

In Remières Wood the going was not so easy for them; there was all-day fighting among the trees and rocks by remnants of squads and platoons. The Germans had reached their first targets around 5:05 A.M. By the time a wounded runner staggered into Regimental Headquarters at six-thirty to report the shocking news that Seicheprey was in enemy hands, Major George A. Rau, his battalion of Connecticut militia shattered, had begun his counterattack with what he had left, driving the Germans from the village itself. He was holding on with what he had, his attack spent. His force was a motley one: headquarters personnel of orderlies and clerks, runners, kitchen helpers—the cook went along with a cleaver and was seen to split a German skull before he died—and a detachment of twenty-five Dough-boys from the Big Red One, forlorn yard birds left at Seicheprey for court-martial offenses, their penalty being the job of cleaning up the mess left there by the outfit. (These lost lads had neither service records nor court transcripts with them, but after their work that morning the Yankee division adopted them for the duration of their sentences.)

The French Corps Commander, Major General Passaga, arrived at Brigade and took charge, reducing the West Point brigadier, Peter Traub, to a mere implement of his will; for the French regiment on the right had been attacked, losing four machine-gun posts and a number of prisoners to the Germans. The colonel of the French, a character much admired by the many characters of the Yankee outfit, galloped over on a thoroughbred horse, complaining of the animal's skittishness under heavy shellfire. Colonel Bertrand wore six wound stripes, and his "kitchen battery"—the French did not refer to rows of ribbons as fruit salad—contained all his country could bestow.

Another wounded Doughboy staggered in with the report that Remières Wood was lost, the village of Beaumont isolated, the three battalions split at their junctions. By noon the French thought the situation dark indeed, so sensitive were they to the mystifying demonstrations of Ludendorff's guile. On April 9, he had struck the second blow of his drive on the British Armies in Flanders, with such force that Haig had committed the last of his reserves and was to issue on April 21 his famous "backs to the wall" order, possibly Britain's last fatal stand against the advancing Germans.

Was it possible that Ludendorff would jab now with a steel-pointed finger at French positions around Verdun, to bring the war to a speedy end?

Passaga planned a counterattack for dawn the next morning, Brigadier General Traub making his dispositions at Passaga's directions. A battalion was selected to make the assault, and patrols were sent out in darkness to reconnoiter the ground it would attempt to wrest from the Germans. Specific tactics for the counterattack would have to await information brought back by the patrols. The plans, particularly the timing of the patrols, were impossible of execution because of the confusion that existed in the combined staff—and because out in the darkness men were still fighting hand to hand and no patrol could possibly return. The battalion commander, from the U.S. Philippine Constabulary now transferred to the U.S. Army, waited for them in vain. Some of his supporting elements failed to come up during the night. Half an hour before he was to jump for the woods, he took the matter in his own hands and called the whole thing off, refusing his flank to the French, who were also scheduled to attack. His defection seems like madness; he was subsequently court-martialed, found guilty, and dismissed from the Army.

But in Remières Wood the battle was not lost, in spite of earlier reports. It was the scene of desperate man-to-man fighting in which the tactical skill of the veteran storm troopers counted for little; the Germans had lost their advantage after the first admirably planned shock, and now found themselves face to face with New England boys who had no intention of giving up the wood. Without reinforcements they drove the Germans out of the wood and recaptured the difficult Sibille trench beyond it, which the Germans had organized for defense, and where the heaviest American casualties had taken place. After the inept battalion commander had been relieved, elements of the counterassault team had little difficulty in clearing out the remaining enemy.

The Germans withdrew, taking 136 prisoners, leaving behind 60 percent of two infantry companies and one machine-gun company killed or wounded; they had also inflicted heavy casualties on advanced posts held by twenty-five men under a lieutenant.

Remières Wood was a picture any Doughboy would long remember. A machine gun might have its gunner and his helper still at the gun, the dead boy's hands still on the spade handles, the helper with a feed strip of D.M. cartridges still in the attitude of trying to feed it into the guides—caught at this second's pause by two Germans who were now lying dead before the gun, with helmets of evacuated German wounded on the ground marking the field of fire. A platoon reduced to eight riflemen, all wounded, lowered rifles and hailed their rescuers. The guardsmen, new to slaughter, set about burying 160 Germans whom they regarded as vermin—carrion the hardened Doughboy would later leave to the vultures and bluebottle flies. The Germans on the other side admitted six hundred casualties, and they had yielded one hundred prisoners to the Doughboys. Still, they claimed a victory over the ignorant Americans and turned it to propaganda uses. The Yankees thought otherwise. Green troops, they had been placed in positions to be held at all costs, had been savagely molested, and had recovered them against the cream of German assault troops. Their morale was sky-high.

The Yankee colonels visited various hospitals to encourage the recovery of the lightly wounded, who did not always report back to their home division. The New Englanders maintained their dignity and independence. One colonel from Seicheprey came to the cot of a wounded Doughboy, who regarded him sullenly. What was wrong? The boy said he had no money to spend because he was still paying off a court-martial fine. Who fined you? "You did," said the boy, and the colonel turned red. The boy had been among a group that had swapped uniforms with some poilus and, looking ridiculous, had tried to get past the Iron Commander's sentries guarding a whorehouse door. . . .

Colonel D. K. Major, Jr., a Leavenworth General Staff officer who had come to Seicheprey to purge headquarters of its National Guard spirit and make it more like the Big Red One, went back briefly to the staff school at Langres to lecture on what the Guardsmen had done wrong in the engagement. Not one of the Yankees gave a damn what he said until he criticized the "faulty dispositions" of their "beloved leader"—which was the way they referred to their own West Pointer, General Edwards. Then, if the colonel had cared to strip the silver eagles from his shoulder straps behind the latrine, 26,500 men would have stood in line to fight him.

Back home, Seicheprey was hailed as a great victory, coming just in time to stimulate sales for the Third Liberty Loan. In the Toul sector, the Germans cunningly continued to harass the troops who had dared to contest their supremacy. April, May, and June in this "quiet" sector cost the Yankees, in killed, wounded, gassed, and missing, 2,891 casualties.

But the New Englanders were now battle-tested and they had distinguished themselves. Their deficiencies and their success were further steps in forming the army that Pershing, despite British entreaties, still refused to piecemeal in Flanders, where Haig was scraping the bottom of the kettle with a last line of cadets, household troops, military valets, the last British infantry available in France. Seicheprey was the first engagement of Doughboys in any sizable force, and it was a picture in miniature of what would happen to a million of their buddies in 1918 from the Swiss border to the English Channel.

Chapter **4**

PRACTICE AT CANTIGNY

With calmness and certainty . . .

When the Doughboys of the 1st Division, soon to wear the shoulder patch of a big red 1 on a brown tabard, moved into the Picardy sector the last week in April, 1918, they were not expected to make an assault on the Germans. They came to reinforce General Marie Eugène Debeney's exhausted French First Army which had barely succeeded in stopping the brilliant Oskar von Hutier's March 21 offensive after the German Army had smashed forty miles westward from Saint-Quentin, establishing a new salient around Montdidier and the spearhead village of Cantigny. Cantigny was a little village of two hundred souls, situated on slightly rising ground three miles west of Montdidier, in a pretty countryside patched with innumerable small forests capable of concealing ninety German batteries. The Germans intended to hold Cantigny until Ludendorff was ready to strike again and shortly after the Doughboys arrived and had been assigned to Major General Vandenberg's corps they were given the full treatment. On the night of May 3, the 18th Infantry was doused with a massive bath of high explosive and toxic shells; two hundred men were killed and another six hundred wounded or gassed. So great was the devastation from fifteen thousand artillery rounds that long lines of Doughboys were evacuated like blind men, hands upon the shoulders of the man ahead, retching and coughing and vomiting, lobster-pink swellings at armpit and scrotum, eyes sticking shut. So great was the poison in the air that the French had to send up khaki clothing to replace the envenomed outfits of the 18th's survivors.

Major General Robert Lee Bullard had taken over command of the 1st Division when Pershing had decided that his predecessor, Major General William L. Sibert, a brilliant engineer officer, had been too long away from troops to direct 26,500 men in combat. He sent Sibert home, where he became an excellent Chief of Gas Warfare, and appointed Bullard, who had lived his life with troops, to take his place. Bullard was distressed by the mounting curve of casualties as a result of the German shelling. He scolded platoon leaders for what he believed to be laxity or carelessness in exposure to enemy fire. The Doughboys were losing two to four times as many men as the French outfits on either side. But Bullard had no way of knowing that Ludendorff had given orders that whenever Pershing decided to send one of his untried divisions into an active line, it was to be subjected to all the varied kinds of hell the brave and sagacious Germans were capable of administering. Bullard did not know either that there was method in the madness of this nightly din: Ludendorff wanted Ferdinand Foch to be- lieve he was going to resume his offensive there, though he had another sector in mind. Thus every road, communicating trench, battery position, engineer working detail, was stalked by death each night, while daytime showed nothing but sleepy Picardy, spring-green fields of wheat rippling in the sunlight of approaching summer.

Cantigny, its church steeple a slated finger against the sky, lay quiet in the daytime. But the nightly orchestra was always there, and the three ar- tillery regiments of the Big Red One were never quiet, its guns never cool as gunners fed the 75s and the 155s in relays, sending the Germans more than ten thousand shells every twenty-four hours, seeking in vain to silence hidden German batteries in the pretty woods. One battery of four Doughboy guns was knocked out in a single salvo, for the German artillery owned the high ground, and fought skillfully to hold it. The two ambulance companies, the three field hospitals, gained much clinical experience each dawn when the spate of wounded was brought in. The French on either side, hardly molested, said it was like Verdun in the great holocaust of 1916.

Major General Vandenberg was Debeney's ablest corps commander. He liked the way the Doughboys handled themselves in this nocturnal bedlam. He knew from the way the division had behaved during its tour in the sleet at Seicheprey, its freshness in man-to-man combat in the face of a savage enemy, that its Doughboys had shown qualities of troops that did not have to be driven forward, and he had no doubts about American fighting ability. He also knew that no war could be won without resort to the offensive, an ordeal that no Yanks had experienced in the fifteen months since Mr. Wilson asked for war, and he itched to try his hand at directing an American attack, to show his exhausted compatriots that the Yanks could turn the tide. At once he began to subject the 1st Division to patrols and raids, much as a manager sends his young fighter into the gymnasium ring to learn the tricks of the profession at the hands of the old, cunning pros. On May 12 he told Debeney that the Doughboys could stand the gaff as assault troops, which was the highest compliment he could pay them.

Impressed by Vandenberg's compliment, on May 15 Debeney ordered Bullard to take Cantigny. Its capture would not greatly improve the French position; Cantigny was a mere wart on the hide of the God of War. Debeney wished mainly to learn if the Doughboys could live up to such praise; and after he gave his order to Bullard all Frenchmen held their breath. If the Doughboys failed, then all the hullabaloo of French politicians assuring a flagging French Army that America's strength would turn the tables would prove to be so much malarkey, and the game would be up. There followed thirteen days of planning.

Bullard chose the 28th Regiment to lead the assault largely on the strength of its commander, Colonel Hanson E. Ely. Ely was not only a strong character; he was tougher than an alligator steak, as hard-boiled as a picnic egg. He was six-feet-two, with 220 pounds of bone and gristle. When he became a major general he sewed the black woolen sleeve bands of his rank on his trench coat. Even in a driving rainstorm, let no hapless brigadier forget that Ely was now a two-star general. Bullard had known Ely fifteen years before in the Philippines. If Ely asked his mess attendant for a cup of coffee, the request had the tone of a battalion fire chief ordering a hoseman back into a burning building. When he was silent, which was not too often, he continually worked the leathery muscle at the corner of his jaw, as if banking the fires that smoldered in his rasping vocal chords. He had arrived in France the year before, organized the first Military Police, and then was made chief of staff of the 1st Division under Major General Sibert. Bullard had hardly cushioned himself in a farmhouse chair after relieving Sibert before Ely began bitching. Why was he still a colonel? He could name four colonels who got the star of a brigadier general, and who could not hold a candle to Hanson E. Ely. It was a lousy oversight.

Bullard was nothing timid; he had the three kinds of guts that distinguished a born commander—combat guts, staff guts, and man-to-man guts. He would not sack this fighter or transfer him out. Instead, he relieved him as chief of staff and gave him command of the 28th Infantry, happy to be far from that maddening voice. If Ely wanted a brigadier's star, and felt himself unjustly left out of that swelling galaxy of luminaries, then by God let him win it on the field of battle by sticking his neck out like any other Doughboy. And so Ely, not so much the 28th Infantry, which was rivaled in excellence by the three other infantry regiments of the division, was chosen to lead the Doughboys, new to the assault, against the accomplished deviltry of the old German pros.

Bullard was well fixed for his other higher officers, too—no division anywhere ever knew better ones. His cast included a genius in the timing of warfare movement, work known in the jargon of the trade as logistics. He was a tall fellow of Southern speech, a graduate of the Virginia Military Institute, and a General Staff officer. Lieutenant Colonel George Catlett Marshall, Jr., was an assistant chief of staff to the 1st Division in the field of operations. The man in charge of his artillery was Bullard's special pride. The division commander had seen Charles P. Summerall in some Luzon fighting when, as an artillery lieutenant, he brought his single gun up to Captain Bullard's infantry line. Now a brigadier general, he was known widely for his manners and his courtesy. He was also known as a stickler for detail, speed, and devotion to duty, harshly unforgiving of shoddiness and timidity. "General Summerall may be a son-of-a-bitch," some of his gunners said, "but thank God he's *our* son-of-a-bitch."

"It is interesting to record," Pershing noted in his memoirs,

that of the officers of the 1st Division to participate in this battle, Bullard was later to command an Army; Summerall and Hines, Corps; Buck, Ely, Parker, and Bamford, Divisions. Two members of the division's staff, King and Marshall, were to become chiefs of staff of corps. Many other officers then with the division would have undoubtedly reached positions of command had they not sacrificed their lives at Soissons.

Soissons was seven weeks ahead.

Five days before the attack, the 28th Regiment marched back to some pleasant fields, untorn by war, to begin rehearsals on terrain similar to that fronting Cantigny, covering every conceivable aspect of the proposed battle. French observation planes returned from photographic missions with pictures of German positions, and trenches were dug that precisely duplicated those the Doughboys must capture. Airplanes from a French squadron flew over the rehearsal grounds, dropping practice messages to show the Americans how they must be recovered for liaison. Companies from the ambulance outfits, field hospitals, rolling kitchens, were drilled on farmland turned now into a stage for the cast of amateurs to learn in detail this ballet of stale trench warfare.

Bullard, summoning up his memories of boarding-school French gained at the West Point of his day (the Regular Army was fluent in Spanish), found himself in the fields during these rehearsals, speaking French and pantomiming to platoon commanders to illustrate the language of the instructors in horizon blue, a major general going through monkeyshines to inform a group of college boys on how to fight a war.

The French thought the American division was too brawny, too large for disposition under one major general such as Bullard. The French and the British ran thirteen thousand men to a division—now reduced by constant warfare and diminishing manpower to about six thousand rifles, plus the supporting elements. The Big Red One's two infantry brigades were each larger than a French division. A regiment such as the 28th would have been a beefed-up French brigade, yet it was commanded by a colonel. A great stickler for staff orthodoxy, Debeney solved his quandary during the exercises by treating Bullard as a corps commander, bringing him back to Army Headquarters for a *pourparlez* along with the French corps commanders. Debeney could move a French division with thirty-five freight trains, each with its string of boxcars holding forty men or eight horses. Bullard would have needed sixty freight trains to bring the men and the gear of the Big Red One into Picardy, crowding the Doughboys in; and so he had marched them in instead. He had nine hundred officers, a great number of his company captains of the line with less than one year of Army service, and these never having seen an attack, let alone led one. Three-fourths of the men were last year's rookies.

Aside from the rifles on their shoulders, the packs on their backs, the pistols at their belts, the Doughboys still possessed few weapons given them by the Americans at home. They had no airplanes of their own, no flame throwers, no tanks, no field guns, though they did have a few observation balloons. Their automatic rifles were Chauchats, said to be made of battlefield scrap but believed by Doughboys to have been fashioned from rusty sardine cans. Their heavy Hotchkiss machine guns fired a French D.M. cartridge; American Springfield rifle ammunition would not fit them. The infantry of the richest nation on earth had three kinds of small-arms ammunition, supported by French automatic rifles and machine guns, reinforced by British Stokes mortars. The French set great store by their flame throwers in the taking of a town, and poilus showed up at the practice grounds with these lethal tanks strapped to their backs like fire extinguishers, the hose and nozzle section running under the armpit to the hands which directed a spray of flaming oil. (The Doughboys of the 28th Regiment knew of these devices—six weeks before, in the sleet at Seicheprey, some untried buddies had been burned to death by German *Flamenwerfers* which suddenly appeared on the parapets during a brisk enemy raid.) The French, desiring live Germans for interrogation, wanted flame throwers with the center battalion destined to move into the village itself; there was nothing like a little spurt of flaming oil down a cellar stairs to bring men out with their hands up.

French Intelligence knew that tanks, since the Germans of the 82nd Reserve Division had never seen any, would be a factor in spreading panic. Accordingly, Debeney contributed twelve of these infant terrors in the growing arsenal of war. The French crewed them, too, supplying men who had stayed alive for more than three years. A man might remain in one less than an hour before fainting in the 140° temperature. But the vulnerable tracks, the thin armor, of the new weapon made it unlikely that a light-tank driver would last that long anyway. Of the twelve tanks, not one would enter Cantigny, but German Intelligence—in the subsequent exchanges between colonels and generals—mentioned that the sight of them, lumbering across the fields toward the town, contributed to the confusion there. The Germans had no antitank weapon, not even the African elephant guns supplied to German forces as the war progressed—great hunting pieces with a recoil capable of breaking a man's shoulder if he held the piece for accurate fire.

The French knew by now, better than any other troops, after nearly four years of appalling slaughter, that brave hearts and ready rifles could not take the town of Cantigny without overwhelming artillery support directed by airplanes and observation balloons. The 1st Division had its own three regiments of field artillery—two of French 75-millimeter and one of 155s. The French saw to it that the Doughboys would have in addition a total of 132 little 75s, which Doughboy gunners had learned to fire with a rapidity that both astonished and alarmed the French. Then there were thirty-six of the heavier 155s. Farther back in bunkers they provided the roar of 178 guns and howitzers.

Also attached to the division at the outset of its Cantigny tour were elements from more than half a dozen French artillery regiments, ranging from battalions of the brisk little 75s to one terrifying 280-millimeter trench mortar battery.

The Germans, from aerial reconnaissance, knew something was up. German guns from the small forests were ranging and probing deeper each evening, forcing the French villager around Maison-Tuileric, where the Americans were training for their attack, to gather his family around him at sundown and take to the open fields for what rest he might find under the nightly screams of the shells. The big guns were taking part now; sometimes officers, men, and horses of the 1st Division's wagon trains were wiped out by a hogshead shell, or an aerial torpedo dropped from a Gotha during a moonlit excursion twenty kilometers from the front line. But shelling was not enough; the Germans wanted prisoners. They did not believe the Americans audacious enough to stage a full-dress enterprise, but perhaps a massive raid was in rehearsal, so they planned raids of their own to take place on May 27. That they picked this date, one day before the Big Red One planned its first attack, was not a coincidence. On the same day to the east, between Soissons and Reims, Ludendorff had planned to send General Max von Boehn's Seventh Army and portions of General Bruno von Mudra's of thirty elite divisions in a massive feint against the Allied lines on the Chemin des Dames. A diversion at Cantigny would help to confuse Foch as to his real intentions.

The commander of the 272nd Infantry Regiment gave the code name of *Tarnapol* to his raid. The general of the other reserve division in support called his early-morning caper *Tannenberg*. Both recalled victories against the Russians, and both were launched on the morning of May 27. After an hour and a half of a heavy mortar barrage and shelling by night *Minen-werfers,* the two raiding parties, the best men picked from many companies, came over. These attempted to drive over the forward positions of the 28th, which had returned from rehearsals, and its brigade companion, the 26th Infantry.

The group raiding Yank infantrymen in the Belle Assise Farm positions on the American right was annihilated before it reached the Doughboy lines, but there was severe fighting in the area called Casablanca. German raiders got into the front line before they were driven back by Doughboys rushing up with bayonets from second-line positions. Even so, they began their rush back to their own lines carrying a stunned Doughboy along with them. His buddies pursued the raiders, bayoneted and killed them, and the captive was freed. Three Doughboys in listening posts before the Belle Assise Farm trenches were wounded and dragged back to German Intelligence officers. Not one of them talked of the forthcoming attack on Cantigny. A tougher German division, such as the elements then rushing across the Aisne River, might have pried the secret of Cantigny from them in time.

The German raiders were met with such spirit that some of the defenders ended up in possession of the jump-off trenches employed by the Germans, though in a small way (to a Britisher or a Frenchman a very small way indeed) the Doughboys had begun to pay the price, a single engineer company losing thirty-three officers and men. But the Germans got no information and left three German prisoners in Doughboy hands. During the night before the attack on Cantigny, carriers brought out the dead, the wounded, and the prisoners, and the men of the 28th tried to get a little sleep in spite of the loud screams of 75s and 77s exchanging fire from forward batteries.

Among the raiders the Doughboys captured in the *Tarnapol* raid was Corporal Karl Feltporch of the 83rd Reserve Regiment in support of the two German regiments holding Cantigny. He was from a group of 120 lads picked from the four companies of his battalion, and as he was fed Hershey bars and proffered packs of Luckies and Fatimas and Camels he told Shipley Thomas, Intelligence lieutenant of the 16th Infantry, that there had been no rehearsal for the raid, and little preparation. Corporal Felt-porch and his buddies, many of whom were killed, were informed that "only green American troops are opposing us." While he was doubtless happy to be *hors de combat*, he no longer had any illusions about American fighting qualities. His fellow Germans still holding Cantigny would lose their illusions in the next few days.

The morning of May 28 came early, with a light haze upon the ground before the town. At 4:45 General Summerall's artillery began tuning up, checking the registers and making adjustments. Thirty minutes later, guns were firing in furious cadence, and no Doughboy in the assault could hear anything. Platoon leaders moved along the new trenches of the first wave, pantomiming while checking equipment. Sleepless men blew sand from cartridge clips, looked to bayonet studs and catches. Automatic riflemen with the French Chauchats prayed that they would not jam. Carriers knew what to do if a man in the heavy machine-gun sections was shot down; his body had to be looted of his musettes, for American ammunition would not fit the French gun.

There was no elation now, only swift hearts and dedication. There was a solemnity about it. Some lads opened khaki-backed Bibles and turned to such solace as the Ninety-first Psalm: "A thousand shall fall at thy side, and ten thousand at thy right hand; but it shall not come nigh thee." At 6:45, after ninety minutes of the thundering guns, a curtain of fire, a rolling barrage, came from Summerall's guns, exploding one hundred meters beyond the men in the first line of trenches. The infantry, burdened under heavy packs, each man's shovel protruding above his left shoulder, began walking across the fields for a distance of about ten city blocks to Cantigny and its outskirts.

French divisions on either side of the 1st Division now turned their artillery to the limit of range upon the sector held by the two German regiments. The machine-gun elements of these two neighboring divisions advanced to the flanks of the Americans, ready to dispel—in the German counterattacks—any notion of outflanking the newcomers. The Doughboys themselves advanced their own French-made Hotchkiss machine guns farther than the French thought prudent. All three battalions of the 1st Division's machine gunners came up now to support the attack, while the regimental machine-gun companies of the 16th and 18th Infantry arrived to contribute their bit of chattering hell to the ensemble. One of these companies fired 100,000 rounds in the next forty-eight hours.

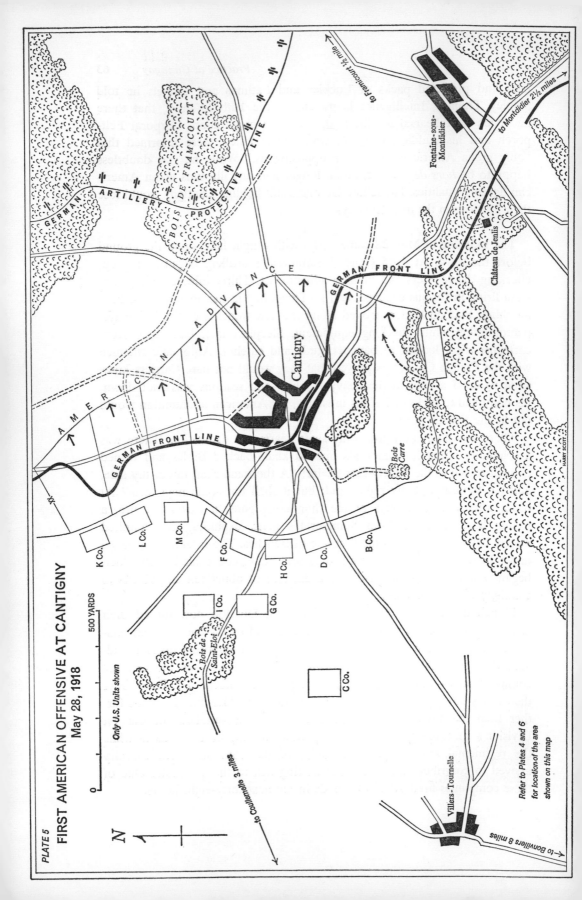

PLATE 5

FIRST AMERICAN OFFENSIVE AT CANTIGNY
May 28, 1918

N

Only U.S. Units shown

0   500 YARDS

to Coullemelle 3 miles

Refer to Plates 4 and 6
for location of the area
shown on this map

to Bonvillers 8 miles

Villers-Tournelle

C Co.

I Co.

G Co.

Bois de
Saint-Eloi

K Co.

L Co.

M Co.

F Co.

H Co.

D Co.

B Co.

GERMAN FRONT LINE

A M E R I C A N   A D V A N C E

Cantigny

Bois
Carré

A Co.

GERMAN FRONT LINE

GERMAN   ARTILLERY   PROTECTIVE   LINE

BOIS   DE   FRAMICOURT

to Framicourt ½ mile

Fontaine-sous-
Montdidier

to Montdidier 2½ miles

Château de Jenlis

HARRY SCOTT

During the night of May 27, men of the 18th Infantry and of the 1st Engineers had dug two lines of trenches before Cantigny, one for a dummy jumping-off place to draw harmless artillery fire. The Stokes mortars came up and dug in less than three hundred meters from Cantigny. Everyone knew now that the attack could not fail; it was a matter of how well it might be executed, how much confusion there might be in the taking of the town, and what would be the outcome of the inevitable counterattack.

The first wave of the center battalion had more than a kilometer to go to form a protecting screen of automatic riflemen beyond the village to the left. The barrage lifted every two minutes, advancing another one hundred meters—a distance an Olympic sprinter might run in less than eleven seconds. The right of the battalion paused in Cantigny long enough to kill, wound, or capture every German there, troops of a reserve division emaciated, half-starved, and deafened by Summerall's guns over weeks of cannonading. Germans were killed in cellars, in trenches, in the village square, in farmhouse parlors musty with the smell of old velvet draperies. The Doughboys used all their types of arms save the French rifle grenades. A man had no need of them—a French flame thrower in a German's face, an American bayonet through his body, a British Mills grenade into his shell hole, Chauchats chattering their curious, hiccuping burst of fire, a Springfield rifle with a quick trigger man—these did the short work. Then they moved on, but not until some neglected Germans in deep trenches on the right of the village opened fire on a platoon, killed its unwary leader, and decimated the rank-and-file before they in turn were relentlessly killed. (It was too late then for them to cry *"Kamerad!"*)

The battalion on the left, moving at the same pace with its French tanks, marched straight to its objective in the fields beyond the village, bayoneting out the enemy trenches and tying into the center outfit, where it now began digging furiously, its shovels the prime weapon now, curving back until it had anchored its left flank to the Frenchmen of the 152nd Division. The latter observed all this with seasoned approbation; it was Bullard who remarked, "A Frenchman never rested until he had dug a hole, and after that he never rested anywhere except in the hole."

The battalion on the right, moving to the east of Cantigny, had some trouble with a small ravine before it, too, found its flank on the center battalion. By seven-twenty all objectives were reached. The second wave strung barbed wire; signalers and engineers ran telephone lines to Colonel Ely's post of command and thence to battalion commanders. Out beyond Cantigny, many Doughboys set to work with their shovels consolidating German trenches. Above, a French squadron commanded the air, and wherever an aviator looked down upon the lines he could see Doughboys digging. Meanwhile, Summerall enclosed the area in a box barrage to seal off the 2,200 meters the small Cantigny countersalient covered in a depth of 1,600 meters at the apex of the curve.

Everything had gone according to plan, with few Yank casualties, the killings in Cantigny and adjacent trenches so overwhelming that German reserves in the woods to the north as yet did not know Cantigny was no longer theirs. Around eight o'clock a small force, about fifty of the enemy, tried to discover the true situation in Cantigny. Riflemen dropped the shovels and shot them down. At nine-thirty perhaps one hundred Germans repeated the maneuver in a spiritless fashion and were destroyed by automatic riflemen now deep in their holes. The Germans knew now they had lost Cantigny, though they believed only temporarily. The new American touring company, with a cast largely selected from amateurs of a year ago, had successfully performed the first act of the drama.

After their second probing of the American position on the morning of the twenty-eighth, the Germans in the supporting lines began streaming in small groups to forward positions in villages and woods north of Cantigny. They were not suited for the savage work of counterattacks. Major General von Mohn, commanding the 25th Reserve Division, backing up the unfortunate 82nd Reserve Division, commanded by Lieutenant General Baron von St. Ange, had not been expected to make much of a fight anywhere with his aging men, his hollow-cheeked boys. Their raids, such as the *Tarnapol* and *Tannenberg* operations, the heavy shelling, were all part of various feints made under the code name of *Manfred*—"to divert the enemy's attention from the ensuing main attack of the Seventh Army."

Now, however, not only had the German raiders been repulsed, but the village of Cantigny had been lost, the Yanks giving Debeney's observers a high-ground view of German-held positions along the Aisne. It had to be retaken if *Manfred* ruses were to continue.

The old garrisons that had been relieved by the 272nd and 271st Reserve Infantry Regiments before daybreak that morning had hardly reached rest areas in the protective woods, the cellars of small villages sprawling before the big town of Montdidier, hoping for a bath, for hot food, for a relief from the incessant shellings of Summerall's artillery, when many companies were at once ordered to assemble in the woods by young captains who themselves did not envisage a counterattack—not with these sedentary troops. They believed they were taking up defensive positions. Nobody knew exactly what had happened at Cantigny; the American bombardment had been horrendous and communication lines had been cut. There were no signals from the town. A flight of Fokkers—about six in number—flew over the Cantigny battlefield around 10 A.M. and were driven back by a swarm of French Spads, but not before they had seen the lines of Doughboys digging in to the north of the village, had identified paths and trails leading into small clumps of woods alive with Americans. Observation planes then began true reconnaissance flights.

Weary German battalion commanders began to group their infantry companies—some of them down to seventy rifles—for an assault against the green Americans. They did not know that Ely, busy on his telephones in the woods to the right of the village, had 3,500 brawny, well-fed men in his own regimental lines, his flanks bolstered by one thousand from a battalion of the 26th Infantry, by fifteen hundred men from Colonel Frank Parker's regiment, machine-gun companies everywhere. These innocent captains, sergeants, and privates from America, new to slaughter, naïvely brave, fresh and prideful, guided by superb staff officers in a textbook operation, would have to be killed and gassed by a score of thousands in massive artillery preparation before elements of two German reserve divisions might have a chance to retake the village of Cantigny. The morale factor that long, bloody day was tremendous. The German Reservists were fighting for a ruse; the Doughboys were fighting for their own pride of manliness.

Across the fields, Colonel Ely—an incessant telephonist—let his brigadier, Beaumont Buck, know the simple score: small losses, everything going according to plan as of ten o'clock that morning. Lieutenant Colonel G. C. Marshall, Jr., G.S., A.C. of S., G-3, arrived about that time in the small Bois de Saint-Eloi north of the town and reviewed Ely's movement. "Our losses are about three hundred," Marshall told Bullard by field message as he picked his way around shell holes, finding cover on high ground to turn field glasses on woods where the young German captains were now assembling their *feldgrau* outfits. Marshall estimated the German dead as around eight hundred, counting those corpses in the fields beyond. Some wounded may have crawled back to the deep German lines. Prisoners would run around two hundred, with several officers.

French aircraft dropped notes telling where scuttling Germans, sometimes in patches of five and ten, were assembling behind German lines in companies of one hundred. Marshall picked his way back to divisional headquarters at Le-Mesnil-Saint-Firmin, where Major General Bullard had not yet begun to chew his nails. Marshall, with his ability to discern the routes by which troops must invariably move, thought the counterattacks would issue from the trees of the Bois de Framicourt and its ravine to the north; from the town of Fontaine-sous-Montdidier to the east; from the landscaped park of the Château de Jenlis to the south. Marshall ordered Summerall to plaster Framicourt, Fontaine, Jenlis, and to keep up a fire of interdiction during the night.

Around noon, the raw-hided Ely began bitching a little. He had begun to lose men copiously from murderous artillery fire. He had been given very little help by airplanes, and was getting less. His own post of command was being shelled, the German observation planes having noted the traffic around his P.C. He wanted more counterbattery work against the big German guns. Ely did not know that, ninety minutes after he captured Cantigny, the airplanes and big French pieces had pulled out, rushing eastward toward the Marne. The French tank battalion, as if expecting to be used in a counterattack to retake positions which Ely would probably lose, patched up its gear and withdrew to reserve areas, minus only one lieutenant killed among its crews. Around two in the afternoon, Ely, still sure of himself, reported he was doing all right, but his A Battalion, cleaning out the ravine south of Cantigny, had taken some casualties, one company having all of its officers down, and a third of its men. He needed more officers in his B Battalion. Its commander, Lieutenant Colonel Robert J. Maxey—his outfit spelled it *Moxie* for good reason—had stopped a bad one, and would die.

Before they ever went into battle, Pershing had told Maxey and nine hundred other officers of the division circled about him in a glade to throw away their textbooks, judge every situation in its own light, and set a personal example of sacrifice to be followed by all other officers in the swelling American Expeditionary Force. And now Maxey was down, two of his captains killed, four lieutenants wounded, and about eighty men—one officer for every eleven men. Cantigny was that kind of a fight. There were no remnants of companies led by freckle-faced, buck private kids suddenly born to leadership, no shattered battalions collected and thrown forward against caves and rocks by sergeants and shavetails. Fighting was in the clear, and there were officers ready to lead and to die wherever enlisted men burrowed in the earth. The Big Red One, officers and men, were all aware that this was a world premiere, albeit in a village theater. By two-thirty in the afternoon Ely was receiving the unwelcome news—if ever notice of an impending fight was bad news to that belligerent Irishman—that he was going to be counterattacked according to Marshall's forecast. The German assault from Framicourt would probably strike between Ely's flank and that of the 26th Infantry's A Battalion, directed by Major Theodore Roosevelt, Jr., eldest of four sons the great Teddy Roosevelt had sent to France, which had jumped off as Ely entered Cantigny, to throw a flank guard on the right of Ely's newly won positions.

By three o'clock, St. Ange was moving toward the Cantigny area, making the air blue with his displeasure. Colonel von Friedrichs of the 272nd Reserve Infantry Regiment, who knew little of Ely's dispositions, selected Major Herzberg to lead the first wave "with calmness and certainty." The major had no inkling of the mettle he was going to test.

Herzberg chose to move forward in three waves around 6 P.M., following a barrage of heavy mortars to soften up the enemy lines, behind the cover of a fire curtain provided by lighter trench mortars. Corps artillery around three o'clock opened up to shatter Ely's second line. Its fire was directed by graduates of Colonel Georg Bruchmüller's staff, the greatest master of all German gunners.

Around five-thirty in the afternoon, thin waves of Germans came into the open, pioneers and explorers with Bangalore torpedoes, steel pipes stuffed with dynamite, to blow open lanes in the barbed wire strung upon screw pickets by engineers and infantry in Ely's second line. The 28th Infantry's Chauchat men and Springfield riflemen, upright under mortar fire, shot them down. A few minutes later, Major Herzberg stepped forth, simulating calmness, with his first wave behind a rolling barrage of light mortars. Some reached the Doughboy front line before they were killed or cried *"Kamerad!"* By the time the second wave followed, the lads from Bullard's Signal Corps battalion had repaired telephone lines, and Summerall's gunners were finding the range. The second German wave fared worse than the first; riflemen, automatic riflemen, machine gunners, mortarmen, and artillerymen were tearing *feldgrau* uniforms into bloody shreds, and the sleepless Reservists were shot down before they traversed half of No-Man's Land. The third wave died aborning. Cantigny had been denied Major Herzberg; but there would be a tomorrow, when the folly of this first, unstudied sortie would not be repeated.

Meanwhile, the 28th's hastily burrowed trenches were covered in great swaths of shellfire, the front line no longer a line, but a series of shell holes, where wounded lay with first-aid bandages stiffening in the night air, mouths cottony with the spittle of bleeding men, shuddering pain arriving as the shock of the wound diminished. Ely began calling for carriers to get these men out. Detachments of ambulance companies and field medics which went forward with the 28th Infantry were not enough; these were wounded, too. After Major Herzberg's waves had been repulsed, his guns still raging, Ely reported to his brigadier: "Two officers left in one battalion. All men in one company gone but twelve. He will stay but should be allowed to reinforce."

Who was HE, with his eleven other men, who sent word to Ely that he would stay? In the 1st Division history, the towering stack of war diaries, HE remains nameless. It was enough for the chroniclers and historians to say that HE was a Doughboy new to the attack and some three thousand miles or more from home. Bullard immediately ordered Beaumont Buck to "tell Colonel Ely to relieve the remainder of the company that suffered so with a company he has in reserve. Then give him C Company of the 1st Battalion," from the brigade line. One major reported that he had only two officers left in his battalion. He needed many men for carrying parties to get his badly wounded back to collecting stations. The division machine-gun officer, Lieutenant Colonel A. S. Bowen, reported: "Line in front Cantigny probably lost. Our troops to counterattack when barrage starts."

Colonel Bruchmüller's staff, past masters from the Russian front, with the veteran artillery of Hutier's army able to shift about the rear areas without much regard for counterbattery fire, began sending Ely's outfits everything they had in the way of high explosives and toxic shells before sundown the following afternoon. Lieutenant General Baron von Watters had been told that "American resistance would be weak" if the next counterattack was properly mounted. Around suppertime of the second day, Ely, barking at his lieutenant telephonist, sent word to Bullard: "Front line pounded to hell-and-gone, and entire front line must be relieved to-morrow night or I will not be held responsible." Watters was searching for Ely with strong concentrations of his quick-barking little 77-millimeter rifles, with massive doses of fire from concentrations of 105s, 150s, and 210s. St. Ange went after him with infantry three times that second after-noon. Ely sent word that it might be necessary to draw back, giving up his front lines. Major Davis, commanding the 3rd Machine Gun Battalion, had told the Big Red One's machine-gun officer that now "our position is prac-tically untenable here but we are bound to stick it out and hope our barrage is a help." The second night descended, bringing with it the fog of war and the darkness which renders all armies ignorant.

Ely had used up his reserves. Bullard sent fresh troops into his support line. "You are not to thicken your line with them," he sent word to Ely. (The French and British staffs, throughout the Doughboy's War, criticized the Yanks for putting too many eggs in the front-line basket.) Bullard was warning Ely in his first engagement that reinforcements were only for a counterattack to be used solely at the discretion of the brigade commander. St. Ange made one more feeble attempt in the small hours of May 30. Bullard knew that Ely, who had enough fight in him to satisfy a warren of badgers, should be relieved and be given time to lick his wounds. He told his chief of staff, Campbell King, to get Ely's outfit out of the lines that night, May 30-31.

The 16th Infantry, 3,500 strong, moved in with no quiet files of men stealthily under the stars. It was a combat relief, perhaps the most difficult of operations for new troops. Ely and his 28th, with reinforcing elements from Roosevelt's and Parker's support, marched back to villages miles behind the lines.

The Doughboys, in the first offensive action, had not only taken a position the Germans had never meant to lose, but had held it against three determined counterattacks. They were there to stay.

Pershing had put his best foot forward in every echelon with the Big Red One. The chief of Sanitary Train since the division first arrived in France was a Colonel James Irving Mabee, an old Regular who had been a small-town doctor in the Michigan of 1900, had married a pretty girl named Lenore Allen and had taken down his shingle and lct out for Luzon and adventure. The field medics with the 28th Infantry, the carriers and ambulance men he sent forward in answer to Ely's demands after the first counterattack, had no easy time under Mabee. He complained bitterly of their ignorance, of their softness, when he first caught sight of these innocents shipped him from the States. They knew nothing of first-aid work such as hemorrhage control, bandaging, shock, splint application. As for the softness —he secured some old sergeants of the Regular Line to monkey-drill them until they were acrobats. "There's no maybe about Mabee," was their stock pun. The colonel had to follow the slow French currents of evacuation, which he did not like. The French corps field hospitals had the good sites. He had to find room for his own three spread out somewhere along the single shell-marked road, and it was a long way back to Villers-Tournelle for a bleeding man. Mabee had two makes of trucks and ambulances: a General Motors heavy rig and the historic Model-T Ford. The General Motors rig was a bigger, faster, better vehicle, but it did not have the jittery sprightliness of the Tin Lizzie with its wishbone springs and a planetary transmission enabling the driver to stamp down on the reverse pedal for a bone-shattering stop.

Mabee found a way to get the Fords into Cantigny itself: they moved along the main road, having to turn out for ammunition trains, always a priority for men under fire, and then driving hell-for-leather up a ravine, dodging shell holes and skirting craters, much as millions of farmers had pushed these little beasts over eroded hills. However, farmers could leave their headlights on; Mabee's drivers were in darkness except for star shells and Very pistol flares searing the night sky. Ambulance drivers, for some reason never justified, drove as fast as possible when a road was being shelled; though a Ford might be dodging one shell only to run faster into another. Advanced dressing stations were established at Coullemelle and Villers-Tournelle, the Fords turning their casualties out there, and the General Motors trucks taking them to Bacouel. There the ambulatory wounded were packed like sardines into stake-bodied trucks for Field

Hospital No. 3 at Froissy. Men whose lives hung in the balance went to Field Hospital No. 12 in nearby Bonvillers. Gas casualties were transported to No. 13, the third of Mabee's hospitals, at Vendeuil-Caply.

It was a long road home for the lads of Cantigny, and a Doughboy with broken bones, bouncing along pocked roads in a Tin Lizzie, needed to chew the edge of his blanket to keep from crying out. He was at home, though, when he looked into the smiling, half-serious eyes of an American Army nurse. He never forgot her. In his war diaries, Colonel Mabee kept the score on the mustard gas men. Poison gas was, despite the horrors implicit in its use, the least lethal of weapons. Of 507 gassed men that Mabee brought back from Ely's attack, 313 were soon returned to duty, these afflicted merely with superficial burns and yperite conjunctivitis. Yperite (the British version) reminded a Doughboy of the Coney Island mustard he put upon a hot dog. Dichloroethyl sulphide, in massive inhalation, brought about a lung corrosion that resulted in bronchial pneumonia. Mabee had only twelve men die of it. Of the 507 gassed men, 182 remained in hospitals for varying times of convalescence, some of these knowing that, henceforth, they were on borrowed time when the rainy seasons began.

There were few casualties among the wounded as the enemy shelled the rear areas, though here and there a nurse cried out in anger over a dead boy, a disemboweled Army mule screamed in his death agony. The seriously wounded, looking at canvased roofs crimsoned in the glare, unable to fight back, cursed all Germans. Woodrow Wilson had told them they were making war, not upon the German people, but only upon Kaiser Bill and his coterie of villains. Doughboys had left America with an attitude of goodwill that was much frowned upon by staff officers; all the Doughboys in those tents had known American citizens of German birth—the quizzical professor, dreamy musician, kindly doctor, the bartender of a friendly saloon. This attitude of goodwill was changing now; the fears of commanders vanished. The 134 officers and 4,338 men Mabee ferried back to his tents in the long Cantigny operation thought of the 41 officers and 867 men who never made it. Kaiser Bill and the War to End War were forgotten. Among the great passions that seized mankind, sometimes the thirst for revenge seemed to the Doughboys the noblest.

The Germans summed up the reasons for their failure to retake Cantigny on the use of troops left too long in sedentary Reserve divisions, on launching their counterattack too soon before their artillery batteries had time to silence American guns, and on the heavy casualties among German officers. Many officers had been killed or wounded. (Doughboy riflemen were indeed eager to obtain a Luger pistol or a pair of Zeiss binoculars; the pistol could fade thirty dollars in a crap game, and the binoculars were worth a hundred dollars in a Red Dog jackpot.) Yet the considered opinion of men who had now been at war nearly four years was this: *Had the counterattack been properly timed and organized, the Doughboys of the 1st Division would have been driven out of Cantigny, as the French had been twice before; for it was felt that American powers of resistance were weak.* Thanks to all these explanations, there is no record anywhere that the German High Command saw the handwriting on the wall that evening in Picardy. The Doughboys, ferrying out their dead and wounded, would have disputed this estimate of weakness to the last man. Yet the Germans could not be taken to task for this erroneous conclusion. Great things were going for them elsewhere. "It cannot be said," General Pershing wrote long afterward, "that German hopes of final victory were extravagant, either as viewed at that time, or as viewed in the light of history."

Only the corps commander, Baron von Watters, seemed to have sensed the true impact of the modest Cantigny reverse. "I am under the impression," he wrote Hutier, "that the troops should be given particularly firm commanders of strong character in order to overcome quickly *the influence* of the recent operation." Watters was politely saying to Oskar von Hutier, a great soldier of whom he stood in awe, that unless the Doughboys were promptly slaughtered in a return engagement, there was no telling where the thing might end. And across the line, Ely, filing his report, warned the A.E.F. that the Germans he had defeated were not first-quality troops, the companies assaulting him seeming driven to the attack, with no stomach for fighting, 80 percent of them boys, and 70 percent of these ill-nourished and hollow-cheeked. But weak opposition or not, as a result of their showing no Army commander, British or French, ever wanted to relinquish one of these big, raw-boned American divisions, cantankerously ignorant though some may first have been.

Captain W. G. Livesay, Ely's regimental adjutant, totaled up the 28th's share of the cost of taking an obscure little village from German Reserves. In the photographs which Ely, still beetling, had made of himself and his staff, Captain Livesay shows up as a big boy with a moon-faced smile without a line in his face after those three days within the sound of Hanson E. Ely's voice and the thunder of the guns; a lad made of steel, with a foam-rubber cushioning. The 28th jumped off the morning of May 28 with 122 officers and 3,757 men. Three days later, the regiment sprawling exhausted around the villages of Froissy, Saint-Eusoye, and Maisoncelle, Captain Livesay reported the body of one officer missing, thirteen killed, and thirty-one wounded. The men in the 28th's ranks alone had paid for their victory with 187 killed and 636 wounded. How easy this fighting would soon seem to a regiment such as the 28th, now fully acquainted with the stagnation of trench warfare.

Back home, the newspapers broke out banner headlines to announce an American "first," the capture of Cantigny—though censorship permitted no mention of the Big Red One. In London, Prime Minister Lloyd George made brief mention of Cantigny as a bright patch in an otherwise melancholy sky. Ferdinand Foch, Supreme Commander of all Allied Forces, had no time to praise the Americans—he had guessed wrong and was in serious trouble at Château-Thierry on the Marne.

Desperation

Chapter 5

PLUGGING THE CHÂTEAU-THIERRY GAP

Retreat, hell. We just got here.

Ludendorff was unquestionably the finest tactician on the Western Front, but his strategy in the spring of 1918 was transparent; all knew he had to drive the British into the sea to conquer France. He had struck an almost mortal blow at Saint-Quentin in March at the juncture of the French and British lines, driving west all the way to Montdidier, and had followed it in April with a second well-nigh fatal smash at the British in Flanders before he was checked north of Hazebrouck, only a day's march from Dunkirk. While events had gone very well for the Germans to this point, the Allies were still hanging on, their lines still joined, with a reserve "mass of maneuver" around Compiègne built up to prevent a split between their forces. In an effort to separate them, Ludendorff planned a ruse farther east by sending General von Boehn's Seventh Army in a powerful smash against the French lines north of the Aisne River along the Chemin des Dames from Reims westward to Soissons. He had no intention of fighting his way south across the Marne at Château-Thierry or on to Paris, only an hour away, but he wanted to compel Foch to move some of his reserves eastward and away from the British. Then, with the French and British divided, the Crown Prince of Bavaria, with three armies, would drive the latter into the sea, and subsequently the Kaiser would fight his way leisurely into Paris. If Foch did not swallow the bait and

77

rush his reserves to the defense of Soissons, the Vesle River line and the French capital, Ludendorff hoped that a terrified Clemenceau would overrule the Supreme Commander.

German Intelligence told Ludendorff that Major General Duchêne, commanding the French Sixth Army along the Chemin des Dames, had learned nothing of elastic defense in four years of fighting, and had crowded his forward lines with troops on a vulnerable ridge easily flanked on its western fallaway. The great ridges between the Aisne and the Vesle, which should have been the French Main Army Line bristling with pillboxes and guns, tanks lurking beneath trees, were lightly held. It was a situation made to order for Ludendorff's tactical genius and one which might have been anticipated, though only briefly, if the French had accepted the opinion of Brigadier General Dennis E. Nolan, chief of American Intelligence. Two days before the 1st Division struck at Cantigny, he went to Soissons with Pershing's permission to tell the French that he was convinced the Germans had massed forces to break the French lines on the Chemin des Dames. The French told Nolan politely he was mistaken, and Nolan returned to Chaumont to be routed from bed the next morning, May 27, by a message that upwards of thirty German divisions were crossing the Aisne River before the French had had time to destroy the bridges.

General von Boehn had prepared his assault with great secrecy; axle boxes on caissons and wagons were muffled against clacking; horse hooves were bagged with gunny sackings; and every harness buckle was greased against jingle or glint. Three hundred thousand men of his Seventh Army had moved along side roads in darkness, lying hidden in forests throughout the airplanes' daytime hours, every spring and well protected by sentries against daylight thirsts, each man supplied three days' iron rations of canned horsemeat goulash in his rucksack. The troops had worked out their forthcoming assault with live ammunition in rear areas under the direction of the artillery entrepreneur, Colonel Bruchmüller. Before dawn on May 27, Bruchmüller surpassed himself, letting loose a murderous barrage that thundered without the slightest warning on the crowded defenses of the French Sixth Army, on the Chemin des Dames. Whole divisions soon ceased to exist, many poilu prisoners led back to German cages with brains so scrambled from concussion that they never regained sanity.

The swarm of old German professionals swept forward toward Paris on a thirty-mile front, gobbling up the great railway yards at Soissons, seizing airplanes, shops, stores, 650 guns, 2,000 machine guns, and 60,000 prisoners. When they found bridges over the Vesle River at noon the first day still intact, they swept on, taking 45,000 hospital beds—a critical shortage for the French—and heading for the Marne. The Marne River, gathering

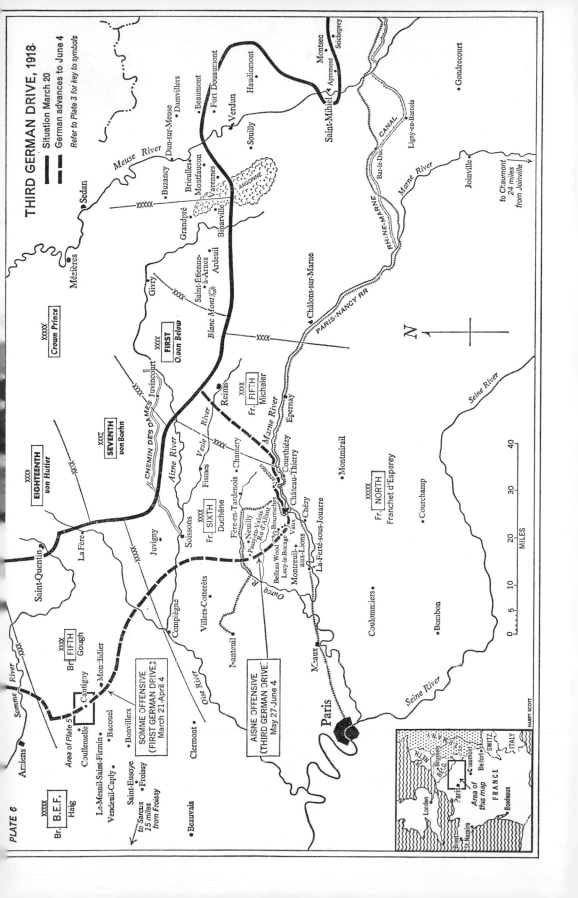

PLATE 6

THIRD GERMAN DRIVE, 1918.

━━━ Situation March 20
╍╍╍ German advances to June 4

Refer to Plate 3 for key to symbols

strength in eastern France, flows northward past the Vosges Mountains, turns westward until it reaches Château-Thierry, which lies on both sides of the river some fifty miles northeast of Paris and about thirty miles southwest of Reims. Here the hills turn in abruptly southward in a left-angle bend to flow into the Seine at Paris. Elements of von Boehn's Seventh Army were heading now for Château-Thierry, important as a communication center, and the bridges scattered along the Marne to the east of it. Major General Mondésir's desperate French XVIII Corps was falling back across the Marne while the Germans took possession of impregnable positions in the 150-meter hills north of the river. Foch was not fooled by the ruse and said, when Boehn first struck, that this was a feint—although a massive one—to draw French reserves away from their positions behind British and French lines. But the feint had turned into an astonishing victory and there was no controlling Ludendorff's tactical greed. Somehow, Foch had to find troops to stem the German tide.

Pershing went to see Sir Douglas Haig as soon as possible after the assault began, arriving for breakfast May 30. He found Haig boiling with anger because three British divisions, sent at three-fifths strength to the Soissons area as reserves to recuperate from the battering of the previous March, had been in the front line with four French divisions and had been shattered by the German avalanche. Haig said he would like to criticize the French, but he had himself been twice caught off balance the same way in the spring. Haig knew the situation at Château-Thierry: three British and four French divisions virtually no longer existed; thirty-five French infantry and six French cavalry divisions had been scattered, all the reserves now committed.

The Iron Commander went about the British area inspecting Doughboys in training there, knowing he would soon have to use them, hoping he would not have too much of a wrangle with Lloyd George, Lord Milner, and his friend Sir Douglas when he had to take them away from the British and set them in motion toward the Marne. He liked the Kansas and Missouri boys of the 35th Division, who were corn-fed and bigger than average, the "All-American" draftees in the 82nd, and the New Yorkers of the 77th. He thought the Pennsylvanians of the National Guard 28th and the "Regulars" of the 4th would be able to prove themselves. Their respective major generals, Wright, Burnham, Duncan, Muir, and Cameron, all sang the same tune: "Sir, the general isn't going to leave us here with the British? We're going to have our own army, aren't we?" In the present emergency Pershing knew an American Army, as yet unformed, was out of the question. It must have pained him. Pershing did not even consider the 3rd Division of "Regulars." It was only then entering the highest plateau of its training, with three machine-gun battalions and regimental machine-gun companies scattered over a wide area from Courthiézy in the east to La-Ferté-sous-Jouarre in the west, the latter only a short march from Château-Thierry; its indispensable 6th Engineers still undergoing training with the British near the coast; and its three artillery regiments, still inadequately equipped with makeshift French guns, specifically exempted from active duty until further training had been completed. But its infantry of seventeen thousand men—still not deemed first-quality troops—was nearest to Château-Thierry.

After he left Haig on May 30, Pershing went to dine with Foch at Sarcus. Before leaving, he granted Foch's request to bring his five green divisions into the Marne area, and he ordered the 3rd Division to move up behind Mondésir's shattered French ranks. He also submitted that the German right flank at Soissons was going to be vulnerable to an Allied—American—counterattack once the front was stabilized. The marshal replied dolefully—a rare mood for him when the word *attaque* was mentioned—that he had such a thing in mind.

Late in the afternoon of May 31, the first of the American reinforcements, fifteen Doughboys of the 3rd Division carrying two Hotchkiss guns, rushed across the wagon bridge over the Marne and into the town of Château-Thierry. They were led by Lieutenant Bissell, a recent graduate of West Point. His mission was to discover the situation around the approaches to the bridge which was being defended by remnants of a French Colonial division of black Senegalese—magnificent assault troops, and looters beyond compare. While John T. Bissell was shifting his two guns from house to house, from street corner to courtyard, elements of his 7th (motorized) Machine Gun Battalion were digging gun emplacements across the river on the south bank of the Marne. The battalion moved up through roads swarming with refugees, and clogged with retreating French soldiers. Like all troops shattered by defeat, they assured the Doughboys that all was lost. It had been almost a year since Captain Stanton had cried, *"Nous voilà, Lafayette!"* And now: *"Enfin, voici les américains!"* Alas, said the poilus, they were too little and too late. Everyone thought so except the ignorant Americans. The fleeing French Colonials paused only long enough to loot the baggage and the field packs of their brave comrades.

As darkness came on, Major James G. Taylor arrived to find that his executive officer, Captain Charles F. Houghton, had placed eight Hotchkiss guns in brush on the south bank of the river covering the wagon bridge and nine guns commanding the railway trestle five hundred meters upstream. In spite of the frantic confusion en route, by midnight all machine guns were emplaced, a tribute to the persistence and energy of such sergeants as Robert Gould, Ezra Muse, and Cletus Montgomery—who won the Distinguished Service Cross—and of buck privates like Jimmy Punco, to whom the French gave their highest award, the Médaille Militaire. These expendable Doughboys were digging two alternate emplacements for each gun already in position, with a fourth position kept secret and known only to platoon leaders. (It was discovered six weeks later from captured Germans that these positions were plotted on the enemy's assault team maps. There were spies and traitors everywhere.) From time to time the diggers dropped their shovels and fired streams of bullets into the town square across the river, but they had to be careful not to hit the retreating Colonials. By ten o'clock on the night of June 1, the Germans had reached the river's edge, driving what remained of the French Colonials onto the wagon bridge. When the fighting reached the middle of the span French demolition teams, having placed all their charges, blew up the bridge, sending attackers and defenders into eternity with the same breath of fire. No one then knew if Bissell and his fourteen buddies had been on the bridge.

From the hills across the Marne German Intelligence officers, with data from patrols, telescope stations, observation balloons, and spies, soon gave their estimate of the American enemy who had kept them from crossing the river. "They have a healthy and vigorous appearance . . . engaged on the front for the first time . . . the division is to be considered altogether a good one . . . fighting value will increase with wider experience in warfare." On the south side of the river defenders were digging positions in the poppy-strewn wheat of rolling farmland where there were good communicating roads. There were still no defensive lines except some clever ones that the French drew on paper and presented to the Yanks. The 3rd Division's infantry filtered in amid sniping and cannonading, with many aerial dogfights overhead, and immediately, with French help, drove back across the Marne's pontoons those Germans who had crossed the river south of Jaulgonne.

On the night of June 2, a lieutenant named Cobbey thought he heard someone calling his name from the brush at the base of the bluffs across the flow of the meandering, picture-book river Marne. Cobbey took the chance it was not a ruse (what German had ever heard of E. W. Cobbey, 2nd?) and crawled over the ties of the railway bridge, bringing back his friend, Lieutenant Bissell, and thirteen Doughboys. Both guns and one man were missing in this first feat of outstanding valor at Château-Thierry, where such performances in the 3rd Division were to become commonplace.

Lieutenant W. R. Flannery of the 7th Infantry won that outfit's first French decoration when he heard a wounded poilu crying piteously in the brush along the north bank of the Marne. Flannery first thought of taking a patrol across the river, but he knew that many Germans could imitate the cries of a wounded Frenchman. And so he stripped down, his Colt 45 lashed on top of his head, and swam the fifty yards of darkness. He swam back with a Frenchman's hands upon his shoulders to field medics who waited on the south bank.

General Mondésir now had seventeen thousand American infantry and machine gunners to piecemeal among his troops. This was against everything Pershing had fought for, but by this time the issue of an American army was in doubt. The French general began shuffling his deck of cards with the Doughboys, big, new and eager, whom he regarded as his trumps. Only the rare spirit of these lads, Regulars then in name only, saved the 3rd Division from ignominy in the next two weeks. The regiments were shifted constantly, and sometimes battalions of weary French separated battalions of fresh Americans. Only the 38th U.S. Infantry, under a pugnacious colonel whom Bullard had sacked from the Big Red One because of his profane refusal to believe that the French could teach him anything about war, was not shuffled by Mondésir. It would have needed a brash Frenchman indeed to break up the regimental front of the 38th in the teeth of scathing disapproval from Ulysses Grant McAlexander, who was as solid as an icebox set on two fire hydrants. Before he left the Marne, the modern Ulysses—like Homer's original, "he was more majestic when seated"—found the 38th enjoying the finest day in the regimental histories of the American Expeditionary Force. (Visitors to the state capitol at Austin will find a full-length oil of McAlexander there entitled "The Rock of the Marne." There is nothing farfetched about the sobriquet.) It was not until the middle of June, its artillery having come up, that the 3rd Division was given its own sector, a front of seven river miles along the south bank of the meandering Marne from Château-Thierry eastward to the outskirts of Varennes.

About the hour that Lieutenant Bissell and his buddies were dashing across the wagon bridge to Château-Thierry, a full American division was moving forward to their left to engage the onrushing Germans of the Group Conta in Boehn's German Seventh Army. If the Group Conta could turn the corner of the Marne at Château-Thierry in a direct drive over no natural obstacles, the 3rd Division and all the others in Mondésir's corps would have the Germans across the river tearing them to shreds on their left flank. The French had known no nightmare like this since Galliéni's taxicabbers and the Old Contemptibles and various French corps had driven von Kluck's uhlan patrols out of Meaux in 1914 in the First Battle of the Marne.

The 2nd Division, 1,063 officers and 25,602 men in its twin brigades of Regulars and Marines and their supporting elements, had been alerted for May 29, its commanders given maps of the Beauvais-Rouen area, its destination the capable Debeney's French First Army at Cantigny, where it was scheduled to relieve the Big Red One. All artillery and combat trains were replete with ammunition, all ammunition belts filled, each man carrying two days' rations, with three in regimental reserves. However, they had neither trench mortars nor hand grenades, critical shortages. It was to be a routine operation, the movement to begin on May 31 by rail and bus, with motorized elements to follow by marching. But around five in the afternoon of May 30, a French staff officer appeared and ordered the division to move instead at five the next morning to the Paris-Meaux area, transport being French camions. The American government, properly, had to pay the Doughboy fare, and some Marine units were late shoving off because a French transport officer, who had the soul of a bus conductor, insisted on counting Leatherneck noses before their camions could move toward a life-and-death appointment in Belleau Wood. The motorized elements and horse-drawn impedimenta were to be shipped by rail.

Private Bailey, Chauchat gunner of the 9th Infantry, 2nd Division, was crowded with nineteen buddies in the stake body of a small blue camion with its driver from French Indo-China, a little brown man who spoke no European language, and whom paymasters knew only by his thumbprints. Seventy-five camions bumper to bumper extended for a mile to transport a battalion of U.S. Infantry and there were twelve battalions in transit. Private Bailey remembered that on the morning of May 31, having marched some miles at early dawn to catch the bus, he saw the Eiffel Tower on his left but had no knowledge of his destination. He only knew that the French had been defeated north of Château-Thierry and the division's orders had been changed. When the buses made a right turn, the signs pointed toward the railhead of Meaux, but he had no notion of its whereabouts. The roads were shrouded in white dust, the olive-drab uniforms of the Doughboys soon gray with a mantle of chalk. Sometime around noon, the caravans halted for the men to eat a salty bacon sandwich. Thirst began its annoyance shortly afterward. An hour before dusk, the camions rumbled through the deserted town of Meaux, where guards stood before stores and shops half-looted and swarms of refugees jammed into boxcars en route to camps. The camions swung up the road toward Château-Thierry, and the Chauchat gunner, after nearly a year of quiet villages between tours of the inactive sectors, saw the backwash of war. "One who saw that stream of misery can never forget it," Private Bailey wrote.

There were people of all ages except men of military ages; there were children riding on the creaking wagons, held in place by their feeble grandparents; everyone who was able to do so was compelled to walk. There were carts drawn by every conceivable animal: cows, oxen, dogs, and horses. The other cattle were driven along by the side of the wagons. The procession was noiseless, for the marchers were too miserable to more than glance at us as we passed and probably thought: *a few more for the Boches to devour.* Alongside the road, too tired to go farther, was a leathery-faced old woman with all her remaining property piled on a wheelbarrow . . . each procession occupied half of the hot, white road from which there rose a cloud of bitter dust—the young going up to slaughter and be slaughtered; the old and their youth fleeing from the *furor Teutonicus.* Each half pitied the other, and the fresher half swore to avenge the feebler.

By midnight May 31–June 1, the infantry was marching somewhere on the road to Château-Thierry. Bailey's squad, burdened under two Chauchats, ammunition clips, Springfield rifles and bandoliers, heavy packs, field rations, and two hundred pistol rounds, stretched upon the cobblestones of a deserted town square. Eighteen hours of standing hip to hip with a seventy-two-pound pack, dry-throated in a cloud of dust, had wearied them. Most men lay in full equipment on the cobbles and slept, but some scroungers with keener noses smelled brandy. "If there is a brandy distillery there," Bailey recalled, "then the place might have been La-Ferté-sous-Jouarre. Some of the fellows for a while forgot their fatigue." By dawn, remnants of French regiments were streaming through the square as Doughboys tightened belts and fell into company lines. "Many of the men told us we would never stop the Boches. Pointing dramatically at the bloody bandage on his head, one of the Frenchmen shouted: *Voyez ça? J'ai tué trois boches avant de la recevoir.*"

The Chauchat gunner and his squad were soon marching northward again in summer heat through the disheartened and retreating Frenchmen. The gas saturation in the inactive sectors began to tell on men returned from hospitals. Private Gilbert's face turned a ghastly green. Frothing at the mouth, Gilbert fainted onto the side of the road. None believed him a malingerer. (Gilbert returned to the 9th Infantry, was twice wounded, and then stopped a fatal one in the Argonne.) By noon the column saw no more of the defeated French. The furious pace slackened when the Doughboys began to pass forlorn poilus at siege guns firing by map into fields and woods beyond them. The column then halted for a brunch of corned-beef hash eaten from the cans. It aggravated thirst, but Lieutenant Janda drove Bailey's platoon from a small stream which he believed polluted.

The regiment halted in the abandoned town of Montreuil-aux-Lions in the early afternoon of June 1, and word was passed to forage liberally—

for the first time since Sherman gave the word to his Georgia bummers. Cider, wine, and brandy were in many abandoned shops, and the 9th Infantry had a brief carouse before resuming the march, inebriated comics in some squads now caparisoned in corsets, lace-trimmed drawers, and large organdy hats. Bailey carried a live chicken with trussed legs, and a buddy had an iron cookpot. Bailey had been unable to raid a kitchen garden for a chicken stew, being barred by a poilu sentry who was saving it for his general. "Tell the general," said the Doughboy, congenial after so much hard cider, "that I'll take the house next door." The battalion turned again and soon was single file in a patch of woods. The German was ahead and coming on. Thanks to the fortunes of war, Private Bailey was permitted to snatch a few hours' sleep in a clump of woods, though he was roused every two hours to serve as sentry on the gas guard. It was June 2 before his regiment found itself on the fighting line.

So great was French confusion in constantly changing combat orders for the 2nd Division that Germans who later interrogated their first U.S. Marine prisoners were astonished to discover that wounded sergeants with three hash marks did not know how the Leathernecks and Doughboys reached the wooded patches due south of Belleau Wood. "They are kept in complete ignorance," Lieutenant von Buy of Intelligence reported to his commander, General of Infantry von Conta at Fère-en-Tardenois. "They cannot name the towns they have passed through." Had the Germans been able to capture Brigadier General James G. Harbord, Pershing's ex-chief of staff at Chaumont, who led the Marine brigade from rest areas behind Verdun to Belleau Wood, General von Conta would have been staggered to learn that Harbord did not know either. When Pershing gave Harbord the Marine brigade, he said it was the best in France and if Harbord failed he would know whom to blame.

Around two o'clock on the afternoon of May 31, the first Order of Battle came from the desperate General Duchêne, French Army Commander: "The American 2nd Division is placed under the orders of the general commanding the French VII Army Corps for the initial purpose of closing the gap at Ru d'Allant and then to counterattack as soon as possible in the direction of Passy-en-Valois"—names quite unfamiliar to the staff officers of the 2nd. When the Americans arrived at Meaux the French corps commander, Major General Georges de Bazelaire, directed one brigade to set up headquarters near the French 4th Division at Chézy to the northeast, a bridgehead to Ludendorff's right, five miles downstream from Château-Thierry toward Paris, "and form for attack in the rear of the front held by the French." Colonel Mourruau, Bazelaire's chief of staff, could not say just where the French front was around Chézy, but the

omission was excusable since there was no front; and so he had no orders
for the other brigade. There were only roads choked with refugees, troops,
and limousines of staff officers falling back to form a line of defense. The
chief of staff of the 2nd Division, breasting this flood in an effort to reach
Chézy and indicate a line, was soon turned around again. For Duchêne
had found a new urgency, and the American 2nd Division was now given
a second set of battle orders, transferring to Major General Jean Degoutte's "XXI French Corps as reserve." Degoutte, a much younger man
than the elderly Duchêne, was something of a hatchet man for Ferdinand
Foch in his occasionally sour relations with Black Jack Pershing, and
now he had 26,665 Americans to do with as he chose. Degoutte's chief
of staff found the 2nd's chief of staff at midnight and pleaded that someone
throw a Doughboy regiment—any one he could lay his hands on—to plug
a four-kilometer gap in the shambles of the French 43rd Division, piecemealing the regiment into the French division under command of Major
General Michel.

The French next issued a third set of battle orders which counter-
manded the other two. Cynical Marines on Harbord's staff had urged
their new brigadier to obey neither the first nor the second battle order.
"When it comes to the French, General Harbord, a good Marine never
goes into motion until he gets the third edition." And they had already
begun to look upon Harbord, the old ex-enlisted cavalryman from Kansas
State Agricultural College, as "a good Marine." (The adjective had no
comparative or superlative. Nobody since 1775 had ever been better than
a good Marine.) Harbord only knew that he was standing on the Paris
road between Meaux and Montreuil-aux-Lions, throwing rations and field
packs out of French camions crowded with Marines and jamming more
Marines and ammunition in. Presently he was in marching contact with
the 9th and the 23rd Infantry of the Regulars and their Brigadier General
Edward Lewis; and the colonel of the 2nd U.S. Engineers was looking
through pitch blackness at ground he had never seen before and for which
he had few maps. Later, Harbord was setting up headquarters in the
doomed village of Lucy-le-Bocage, where General Michel's retreating
personnel were busily looting, ripping open parlor sofas in search of
hoarded gold, throwing furniture from windows, stuffing their musettes
with laces and linens, and battering in the doors of wine cellars. (If they
didn't loot it, the Germans would.) Michel was quite ready to take
command. He hoped he still had some troops fighting in the Bois de
Belleau, west of Château-Thierry, and he was not whipped yet. He proposed an immediate counterattack in concert with the Marines.

At this proposal the American chief of staff, Colonel Preston Brown,

USA, an old General Staff officer, told the Frenchman off. "The proper way to stop an advance is to form a line and hold it," said Brown. Douglas Haig, superb only in this field of operations, would have agreed with the tough-minded Brown—a polo player like Haig, and a celebrated Dapper Dan from Yale. But the French general was an apostle of the fiery Ferdinand Foch, who for the first years of his war held to Grandmaison's doctrine which, stripped of military jargon, said that when in trouble the only gutty thing to do was to rush blindly into a fight. The Frenchman found Degoutte, who indicated a line but kept secret his own decision that as soon as the line was formed he himself would order the counterattack. A French colonel advised Colonel Wendell C. Neville, an Annapolis graduate commanding the 5th Marines, that the best thing to do was to retreat. Neville, who wore the Medal of Honor, replied, "Retreat, hell. We just got here." Meanwhile the French general walked away from Harbord without a parting word. "Where are you going, General?" Harbord asked him. "To supper," replied the Frenchman, and whistled off into the darkness toward the sentry who refused Private Bailey his vegetables.

Degoutte was desperate. Northwest of Château-Thierry, elements of French cadres were still trying to get out of the villages of Belleau, Torcy, Vaux, and Bouresches, extricating themselves wherever they could to seek safety along the Paris road. No one knew where the enemy was in this area. Across the river, the 3rd Division held the south bank of the Marne inviolate for seven miles.

Major General Omar Bundy attempted to place the 2nd Division into line, in as many lozenges as an Afghan shawl, but Harbord graciously asked to keep his Marines in one piece. Preston Brown had found the 23rd infantrymen sleeping on the Paris road and rushed them with a battalion of Marines and two Leatherneck machine-gun companies into the pitch blackness of Michel's gap, where the oncoming Germans had torn a hole in the remnant of the last French division between them and Paris. By dawn of June 2 the line ran: 23rd Infantry on the left, 6th and 5th Marines in the center, 9th Infantry on the right. Everyone hoped that somewhere to the right of the 9th, the French 10th Colonials, those who had escaped Château-Thierry, might form strongly enough to give them a flank hard by the town itself. Degoutte warned that he did not know where his left flank was on June 2 "since it is possible that the advance of the enemy will not permit this regiment [the 23rd] to arrive in time on a predetermined line." The Doughboy regiment and the Marine battalion beat the Germans by four hours.

It was a near-miracle that the 2nd's officers, Regulars and Marines, had been able to form a strongly integrated line with few maps, without knowledge of the situation. Paul Malone, colonel of the 23rd U.S. Infantry, now virtually on his own, knew he had a position somewhere to the southwest of a patch called the Bois de Belleau; that the Marines on his right faced this wood and its pendant village of Bouresches; and that somewhere far to his right was the other regiment of the Doughboy brigade. His own left flank was in the air; whether Germans would strike him on his blind side as French streamed past his flank, machine guns in disorder, was all fogged in war. By dawn, June 2, fierce German elements came after the lonely Malone, and at the Marine center. They were just as fiercely beaten back, and the fight was on.

"Thanks to the arrival of the American 2nd Division," reported Degoutte in a bulletin to his own troops on June 2nd,

it has been possible to stiffen the entire line of the Army Corps, by means of a solid line, occupied at present by American regiments. The American regiments should fully understand that they are to hold in place and that French elements driven back by hostile attack are to be allowed to pass through American lines, in order that they may be reorganized under the protection of their American comrades.

He ordered his ghostly poilu tatterdemalions "regrouped as small, homogeneous reserves" far in the rear, fearing they might be taunted—or might volunteer—to join the Regulars and Marines on the line. The French Degoutte as yet had no sure faith in the Yanks. A French aviator reported that he saw a wavering line falling back near Triangle Farm in the fields south of Bouresches and Degoutte angrily telephoned the Marine's new brigadier. Harbord in turn queried Major Thomas Holcomb of the 6th Marines. "When I do any running," a testy Holcomb replied, "it will be in the opposite direction." Degoutte's fear that the Yanks were bolting along with the French angered Harbord. He reported to his superior: "Nothing doing in the fall-back business," which must have given some French translator a difficult time.

On the morning of June 3, General Michel informed the 2nd Division that he had lost Belleau Wood during the night. But Degoutte had his brawny Americans to squander as he chose, so he informed the 2nd Division that "General Michel is actually preparing an operation to retake the lost ground." The Yanks on their established defensive line had no say in the matter; they were cannon fodder. The German 28th Division was cutting down poilus from village to village, slope by slope. It was a crack outfit—Jägers, Fusiliers, and Body Grenadiers much admired by the Kaiserin, whose husband had telegraphed her May 29 after Boehn's break-through that "the 28th Division has again distinguished itself." The German Crown Prince, commanding the Group of Armies, had ordered

Boehn to halt his forces June 3 at the Marne River from Château-Thierry eastward. A subparagraph ordered the Group Conta to persist until it too reached the Marne. It never did.

The Yanks had accomplished their paramount mission. They had stopped the Germans in fields five miles west of where the Marne crooked abruptly south, but Degoutte had no river barrier before him as did his fellow corps commander Mondésir with his American 3rd Division. During the days of June 4 and 5, the Doughboys and Marines beat off attacks by the inquisitive Germans and improved their lines. Brigadier General Lewis managed to sideslip Malone's 23rd Infantry toward his 9th Infantry wing near Château-Thierry, the Marines in turn inching westward as a brigade. By June 5, the 2nd's artillery had come up and the four field hospitals established where Army nurses and medical corpsmen on all-night shifts were rolling bandages. The race-horse brigades, now in proper order, were in a line of battle for thirty days of savage fighting. Before them, the Germans held rocky, wooded positions on the line Belleau Wood–Bouresches–Vaux running southeast toward Château-Thierry.

On the night of June 5, Degoutte passed the word. He was going to counterattack around Belleau Wood—counterattack blindly for he did not know the enemy strength or disposition there. Around that midnight, regimental commanders began receiving orders: the Marines would attack at dawn next morning, June 6, seizing positions in patches of trees and on hillocks facing the wheatfields that stretched north to Belleau Wood. The 23rd Infantry would advance to support their right flank, but *had received no orders* in the confusion of French ascendancy at Major General Bundy's headquarters. The 9th Infantry would hold fast a thin line, its main elements in reserve. After attaining this attacking position, which Degoutte outlined in Paragraph 2 of his order, the Marines would then, at 5 P.M., execute Paragraph 3 and cross the wheatfields to seize Belleau Wood, the position just lost by General Michel. The Marines had rifles and bayonets, Chauchats, and Hotchkiss guns. They had neither mortars nor hand grenades, nor did they have signal flares or Very pistols. It was a far cry from Debeney's massive preparations at Cantigny and Vandenberg's mother-hen care. It was nearer to San Juan Hill, except that no spiritless colonial garrisons awaited the Americans. Degoutte's name looms large in the history of the Château-Thierry defense and in the attacks which crossed the Vesle to clean out Boehn's salient in July, August, and early September. It bears no luster in the memories of those whose buddies perished while serving under a Frenchman who—unlike Mangin, Gouraud, and Debeney—was profligate with American blood when all other corps troops in the Aisne-Marne area were digging in to await Ludendorff's next assault.

Led by lieutenants in Sam Browne belts, prime targets for machine gunners and telescopic riflemen, the first movement went off with dash and verve. But it grew very rough around the square of woods fronting Lucy-le-Bocage; it was, in fact, rough everywhere, with furious fighting until noon. Messages told the story: "We have reached our objective and are entrenching," Major Julius Turril sent word from his battalion. He could not as yet count losses, but he let his colonel know they were heavy as indicated in his second sentence: "Williams is up on the left with three platoons—Hamilton in the center and Winans on right—the remnants of other companies have joined the other two." An outfit without grenades or trench mortars had recourse to the bayonet.

"Y.M.C.A. working beautifully as far down as the front line," a satisfied Major Roberts sent word to Intelligence Chief Dennis Nolan at Chaumont. The chief liaison officer from Chaumont informed Nolan that the operation was "an entire success." He added that the replacement problem would be easy: more than half of them would come from the Marines. "I forgot to say," he concluded, "that the animals of the 2nd are coming strong." There were seven thousand horses and mules. "I spent a good part of my time looking up and watching the M.P." On his recommendation, the Army officer commanding the Military Police was sacked, and a Marine major put in his place. Later a Leatherneck runner unable to find the colonel of the 6th Marines (the colonel, Albertus Catlin, had stopped one in the shoulder and was on his way to a field hospital) encountered a Doughboy military policeman near the front. The runner asked the M.P. why he was so near the front. "To keep you Marines from running away," said the Doughboy. They were still rolling in the dirt when an ambulance crew pried them apart.

Shortly after noon on the sixth, Degoutte, satisfied with developments, sent the following message to Harbord: "The first part of the operation prescribed in Paragraph 2 having succeeded, the American 2nd Division will execute, this evening, the second part of the operation described in Paragraph 3 of the same order," which was the proposed capture of Belleau Wood.

Lieutenant Hadrot, French Air Squadron 252, dropped a field message: ". . . it is uncertain who holds Belleau Wood." The Marines had taken 150 prisoners, mainly machine gunners, who could have told Hadrot that one German battalion held the Main Line of Resistance in the woods, sacrificial units in thin lines ahead of it, with another battalion in support. Each company had four light Maxim machine guns in the line, with two heavy ones with their gun teams in support. There was a reserve line of heavy machine guns behind the two German battalions but no deep trenches, as they did not intend to remain there after more artillery came up. Machine gunners were behind huge boulders in small ravines, hidden in amphitheaters in the second-growth timber, echeloned in the mass of brush that carpeted the wood, all unseen, with flanking field of fire. The German prisoners knew nothing of Bouresches, a village of one thousand souls which was a key position to be assaulted and captured as per Degoutte's Paragraph 3. It lay at the southern tip of Belleau Wood—which was shaped like a sea horse, its head and curling tail facing west, a crown of rocks the mane of the horse's head and neck within a square mile of machine guns.

Private Bailey saw the first evolutions prescribed in Degoutte's Paragraph 3, where he lay in support near Lucy-le-Bocage south of the wood. He was well dug in, with captured pigs and rabbits numerous for the cookpots. Someone even found a barrel of hard cider, bringing it back lashed between the wheels of an old baby carriage. The sun shone brightly that day, recalling to Bailey the war poems of Alan Seeger, the New Yorker killed as a volunteer with the French Foreign Legion: "the slant sunshine of October days. . . ." All day Private Bailey listened to "the hellish clatter and roaring of our guns" on some woods beyond his position.

For the last few minutes before five the fire was terrible. At exactly five there was a silence . . . then the guns were directed to the fields behind Belleau Wood to prevent the Germans from bringing up reinforcements . . . we could see the long white line of explosions, but we did not watch that for long . . . there were some yells to our left towards Lucy-le-Bocage. We saw the long lines of Marines leap from somewhere and start across the wheatfields toward the woods. Those lines were straight and moved steadily, a few paces in front of each its officer leading, not driving. The attackers went up the gentle slope and, as the first wave disappeared over the crest we heard the opening clatter of dozens of machine guns that sprayed the advancing lines. Then we heard some shrieks that made our blood run cold. High above the roar of the artillery and the clatter of machine guns we heard the war cries of the Marines. The lines continued to go over the crest and, as the last disappeared, we began to notice that a machine gun would go out of action. This meant that the Marines were either shooting the gunners or crawling up and bayoneting the crews. . . . How long this took I do not know, but it seemed less than half an hour before all the machine guns had stopped firing. . . . Directly in front of us, though concealed by some woods, the Marines had attacked and captured Bouresches.

As night fell, messages told the story of the charge through the wheat: "What is left of battalion is in woods close by. Do not know whether will be able to stand or not. Increase artillery range." This was from Major Berry of the 5th Marines. "Unable to advance farther because of strong machine gun positions and artillery fire. Have given orders to hold present position at far edge of woods. Losses already heavy. Await instructions.

Berton W. Sibley, Major, USMC." Meanwhile, Holcomb had begun his "running in the opposite direction." He reported: "Robertson says he holds Bouresches and woods to right with most of company. Needs reinforcements." Major Edward B. Cole was the Marines' "Harvard man." There were many lieutenants from Cambridge, but Cole was a veteran and a machine gunner of merit, a favorite fated to take a fatal wound before the week was out. "Have just come back from the Bois de Belleau. When I left, about sundown, the whole outfit was held up in the north edge of the wood by machine gun nests. . . . They should be furnished with trench mortars and hand grenades, if possible. Had these been furnished, they would have been over with it two hours ago."

On the right of the wood, the Doughboys of the 23rd Infantry received Degoutte's orders only fifty minutes before the Leathernecks jumped off. The regiment was to support the Marine right, its left platoon keeping contact with the adjoining Marine platoon. Colonel Malone drove an automobile into the front line in his haste to make sure his two battalion commanders there got the proper word, sketching positions on their maps before he was recalled to Brigade Headquarters. But the right-flank platoon of the Marines was under orders to hold fast. A foul-up resulted and the men of the 23rd were unable to restrain themselves when so many buddies on their left were fighting for their lives. In the late twilight of a French June they broke over with wild shouts and went after the enemy; this became a habit with Americans which would persist through dozens of battalion actions until the Armistice. "The Marines were seen advancing in splendid order and the spectacle was inspiring," Malone explained in his report of this excessive gallantry.

The men of the 23rd Infantry could not be restrained when they reached their objective, the Marine flank. They rushed on, driving their way deep into German lines. There were spontaneous fights conducted with great skill and courage, Malone reported of this regrettable action. The Germans broke through to shatter M Company on the left flank, destroying the Doughboy platoon that refused to halt by the Marine platoon, but Malone brought up reserves and drove them off, later in the night extricating the impetuous battalion and bringing it back to the original objective. The battalion and its support suffered 27 killed, 225 wounded and missing. Major Waddill might have been court-martialed and his career closed out. Instead, Malone wrote a report which he knew the Iron Commander would study. "It is highly undesirable to check the fine spirit of fight in such troops. Experience will instill caution rapidly enough." He gave notice that Major Waddill would receive a few blasts from the chicken colonel.

"The tactical lessons learned in this operation will be imparted to those needing them. . . ."

Thus ended the hardest day in American history since Sheridan broke through at Five Forks and overwhelmed the relics of Lee's army. In view of the days ahead, it was a cloud no larger than a man's hand. The 2nd Division, taking a leading part on all subsequent battlefields between Soissons and Sedan, would know bloodier ones, but by naked courage Marines had gained a foothold in the wood. Malone's 23rd Infantry was little remembered for its fierce accompaniment on the right flank, the 9th Infantry to the left undergoing bitter frustration and taking heavy casualties where it blocked the way to the south-flowing Marne.

Chapter **6**

BELLEAU WOOD AND VAUX

Oh, the headline-hunting bastards!

On the morning of June 6, 1925, two retired officers returned to the village of Bouresches, more out of curiosity than sentiment, to see how two friends, Lieutenant James Robertson and Lieutenant Clifton B. Cates, had stayed alive while leading platoons across the field from Triangle Farm. Neither of the two visitors, one a major with a withered arm, the other a captain with a foot made of Idaho willow, knew much about Bouresches, though they had spent some time in garrison there seven years before, after relieving Robertson's outfit of Holcomb's battalion. In a disputed town there were few daytime vistas, and Bouresches in mid-June, 1918, was an ideal place to get killed if one so much as threw his shadow across a doorway.

The major was desirous of seeing two things in Bouresches. He wished to see if the old man who kept his blind wife in the cellar throughout the fighting was still there; and further, he wished to see if the people in the first house to the right as one entered the village had restored the fine old fruitwood case of a grandfather clock in the parlor. The French, falling back during the brief time they held Bouresches, had desecrated this clock, overturning it and using the case as a privy seat, with velvet portieres nearby to do the office of toilet tissue. The major had seen war at Vera Cruz, and amid the savage fighting in the jungles of Haiti; but this vandalism had shocked him beyond anything else he had ever seen. He had been in great pain at the time, having been shot through the left elbow the week

95

before, and his arm was in a sling and swollen like a football. The major had refused to leave the field on June 8, and was led away June 22 when the enemy got to his other arm.

The captain with the Idaho willow foot wanted to see the apple orchard in the garden next to the house at the left side of the main street. He had managed a few hours' sleep there that busy week, but only knew its walls of flint and fragrant trees by night. German snipers in the railroad station on the embankment beyond the village would have killed him in five seconds had he visited the orchard by day.

The two friends drove into Bouresches and were saddened to find the warm tile of yellow roofs now repaired with galvanized iron, hideous where it glinted blue in the sun. They found the *estaminet,* ordered wine for the mayor and sundry farmers, switched to brandy, and soon had the villagers, none of whom they had ever seen before, almost feloniously drunk. The major learned that the old man had taken his blind wife farther south, after his days of attending her in the cellar where runners gave her chocolate bars purchased from Y.M.C.A. carts and, surprisingly enough, cigarettes. The mayor called the captain aside and walked him to a nearby barn, where deep in the gloom he could see a U.S. Army 1918 Dodge, property of the infantry brigade. His Honor set the spark and the throttle levers on the steering-wheel quadrant, and twisted the crank. The old Dodge began tickety-ticking like a watch. *"Bonne voiture!"* belched the mayor. In what patch of woods had the mayor been hiding? Had he stolen the Dodge? Unlikely, M'sieu. Some Marine had sold it to him.

The orchard was small and plain, and much as the captain had imagined it, apple trees above a fine stone wall six feet high with a broken-glass crown to thwart any urchin who did not have a corduroy jacket thick enough to pad the jagged teeth. Someone had replaced the gate on its iron strap hinges, the gate he had removed for speedier access to Chauchats, Hotchkisses, and a captured Maxim placed there to repel the many probings in the dark. The two friends pulled the bell rope and a young woman appeared, auburn-haired, pale from a recent confinement, a pallid baby blinking at her breast. The two friends explained that they had done some fighting around the orchard and would like to sit there for time to smoke a cigarette.

"Then it was you who defiled our orchard," said the young Frenchwoman, narrowing the distance between gate and gatepost. The captain wanted to say that he had left no German dead in the orchard; they had been dumped into the streets after the bestial frenzy of night fighting beneath white parachute flares and many-colored rockets, fighting amidst hoarse screams and exultant shouts so intense that a man was enervated for hours afterward, shuddering at the thought that, had he stopped to put a fresh clip in a pistol instead of seizing a shovel and splitting a raider's skull beneath his pillbox cap, he would not have survived.

"You did not save my village, M'sieu," the young mother went on. "You ruined the soil of the orchard. Every year we dig up the empty *cartouches* from *les mitrailleuses*. The brass can be tasted in the fruit itself, M'sieu. When you left, why did you not clean up our orchard? Take your sordid *cartouches* with you?" She closed the gate without haste.

"I don't think I'll try to see the grandfather clock," said the major.

The major climbed the railway embankment for a German's-eye view of Bouresches and marveled that Robertson had ever taken the town with rifle and bayonet and lived to tell Holcomb. And that business of Lieutenant Moore and Sergeant Major Quick driving a laden ammunition truck in daylight over open fields into the town. . . . Some men, such as the sergeant major, possessed the maximum durability, fortune always at its peak, that Almighty God sometimes vouchsafed a soldier. At Guantanamo in 1898 when the U.S. Fleet began firing on his battalion's positions, Quick stood on ramparts to signal "cease firing" for an hour before a quartermaster happened to read him.

The captain, sticking to level ground, came upon a long-forgotten hedge. There had been a badly wounded Doughboy officer lying beneath it one mid-June night, come with a company of the 7th Infantry of the 3rd Division to relieve the exhausted Marines in a hell of high explosives and toxic shells. He had not made it, this officer, but he had offered his life to relieve his unknown friend. What was his name? *Lieutenant Loucks*: the name came back after seven years.

Near the town there was a cemetery of German dead, crosses creosoted black by the thrifty French, names stenciled in white, home towns included in the legend. The name of Mulhausen was prominent: these boys came from the country around Strasbourg, which was German from 1871 to 1918; represented the 250 men who broke into Bouresches one night and almost won it back. They left fifty dead in the streets and orchards before being beaten off, uncounted others in fields behind the village. The two friends drove by the German cemetery without a word, and entered Belleau Wood.

Seven years before on the evening of the same day, June 6, elements of the 2nd Division's Marine Brigade lay shattered and exhausted in the confused tangle of the Bois de Belleau, having seized about two-thirds of the forest at awful cost by overwhelming enemy machine-gun nests with rifle and bayonet. Unable to advance farther in the dark with their ranks so depleted, uncertain about the future when the Germans struck back, as they assuredly would, the Leathernecks had merely set the stage for a long nightmare that could have been avoided with the help of one weapon. The British Mark IV tank was the key to unlock the gates of Belleau Wood in fifteen minutes, but it was never available to the Yanks. Had the Marines possessed two companies of these tanks, clumsily lumbering over scrub and brush with field guns in their snouts, machine guns for antennae, Chauchat gunners, riflemen and grenadiers swarming around, the name of Belleau Wood would not have been long remembered.

On June 7, the Marines and the 23rd's Doughboys attempted to consolidate their lines, to tend to the wounded and bring up ammunition and food; and the Marines tried to pinpoint the German strong points in the total and gloomy confusion of the forest. The latter proved impossible; no one knew exactly how much of the wood was in American hands, or where or in what strength the enemy lay. It was to cost them dearly to find out.

Fortunately, Conta's last attack in force in an effort to reach the Marne did not strike Belleau Wood till June 8. The Marines, with Degoutte always anxious to attack, answered by sending up troops to be slaughtered in driblets in a continuous series of brutal actions, and the contest seesawed during six days of cruelties. The fighting in the wood was such that, on June 12, messages read like this dispatch from Lieutenant Colonel Frederick Wise: "A dying German officer states that a fresh division is in and the plan was to attack tonight. . . . We are in full spirits. Have only 350 old men left and 7 officers. They are shelling very heavy."

True to the dying officer's warning, the Germans put up another ugly fight in the small hours of that night, in a confusion of fallen trees, huge boulders, bloody gullies. "We have a runner in from the battalion on my right stating that the enemy has taken Bouresches," Harbord reported before dawn, on June 13, in a field message to Division. The runner was Lieutenant Davies, who had been ordered by his wounded captain to tell Harbord that all was lost. He had run the gantlet to Triangle Farm, and being suspected unjustly of having panicked was subjected to a day of hard questioning before he was cleared and returned to the lines. Major John Hughes sent word from the woods at 5 A.M.: "Have had terrific bombardment and attack. I have every man, except a few odd ones, in line now. We have not broken contact and have held." Two minutes later, he sent another message which read in part: "Estimate casualties at under 20%, including Captain Fuller killed and Captain Burns wounded. . . . Can't you get hot coffee and water to me by using prisoners?" At the same minute Harbord was ordering two companies out of reserve for a dawn attack to recapture Bouresches. Eight minutes later Harbord canceled this order. "I have a message, received at 5:25 from my major in Bouresches that we still hold it," he explained. "There is nothing but U.S. Marines in the town of Bouresches."

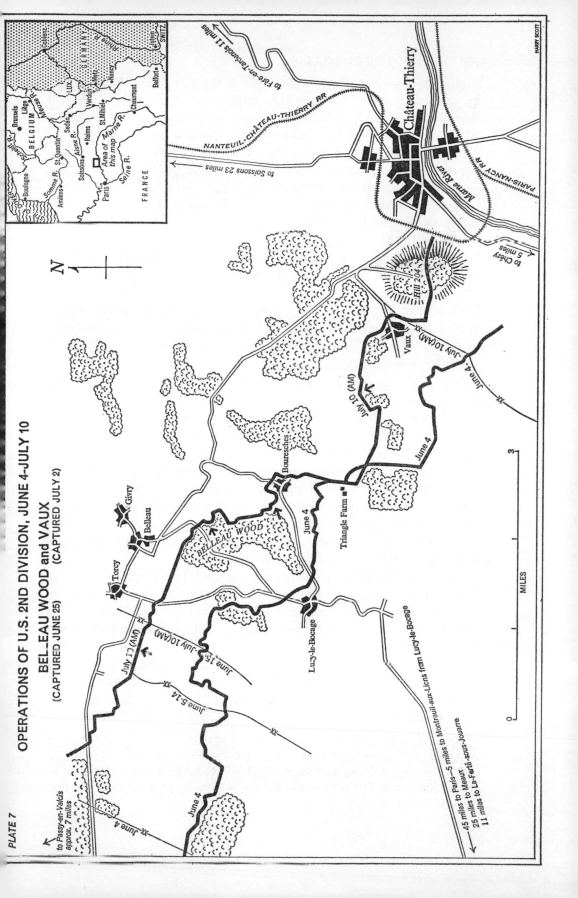

PLATE 7

OPERATIONS OF U.S. 2ND DIVISION, JUNE 4–JULY 10

BELLEAU WOOD and VAUX
(CAPTURED JUNE 25) (CAPTURED JULY 2)

HARRY SCOTT

Harbord now began sending messages to the Regulars at Division that he, an old Regular, alone could have written—no Marine brigadier would have done so. His brigade had been fighting thirteen days, not a man having taken off his shoes, and few of them the recipient of a cup of hot coffee. He demanded that his brigade be relieved, citing the British and French practice of never subjecting an outfit to more than four or five days in the hell of an incessant attack, with battalions leapfrogging forward over one another in turn. His demand went all the way to Chaumont, where Fox Conner, Pershing's G-3, informed Major Richardson, Chaumont's liaison officer with Degoutte: "On that question of relief, leave that matter entirely to the French. Do not insist on any relief. The reports that we have show that conditions are not very bad. Do nothing further in the matter." Degoutte then informed Harbord that there could be no question of relief until June 25, two weeks later. (The French poilu of 1918 would have picked up his musettes at this point and decamped in a civilized manner.) Degoutte issued a bulletin in precise French style, reviving the murderous follies of 1916, Paragraph 3 reading:

With a view to continuing the impression of the enemy that he is being threatened by an attack on our part and thus compelling him to engage, as heretofore, fresh units needed for battle, the Army Corps will preserve the offensive attitude which it has adopted since 1 June.

Preserve this attitude against fresh German divisions, replaced every four or five days, preserve it with a brigade where a battalion reported, "About out of officers." Just as no Marine brigadier could have challenged Chaumont, so no Marine officer would appeal to Brigadier Harbord summarily, though messages could read: "Lost a great many men. . . . Everything running smoothly and in fine shape but . . . I am afraid of reaction. This is a different outfit from the one of yesterday."

The 23rd U.S. Infantry, continually whipped into tactical superiority by a born teacher, Colonel Malone, was having its tribulations on the right of Belleau Wood. It daily met and repulsed countless assaults, improving its position and taking heavy casualties. A battalion commander in the 23rd grew weary of the constant stream of memoranda telling him what to do. It was indicative of the birth pangs of a combat outfit. "As some of the requests, orders and reports of some of the staff are so absurd, ludicrous, and in many cases impossible," Major Charles E. Elliott informed Colonel Malone,

I request that the following officers visit my C.P. as soon as possible to see situations for themselves: Regimental Gas Officer, Regimental Intelligence Officer, Regimental Signal Officer, Regimental Surgeon. For instance, to receive instruction that no one will sleep within 1,200 yards of the front line unless in a gas-proof dugout, and with gas sentries over each dugout, would keep us awake all the time, as such things are not possible. . . . Another is that a man who is exposed to mustard gas should have a warm bath with soap and water, and a change of clothing . . . we don't get enough water to wash regularly . . . some of us are about to fall through our clothes . . . it becomes exasperating to receive so many requests and orders which someone has "doped" out of a book. . . . They must remember the actual defense of this position must be considered.

Major Elliott had been fighting nineteen days by this time, his Doughboys unwashed, half-fed, and always thirsty. He ended a fighting man's rebuke to staff officers with the sarcastic remark that defense of his line "takes some time each day." About twenty-four hours each day.

By June 25, Malone had reported 855 casualties in the 23rd Infantry, 334 of them caused by gas. He estimated that 4,000 gas shells had effected these, whereas a total of 116,000 rounds—cannon, mortars, machine guns, and enemy rifles—had caused the remaining 521 casualties. Only two gassed men died, but the others were out of action for two weeks. Masks would protect a man's respiratory system against mustard gas, but not his hide.

Long before June 25 Harbord became insistent: he was afraid of no one at Chaumont, and the idiotic remark by Fox Conner "that conditions are not very bad" infuriated him. A one-star general, he demanded that two-star General Bundy—and to hell with the French—find relief for his brigade. Major General George H. Cameron's 4th Division had now been moved into the rear area. One of its regiments had no rifle practice and none of its Doughboys had ever fired a Chauchat or a Hotchkiss. Cameron, destined to be one of Pershing's best before he wore himself out, offered to do what he could, but the Iron Commander would not release his division to Degoutte. It would have been murder to send Doughboys just arrived from Camp Greene, North Carolina, into woods fighting with weapons they had never fired. Major Richardson, Chaumont's liaison, now told Fox Conner that relief was imperative. Timid little Bundy finally went across the Paris road to Mondésir and borrowed the 7th Infantry of the 3rd Division from the Frenchman for five precious days. The 7th Infantry, which had not yet finished its training behind the bridgehead at Château Thierry, began moving into Belleau Wood the night of June 16.

The Doughboys were appalled by the difficulties of the relief. The foxholes were so randomly placed that some elements destined for the 5th Marines found themselves led by confused guides in darkness to the rear of the 6th Marines, who were continuously exchanging fire fights with German machine gunners. Every depression there was nauseating with stale mustard gas. (The belch of mustard gas was a sickly one, like a bonbon stuffed with perfumed soap.) Two days later the Marine brigade, having been relieved, was in division support, one battalion minus 64 percent of its original members, lying on wet ground in thick forest, sleeping just forward of French corps artillery. The blast of these hot-mouthed monsters went unnoticed by the men, who slept constantly between hot meals and coffee brought from rolling kitchens in heavy French marmites (clay vessels capable of keeping food warm a few hours).

The Germans still ruled the air, three of their balloons always visible to anyone who walked a mile to Brigade Headquarters; and their artillery still sought the weary battalions hiding in the wood. Sometimes German observers flew so low seeking targets for artillery that men motionless under the trees could see the goggles of the pilots and make out the small Iron Crosses painted on the fuselage. There was one great day when two enemy Rumplers were suddenly set afire by a small French Spad that, like a bolt from the blue, appeared between them with crackling guns. As the two flaming enemy ships began their dive to earth, the Frenchman vanished. The next afternoon, Father Frank Brady brought into the forest a Paris *Herald* which proclaimed that Captain René Fonck had destroyed five enemy planes in his greatest day above the Marne.

As soon as the 7th Infantry was in place on June 18, orders came for it to attack, carrying out Paragraph 2 of Degoutte's order under the direction of Major General Stanislas Naulin, Degoutte having been promoted to command Duchêne's army when the elder general was sacked. The 7th Infantry was in no condition for such an enterprise, yet in due course a series of attacks on a battalion scale were begun, and inevitably they failed. (Marines were not surprised when they learned of this. They had failed to advance on similar sanguinary occasions.) Harbord had no choice but to follow French orders for persistent attacks to recapture Belleau Wood. "Your battalion will be relieved tomorrow night," he told a 7th Infantry officer June 20. "Tomorrow morning is its only chance to redeem the failure made this morning. If you clear the northern half of the Bois de Belleau, the credit will belong to the 1st Battalion, 7th Infantry, and will be freely given. The battalion cannot afford to fail again."

How a newcomer felt about this hopeless piecemeal action was expressed in a message, privately directed, from Lieutenant Colonel John P. Adams to Harbord at Brigade Headquarters. Adams, commanding the 7th Infantry's 1st Battalion, was from old Regular Army stock and just as feisty as Harbord. If Elliott in the 23rd thought some orders were senseless, Adams pointed out the worse folly, he thought, of the whole Belleau Wood affair.

First, he agreed that A Company, led by Lieutenant Helm, would lead the first wave at three-fifteen in the morning, but it was absolutely necessary that he be given one thousand hand grenades and five hundred V.B. rifle grenades at once. Inasmuch as his men had little to eat for twenty-four hours, he wanted some food sent Helm's company by 11 P.M. Accompanying these sensible demands was the following message: ". . . I do not believe any attack without a heavy artillery fire preceding can move the guns from the woods. They are all emplaced and strongly held. The woods is almost a thicket and the throwing of troops into the woods is filtering away men with nothing gained." Adams then recommended withdrawal of two companies from the line, leaving Helm holding with only one company, and a murderous shelling given the machine-gun nests, and then an advance made. "I can assure you that the orders to attack will stand as given, but it cannot succeed. This is only my original expression and has not reached the ears of anyone else." He then told Harbord that after such an attack as he was ordered to make his line could be crushed at any time, leaving the woods, bought with Marine blood, open to the enemy. The battalion had only two trench mortars. (The Marine brigade's six infantry battalions had none on June 6.) In a postscript, Adams added: "The two Stokes guns won't even worry the German machine guns." Adams kept his word next morning, June 21, at 3:15, and everything he had written Harbord came to pass. The battalion was broken, and the woods were left open; though the Germans in their own confusion did not learn of it before nightfall, and by that time the lice-infested Marines, who hoped never again to enter Belleau Wood, were moving into its legendary hell once more.

No one knew where the lost positions were in the dark shambles ahead. Some of the Leatherneck outfits took a chance and moved by the flank through wheatfields, long files of men freezing motionless lest moving shadows betray them when enemy parachute flares, daylight-white, burned long in the sky. The 7th Infantry guide, after his four nights of horror, could not regulate his pace when ranging shells roared into flame a hundred yards away. When he quickened his step almost to a dogtrot, the files were broken and the company halted perilously to repair the break. The leading officer after three such breaks said harshly, "Do I have to shoot you in the ass to slow you down?" The Doughboy was anguished, "Officer," he cried, "don't shoot me, officer! I got no business here. I only been in the United States Army five weeks." He kept his pace thereafter and found his old position. The next morning in a foxhole his new friends were teaching him how to work the bolt on his Springfield rifle. He begged to stay until he had killed "just one Joirman" but was sent back with a runner that night, and a note of thanks to whomever it concerned in the 7th U.S. Infantry. "The sergeants among the replacements," the Chaumont inspectors noted, "know less than privates here in the line. . . ." Everyone liked the guide. "If that little guy learns to keep his head down, he'll do all right." He and his buddies would do better than all right three weeks later at Mézy.

Where the 9th Infantry's 3rd Battalion lay in reserve, Private Bailey and his buddies thought that inaction while their friends were fighting and dying was more bitter to endure than the trials of the combatants themselves. (Why were they not sent in to relieve such battalions as Elliott's of the 23rd Infantry? That was something the inept Major General Bundy would have to pay for.) The Germans had brought heavy guns into play, and they ranged and searched wooded patches for Bailey and his friends, maintaining a harassing fire of high explosive and toxic shells. Bailey heard one of their heavy shells coming the evening of June 15.

There was something unusual about the sound of this particular shell. It seemed to be coming closer than the general run of shells. I was certain that no shell could fall in this sheltered spot but I thought it best not to trust my judgment too far. Then I considered whether I would try to get to my dugout or lie down where I was and take my chances. . . . I decided I would try for my dugout. . . . I was diving through the air and just as I was about to disappear . . . the shell exploded. . . . I felt a stinging sensation in my right elbow. . . . At noon the nurse came around and told me I was to have the dressing on my wound changed. . . . I looked and saw that the little hole that had been there the night before had been enlarged to a cut that extended from a couple of inches below the elbow nearly to my shoulder and was into the bone.

Three days later, strolling in pink pajamas and robe outside the hospital gates, he saw some green 4th Division lads trying to figure head or tail out of French Chauchats they had just been issued with instructions in French. Private Bailey's fighting days were over before he ever saw the enemy, but he had also served, and he continued to do so as he sat on the ground and with one arm conducted classes in how to affix a half-moon clip of flimsy construction to that beastly-looking weapon. (Long after a later war, he brought his grandchildren to Soulaucourt for a visit.)

The French frenzy to seize Belleau Wood again revealed itself in the situation there. In the days that followed the first assault on June 6, Harbord's brigade had been driven, inch by inch, into a crescent, with its deepest penetration against the last three hundred yards of machine guns in the rocky amphitheater of its northern edge. "The situation is intolerable," Harbord messaged Major Maurice Shearer of the 5th Regiment. The Germans could pour enfilading fire into every trench and foxhole, making great use of their fiendish little one-inch cannon, a toy much liked by their snipers. Shearer was told on June 22 he "must clean out the woods by tomorrow night" by means of the kind of attack which Lieutenant

Colonel Adams had said would fail: hand grenades, rifle grenades, Springfields, Chauchats, Hotchkisses—and no massive artillery preparation.

Thus on the afternoon of June 23 the 3rd Battalion tried again for Shearer, and soon ambulances were ferrying shattered men into field hospitals. The division organization provided forty-one ambulances, but another 159 Fords had been found somewhere to carry the overload. The attack was spent by eleven o'clock that night, survivors digging in as possessors of a few more meters of fallen trees, rocky traps, and some captured Maxims. "Things are rather bad. One company almost wiped out," Colonel Neville informed General Harbord after midnight. Men in supporting platoons, inching forward to plug the gaps in a decimated company where there was no artillery roar to drown the cries of human beings, sometimes thought this duty the worst of war's alarms. The cries of men as blood drained from them and they lost self-control were almost not to be endured. Officers restraining men who wished to administer first aid to such sufferers felt themselves unconscionable brutes as they hazed the kindhearted into gaps littered with corpses, crawling forward hugging the ground, the blood of other men on their sleeves, their hands, their faces. Wounded lads on their backs, a kneecap still on its ligaments caught in brambles where it had been shot out of a leg, begging for someone to release it so they might inch back farther to some slight depression, might find succor; but the ones who needed tourniquets and compresses—and precious time—could not be accommodated. The gaps had to be plugged. This last failure in Belleau Wood would be remembered by some as the worst afternoon of their lives no matter what fortune later befell them.

One company estimated that, advancing twenty yards, it had faced sixteen heavy and thirty-five light machine guns. It was now time someone at French Corps Headquarters accepted the facts of the situation and the need to proceed along lines recommended by Lieutenant Colonel Adams of the 7th Infantry, who by this time had returned to the other side of Château-Thierry to rejoin the 3rd Division. "The Marines fighting in Belleau Wood are magnificent," Major General Dickman, his commanding officer, told Adams, "but theirs is a useless sacrifice."

The next day, June 24, Shearer, as strong as a plow horse and as imperturbable, moved his battalion post almost into the front lines. At nightfall the lines were pulled back two hundred meters and gunners on both sides resumed their deafening arguments. Runners from Regimental Headquarters passed along the scuttlebutt that this was the last attack, and that battalion survivors would parade in Paris on the Fourth of July; but there was little speculation as to who would survive. Once again exhausted men fell asleep supperless, thanks to German fire of interdiction so fierce that ration parties carrying marmits of hot beef stew could not make their way up "Gob Gully," the supply route. The marmits arrived the next morning, the stew cold and sour. Men about to die that afternoon ate it greedily for breakfast.

All day the big guns plastered the woods in front of Shearer's position in preparation for the final attack. When the heavy shelling stopped and the creeping barrage crackled on the mass of brush and fallen trees a hundred meters ahead, the curtain of fire almost singed the first wave at 5:15 P.M. as it climbed the bank of a sunken road and started for the machine guns among the rocks in the horse's head.

Buck Sergeant Alison Page held a grade unattainable for a nineteen-year-old in the peacetime Corps. He was a tall boy, popular with his two-squad section of the 47th Company, with a darkly handsome face that seemed incapable of showing any meanness. He was from North Carolina, a college boy enlisted at Wilson's call. His uncle had spent six years as Ambassador to the Court of St. James's, three of them dedicated to provoking American intervention in the First World War. Some historians looked upon the actions of Walter Hines Page in London as treasonable, in his disloyalty to Wilson's demand that Americans remain neutral in spirit as well as in deed; but this was no concern of Sergeant Page. He was exactly in the center of the 47th Company at five o'clock on the afternoon of June 25, and the company was in the center of the full battalion attack. The corps artillery was in such fine fettle it did not seem possible that any living thing could have survived its night-and-day bombardment, but the moment Sergeant Page stepped out, the machine gunners were beaded on him from four hundred meters away. He was killed instantly; and many times thereafter the officer with the Idaho willow foot who led that first wave was besought by Red Cross workers to describe just where Sergeant Page fell, so that salvage sections might recover the boy's rifle for the Ambassador. It was not possible to denote the place for Mr. Page's emissary. In the shattering confusion of the attack it was impossible to recall where everyone fell.

The officer himself was twenty-three, and he did not know whether he was a second lieutenant, a first lieutenant, or a captain in the expanding Regular Line. But he was gas-sick, he had a piece of steel in his left leg, and he did not care. Having lost a spiral legging while crawling, he had cut his left breeches leg short, and his beautiful forest-green uniform was held together with strings. He still wore his Sam Browne, spit-shined to conceal his cowardice in having to wear it, and his Colt .45, cocked, was stuffed into his shirt front. His company commander had been badly wounded, and Colonel Neville had assigned an old-timer, Captain Gaines Moseley, to back him.

The attack took the shape of a fan: the 47th Company in the center, with the longest distance to go to reach the north end of the wood; the 20th plus two platoons of the 45th on the right; and the 19th on the left. As the barrage lifted, the scarecrow leader and his men moved forward, Moseley following a hundred meters behind, watching him like a hawk. At the first hundred meters someone from forty yards away threw a potato-masher grenade at the scarecrow's feet. He dropped, but not before its explosion had driven fragments of his tin hat into his right cheek. He was up immediately, with ears ringing, for Harbord had said at Shearer's old command post on the 24th, "When you reach the curve [drawn correctly to denote the north end of the wood by Lieutenant Colonel Logan Feland after a very perilous reconnaissance that morning], pick up a rifle and lead with steel."

Feland had asserted, correctly, that there were no deep trenches at the end of the wood, only six-foot rifle pits about twelve feet in length and about three feet apart, scattered among boulders that dotted the area. On reaching the rifle pits the gas-sick boy jumped in and began fighting his way from pit to pit, diving headfirst over the undug links. The barrage had done almost nothing to the expert riflemen defending their posts, or to the light Maxim gunners deployed before them. Only twice, in diving from pit to pit, did this officer fall on the shell-shattered body of an enemy soldier, and the German survivors, knowing it would be death to raise their hands, were very stubborn.

The 47th Company reached its center objective, the curve at the north end of Belleau Wood, with about seventy survivors, and was preparing to hold it against a counterattack when the scarecrow received his first and only suggestion from Captain Moseley. Lieutenant Jacob Heckman, leading the left platoon, had sent word by runner that he had reached some high boulders short of his objective with only twenty men left, and could not survive a counterattack, and would thus uncover the right flank of the 19th Company that was being bitterly opposed on the left spoke of the fan. "You must try to uncover Heckman," said Moseley. "Take as few as you can, begin your demonstration, and I'll get word to Heckman, when he hears you, to go in with what he has left."

The young officer took nine men, leaving the rest to hold the curve, and moved west by south, now out of the woods. He did not last two hundred meters. Awaiting him were about 150 troops of the counterassault teams, untouched by the bombardment. Half an hour later, well tourniquetted, he sat up and gave Major Ralph Keyser of the leapfrog battalion their exact position, and soon heard the shouts, shots, and screams of the mopping up.

In the aftermath there was only a broken wood of second-growth timber where dead men lay in pools of blood, the red trickles thinning out until they formed into pools again around rocky nests where both Germans and Americans slumped across machine guns, with trails of wounded leading farther on to the edge of the woods. There were shallow trenches along this skirting fringe of trees, and frantic victors, lifting the weight of German dead, stretched bayoneted corpses lengthwise in lieu of sandbags for a parados against inevitable counterattacks. All through the wood the U.S. Navy's hospital corpsmen swarmed, here and there a captured German medic aiding. To these latter, there seemed to be no change in a four-year situation. It was all a matter of applying sponges and tourniquets wherever they might be; of crying *"Langsam . . . langsam"* to prisoners lifting Yanks on stretchers made by slinging a blanket between two Mauser rifles, barrels still hot from the intense fire directed at the Leathernecks. As the medics and wounded awaited the arrival of more prisoners for carrying parties— there were gangs of them in groups of twenty and thirty—shots, screams, and battlefield yells told them where the fighting continued in the twilight of isolated glades and wooded patches. Wounded men became alarmed when some German *brancardier* would stoop to loosen a tourniquet and bleed a man a little. *"Es vas besser,"* these veterans would explain. Some lad from Milwaukee would sit up and translate: "He does it so you won't fester and get gangrene." Around nine o'clock Colonel Neville messaged Harbord: "Woods now *U.S. Marine Corps* entirely."

Harbord was sick of slaughter. In a moment of indulgence he had permitted his headquarters first sergeant, always nagging the general, to participate in an attack, and now he had to send out searchers to find the body. He had given his favorite messman the same permission, this for the afternoon attack when the eager messman pleaded that he had found a buddy who would take his place if he were late getting back to supper. He, too, was killed. Harbord had never ceased to scold officers for getting themselves killed in droves, saying the proportions were now reaching the tragic percentages of the Old Contemptibles in Britain's early days; and now the 3rd Battalion was almost bereft of them. Even the last of the young Doughboy officers, Lieutenant Coppinger, who had been lent to the battalion to take the place of fallen Marines, had been killed. Doughboy Lieutenants Hale and Russell had made it to hospitals, where they survived. Harbord read Neville's message. Words like glory were not in his lexicon. He merely replied: "Your Shearer Battalion has done splendid work." And this was the capture of Belleau Wood.

Even without tanks, Belleau Wood might have been won on June 10, with many lives spared, but for an incredible error on the part of a brave and otherwise competent officer. Lieutenant Colonel Frederick "Dopey" Wise had led a costly battalion attack by the 5th Marines that evening and had completely misread his map, had veered off to the right, and had emerged from the forest to stare in the darkness at the Yank-held village of Bouresches to the southeast, believing that he was looking at the village of Belleau to the northeast. He then reported that he had captured Belleau Wood. There was only brief elation at Brigade; but "Dopey" Wise, a blustering officer who did not lack for guts, persisted in his claim, and when confronted by true bearings, tried to foist his error on some of his lieutenants.

How could he mistake a village only a carbine shot away for one a good long mile at his back where a Springfield sniper in an advanced blind needed a thousand-yard carry to move an exposed enemy in the village streets of Belleau? The answer remains in historical limbo. Harbord scolded furiously, and thereby won the ill-deserved reputation in some quarters for being as conscienceless in his bid for power as was Degoutte. It was possible that Wise, an experienced soldier, was suffering from delusions caused by shell shock. He must have been a stable officer on other fields, because when transferred out of the brigade he was given a Doughboy regiment in the 4th Division under a granite major general, John Hines, as taciturn as U. S. Grant, who would have sacked him with a grunt had he misfired on his boundary. But Wise became a chicken colonel, and was successful through the Argonne-Meuse fighting. Seven years after this abortive action it not only still seemed incredible to those friends who returned to look over the ground; it also seemed miraculous that Lieutenant Colonel Wise had not been sent home. His name bears no fame with the survivors of the 2nd Battalion, 5th Marines, remembering those buddies who had fought for him to the death. It became a matter for topographers at Quantico, in field surveys with young officers, to discuss behind trees.

There were many views as to the value of Belleau Wood, though all historians say that, whatever its tactical value, the fighting there was a tocsin to the failing French, who had suffered 400,000 casualties since March 21. Lieutenant General Robert L. Bullard, who knew the French best, was of a stronger opinion. Bullard was friend to Gouraud, Debeney, Mangin, and Pétain, making the rounds of their homes after the Armistice as a house guest, and he understood their character. Bullard wrote that had not the 2nd Division Regulars blocked access to the Paris road the night of May 31, with the Marine brigade in the center, the war would have been over, Group Conta crossing the Marne at will. Bullard said it was a matter of four hours at that midnight hole in Michel's 43rd Division.

Boehn's subparagraph orders to Conta bear Bullard out. When Crown Prince Friedrich Wilhelm ordered Boehn's hordes halted on June 3 to regroup, to advance no farther, the advance was yet to persist "on the right wing as far as the Marne." Only on June 8, after five days of constant attacks, did the Group Conta's six advanced divisions call off their offensive attitude, having been brutally molested by the Americans who were the equivalent of two and one-half French divisions. That afternoon Conta's forward divisions received word to assume the defensive: "It is urged that the distribution in depth, ordered for defensive battle, be carried out in every respect. Should the enemy penetrate the main line of resistance, the counterattack will be launched automatically." Feldtkeller, major general commanding behind Belleau Wood, called off his automatic counterattacks after losing 7 officers and 433 men in the final capture of the wood, and yielding about 200 as prisoners the next dawn. He had seen six German divisions mauled there in their turn, among them the 5th Prussian Guards. "In the fighting on our front," Conta had ordered, "should the Americans even temporarily gain the upper hand, it would have the most unfavorable aspect for us as regards the morale of the Allies and the duration of the war." Conta warned that "this or that unimportant wood or village" (Belleau Wood or Bouresches) was to be retaken whenever Americans captured it. But Feldtkeller called it quits.

Degoutte did not call it quits after Belleau Wood was his. Actually, he tried to fight his French divisions just as cruelly as he had his American. He reconstituted them and drove them forward, though they frequently left American flanks isolated. Eventually they would come up; though Malone and other 2nd Division colonels could report that French infantrymen had not taken certain patches of ground even when threatened by their own colonels. "There are too many machine guns there," they said blandly. "So we gave up the attack." On the other side of the line, Lieutenant von Buy, examining prisoners from the 2nd Division, informed his group commander that the Americans were "of assault quality." "The various attacks by both of the Marine regiments were carried out with vigor and regardless of losses. The moral effect of our firearms did not materially check the advance of the infantry. The nerves of the Americans are still unshaken." Of the Doughboy replacements he could say:

Millions were ready to take their places. The personnel may be considered excellent. They are healthy, strong, and physically well-developed men from eighteen–twenty who, at present, lack only the necessary training to make them into a very worthy opponent. The spirit of the troops is fresh and one of careless confidence. A characteristic expression of one of the prisoners is "We kill or get killed." The prisoners made a wide-awake, agreeable impression; but they were entirely disinterested in military matters.

Lieutenant von Buy—an intellectual with the Burgundy stripe of the General Staff—was amazed at a salient characteristic of his captives. They considered themselves Americans! "Only a few of the men are genuine Americans by ancestry, the majority is of German, Dutch, or Italian parentage; but these half-Americans, who with few exceptions were born in America, and who never before had been in Europe, consider themselves unhesitatingly as genuine sons of America." This was also the view of John J. Pershing, who had been hoping to persuade the Allied commanders to accept these simple truths set down simply by a German lieutenant at Fère-en-Tardenois, June 17, 1918, at headquarters of IV Reserve Corps, Group Conta.

Harbord had Belleau Wood but he knew that relief of his Leathernecks was not imminent, even though it had been promised for June 25. A product of the Regular Army, familiar with its ranking personnel, whom he first knew as an enlisted man, Harbord jestingly told his Leatherneck staff that the Doughboy brigade would never consent to relief until it was identified with a show all its own. (Actually, Colonel Malone, on June 25, made a forceful demand for the relief of the Doughboy brigade.) As if to prove Harbord's jest, Degoutte singled out the town of Vaux, one mile west of Château-Thierry, as the next objective.

It was the sort of village that made the French provinces ripe for literature. Its two hundred souls were people of means who lived in fortress-strong houses with fine gardens behind heavy walls, establishments built of stone to last out the ages. Few doomed villages were ever so thoroughly reconnoitered before being reduced to rock piles. All soldiers of the 23rd Infantry, and those of the 9th Infantry who had sought and been given a piece of the action, knew the nature and location of every machine-gun pit ringing the town, every house in it, and some even knew the names of the occupants, long since fled. The principal house belonged to a wine merchant, and though no one held any hopes that a bottle of wine was left in the deep cellar of the Maison Dubois, the Doughboys knew how many Germans now occupied it and they intended to kill them all.

The Vaux attack on the night of July 1 went off with dash and style, much in the Cantigny manner. Colonel Malone of the 23rd Infantry directed it, and the Doughboys displayed much daring on the wooded flanks where the French, in their now cautious style, failed to move up in time. Elements of the 9th Infantry suffered from enfilading fire from the enemy on their right awaiting the French assault on Hill 204 dominating Château-Thierry. The French wanted no part of these long, almost treeless slopes to the north and never did take them. (Hill 204 was a part of the unfinished business which was to confront the New Englanders two weeks later.)

When a French machine-gun outfit arrived tardily on the right of Vaux and tried to expropriate some Germans captured by the Doughboys—to make a token showing—a Yank lieutenant overrode his sergeant's blasphemous objections. "Oh, let 'em keep 'em. We'll catch some more." Vaux itself was the target for Major Elliott's battalion, the same Elliott and the same battalion that had just finished a month of continuous fighting while being pestered with staff orders which he had called "absurd and ludicrous."

The battalion was angry in three directions all at once, chiefly angry with the Paris *Herald,* which, by a censor's lamentable slip, had reported that the Marine brigade was fighting in Belleau Wood five miles west of Château-Thierry, the first and last mention of an infantry cadre by designation. It opened the floodgates of a managing editor's fancy in every American city; and to them nothing but Marines were fighting in the Château-Thierry area, though the Marines, never ones to hide their fierce light beneath a censor's bushel, claimed nothing of the sort. (The feeling that a censor's lapse engendered still endures, though Pershing lopped no head because of the slip; he knew the fanfare would cause every sergeant in France, Regular, National Guard, or Selective Service, to die rather than suffer by comparison.) Secondly, the battalion was angry with officious staff officers whom Major Elliott had called foolish; and to some extent the Doughboys were even angry at the Germans opposing them.

Many were its shooting gallantries that night in the crumbling streets of Vaux and in the woods to its left. No one ever knew how many Doughboys were in the assault teams that night: men played hookey and went along, engineers, signalers, artillerymen, and mule skinners included, in a "show of their own." The maddening headline of the Paris edition of the New York–Paris *Herald,* which ran a week of U. S. Marine exploits before Pershing stopped the show, had stung the Doughboys to a fury that the unfortunate enemy in Vaux had to sustain. "We have fought the Canadians and Australians," a captured officer said, "but you fellows are rougher." Everyone beamed, and the officer was showered with cigarettes.

Marine casualties lying in tents around Coulommiers saw the glare and listened to the faraway fury. The first ambulance clattered up around dawn. Bedridden men knew the scene outside: rows of stretchers bearing faintly moaning men leading to the operating trucks of Mobile Hospital No. 1, where Army medics instantly clapped wood battens upon a wounded man to restrain his first revulsion to sulphuric ether, big hands slapping vaseline on the patient's face to avoid burns, and then the ether cone. Two breaths later the production-line speed came to a halt. The surgeons in their blood-soaked gowns took their time.

The first messenger bearing tidings from Vaux to the Marines in one tent was a giant Doughboy captain, legs now in splints, overseas cap with the infantry's blue cord for piping still on his head. He sat erect on his stretcher, drunk on ether fumes, shouting happily as orderlies lurched down aisles of grass toward the row of beds prepared at high speed by Army nurses from Council Bluffs, Iowa. "Oh, the goddam sonsabitches!" the captain shouted joyously. "The headline-hunting bastards! We showed the sonsabitches how to do it!" No one in that tent thought the captain's remarks applied to the sonsabitches in Colonel General von Boehn's German Seventh Army. . . . By noon, awaking thick-mouthed to gag down his tin plateful of an eye-stinging salmon salad—one part salmon, one part chopped onion and no fuel to boil any potatoes for it—the Doughboy captain was courtesy itself to the Leatherneck runner of Italian origin minus a leg in the neighboring bed. Had not Lieutenant von Buy said that all considered themselves unhesitatingly as genuine sons of America?

Two wars later it was still true. The 23rd U.S. Infantry was crouched forlorn with MacArthur's handful behind the fatal parallel in Korea, shaken by appalling casualties when it was relieved by a regiment fresh from the Inchon landing. The old pros of the 5th Marines were giving some buddies from Belleau Wood days their turn to rest in the loud Korean woods.

Chapter **7**

VIOLENCE ON THE MARNE

While anyone's left alive, let's give them hell!

The German setback in the Château-Thierry area was the only blot in three months of Prussian glory unprecedented in the West since 1914. In fact, Ludendorff's feint against the Chemin des Dames had proved so unexpectedly successful that now he decided to exploit the break-through to the Marne which he had achieved. The German nation, elated by its victories, expected to win its war before the end of July.

The turning point was to be an attack by three armies numbering about 2,352,000 men, a two-pronged assault on a scale of firepower never before witnessed in man's long record of bloodshed. Two armies, commanded by General Guenther von Einem and General Bruno von Mudra, supported by one-third of all German artillery, would strike at the French center in the Champagne on a thirty-mile front between Reims on the west and Verdun on the east. The German right under von Boehn would push the Marne salient southward, crossing the river on a thirty-mile front east of Château-Thierry, make a junction with von Einem and von Mudra, and then push down through the Surmelin Creek Valley to seize the highway to Paris.

Nor had the British to the northwest been forgotten. Once below the Marne, von Boehn was to pause long enough to send more artillery and rifles to the armies of Crown Prince Rupprecht, 1,182,000 strong and poised before Hazebrouck, so that the latter could strike Sir Douglas Haig a fatal blow. Ludendorff named midnight of July 14-15 as his H-hour. It was

114

now or never with the Germans. With their great divisions returned from Russia, their armies in the West were at their peak strength of 3,534,000 men, and Ludendorff could still draw 450,000 from his civilian population.

Facing the Germans were 1,239,000 British, including 130,000 new men sent to France in June, dragooned from the depths of malnutrition and poverty, undersized and hastily trained. (There were still some excellent troops in the British Isles, but Lloyd George was afraid Haig would send them forward to mass murder if he delivered them to the Scot—a comment on Lloyd George's lack of guts in dealing with Haig as much as on Haig's ruthless war.) There were 1,670,000 French extending from western France to the Swiss Alps, but the French were short 80,000 men in their front-line units, with only 60,000 in the civilian reservoir. Neither the British nor the French could draft more men before October, when youths of seventeen would be available from the 1919 class. So there was a total of 2,909,000 Allied troops to oppose the German assault, not including Pershing's growing force.

Clemenceau and Foch came to Chaumont to see what Pershing could do about this manpower shortage while Doughboys and Marines were still fighting desperately in Belleau Wood. The Iron Commander noted in his diary that it was a beautiful day in the foothills of the Vosges, the sun rising early and gilding the blue of the forests. Clemenceau, after pushing through ten thousand shouting townspeople—he was the shield of France—finally reached the *hôtel de ville*, made a speech, and joined Pershing for a drive in his new Cadillac. Then the two men returned to Chaumont to meet with Foch and settle the course of history. The Supreme Commander announced that the Germans would attack again sometime after July 20 (he did not say where, but he secretly expected it to come at the Marne), and he asked Pershing to ask Woodrow Wilson for a total of one hundred Yank divisions, all to be in France by April of 1919. Realizing that French morale was dangerously low, Pershing reluctantly signed a joint cable with Foch asking for one hundred divisions, telling the harassed Newton Baker he wanted eighty in France by April, 1919; 3,200,000 Americans in combat lines, with about half that many more in France to keep them supplied with food and ammunition. The Secretary could have until July, 1919, to supply the other twenty divisions; but in his diary the Iron Commander wrote that he believed eighty—the equivalent of 160 British or French divisions—the American limit. The conference was unusual in that there were no quarrels, but these were perilous hours.

Two weeks after the conference at Chaumont, in early July, Foch sent Pershing his dispositions for the American divisions. He requested that the 42nd Rainbows, the third of the four trained outfits (1st, 2nd, 42nd, 26th)

Pershing had promised him, be given to General Henri Gouraud, defending the line that ran from Reims toward Verdun. Foch relieved all the elements of the 1st and 2nd Divisions—replacing the latter, now holding Bouresches, Belleau Wood, and Vaux, with the 26th, which had had three weeks' rest after its quarrels around Seicheprey and Montsec—and moved them to rest areas below the Marne, where each had to absorb about eight thousand replacements. Foch then asked Pershing to give General Degoutte another division as a last-ditch reserve below the Marne, and Pershing sent him the untried 28th Division of the Pennsylvania National Guard.

The Pennsylvanians, commanded by Major General Charles H. Muir, were physically the equal of the New Englanders, but they had not gained the experience of the latter, not all of them the marksmen that characterize great infantry. They had been strengthened by drafted men who learned to fire a rifle by shooting at tomato cans set on sticks in the Somme fields at Crécy, or with their rifles cracking against hillsides that looked down upon a meadow where Henry VIII faced François I on the Field of the Cloth of Gold four hundred years before.

The Pennsylvanians had their proud traditions, among them a monument to the Philadelphia Brigade's stand at Gettysburg, where it broke the back of Pickett's charge and the heart of the Southern Confederacy. They had their National Guard characters, too, a celebrated one being George M. Orf, who had arrived in France as a captain only to be informed that he was physically incapable of wearing a uniform and must come home at once. The *ci-devant* captain promptly tore this order to shreds and, under the affectionate and derisive sobriquet of Mister Orf, continued with the trade of war through one counterattack and two assaults before Washington caught up with him.

With the help of such as Mister Orf and his buddies, and the more experienced men in the four other American divisions, Foch not only expected to blunt Ludendorff's next attack but to drive von Boehn out of the Château-Thierry salient by some September attacks, and win the war in the summer of 1919.

Allied airplanes had been aggressive in June and July trying vainly to discover the mass of Boehn's troops. The air was alive with British and French airplanes, and Americans flying French pursuit craft fought to protect the work horses of the sky, the photographic reconnaissance ships; by this time the air war had changed from a romantic gallant adventure to a grim business of kill or be killed. In the second week of July the first American ace made his fifth kill above the ruined bridges of Château-Thierry.

Douglas Campbell, a graduate of Groton and Harvard, had spellbound Captain Edward Rickenbacker, America's eventual ace of aces, with his flying ability. With almost no dual instruction, he digested all the available knowledge on aerodynamics, and soloed in a French Nieuport, a tricky little vixen with a habit of shedding its linen skin if piqued too savagely. By the time Douglas had made his fourth kill, mastery of the sky was being contested by the legendary Baron von Richthofen's squadrons, who brought their red-nosed Fokker *Gruppen* into the aerial arena, some of the Germans flying seven sorties a day. But Campbell's fifth victim was a sitting duck, a Rumpler observation craft, throttle wide-open in a run for home with photographs of Doughboy dispositions on either side of Château-Thierry. The observer in the rear seat was standing arms folded, a sign that he had no more ammunition. A few years earlier a pursuit pilot would have saluted the bulletless pair and given them their lives, but this was 1918 and such chivalry had to be forgotten in the interests of men fighting on the ground who might be shattered by a bombardment if the photographs were distributed to Bruchmüller's gunners. When the Germans made no attempt to turn 180 degrees and be shepherded as captives to a French field, Campbell put the torch to them.

A few days later, around ten in the morning, July 14, Doughboy gunners at the bridge at Château-Thierry must have seen a flight of Spads, the best airplanes of the war, in a bright sky above the ruined town. The last aviator in the flight was Quentin Roosevelt, just finished training with many fledgling Yanks, at the great American field of Issoudun. Unlike most Roosevelts, he did not possess the vivacity of his famous clan. He was a well-liked, deliberate boy with thorough ways, well-set and sandy-haired, who had not progressed as rapidly as some in his flight training. He was the sort of pilot, his friends said, who, given time, would be a great one; the tortoise who eventually outsped the hare. As the Yanks swept over Soissons, they saw a flight of red-nosed Fokkers coming head on, possibly ten of them, though figures in the air were never verified. As the new American boys went forward to meet them, Quentin, swiveling his neck from left to right as tail-end Charlie, saw a flight of perhaps a dozen Fokkers at eleven o'clock, over his right shoulder. He broke off and, a single plane, kicked his rudder and began his Immelmann, rising to meet them. Rittmeister Manfred, Freiherr von Richthofen, killed seven weeks before, had taught his squadrons always to plan it that way. "Let the customer come into the store" was his constant injunction.

The Germans buried Quentin with military honors in a field by a farm road leading to the village of Chamery, honors paid not only because they remembered the Rough Rider President, but because they knew their

Kaiser was an admirer of Teddy Roosevelt. They knew, too, that it had needed guts on Quentin's part to meet his death that way, and for a grave marker they made a figure of his airplane's two wheels between the propeller, with the legend, QUENTIN ROOSEVELT, AMERICAN AVIATOR. On a nearby landing field the squadron artificer painted another Iron Cross on the fuselage of Sergeant Johannes Thom's red-nosed ship; Quentin was the sergeant's twenty-fifth kill. Four weeks later, patrols of the American 32nd Division came upon Quentin's grave and, though under fire—on their way to the terrible gallantry of the Soissons–Saint-Quentin road—they built a fence around it, landscaping it with field flowers. There was something special about this grave; perhaps they sensed that they were all sons of Teddy Roosevelt. Thereafter, so many Doughboys of the 32nd turned aside to pray at Quentin's grave that commanders placed a *cordon sanitaire* around it, for German guns were still ranging at anything in open fields thereabouts.

Degoutte's Sixth Army line was a half-moon, with its left horn resting on the 26th Division to the left of Château-Thierry, then curving some five miles back of the Marne to the gateway in the last heights before Paris, and continuing eastward until it horned up into Gouraud's left flank anchored in the city of Reims, some twenty miles above the river. By July, the 3rd Division was holding down seven miles of river front from Château-Thierry to the outskirts of Varennes. Unlike the 2nd Division, which had been plunged into action at Belleau Wood in a matter of hours on June 1, the 3rd had had five weeks to dig in and get its bearings, though its elements had suffered at the outset from the inevitable French shuffling and shifting at the hands of the corps commander, General Mondésir.

Once free of French interference, the division commander, the able Major General Joseph T. Dickman, a portly cavalryman with a painter's eye for landscapes, a gourmet's taste for wines, and a soldier's eye for ground, took stock of his seven-mile sector. Behind it, the Paris-Nancy railway and the Paris aqueduct ran parallel to the river; and on the extreme right was the open plain of Le Rocq, a mile-deep plateau which Dickman knew would be greatly prized by the Germans as an assembly ground. Between the plateau and the river was a square mile of wheatfields, wooded patches, and small ravines of the Surmelin Valley, where its sluggish creek wandered into the Marne. The meandering Marne thrust itself toward the Western end of the line near Château-Thierry; it was not a likely spot for a German crossing. The ideal ground on the south bank was to the east.

Dickman decided to force the enemy into a battle of maneuver before the Rocq Plateau on the east. There he placed only one battalion of infantry of each regiment in his first line before and behind the railway embankment. He placed another battalion in strong points for support in counterattacks, and he made the last battalion the "woods line," hidden beneath the trees in July's verdure. His artillery was well forward, his regiment of 155s deployed throughout his front, with instructions to fight its guns to the death rather than withdraw, his two regiments of 75s deployed behind his infantry brigades.

On the left, its left flank resting on Château-Thierry, Dickman placed the 4th Infantry Regiment; next to it on the right the 7th, then the 30th. For the crucial right wing, its eastern flank touching the French division at Varennes, he assigned the 38th, commanded by the stocky Ulysses McAlexander. Dickman knew the critical spots would be the juncture of his 7th and 30th Regiments, and between the 38th and the French to the east.

Noting that Mondésir was packed up bag and baggage, ready to run for it, Dickman told his staff that if he himself packed up and Pershing dropped around with his observant eye, then the city of Blois, where the Iron Commander sent the many officers he sacked, would not even be a whistle stop on Dickman's progress to the Sahara Desert. Everybody in the 3rd Division was there to stay.

Well pleased with his disposition, Dickman was visited by Degoutte, who said he did not like Dickman's thin front line. The way to defend a river was "with one foot in the water." Dickman offered to give ten thousand Germans free passage across the Marne and guaranteed he would "kill every damned one of them." Degoutte was talking a kind of defense that no sensible Frenchman at that time would undertake. The new tactics of Debeney and Gouraud, borrowed from the German, consisted of a series of defense lines that grew progressively stronger in depth, against which the attackers gradually would be worn down by shattering artillery fire and sacrificial machine-gun units until they were so exhausted, divided, and disorganized they would be unable to carry the bristling main army line of defense or resist a counterattack from a powerful pool of fighters waiting in reserve. But Degoutte was adamant and ordered Dickman to obey, and to avoid controversy and inevitable French charges of insubordination forwarded to Pershing at such a grave hour in European history, Dickman pretended to comply. When Degoutte left, Dickman went back to his original dispositions while Corps Commander Mondésir politely looked the other way.

The Pennsylvanians were not so fortunate in their dealings with French staff interference. When he got the 28th Division as last-ditch reserves in

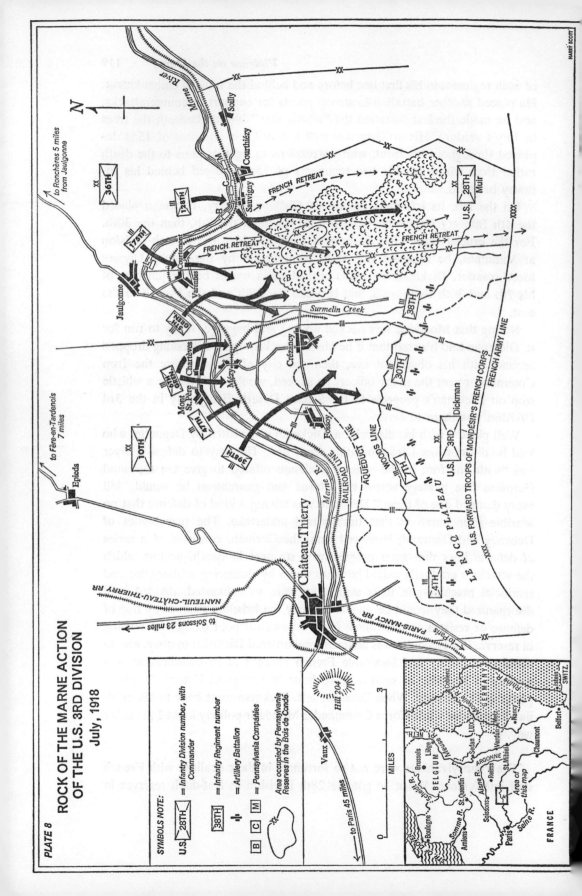

PLATE 8

ROCK OF THE MARNE ACTION
OF THE U.S. 3RD DIVISION
July, 1918

SYMBOLS NOTE:

U.S. 28TH = Infantry Division number, with Commander

38TH = Infantry Regiment number

⊹ = Artillery Battalion

B C M = Pennsylvania Companies

⬭ Area occupied by Pennsylvania Reserves in the Bois de Condé.

HARRY SCOTT

July, Degoutte first put them in a second line, the 56th Brigade close behind Mézy and Froissy, where McAlexander's 38th Infantry held the advance line, the 55th Brigade behind the French division to the right. But it was not long before Degoutte began to tamper with their dispositions, as he had with those of the 3rd. First, he moved it much closer to the river than any others of his main body, even closer than the French divisions that flanked it. Then he decided to mix in some Pennsylvania companies as cement to fill the interstices between his own sparse battalions, and on July 14, just before von Boehn's attack, he ordered four companies of the 55th Infantry Brigade into the French front line to the right of Dickman. This was in defiance of everything Pershing had fought for, but like Dickman, Colonel Brown of the 109th and Colonel Kemp of the 110th Infantry knew they had no choice but to obey at this perilous hour. Thus, four green companies that did not understand the new defense tactics of Debeney and Gouraud found themselves scattered over two miles, with no French liaison and no Doughboy officer who could understand French.

During the weeks preceding the German offensive, activity along the Marne was limited to continuous patrol action. The width of the Marne was a hazard to patrols from both sides, and the Doughboys had great difficulty at first in securing prisoners. One eager beaver in the 3rd Division, Captain F. M. Lasseigne, came back empty-handed twice, but on June 17 he returned with five live and talkative Germans in his pontoon boat. Patrol action continued all along the line, and it was as a result of a daring patrol on July 14 on General Gouraud's front east of Reims that one of the great pieces of good fortune ever to befall any army fell into Foch's hands. A German major was captured whose papers revealed the German plan of attack. (The Hohenzollern Crown Prince later said this officer was a traitor.)

Bruchmüller was to open the bombardment at ten minutes past midnight on July 15, about six hours thence, and about five days earlier than Foch had told Pershing he expected Ludendorff's next push. At 1:30 A.M., fourteen German divisions under von Boehn would begin crossing the Marne between Reims and Château Thierry, with fourteen to follow. The gateway between the heights five miles south of the Marne would be gained later in the day by an attack spearheaded by a rolling barrage from eighty-three batteries plastering the Rocq Plateau at 11 A.M. East of Reims, and up to the brow of Fort Douaumont at Verdun, two German armies would hurl themselves upon Gouraud with Châlons-sur-Marne twenty-five miles south as their goal. It was all excellently planned. With two thrusts at the heart of Paris, Foch would be forced to shift east to its defense, giving

Crown Prince Rupprecht with three armies the chance to strike Haig at Hazebrouck. "We expected great things in Paris by the end of July," the Reich's Chancellor Georg Friedrich, Graf von Hertling, wrote in his memoirs.

Foch put his faith in Gouraud's intelligence. A quarter of an hour before midnight on July 14, only a few hours after the four doomed Pennsylvania companies had eaten their corned beef—a gift of the French, who called it *singe*, or "monkey meat" in Doughboy translation—every Allied battery south of the Marne opened on the German troops who were hurrying in the night toward the north bank of the Marne. It was a breath-taking move in the gamble of war, for Foch thus revealed the whereabouts of his own massed guns. Had the captured German papers been a piece of counter-intelligence, the German major a plant with false plans, the game would have been up. The French had twenty-five agonizing minutes to wait. Then brilliant star shells burst above the French, and Bruchmüller's orchestra crashed in reply on schedule. Behind this great mass of guns throwing shells twenty miles over a sixty-mile front, Karl Rosner, correspondent of the Berlin *Lokal Anzeiger,* and wartime Boswell to the Hohenzollerns, tele-graphed his paper that "the Emperor listened to the terrible orchestra of our surprise fire attack and looked upon the unparalleled picture of projec-tiles raging toward the enemy positions." Rosner and his Kaiser did not know about the captured order; there had been no surprise.

Despite the punishment many regiments received in the unexpected French bombardment, Boehn's men began launching their pontoon boats from the north bank of the Marne at 1:10 A.M., and crossing the river with skill and daring in the great tradition of their infantry. They were a handsome lot, all equipped in new uniforms and accouterments, and the sedentary troops they had passed through on their way up could see that they had new leather belts and boots, rarities in a country suffering from the stranglehold of the Royal Navy's blockade. The gunners were riding postilion-fashion on batteries whose horses were sleek from the summer's grazing, and the shepherd dogs pulling machine-gun carts looked to have been meat-fed. This was the *Friedenstürm,* the "peace-storm" of the last battles before the Master Race ruled the great plain of Western Europe. They were professionals, the best that Ludendorff had left after Falkenhayn lost 650,000 German casualties in the Somme battles of 1916, where the British civilian armies and veteran poilus had destroyed the trained fabric of skillful captains and noncoms that make an army great—and been de-stroyed in turn. Neither side now had troops like that lost host.

On the right of the U.S. 3rd Division, the six French divisions fought frantically for a short while and then decamped, stopping only when they reached Degoutte's half-moon. The first that Captain Cousart, commanding L Company, one of the four doomed companies of the 28th Division, knew of the French withdrawal was when he realized that he and his headquarters detachment were now fighting on *four* fronts—Germans before him, to his left, to his right, and on his back. The war was over for Cousart and his handful of buddies. They were led away captives, crossing a river bobbing with German corpses.

The other flank of L Company suffered the same misfortune. Lieutenant James Schloch, second-in-command of L Company, found his best sergeant, Frank Benjamin, kneeling nearby working his Springfield bolt in next-to-nothing and firing at Germans on his right. Schloch had never before been in a fight, but he realized the French had withdrawn and he knew what had to be done. With Benjamin, he rounded up forty men left and moved rear-ward in a rough square, fighting in all directions, collecting others from L Company in the woods along the way, each man firing Indian-War fashion from behind trees, using bayonet and throwing grenades. Schloch was in the midst of a victorious Prussian regiment, but four hours later he saluted Colonel Brown at Regimental Headquarters. "Sir," he said, "L Company reporting for duty with sixty-seven men."

The other three companies of Pennsylvanians suffered a similar fate. In the midst of the fight, a German battalion broke M Company of the 109th Regiment into three segments. Many Doughboys disappeared fighting into a swirl of Germans, but some, like Captain MacKay with a dozen men, Lieutenant Tom Fales with thirty-five and six German prisoners, and Lieu-tenant Martin Wheeler with a shattered hand and half a platoon, eventually made it back to regimental lines. Perhaps the pluckiest of a plucky lot was Lieutenant W. M. A. Crossman. He got back with only one man, a corporal with broken legs, whom he carried piggyback for two miles through woods alive with Germans, setting the corporal down from time to time to fight a one-man rear-guard action. In the two separated companies of the 110th Regiment, Captain Fish and Lieutenants Claude Smith and Gilmore Hayden eventually made it back with 123 men, twenty-six of them wounded, some carried on blankets slung between rifles, after a running fight in which they bagged six prisoners.

C Company lost many men to the Germans, but were any soldier to be singled out in this outfit, it would have to be Corporal Alvey C. Martz from Pennsylvania's lonely Somerset County, who was stringing barbed wire on the river bank with a patrol of six men when Bruchmüller's guns opened. (Why this lad, who had never been to war, who had never under-gone a patrol exercise in a quiet sector, should have been placed there at the known zero hour is something that Degoutte, who all along had wanted the Yanks to fight this way, could never explain to Pershing.) Martz and his six buddies dropped into shell holes. When the bombardment lifted and Germans swept around the wire, Martz was left alone. Concealment was impossible; Martz and the others suddenly reared up on signal, shouting, throwing grenades, and firing rifles into the backs of Germans between them and where they last had left the company. The Germans fell back into defensive positions to analyze this surprise, and Martz with his six buddies gained a clump of protective lindens. After two hours of tree-trunk fighting, they ran into Sergeant Bob Floto, of their company. Martz turned his army of six Doughboys over to Floto, who now commanded an army of fourteen men in the midst of seven German divisions. Soon they sighted six Doughboys marching single file, a German leading and another following the file. Martz, the deerslayer from remote Somerset County, and another boy circled through the woods and ambushed the file, and Sergeant Floto now had an army of twenty men. Two hours later, they encountered Captain Charles L. McLain with a handful of men. The Doughboys proposed to fight their way back to their company by the river, but McLain knew it no longer existed. Then, moving cautiously with points and patrols and giving Martz the honor of commanding the rear guard, McLain worked his group back to Regimental Headquarters after thirty-six hours of continuous fighting.

Not one of the four doomed companies had been notified that the French were falling back, though Ulysses Grant McAlexander could have told them that when the sagacious French poilu said, *"Nous resterons là,"* he was uttering so much mannerly malarkey. Such incidents set Pershing's resolve to resist French demands for piecemealing Doughboys among French units, even though he realized that the action had been due not to betrayal but to the failure of liaison. Yet so high was the morale of the Pennsylvanians of the 28th Division that the other ranks, dug in on a secondary line behind the French now streaming rearward, envied the survivors of the four companies and almost wished that they too had been abandoned that day beside the river. Some of them had their chance to shine almost immediately.

Early in the fighting, McAlexander of the neighboring 38th Infantry, 3rd Division, requested they throw a block to hold the Bois de Condé on his right flank, a critical position abandoned by the French. When the Germans came on, breaking into small groups to assault the line, they found it held, surprisingly enough, by Americans of the 109th Infantry, Pennsylvania National Guard. Platoons of Pennsylvanians now began learning the art of war as Pershing had intended, fighting fiercely in the ravines of the wood and suffering many casualties; and they held the position inviolate, all three badly wounded captains refusing to quit the field.

The 28th Division is little remembered in this baptism of fire; its performance was overshadowed by Dickman's 3rd. But the Pennsylvanians fought valiantly against the German assault, and later in the counterattack with the French drove the enemy off.

Captain Jesse W. Wooldridge received the warning of the German attack around suppertime beside the Marne, where his company of the 38th Infantry, 3rd Division, lay in wait to the left of the Pennsylvanians and the French. The captain, a young man with glasses and a sandy pompadour, was a long way from his home on Turk Street in San Francisco, where the year before he had been a young businessman much interested in Woodrow Wilson's warning to the Germans about unrestricted submarine war. Had he been told then that a year later he would be regarded by General Dickman as an infantryman with a flair for minor tactics he might have dismissed the notion as fantasy; for Mr. Wilson had insisted that Wooldridge and everyone else must be "neutral in thought as well as in deed"—a feat Homo sapiens has never been able to perform. Even less credible would have been the notion that a Colonel U. G. McAlexander, who seemed to know the innermost qualities of some 3,500 Doughboys in the 38th Infantry Regiment, would regard Wooldridge as a cold-blooded killer capable of fighting a battle of maneuver with four platoons against anything the Germans might send his way.

Wooldridge, McAlexander, and the men of the 3rd Division had one thing working in their favor that would be very valuable in the hours ahead. Pershing had insisted on teaching his troops open warfare, and he had stuck to this resolve in the face of continuous criticism from the British and French, who considered such instruction an unnecessary waste of time in the light of the trench warfare prevailing on the Western Front. Thus every man in the 3rd Division, and every division which, unlike the 28th, had finished its training, knew Pershing's "open book" by heart and had had a chance to practice its precepts. In his "Combat Instructions," Pershing pointed out the difference between trench and open warfare: "Trench warfare is marked by uniform formations, the regulation of space and time by higher commands down to the smallest detail . . . fixed distances between units and individuals . . . little initiative." (The Germans, accustomed to a high degree of regimentation in their social scheme, excelled at the discipline of trench warfare; the British and French, accustomed to greater individualism, must have found it difficult; Americans, Pershing may have believed, would not countenance it.)

Open warfare is marked by . . . irregularity of formations . . . comparatively little regulation in space and time by higher commanders . . . that greatest possible use of the infantry's firepower to enable it to get forward, variable distances and intervals between units and individuals . . . brief orders and the greatest possible use of individual initiative by all troops engaged in the action.

The Doughboys of the 3rd would find Pershing's insistence that they master the art of open warfare saving many lives.

McAlexander set up a three-company battalion front, and he gave each company commander *carte blanche* to dispose of his strength. He placed Wooldridge on the left, holding the 38th Infantry's first line where it joined the 30th. He wanted the killer where the Germans would seek to pierce the junction of the two regiments, knowing the fighting there would be sanguinary indeed. In the center, he placed H Company, and on the right, its flank resting on the French in the outskirts of Varennes, he placed E Company. McAlexander positioned F Company in slit trenches echeloned and facing the French to the east. The company was commanded by a shy fellow with the build of a fullback, Captain T. C. Reid. Behind Reid was Hill 231, a slight bulge of woods on a plain where a ten-foot elevation for machine gunners could settle an issue of life and death. He was mortally certain that Reid would deny all Germans access to Hill 231. The men were to stay in deep trenches behind the slit trenches until the initial bombardment passed to the rear, then dash to their fighting positions to protect the right flank from Germans who would inevitably drive the French back. McAlexander realized the French would fall back, sensibly yielding ground and saving lives, and felt no rancor about it. He told his young captains that in time, if the war lasted, Americans would also yield ground, but it was now their part "to so impress the Germans with our fighting ability and *our wish to fight them* that their morale would be destroyed," for they knew millions of Americans were ready to take the place of the 38th's Doughboys.

The stocky colonel thus had about 250 of his 3,500 men "with one foot in the water," where Degoutte had proposed to put about 2,000. The rest were in two lines to the rear; the 1st Battalion about a thousand yards behind the railroad, its reserve echeloned on the right to protect its French flank; the 3rd Battalion hidden on the extreme right of Dickman's "woods line."

Wooldridge, making his own dispositions only forty-eight hours before the attack, did not believe any German colonel foolish enough to attempt a charge through the waist-high, poppy-flecked wheatfields facing him, so he placed only one platoon, under Lieutenant Calkins, in thick brush at the river's edge, pledged to fight there until overrun. He placed his second platoon on the river side of the railroad fill behind Calkins, deep in holes

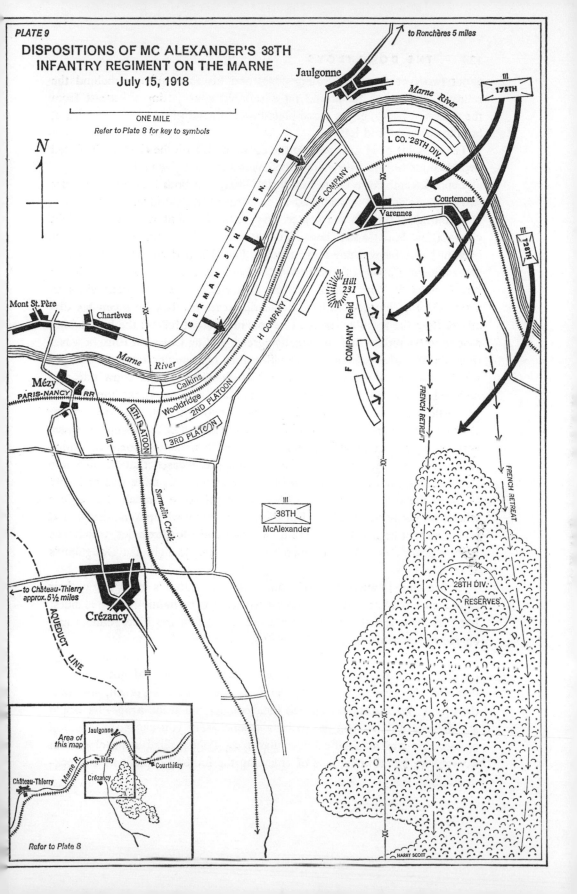

PLATE 9

DISPOSITIONS OF MC ALEXANDER'S 38TH INFANTRY REGIMENT ON THE MARNE
July 15, 1918

ONE MILE

Refer to Plate 8 for key to symbols

N

to Ronchères 5 miles

Jaulgonne

Marne River

175TH

L CO. 28TH DIV.

GERMAN 5TH GREN. REG'T.

F COMPANY

Courtemont

Varennes

128TH

Hill 231

Reid

F COMPANY

H COMPANY

Mont St.Père

Chartèves

Marne River

Calkins

Wooldridge

2ND PLATOON

FRENCH RETREAT

FRENCH RETREAT

Mézy

PARIS-NANCY RR

4TH PLATOON

3RD PLATOON

Sturmelin Creek

38TH
McAlexander

XX
28TH DIV.
RESERVES

to Château-Thierry
approx. 5½ miles

AQUEDUCT LINE

Crézancy

Area of
this map

Jaulgonne

Mézy

Courthiézy

Marne R.

Crézancy

Château-Thierry

Refer to Plate 8

HARRY SCOTT

about two feet from its leading edge, and his third platoon behind the railroad. His fourth he placed on a railroad spur jutting southeast from the station at Mézy, giving three platoons command of all directions of fire, both to the right and left.

The captains of H Company in the center and E on the right each placed two platoons on the river's edge, believing the enemy would assault frontally and determined to delay him to the limit, and both located their other two platoons astride the railroad to conform to Wooldridge.

Wooldridge, now in the center ring of the big tent with the midnight circus a few hours away, began taking stock of his men. None had ever been in battle before, any more than he had. He had confidence in some, and misgivings about others. Private Wilson, for example, was a hothouse boy from New York whose wealthy father had made frequent visits to Camp Greene, North Carolina, demanding that the boy be given his discharge from the Regular Army as he was not a stout fellow; the boy, taking tone from his father, had continually agreed. Acting Corporal Enright was a thorn in Wooldridge's side, a troublemaker continually bitching because senior noncoms of the Old Army pushed ahead of him in chow line and he hated their guts for it. Another New Yorker, from the sweatshop district, spoke little English and seemed to possess two left feet. He was Private Dickman, no relation to General Dickman. There was the company water cart driver, a peewee with an unpronounceable name, whom Wooldridge regarded as absolutely useless. The captain was pleased that Peewee was now two miles back of the line with his cart, where his mule was probably blocking the road, ignoring the blasphemies of some French staff officer whose limousine was held up. But there were many whom Wooldridge had taught all that he had learned from Dickman and McAlexander, which was a great deal. These were the men now preparing to fight the Doughboy's War.

Unlike the doomed Pennsylvania companies, Reid's men knew their right flank would be exposed and they would soon be fighting on three sides, but they were with their own folks, with their own machine gunners and engineers and artillerymen and signalers. Their colonel, the modern Ulysses, knew every inch of ground before him. He had often walked it erect in daytime, frequently being shouted at by sergeants who did not recognize him and who cried, "Get down, you crazy idiot!" or "Get down, you goddam fool!" When they recognized their colonel and stood agape, he would say breezily, "When you get to be a colonel, son, you can go where you please." He was a fabulously popular West Pointer, like some classroom savant who was also capable of creaming the football captain in a knockdown fight.

The Germans had their pontoon boats in the water before the 30th and 38th positions by one in the morning, but things went badly for them at first. They had been told that Bruchmüller's "surprise" bombardment would leave front lines as shattered as those on the Chemin des Dames in late May, that the south side of the Marne would be littered with dead and demented Doughboys. Instead, they had been battered by the unexpected Allied bombardment on their way up, and when they started across the river they found men like Lieutenant Calkins of Wooldridge's company with one foot in the water. Calkins was finally shot down in the dark of 2 A.M., his platoon overrun, though he himself was ferried across the river by his captors for first aid, and he survived.

Corporal Connors, with his squad of two Chauchat teams and their buddies from three companies, killed twenty boatloads of the boys in new leather belts before all but Connors were killed or wounded. Connors had no more clips for his hiccuping Chauchats, but there were still the grenades. He began throwing these into the oncoming boats rather than retire with honors to his company line on the railway embankment, the Marne's silver water crimsoned with red whorls, its surface bobbing with floating bodies and smashed boats. He was still at it, having pulled the pin of another grenade, when a German rifleman killed him and his own grenade tore him to pieces. (McAlexander refused to bury Corporal Connors by the railway embankment. His cross stood by the river's edge.) All five platoons on the bank were overrun or annihilated, though here and there a Doughboy out of ammunition, like Sergeant Hardy who fought his way from the river bank with a Colt 45, managed to regain his company's line, but they had bought precious time and had compelled two regiments of Grenadier Guards to change their course, impressing the first check on Boehn's fine army.

Nevertheless, one of its roughed-up battalions with great skill and courage effected a bridgehead by three in the morning and gained a footing on the railway embankment between the 30th and 7th Infantry. By seven in the morning, three German companies were straddling the embankment, gathered to assault the left flank of the 7th Infantry, which had not been protected like the 38th with echelons in depth. They came on confidently, in platoon front rather than in echelon as fire teams—much as the reservists had begun their first counterattacks at Cantigny—and they met the same mettle, with an additional element of shock. For the platoons of Lieutenants E. W. Gray and A. H. Baker could not be contained. At their first sight of Germans they broke over with wild shouts, hip-firing, brandishing the bright steel of bayonets, using rifles and Chauchats as clubs when out of ammunition, driving into the heart of two German companies on the river side of the embankment, killing and being killed. Gray and Baker, unable to restrain them, joined and led them, Gray being cut down deep in the German masses and taken prisoner. Baker fell in the midst of his platoon and was carried, wounded, back to the 7th's lines by its few survivors. Fortunately, Lieutenant R. G. Butcher, on the far side of the embankment, was able to restrain his platoon, which was well positioned, and settled down to an all-day skirmish and was never dislodged.

The German battalion recoiled under this astounding charge, and by the time more companies joined it, the 7th Infantry had wheeled its right wing to flank positions facing this German penetration. Though it was mercilessly shelled, the 7th Infantry was not molested by infantry on its right flank after eight o'clock that morning, and from Butcher's platoon on the right to Château-Thierry on the left, five miles of the Marne remained inviolate. But there was nothing inviolate farther east along the Marne where McAlexander stood at bay and Wooldridge practiced his new profession.

General von Boehn, having digested the Intelligence summaries regarding the fighting qualities of "these half-Americans" made by Lieutenant von Buy in the midst of Belleau Wood, gave the 2nd Guards Division the honor of putting the Doughboys in their place. The Brigade of Grenadiers, 5th and 6th Regiments, linking two German divisions, crossed the river directly opposite the line Mézy-Varennes, while the other German brigade of crack infantry turned its attention to the French garrisoned around Varennes itself. Two-thirds of them were on the south bank of the Marne before dawn and ready to clear the railway embankment at daylight, still hoping to follow a rolling barrage at 11 A.M. to break Degoutte's Army Line. The first step in their order of battle was to dislodge the automatic riflemen from the river side of the embankment, where the latter employed the advantage of a nine-foot elevation. The grenadiers knew how to effect this dislodgment; they would go forward through the wheat, honeycombed in combat groups, automatic riflemen and machine gunners covering them. They would hurl their grenades and rush the bank. Some would be killed and others beaten back, but eventually there would be many grenadiers clinging to the base of the embankment, the American gunners above them powerless to bring fire to bear upon them.

The first shock of the charge, led by a captain of the 5th Grenadiers, a favorite Guards outfit of the Kaiser's, was met by Lieutenant Mercer M. Phillips of Wooldridge's right platoon, the biggest man in the 38th Infantry. Phillips was wounded in the head and as his corporal, Delsoldart, knelt to bandage his forehead, the grenadier captain was upon him. Phillips was up in a flash with the corporal's rifle, bayoneting the German captain, who, as he fell back dying, put a pistol bullet into the giant Doughboy lieutenant's brain. All day it would be a matter of individual "soldiers' battles" until groups united again on a field of maneuver, with skill and intelligence on both sides.

When Phillips fell, Sergeant Nunley pulled the platoon together and counterattacked, rushing down the embankment, and into the wheatfields. Nunley held his platoon together all day, elements of other platoons clinging to it as the field became, in the words of Wooldridge, "a military omelet." Sergeant Nunley's score of July 15 was seventy-six prisoners, many of them wounded.

Wooldridge presently found he had to drive back the Germans on his changing right flank himself or be enveloped. Planning a counterattack on a German machine gun with a half-platoon commanded by Lieutenant Paul Murray, Wooldridge took the extreme right. The thin line of perhaps twenty men began wriggling through the wheat, pausing to fire, waiting for the signal to rise and go in with the bayonet. Doughboys were dropping all along the line, and when two men between Wooldridge and Murray were killed, Wooldridge crawled over to the lieutenant and shouted that they must keep the right flank up or all was lost. His arm was around Murray when a bullet crushed the lieutenant's brains. Wooldridge, searching for survivors, found only Private Weiner, and together they moved to the left to collect the wreck of the platoon, but all the rest had been killed in the attack. Wooldridge, with the last bullet of his last clip, killed the machine-gun officer who was the cause of all this trouble, and Weiner with his bayonet accepted the surrender of the three surviving German gunners. The captain and the private then regained their lines with their prisoners after their successful counterattack.

Because of such exploits, things were not going well for the grenadiers. Their two regiments had been unable to effect a junction between two German divisions after the French fell back. Their brigadier, who had crossed the river, had been shot, and the colonel of the 6th Grenadiers as well. It was suicide for a German to raise his head "above the ears" in the wheat, a German said afterward. Wooldridge soon killed the staff major of the leading battalion, too. He was not of a mind to kill him at first; he merely shot him in the right hand at a distance of three feet before the German could pull his pistol from its holster. The major, staring at Wooldridge, then slowly moved his left hand across his body to the butt of his pistol. Wooldridge started to raise his knee to boot the fellow to the ground, but the heat of battle was on him and when the German still tried to draw his pistol, he killed him instead.

A Doughboy nearby bayoneted the major's adjutant, who uttered a loud "Ugh!" Shortly afterward, Wooldridge was astonished to see that the peewee of the water cart had made his way on foot two miles through Bruch-müller's bombardment and was now wearing the Luger pistol of a German staff officer. An American staff officer later admired it, and the runt of the 38th's litter presented it to him. "Did you kill him?" asked the staff officer. "Did I kill him? Why, goddam it, you could hang your pack on my bayonet sticking through his back!" That was the "Ugh!" Wooldridge had heard.

It was that kind of a fight, brutal, bitter, hand-to-hand. The grenadiers had fought on many stricken fields, but they had not before seen such an example of Pershing's open warfare, "brief orders and the greatest possible use of individual initiative by all troops engaged in the action." There had been nothing like it since the "Old Contemptibles" swept by Château-Thierry in 1914.

There was valor on both sides. In the heat of the fray a corporal brought a Prussian officer to Wooldridge. As McAlexander's fiercest captain came forward to search him for intelligence, the Prussian drew his battle orders from his jacket as if to tear them up. Wooldridge jammed a pistol against his belly. The German, looking the American in the eyes, tore the papers into bits. Wooldridge let a brave man keep his life, and sent him to the rear. Another time, in the midst of one fight, he found McAlexander between him and the enemy. The captain scolded him: "Colonel, don't you know that nothing can live in this place?" Ulysses shrugged his oxlike shoulders. "Well, while anyone is left alive, let's give them hell."

Wooldridge had the opportunity to observe many of the doubtful ones in action, and later he wrote a monograph in honor of his company. Private Wilson, the hothouse flower of New York society, was observed by Wooldridge in a slit trench with two buddies when three grenadiers got to him. He saw Wilson bayonet the first man, have his rifle wrested away by a second, take it away from the German and kill him. The third he knocked down with his naked fist and claimed as prisoner. The captain hoped that from these feats of strength Wilson would acquire some of the cockiness of his buddies, but he never did, and continued to insist that he was not a stout fellow.

Enright, the troublemaker who hated the senior noncoms, found his squad beefed up to ten men by the fortunes of war. He led a flank movement against five machine-gun positions. When the operation was completed, he brought back his two wounded, and thirty-six prisoners, pretty well shot up, but he had forgotten to destroy the cartridge guides in the German guns—a blooper for which he knew the old noncoms would needle him. Unable to bear this thought, Acting Corporal Enright seized an entrenching tool and went back alone to disable the guns. Portraits of him in divisional records show a long-faced, rather sad boy with the Distinguished Service Cross gleaming on his left breast.

Wooldridge got around to Private Dickman in his reserve platoon, too. The private was in a slit trench with two of the men who had learned musketry by firing at tomato cans. He was calling ranges in fuzzy English like a Regular Army man, firing carefully and coaching the others as he followed his new profession with no more emotion than if he had been at a cutter's table in a Seventh Avenue loft teaching apprentices how to save yardage. No German ever lived long enough to reach that slit trench.

The most surprising of the lot was a comic-strip character named Richardson and called "Eaglebeak" after the original, who was drawn along the lines of Washington Irving's Ichabod Crane. He never seemed strong enough to lift a camp stool, and no amount of gymnastics ever put an ounce on his skinny frame. In his first countercharge, Eaglebeak swept upon a machine gunner with his bayonet. The German promptly took the rifle away from him. Eaglebeak looked like a goner, but he closed with the enemy, rolling in the wheat, and beat the gunner to his Luger pistol. There was a muffled report, and the emaciated Eaglebeak arose, possessor of the proudest trophy a Doughboy could display.

As the daylong fighting went on, the front-line battalion of the 30th Infantry suffered heavily from German batteries on heights across the river. From here, snipers also took pot shots all day at a solitary horseman coursing between the 30th and its artillery support. They killed seven horses ridden by liaison Lieutenant George P. Hays, and on his twelfth sortie they got him with multiple wounds, but he was able to stand on his feet the day Pershing came by to award him the Medal of Honor.

So it went throughout the day. By 6 A.M., McAlexander had committed his second-line battalion and was ordering up his third. Two companies of the 30th's first-line battalion were now engaged heavily on Wooldridge's left flank, its charging men mingled with his and fighting furiously in squad units. Literally everyone was involved in small battles of maneuver on both sides of the railroad in clumps of woods, wheatfields, small ravines, or on the Rocq Plateau. Two Y.M.C.A. men tried to enlist on the battlefield as privates, but were told their work with the wounded was indispensable. A belligerent mess sergeant named O'Connor and an equally fierce chief cook named Maloney, with sundry Hibernian bottle-washers, abandoned their rolling stoves in exposed places far in the rear and joined Wooldridge in the front line, fighting with Irish fury. It was four days before their company had a hot meal, for German gunners shot the kitchens to pieces thinking they were field guns, and the survivors subsisted on horsemeat goulash until O'Connor and Maloney, miraculously alive, "acquired" some French rolling kitchens and large stocks of corned-beef hash and canned tomatoes for a mulligan stew.

"Why're ya makin' so much hash, Sergeant? There's only fifty-nine of us left!" "Listen, buddy, hash ain't no orchid that has to be worn the same day!"

On the 38th's echelon flank facing the French gap, Captain Reid did not commit *his* kitchen brigade until late afternoon, though in the half-darkness of dawn the grenadiers were on his flanks and in his rear—stopped only by McAlexander's skillfully placed slit trenchmen—before he realized the soldiers streaming south were German and not French. The latter had yielded Varennes without troubling to notify him, and by dawn the enemy was astride and behind the railroad fill. So deep was the German invest-ment of French lines that there was little hope of support for Reid from the second-line battalion, now heavily engaged on its own right flank and rear, the fighting so furious that frequently its surgeon, Captain Daniels, dropped his instruments and joined field medics and wounded to drive off enemy combat teams. On one such occasion, the ubiquitous McAlexander was beside him, breathing none too easily from having stepped in a gas pocket, and concealing a wound. Sergeant Thompson, a field medic fighting along-side Daniels, spoke out of turn. "Colonel, aren't you afraid of being picked off out here?"

This was *lèse majesté*. Ulysses combed the sergeant with his eyes and then addressed the surgeon: "Well, Captain, I suppose I should be about twenty miles back with a bunch of orderlies around me and a telephone to tell you fellows what to do. But, hell, I want to see what's going on." Daniels was later killed when trying to recover some of his surgeon's tools after his field station was finally overrun.

Though Reid was denied well-organized support from the second-line battalion, fighting for its own survival, he did get replacements in company driblets, sometimes picking out men he had never seen before and making them corporals on the field to lead squads in counterattacks. For his last counterattack around five o'clock in the afternoon, against the 5th Grenadier Guards on his front, and companies from the 10th and 36th German In-fantry Divisions on his right and rear, he threw in his cooks, clerks, bottle-washers, and typists. The company cook led his last charge, for the mess sergeant had been shot vainly trying to rescue a pal. "My men were mag-nificent," wrote Reid, "easily handled, trustworthy, ready and willing to take any chance I would take with them. Their rifle fire was accurate [he reported a remarkable piece of shooting by Sergeant Fisher, who drilled three Germans of a seven-man machine-gun team *through the head* at seven hundred yards, forcing the survivors to retire behind the railroad embankment], bayonet fighting furious, and valor simply indescribable." Reid was a square peg in a square hole that day, another example of McAlexander's uncanny ability to pick the right man for the right job. His only regret, expressed later, was that he had not, like Wooldridge, killed any Germans himself. "Colonel," he wrote, "I was just too busy."

The 3rd Division's batteries, which Dickman had placed forward to provide close support, were often smashed by Bruchmüller's gunners during the day. But the surviving gunners, along with the 6th Engineers, crossed to the right, helped themselves to abandoned French pieces and ammunition and somehow managed to manhandle them back to their old positions behind Reid's echelons. There they stayed, heeding Dickman's order to fight their guns to the death rather than withdraw. Some of their shells fell among Reid's men—a hazard all troops undergo with close support—but Reid got word to them before many of his foot soldiers were hit, and their support was invaluable.

By nightfall on July 15, half the 6th Grenadier Regiment had been killed or wounded by McAlexander's men, the other half having marched as prisoners to the rear, leaving the shards of the 5th Grenadiers huddled by the river. It was a staggering setback to German hopes. Only in the perspective of hindsight can historians estimate what von Boehn might have achieved if the Germans had been able to take the Surmelin Valley and the Rocq Plateau—their closest penetration to the French capital since 1914. Possibly he might have swept on toward Paris and ended the war. He did succeed in crossing the Marne and massing about 75,000 men in a depth of three miles against the French lines on the heights to the immediate right of the 3rd Division's battleground before he was driven back in three days of fighting. But every foot of the flat country the Germans wanted, defended by Dickman's division, was denied them. By nightfall, the remnants of the German grenadiers facing McAlexander were huddled by the river's edge, being pontooned back to the north bank, their *Friedenstürm* a failure.

To the northeast, still some twenty miles north of the Marne on the front line from Reims eastward, General Gouraud's Fourth French Army, employing Pétain's now famous elastic plan of defense borrowed from Ludendorff—and scorned by Degoutte—was checking the onslaught of the Germans under von Einem and von Mudra, whose purpose was to widen the Marne salient eastward by capturing Reims and pushing twenty-five miles south to join von Boehn at Châlons-sur-Marne.

Assigned mainly to the second line to which the front line withdrew while the enemy was being cut to pieces was the American 42nd Division, the Rainbows, composed of National Guard elements from many states. Under the National Defense Act of 1916, a milestone in our history, the President, when authorized by Congress, could draft the state guards into elements of the United States Army, thus breaking the stranglehold which provincial and partisan governors had upon Abraham Lincoln's conduct of the Civil War. (Grant could not make a New Yorker a general; only the governor at Albany could do that.) When Wilson asked for war, there were seventeen National Guard divisions of some 382,000 officers and men, and they saw more days of fighting than Regulars and draftees combined.

Just as the 2nd Division had its Doughboy-Leatherneck rivalry of brigades, the Rainbows were capable of internecine strife between companies. Its Alabama battalions had fought New York battalions at Gettysburg; Chicago outfits had plowed through Dixie battalions in Tennessee. But the deepest feud was more recent, originating among the iron hills of Anniston, Alabama. There a Manhattan regiment, "The Fighting Sixty-Ninth" of legendary Irishmen, in summer maneuvers showed itself a master of henhouse strategy, reducing the chicken population of the region to the vanishing point, to the chagrin of Southern boys who thought themselves masters of roost and wire. New Yorkers skilled since infancy in palming bananas from a pushcart under the watchful eye of its small capitalist thought of chicken-stealing as moonlight amateurishness.

This outfit was now through A.E.F. organization known as the 165th U.S. Infantry. Some of its colorful personnel were Father Duffy, the Vicar of Times Square, the principal chaplain, and William J. (Wild Bill) Donovan, later a two-star general of cloak-and-dagger fame, who won the Medal of Honor as a regimental commander. The regimental poet was Sergeant Joyce Kilmer, author of the ballad "Trees" so often sung by ladies at chicken-salad luncheons; but the Rainbows knew the fated Kilmer best for his poem "The Wood of the Rouge Bouquet," and were immensely proud of him. A Chicago battery boasted a future playwright who was dedicated to the proposition that all men are equal and that he, under no provocation, would accept a position higher than that of buck private, though he frequently dined with brigade staff. Private Charles MacArthur, sent on a blistering errand of liaison to an Alabama battery that first day forward of Châlons, when inquiring above the barking of the guns where he might find the first sergeant, was informed by a sweating, half-naked gunner: "Yank, this battery ain't never had no goddamn top sergeant and ain't never going to stand for none." There was another MacArthur with the Rainbows. Brigadier General Douglas MacArthur was chief of staff that day.

Even as a young lieutenant, Douglas MacArthur, with a legendary father who was a Yankee colonel at the age of twenty, was becoming something of a legend himself. As chief of staff, his work was infinitely difficult, with the shuttle of battalions moving through French outfits to counterattacks, the flux of battle bringing orders to sideslip, to withdraw, to go forward, making full use of engineers, gunners, signalers, in an exercise of tactical toe dancing in elastic defense. The sanitary train was greatly taxed in ferrying out wounded Rainbows as the French did not have a single ambulance to spare.

With the Americans, that July 15, Gouraud was the most popular general in France. Unlike Degoutte, he did not put his Doughboys in the First Line. Actually, he brought them up to his changing Resistance Lines a few companies at a time, always under division control by their own General Menoher, for counterattacks into the Intermediate Line where they were outstanding for alertness and ferocity. At no place on the front were the Rainbows in the first sacrificial line, though the Germans knew the green Americans were facing them, and employed ruses in three days of fighting. One group of dismounted uhlans came forward in poilu uniforms with friendly calls in French-accented English and were promptly machine-gunned. Another group tried the ruse in the dark; there was not a shot fired when all twenty-one Germans were met in a friendly fashion and then bayoneted by the chicken thieves from Wild Bill Donovan's outfit. The Rainbows took their casualties—about 1,590 of them—in good grace. Days ahead would find this figure a small reckoning.

The Germans sustained heavy losses and their gains were insignificant—they got just exactly as much ground as Gouraud had figured on giving them before they were stopped at the changing intermediate lines, the Rainbows fighting beside the French to plug the gaps. After two days, Mudra and Einem, now possessors of some twenty miles of marshy farmland three or four miles deep littered with futile German dead, called off their attack.

Division histories in armies of all nations are fulsome in self-esteem, but the Rainbows, who came from so many states, never even bothered to write one until 1937. What the French thought of them that July day was found in the diary of an observer, Major J. Corbabon, from General C. M. de Raganeau's French Military Mission, who witnessed three days of fighting. After listing seven successive counterattacks by the 116th Infantry to fill the breaches in the intermediate line, and citing the "most brilliant attack" by elements of the 117th Infantry in concert with a French battalion under General Charles T. Menoher's command—this understandably an intricate feat—he admired the cadence and recklessness of its artillerymen. He wrote:

The conduct of American troops has been perfect and has been greatly admired by French officers and men. Calm and perfect bearing under artillery fire, endurance of fatigue and privations, tenacity in defense, eagerness in counterattack, willingness to engage in hand-to-hand fighting—such are the qualities reported to me by all the French officers I have seen.

The major also thought Douglas MacArthur's staff work, with the "esteem and understanding" he showed his French colleagues in the operation, would result in even greater efficiency in days to come. He appreciated, too, that the 42nd Division not only evacuated 1,150 wounded Rainbows within fifteen hours of the first attack. Their trains brought back hundreds of French as well. The German prisoners, confused by the bigness of the 42nd's organization, said they were opposing the "two best divisions in the American Army—the 42nd Division and the Rainbow Division."

Von Einem and von Mudra were still twenty miles north of the Marne when they called it quits. Von Boehn was south of the Marne with 75,000 men in the wrong end of the sack and facing the wrong way on the wrong side of the river. He would not hold even this unenviable position for long. To the north, a great Allied counteroffensive against Soissons was under way and threatened von Boehn's supply lines. Within two days, he would have to extricate his troops and fall back fighting. They would not threaten Paris again.

While the Doughboys rushed toward Soissons and the course of the war changed irrevocably, General Bliss, Woodrow Wilson's deputy in the Supreme Allied Council, wrote to Pershing that he had heard many Frenchmen in high position say that the Americans had saved Paris. He thought it worthwhile to record this judgment now, he said, for the time would soon come when the Yanks would be forgotten.

Counterattack

PART III ★ JULY 18—AUGUST 12

Counterattack

Chapter **8**

SOISSONS—THE ROAD BACK

You rushed into the fight as to a fete.

When Pershing suggested to Foch on May 30 that together they might strike Boehn on his Soissons flank, the Supreme Commander had been too morose to discuss the matter. "It would be difficult," Pershing wrote twelve years later of that silent dinner circle, "to imagine a more depressed group of officers . . . as they contemplated what was probably the most serious situation of the war." Two weeks later, Foch had recovered his morale sufficiently—perhaps the performances of the Doughboys at Cantigny and Belleau Wood helped revive his flaming spirit as much as Debeney's check of Hutier's infiltrations when the latter made a massive attack (Ludendorff's fourth of the year) toward Compiègne in early June— to write General Pétain in the French Staff's formal style: "I have the honor to invite your attention to the communications net at Soissons."

Providing that Boehn could be held in check at the Marne, the German bulge, stretching south from Soissons to Château-Thierry, curving east along the river and then north to Reims, provided a magnificent opportunity for Foch to trap the Germans. Classic strategy for a counteroffensive dictated that the Marne line at the apex of the salient be held with as few troops as possible and the bulk of Foch's troops be massed quickly and without detection for an assault on the vulnerable flanks in an attempt at a breakthrough, and, possibly, the encirclement of the enemy. It is clear from his dispatch to Pétain that Foch saw the opportunity, but whether or not he would take advantage of it, and had the means to do so, remained to be seen.

Foch's letter went down the ladder from Pétain, eventually reaching General Charles Emmanuel Mangin, commanding the French Tenth Army west of Soissons. Mangin had been a Nivelle Army commander in the Hurtebise Farm tragedy of April, 1917, and had unjustly been called a butcher when Nivelle's pressures on him ended in cemeteries. In due course, Mangin replied with a summary plan for offensive operations, and toward the end of June—Pershing having nudged him once again when he visited Chaumont—Foch let his French commanders know secretly the number of divisions needed for the offensive. Mangin made an exploratory attack June 28 with a few warwise French and British divisions and succeeded in seizing some high ground west of Soissons. He told Foch, again through channels, that the operation "tended to prove" that the Germans would have as much difficulty defending their positions against a surprise attack *without artillery preparation* as the French had experienced when Boehn jumped them on the Aisne late in May. Foch, expecting Ludendorff's next push across the Marne no sooner than July 20, named July 18 as D-day for the Allied assault, hoping to beat the German to the punch.

When Boehn attacked at the Marne July 15 and got seven German divisions across the river to the right of Ulysses Grant McAlexander, Pétain lost his nerve, recalling the wave of mutinies that followed the Nivelle debacle, and the 400,000 French casualties in the Allied reverses since March 21. He despatched a message to Major General Marie Émile Fayolle, commander of the Army Group defending Paris, ordering him to suspend the Mangin operation and send him reserves for the battle south of the Marne.

The indomitable Foch reacted at once. This time he did not say he "had the honor" to suggest anything. His brusque rebuke to Pétain read in part: "There can be no question at all of slowing up, and less so of stopping, the Mangin operation."

Pershing was told nothing of the proposed offensive. He fished for information from Foch, who only said that "studies are being made," and from Clemenceau, who knew nothing. Foch was going to achieve surprise— surprise of place, of time, and weight of mass—and he did not want to wrangle with anyone about an independent American Army, or risk tipping off the Germans about his intentions. But at Foch's request Pershing prepared a list of American divisions that could be made available. The 1st and 2nd, now in reserve below the Marne, had been brought up to full strength and when von Boehn was stopped at Degoutte's Sixth Army line they were ready for anything Foch had in mind. The 3rd and 28th, now mopping up grenadiers and licking their wounds south of the Marne, would be ready shortly, as would the 42nd Rainbows now east of Reims. The 26th, holding to the left of Château-Thierry, was in position to break out of the Bois de Belleau and push northeast. The green 4th, and the 32nd and 77th, finishing their training, completed the list.

Foch had earlier asked that these divisions be transferred to Fayolle's French Armies. For once, Pershing took no part in a violent Allied quarrel that erupted when Foch demanded that Haig relinquish all five American divisions training in British areas, as well as reduce his own forces. (Haig and Foch were never again friends, though when the chips were down, or the cupboard bare, each was capable of magnanimity toward the other in a common cause.) Fayolle would have for the offensive nine American divisions, ten French, and four British; actually, he would be in command of 350,000 Americans, counting supply troops and replacements.

Mangin knew that the July 18 operation was a gamble. His objective was to drive due east on the line of the German salient that extended southeast from Soissons to Château-Thierry, seize the heights dominating the important rail network at Soissons, and cut main German communications lines to Château-Thierry, isolating von Boehn's army on the Marne. To lead the attack, he knew he needed the best assault troops he could get, and he also knew that among the French forces only the Americans had both the guts *and the physiques* for a surprise attack with rifle and bayonet, the strength to bear heavy packs up steep hillsides. To strike at the base of the salient near Soissons he got the 1st and 2nd Divisions, Fayolle knowing from their records they were *"soldats de la première classe pour le combat."* Sandwiched between these two brawny divisions he placed the French 1st (Moroccan) Division, red-fezzed fighters accompanied by bellowing mullahs attesting that Allah was merciful, augmented by what was left of the French Foreign Legion. They were the best French assault troops that Mangin had. Below the 2nd Division, about midway on the thirty-five-mile line of the salient's eastern face, Degoutte located the green 4th Division infantry, commanded by the lean, ascetic Major General Cameron, patch-working its battalions into two French corps. Below the 4th, just west of the salient's point, were the 26th New Englanders, and at the apex, ready to counterattack after stopping the Grenadier Guards, stood Dickman's 3rd Division.

The Yanks of the 1st and 2nd Divisions knew they were going to fight when the artillery began pulling out around July 13. They did not know their destination, but it mattered little to them. In June, during the long cannonading after the capture of Cantigny, the 1st Division's gunners had found the

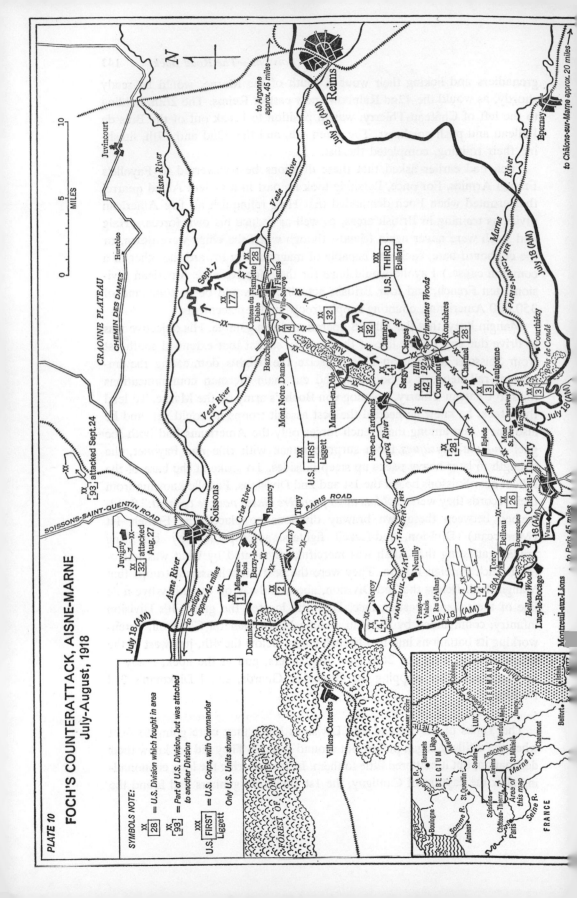

PLATE 10

FOCH'S COUNTERATTACK, AISNE-MARNE
July-August, 1918

SYMBOLS NOTE:

$\frac{XX}{\boxed{28}}$ = U.S. Division which fought in area

$\frac{XX}{\boxed{93}}$ = Part of U.S. Division, but was attached to another Division

$\frac{XXX}{U.S. \boxed{FIRST}}$ = U.S. Corps, with Commander
Liggett

Only U.S. Units shown

time to decorate their gun positions with field flowers from the Picardy countryside. Many bunkers had displayed polished brass shell cases sprouting red poppies, blue lupin and verbena, and there had been flower arrangement contests between batteries, easy pickings for some Italian gardener's son. There had been contests between cooks under fire, too, the prize a trip to a Paris restaurant, and on the Fourth of July there were horse shows—as well as exultant raids by the Doughboys in the bloodstained woods around Framicourt and the Château de Jenlis, where a lieutenant colonel lost his life. The surviving Marines had paraded in Paris, and Pershing also sent battalions from the 4th Division of "Regulars" from all sections of America down the Champs Élysées, just to show the French how the new divisions from overseas, unlike the raw 16th Infantry of a year ago, were now capable of a marching discipline second to none, a warning to Foch that he was no longer a four-star beggar.

Streams of replacements from the 41st Division, now cannibalized into the 1st, 2nd, and 3rd Divisions, embraced fine National Guardsmen from the Pacific Coast, and thousands of draftees, among them a battalion of government clerks from the District of Columbia. Private Bailey remembered that the first of these arrivals were scorned as men dragooned by draft boards when they reported to M Company of the 9th Infantry some time before Château-Thierry. However, one of the clerks soon whipped the company cook in a knockdown fight, always a hilarious sight to men who had to partake of a Doughboy cook's bread and salt. Then another draftee, a baby-faced boy the picture of innocence, reduced the professional gambler of M Company to a state of poverty with a pair of educated dice. This display of soldierly qualities marked the drafted men as "Regulars" and henceforth they were so regarded in all the low-numbered divisions. Heterogeneous mass soon became a homogeneous breed.

Casualties and expansion meant promotion for those who survived, and a combative spirit was rewarded. Pershing was indefatigable in his effort to provide corps commanders—at least for administrative purposes—for troops who now ranged in quality from battleworthy veterans to lads who had scarcely fired a rifle. Many outfits were commanded by colonels and brigadiers never tested in the field. Bullard was named a corps commander, and his gunner, Summerall, got a second star and command of the Big Red One. Major General Bundy was sent into obscurity, and Harbord, ex-Kansas State Aggies, took over the 2nd Division with another star, giving the Marine brigadier's post to his new friend, Neville, of the 5th Marines. Lewis of the 2nd's Doughboy Infantry Brigade was posted with his two stars to Field Marshal Sir Douglas Haig to command the U.S. 30th Division. Private Bailey's battalion of the 9th Infantry saw the last of its Leatherneck major.

He was now Colonel Hiram Bearss, USMC, much disliked at first because he lived up to his Marine sobriquet of "Hike 'em, Hiram," but he had won their admiration by leading a midnight patrol to collar a live German, while shouting in a tone to wake the dead. Bearss replaced a regimental commander of the 26th Division who had been found wanting.

Perhaps the most interesting addition was the new commander for Lewis's infantry brigade of the 2nd Division. Colonel Paul Malone, who should have got it, had offended General Peyton C. March, chief of staff at Washington, and would be a long time, despite constant pressure from Chaumont, winning an A.E.F. star from that embittered master. Lewis's replacement was a new brigadier who spoke through clenched teeth, Hanson E. Ely. (Bullard must have grinned when he reported in.)

And so the old and the new, veteran and replacement, assembled under cover of darkness in the forests of Retz and of Villers-Cotterêts south of Soissons, from which the attack was to be launched.

As the night of July 17-18 fell, Doughboys of the 1st and 2nd Divisions moved forward along uncharted trails through dense forest cover under sheets of rain. Many regiments were without food for twenty-four hours, few had water left in their canteens, and they were bearing heavy packs, burdened with extra bandoliers of ammunition. In the dark tangles of woods many did not know where they were and became intermingled in spite of the efforts of platoon leaders to hold their sixty shivering men together. The old-timers knew that they were going to attack at 4:45 in the morning, but had no notion of what the jumping-off place looked like. Sergeants only knew they must go forward behind a protective barrage; failure to cling to its deafening edges was an invitation to death. On they pressed, soaked to the skin by the torrential rains, hazing the new men, stumbling into gullies. They were paying the price for secrecy and surprise, of being pressed into an army speaking a language they did not understand, under generals they did not know, and of hurrying forward to execute an attack against an enemy whose dispositions were unknown to them. (Boehn had spent five weeks improving the defenses of his tender right flank.)

For the American commanders in the field it was a time of frenzy. Bullard, corps commander without a staff, knew that his duties could only be administrative, so he turned tactical direction over to the French. He did not know anything about the terrain either. After one look at his last-minute orders, he found Harbord and Summerall desperately mimeographing copies for distribution to their colonels, who, in ignorance, had to lead their men through the rain-swept dark. Harbord did not even know where he would find ammunition reserves. Then one of his aides discovered a dump which had been placed there for the 1st Division six miles away on the left. Harbord expropriated it for the 2nd Division.

Colonel Paul Malone of the 23rd Infantry, who had plugged a French hole beside the Paris road in the dark of June 1, had two of his battalions in place before H-hour when one of his staff rushed up to say that the other battalion was missing, having gotten lost when companies of a 9th Infantry battalion, going at cross directions to the front, had mingled with it in the forest. In the darkness, Malone set about straightening them, when another officer shouted that two battalions of Marines were now going across the confusion of the 23rd's Doughboys. Malone and all his staff, with French interpreters, cooks, and bottle-washers, now tried to set them right. Malone found Logan Feland, Colonel of the 5th Marines, and together with French guides they began to straighten fronts and fix boundaries.

Having set the Marines on the right trails, Malone now got his last awry battalion together, gave the French guides the proper direction, and led his men forward. It was now 4:45 and the troops heard the lifesaving barrage burst with a roar three hundred meters beyond them in the open whilst they were still in the forest of Retz—a gloomy stand celebrated for its fifteenth-century monster, Gilles de Rais, who some scholars say was the original of Bluebeard. Malone pushed his stumbling troops forward on the double, and they ran the last three hundred meters to gain the barrage. They broke into the open drenched, exhausted, and without machine guns, with orders to move in three echelons, changing directions twice as they advanced. Employing nothing but rifle and bayonet, they swept on, most of their officers falling as they directed the surge. The first objective of a three-stage assault was a mile away. Doughboys and Marines were masters of it before eight in the morning. To their left, the Big Red One, on the line an hour before the surprise barrage cracked down, moved up the chalky hills, with French tanks leading, bayoneting out clumps of sacrifice machine gunners, losing many officers whom Pershing had destined for higher command, and most of its better-known sergeants.

Once out of the forests of Retz and of Villers-Cotterêts, the two divisions, with Moroccans between them, moving to the northeast, faced a broad plain broken by hills, plateaus, and deep ravines, stretching to the valley of the Crise River, which flowed north into the Aisne at Soissons. By seizing the heights above the valley of the Crise, the Allies could command Soissons with their artillery.

By ten in the morning, the 1st Division had the two objectives Foch had asked for by the close of the day. Yanks crouched upon the two plateaus of Dommiers while to the northeast their buddies needed two more violent days to cut the Soissons-Paris road beyond Missy-aux-Bois and take the ravine beyond it with glinting steel. The onrushing French artillery, revitalized by the Dommiers shock, was on their heels, and by ten-fifteen had begun to play upon the railways of the Soissons communications net with French 155s, the best counterbattery of the war, accurate and far-ranging.

Ludendorff got the news at noon, and telephoned Boehn to get out fast.

Meanwhile, the Moroccans were flagging, and the 1st Division to the left and the Marine brigade to the right thinned their lines, spreading across the gap for a mile until each group of American assault teams could hear the others across the death-struck hills. Then both divisions swept on, the 3rd Infantry Brigade of the 2nd Division leaving its 9th Infantry Regiment's right flank naked in their wildcat assaults. From that moment, the German never took another forward step anywhere in France. It was now possible, as at Gettysburg, to point out the exact acre of artillery ground where the tide of a great war had turned. The Americans did not win a war that day but they saved one.

The Germans, caught flat-footed that first morning, did not use gas. Lieutenant Daniel Bender, regimental gas officer of the 6th Marines, in reserve the first day, went forward on the second day with the first leapfrog wave to check for toxic shells. He was bent over examining a dud shell when a sniper shot him cross-buttocks, injuring his spine. The Dartmouth College wit sent back a field message: "No gas. Shot in the ass. Bender." Charles Emmanuel Mangin, a major general whose career blended literary skill with surpassing qualities in the field, created Bender a Chevalier of the Legion of Honor on the spot. "You rushed into the fight as to a fete," Mangin later messaged his Americans.

Nightfall of July 19, the second day, found the 6th Marines, freshest unit of infantry surviving forty-eight hours of slaughter, facing the town of Tigny, just west of the road leading to Château-Thierry, ready to throw an additional block against Boehn's withdrawal. With them was a rifle battalion of the 2nd Engineers, specialists hard to replace in their technical field. Their colonel had protested, in Belleau Wood, that it was spendthrift folly to kill off his slide-rule men in assault teams, but they were the only reserves available. Harbord's field artillery came up to protect the right flank of the 3rd Infantry Brigade—the 23rd and 9th Regiments—men and horses falling as the caissons came rolling along. Horsemen of the French 4th Dragoons were somewhere to the right and rear, but their commander wisely told Harbord that cavalry should not fight on such a field unless it was a life-or-death issue. Harbord, no longer subject to Bundy's ineptitude or Degoutte's cavalier disregard, withdrew Leathernecks and Engineers to heights a half-mile back of Tigny, commanding the ribbon which was the easiest line of withdrawal for Boehn's artillery. At this point, Harbord demanded that his 2nd Division be relieved. Mangin promptly effected the change-over. The surviving Doughboys and Marines came back in order, passing huddles of their dead comrades along the route. In two days the 2nd Division had advanced seven kilometers, captured three thousand prisoners, seventy-five guns, and sustained about five thousand casualties.

The 1st Division to the left, fighting closer to the Soissons nexus and finding the going more sensitive, was short of its third objective on the eve of the nineteenth. Its lines were now extended and everyone was committed to battle, including its engineers and artillerymen, the latter at times operating over open sights. The Moroccans in the center and the French division on the left were still cautiously exploiting gains around islands of German resistance. The Big Red One swept on to cover much of this French front as well. Everyone was involved, college boys now leading fragments of regiments, sergeants scraping together remnants of companies. Beaumont Buck, Ely's brigadier at Cantigny, having lost all his field officers, was heading his brigade like a platoon leader in front-line sweeps. (All twelve infantry battalion commanders were gone.) Boehn desperately defended the town of Berzy-le-Sec, a hilly French objective which the decimated poilus no longer had the physical strength to iron out.

It was here that Brigadier General Buck, waving his tin hat, took the village on the 2nd Brigade's second try, with Summerall, the new division commander, bringing up his old gunners to work over open sights on German artillery massed there. Mangin then sent in a fresh French division of poilus to replace the Moroccans, and with the Doughboys they cut the Château-Thierry road, halting before Buzancy. The colonel of the Foreign Legion attached to the Moroccans, like his remnants of romanticists and adventurers, and scoundrels from the riverfronts of the world, broken to every known phase of battle, had sought out Brigadier Buck under fire to say he deemed it an honor to be on the field with such companions.

The 1st Division spent two more days in hard fighting before it crossed the Château-Thierry road, and reached a line at Buzancy commensurate with that of the race horses of the 2nd Division's rival brigades. In four days the Big Red One had lost 7,200 men, taken 3,500 prisoners and 68 guns. The two great combat divisions had each now, with Cantigny, Belleau Wood, Vaux, and Soissons, lost around fifteen thousand men, and their war was only starting. Even a division history, which always attributes great feats to all its personnel, could only mention a few men of the thousands whose personal exploits were above and beyond the call of duty.

Bullard, in an angry little book written after reading some disparaging remarks made by Foch in his *Conversations* with M. Raymond Recouly, set down dozens of names he classed as members of "The Solo Club"—

meaning that these enlisted men had, singlehanded, captured a cluster of machine guns. Their names reflect the racial texture of the United States of America, many of them "half-Americans" of Lieutenant von Buy's classification: Stacey Lewis, August Speidel, Misczyslaw Brocki, Arthur Waddell, Charles Cameron, Mike Ellis, Louis Cukela. Cukela was a sergeant who won the Medal of Honor working exclusively with his bayonet and some German potato-masher grenades. He became a famous Leatherneck, and, a retired major in a later war, he descended upon his old battalion commander, Thomas Holcomb, now a lieutenant general and commandant of the Corps, daring him to take off his jacket to decide, in single combat, whether or not he was physically fit to lead a battalion at Guadalcanal. Some of the old-time sergeants assuming command of companies on the second day were capable of dialogue that fiction writers prone to slanginess might have thought stilted. Private Bailey's old top sergeant, Andy Lauer, a New Jerseyman, was such a soldier. "I have been ordered to reach our objective," he addressed the fifty survivors of M Company, its five officers now killed or wounded. "I am going to advance until every man falls, and then go get it myself." Many fell, but the sergeant got it.

Bullard had been on the field to greet the return of his old regiment, the 26th Infantry, which he had commanded as a peacetime colonel. He only recognized one of its leaders, a somber-faced boy leading a company. He had been the colonel's happy-go-lucky orderly on the Mexican border. All the field officers were gone—colonel, lieutenant colonel, majors, staff captains, and all the old-line captains, once sergeants in the regiment, and most of the old sergeants scornful of commissions. The 26th Infantry was now led by a captain with less than two years' service.

Floyd Gibbons was on the field that first day, having escaped the hospital where he had been carried from the charge at Belleau Wood. (He now wore a black patch over an empty eyesocket, his head still ringing from a skull fracture.) Always looking for Cook County copy, he noted that Sergeant Harry Finkelstein of Chicago, a blood-soaked bandage on his head, was driving before him two German prisoners while he munched on his first meal in two days, a piece of black bread taken from a prisoner's pocket. The sergeant had enjoyed a great day despite the hole in his head. He had a medal coming to him, and was looking forward to his stay in hospital. He was wearing seven pairs of Zeiss binoculars on slings from his right shoulder, and five Luger pistols on his belt. Sergeant Finkelstein would enter the washroom dice game as a big-time operator able to buy any part of the action. (Bullard once noted that, in the flotsam drifting back, the Military Police, always alert to check malingerers and stragglers, accosted an able-bodied Doughboy driving before him a single German prisoner. This was prime evidence of a yellow streak, but the boy scoffed at them and pointed to his prisoner's collar devices. He had captured a German colonel and was resolved to deliver him, unlooted, to the brigade Intelligence officer on the hoof. The M.P.s did not send him to the barbed-wire pens they always erected for malingerers, dead beats, scoundrels, and cowards. They let him go on his way.)

Bullard, Liggett, Harbord, Summerall—all the generals speculated that the war might have ended with the astonishing break-through at Soissons at ten o'clock that first morning, if all of Pershing's hefty divisions, scattered about the perimeter of the Aisne-Marne salient, had been somewhere around the forest of Retz and the forest of Villers-Cotterêts north of it. But Foch was calling the strategic shots, and either out of choice or necessity he did not play it that way. Later, General von Boehn, an honorable soldier not given to alibis, said they were wrong. He had plenty of men, and thousands of guns, and he had saved most of his infantry. He was in no hurry to get out. Boehn was incapable of panic. Instead of obeying Ludendorff's summary order, he delayed another two days while making his dispositions for withdrawal to the Vesle, and he intended to molest his enemies severely in his gradual abandonment; he was the first great teacher of the Doughboys. His delay cost him upwards of forty thousand prisoners, but it was worth the price. He had in mind pinning the Americans down to fighting in detail, thus weakening Haig's hope for American reserves, and Foch was playing right into his hands. The main chance for a German victory, now dimming fast, was, as always, the blow to be struck at Hazebrouck to drive the British into the sea, and after the first day Boehn knew Foch had no reserves to exploit the gap at Soissons. It became immediately apparent to Boehn from the ceaseless perimeter bolts that began simultaneously south of Soissons and all along the line, as we shall see, that Foch's plan of attack for the Second Battle of the Marne was, as always, *"Tout le monde à la bataille."* If he could add fresh American blood to his badly drained French supplies and pour it down the *spine* of Boehn's salient, why trouble to pinch both flanks and let the apex die on the vine? Perhaps he felt he did not have the strength for such a break-through, or could not weaken his lines elsewhere for the necessary build-up. But he had thrown classical patterns to the winds and it was going to cost the Doughboys a heavy price.

The 1st Division was relieved by Haig's 15th (Scottish) Division, an outfit of the New Army which, with three others, had been unconquered in Ludendorff's assault the previous April in Flanders. The Scots were not up to strength, but in the rush toward Soissons some of their artillery had managed to come up. The artillery brigade of the Big Red One volunteered to remain at its guns and give support, as did Colonel Mabee's field medics and ambulance drivers. For the first time in history, British, French, and American batteries stood hub to hub in a united cause. But the ensuing Scottish attack, with the attenuated battalions, was not to succeed—through no fault of the gallant Jocks. Their tartaned general was almost in tears as he rode upon the battlefield where the Doughboys had first jumped off. Yank dead lay in hidden pockets where they had first met the Germans, recalling to him the slaughter of his Camerons, Gordons, and Black Watch at Loos in 1915 and on the Somme in 1916.

British historians seized upon his report, and all made use of it to say, and not without smugness, that this revealed the fallacy of Pershing's insistence upon training riflemen for open warfare. Not one British historian pointed out that the British had known the Somme battlefields for two years when they sent forward troops in massed lines to sustain a half-million casualties. Many of the Soissons Doughboys had reached their unknown field of action on the double. Little wonder they were killed some places in skirmish rows. Reid thanked Mabee for bringing out four hundred Scots who might have perished otherwise, and set about reverently burying the looted dead. (The kilted "Ladies from Hell" evoked the admiration of Mabee's medics.)

Pershing had no such conjectures about a total victory, with cavalry rushing into the blue. He had been present at Byng's headquarters that first morning at Cambrai in November, 1917, because some two thousand Doughboy technicians were employed, and he saw Haig's cavalry divisions, fine fighters when dismounted and always kept in readiness for a dash into the blue of Never-Never Land, standing useless while Georg von der Marwitz's Germans drove back the British infantry with cruel losses after their initial churchbell-ringing success with tanks. Pershing "regretted" to his friend, General the Honorable Sir Julian Byng, that he had not seen the old Mounted Arm in which he had spent so many happy years go into action . . . but it was a polite gesture. He knew, like the chronicler in the Second Book of Kings: "The horse is a vain thing for safety; nor shall he deliver anyone by his strength."

Harbord and his chief of staff, standing at the edge of the woods in the late afternoon of July 18, saw a sight to spur the hearts of the old horse soldiers. A division of French cavalry was moving by, elegant troopers walking their spanking horses leisurely, all cap-a-pie in horizon blue, going no faster than French infantry plodding alongside, behind it horse-forage trains blocking the lifeline of the fighters ahead. The colonel of the leading regiment proved to be *très chic,* a wispy relic of the Old Regime. He said he was "thinking about" going into action sometime soon. The jut-jawed Harbord in his cavalry uniform, Marine emblems, and poilu helmet, and the sarcastic Preston Brown exchanged glances at this remark. (For cavalry to exploit the blue, it rushed through a breach in enemy lines while the dying infantrymen who had made it still had time to hear the thunder of the galloping.) When the French cavalry moved on, Harbord asked, "When shall we see him again?" And Brown replied, "When the war's over and we all line up to receive our medals. He will be there." They knew the day of the horse soldier in France was done.

Foch had not sought a break-through, but now had the high ground at Soissons, and his many American divisions, flanked by weary French, were putting pressure on Boehn everywhere. At the hour Malone was shepherding his rain-soaked Doughboys on the double to reach the barrage line, the New Englanders of the 26th Division, thirty miles south, to the left of Château-Thierry, were breaking from the gas-encrusted shambles of Belleau Wood to begin their assault to the left of Hill 204, for a sweep behind Château-Thierry.

When the close-knit New Englanders, having flamboyantly displayed their desire to engage in hand-to-hand fighting at Seicheprey, broke from Belleau Wood, they were the first outfit to be under the tactical direction of an American corps commander. He was not only a good one; he was Pershing's best general, and he owed his presence on the field that July 18 to his fall from a horse.

Hunter Liggett, later lieutenant general and commander of the American First Army on the Meuse, had arrived in France in March to undergo merciless scrutiny by the Iron Commander. It was routine, this sending division commanders to France for a so-called indoctrination tour of the front. Actually, all such two-star officers knew they were preceding their divisions to Chaumont for a searching character analysis, as well as a medical survey. It was not enough to say that Hunter Liggett was portly, or that he had a bulging waistline; he was a fat boy. He was as fat as Fatty Arbuckle, just then throwing pies in Mack Sennett's comedies. He was also a former President of the War College; a West Pointer whose grades suffered because he would wander from library texts on conic sections and ballistics to read *Pride and Prejudice* or the works of Samuel Taylor Coleridge; he was a wit, he was a soldier's soldier, and a tactical wizard. "There is no fat above my collar," he was reputed to have told Pershing. He had arrived with a pomposity of generals. Pershing promptly sent four of them back home, regretting that one was too old, a second too sick, and the other pair too narrow-minded, to eat their hearts out around training camps, but in his cable to Newton Baker he said he was reserving decision a few days on Hunter Liggett.

There was no thyroid deficiency about Liggett. He was an eater. He brought along for a cook an American citizen born in Athens, Greece, who had been a seller of candies to high school students at Seattle before receiving the White House greetings. The Greek may have learned little about arms, but he knew a great deal about Escoffier and Brillat-Savarin, an accomplishment of great importance to Hunter Liggett. Grapevine let Liggett know that his belly, worthy of a department store's Santa Claus, was pressing heavily upon Pershing. How could Liggett make the twice-weekly tours of the first line that the Iron Commander demanded, with all that crawling around in desolate shell holes? After his routine tour of the front, where he attested that the mud of Lee's Virginia, the ooze of Luzon's swamps, the slime of the Rio Grande were nothing to the viscosity of the British battlefields in Flanders, Liggett began violent horseback exercises in hope of reducing his corporation. On one such strenuous gallop, his horse came a cropper, and Liggett was catapulted into a bone-shaking fall. His fellow riders held their breath, fearing the general might have exploded. Someone posted away to bring up an ambulance, but Liggett was up and on his horse before anyone could dismount to attend him. This agility—some fat men are extraordinarily graceful—was reported to Chaumont, and Liggett was given a corps.

When he learned that the American I Corps was also to comprise the French 167th Division, he delighted its French officers—who might have balked at his tactical directions—by giving them a *cordon bleu* luncheon. Everything was laid on, from the dry Madeira to the snifter of Napoleon brandy. The luncheon succeeded so well and Major General Schmidt, of the French 167th, was so complimentary that Liggett was in agony lest Schmidt, in his Gallic way, invite the supposedly Paris chef in for a toast and behold the sweet-seller of old Seattle. In his memoirs, Liggett set down (in polite paraphrase) what he knew the Doughboys were saying behind his back on his front-line inspections: "What is that fat-assed bastard doing up here? What does he know about the hell I'm undergoing?"

An hour before Mangin's spearhead of the 1st and 2nd Divisions raced to reach their protective barrage at 4:45 A.M., July 18, the New Englanders burst from Belleau Wood and smaller clumps thereabouts in fine style, their right brigade larger than the French 167th Division alongside. The time was 3:45, and by nine in the morning they captured the villages of Torcy and Givry, and the château village of Belleau, whose lords of long ago had hunted the now shambled woods. The brigade was Brigadier General Cole's, an officer depressed by the gloom of Belleau Wood with its segments of Leatherneck corpses still in trees where they had been blown sky high. General Cole's brother, machine-gun major, and the Marine's "Harvard Man," had received his mortal wound nearby.

The 26th Division was displaying every evidence of the promise it showed at Seicheprey, infantry putting a great push into its charges against strong points, runners moving across wide wheatfields between Torcy and the woods as dedicated men, with casualties so heavy that frequently a battalion, communicating with its regiment, sent runners in relays, three at one-minute intervals. A Boston lad might pass his Vermont predecessor down and dying, and then a second Down-Easter crawling forward with a shattered leg, the Boston boy knowing that he himself would join these buddies before nightfall. The French were fighting shoulder to shoulder with them. Malin Craig, his chief of staff, messaged Liggett: "Everything lovely."

By nightfall, Liggett was pleading for motor transport to hasten forward his engineers and bridge-building trains; there were streams and ravines to cross, and he had in mind bagging the German garrison in the Château-Thierry area still facing the menacing 3rd Division across the Marne. But German infantry began pulling back slowly for the next two days, fighting sagely. With French divisions fighting skillfully on either side, the 26th Division was bidding fair to duplicate the feats of the Soissons teams. Americans were warned that the warwise French might take their cautious time, but flanks would eventually find them pressing forward to the line of advance.

On the night of July 20, a blue-sky order came from Liggett: "Each division, without waiting for its neighbors if they should be delayed, will push forward at all cost to place the main body of the army along the line of the railroad Nanteuil–Château-Thierry." Each division—and Liggett now had tacit direction of the French division on the left as well as Schmidt's on the right—would fan one regiment of infantry outward as marching outposts to seize the railroad. Corps artillery was rushing up, and the French again brought up a cavalry division for the Never-Never Land of Break-through. "So much depends upon pressing this movement," Liggett sent word to Major General Edwards of the 26th New Englanders, "that every human effort must be made to accomplish it as quickly as possible." The front was narrow behind Hill 204, to the immediate left of the bridge at Château-Thierry. The Doughboys of the 3rd Division were ready to cross the Marne in pontoon boats on the right. Liggett wanted Edwards to breach the left gap with the New Englanders, leaving the French to hold fast on the shoulders of the movement. Then something went wrong.

Edwards, beloved by his National Guardsmen, may have been so emotionally involved that he did not move. Maybe he thought he was a better soldier than Liggett. "At all cost" did not appeal to him. Malin Craig ordered him "to drive forward to the limit of endurance of every man and animal," but he even withdrew his advanced post of command in defiance of Liggett's orders. He had the enemy falling back, and then broke contact.

Grant would have relieved him; Sheridan would have cursed him out of headquarters; Stonewall Jackson would have put him under arrest. The Iron Commander bided his time.

Degoutte, commanding the French Sixth Army, now began a scorching censure in his bulletins. The 26th Division commander had not even prepared orders to advance. Major General Schmidt, Liggett's erstwhile luncheon guest, waited two days—until eight o'clock on the morning of July 22—and then finding that Edwards had not prepared orders, issued his own and threw his slender French 167th into the gap. Degoutte found a staff officer of the 26th Division who said that the four infantry regiments of the New Englanders were static on a single line, no colonel having been ordered to push forward to the railroad. "This officer does not know the order in which the regiments are placed, neither does he know what elements they have had in action or what they have in reserve. He replied to me: 'They are thought to be intermingled.' " Degoutte knew that Liggett was a first-class soldier. He virtually placed the 3rd Division, its infantry spear-headed by the redoubtable Ulysses Grant McAlexander, under Liggett's timing. Knowing the New Englanders from Seicheprey, Degoutte stiffened their flagging morale with their own kind, a brigade of Pennsylvanians from the 28th Division which had been outstanding in its support of McAlexander on the Marne. It was a gracious gesture of confidence in Liggett, despite the failure of Edwards to exploit his fine New Englanders.

After that, all manner of staff hell broke loose. Colonel Duncan Major, Jr., the chief of staff whom Congressman Washburn called a whippersnapper after his staff lecture on the mistakes around Seicheprey, sleeplessly came and went from his duties to reform dejected regiments, straighten directions, lead bayonet assaults. Officers below the rank of colonel moved into commands which constituted usurpation, a brilliant Reserve officer, Major Greenway of the 26th's Engineers, sometimes performing the duties of a brigadier. What had happened was that the devoted old National Guardsmen whom Edwards had permitted to retain higher command when they might have been useful as adjutants at ports of disembarkation had broken down. The rank-and-file of the Doughboys, mercilessly driven forward by the iron will of Liggett, were fabulous in their efforts to redeem the reluctance of their senior officers.

There were many like Private First Class George Dilboy. He was in advance of his exploratory platoon, a solitary point, when fired upon by a machine gun a hundred yards away. He stood erect, returning fire with his rifle until his right leg was shattered. Then he crawled seventy-five yards toward the gun still firing. Before he bled to death, he had killed the German crew. But the New Englanders lacked senior officers with the spirit and stamina of George Dilboy, and the division needed six days, and the 56th Brigade of Pennsylvanians, who helped in the fighting for the town of Epieds, to accomplish what the main attack at Soissons had achieved in two. Its gallantries were legendary, its captures negligible, and still it paid the price of five thousand men. Theirs was the tragedy of misdirected affection, a common fault of the National Guard. Better led, it would have had its prize in the same length of time that the 1st and 2nd Divisions had taken to break even uglier resistance around Soissons. Now it had let the German get away.

Liggett sent no word of disparagement while the superb men of the 26th were still fighting; but after the division had been relieved, Liggett interrogated the captains and sergeants who had held it together, and some colonels who had failed to. Then, August 13 he sent their reports in a personal letter to Chaumont, leaving it up to the Adjutant General to bring it to Pershing's attention if he cared to.

Stripped of its military prose, Liggett's letter said, in effect, that while the division had sustained its part in the action due to the admirable performance of the men, there was a definite lack of prompt obedience to orders, that attacks were not launched at the prescribed hours, that liaison laterally and from front to rear was nonexistent, and that infantry brigade and regimental commanders never knew the positions of their commands. He cited Brigadier General Cole as being especially delinquent in this respect. Commanders asked to be relieved because of the exhaustion of their men, but a spirit of endurance and determination among senior officers would certainly have been reflected by men in the ranks, Liggett went on; and he commended Major Greenway and Colonel Major for their spirit, while deploring the state of mind of General Cole. He had advised the division commander (Edwards) to consider a change in regimental commanders (and Brigadier General Cole) despite their alleged faithfulness and vigor.

It is my belief that the usefulness of the 26th Division as a dependable fighting unit can be restored only after a period of thorough basic training and reconstruction together with such readjustment or substitution among the officers of higher command as will insure a correction and eradication of the faults above mentioned, together with the instilling of a spirit of obedience and obliteration of personal complaints.

The letter was not published in full until 1948, thirty years after the New England press had damned everybody in the A.E.F. except Clarence Edwards; but the higher officers of the 26th Division soon got word of it. General Cole retained his star. He became an old pro; while the Lieutenant Colonel Shelton who "licked hell" out of the Germans at Seicheprey won his star and the other brigade command.

Chapter **9**

ASSAULT DOWN THE SPINE

I would never have believed green troops would advance under such fire.

At the same hour on July 18 that the 1st, 2nd, and 26th Divisions launched their attacks in the Second Battle of the Marne, the four infantry regiments of the 4th Division, about midway in the thirty-five-mile line, never before in combat, not one man having even known a tour of quiet trenches, leaped into the open as battalion cement for French units under old friend Degoutte. (Pétain had impudently asked for fifty such cadres to interweave with the French. He now had twelve.)

Major General Cameron had brought his division from Camp Greene, where Dickman's 3rd Division had had the priority. His was a "Regular" outfit, every day receiving batches of draftees in civilian clothing, rejecting some boys railroaded through the cursory medical examinations of the draft boards, many of which selfishly shipped out the town's unsavory characters or the village half-wit at first call. Some of the old units in Cameron's division had great records—the 59th Field Artillery, springing from the 2nd Dragoons of Andrew Jackson's days, had later broken through the enemy's infantry at Resaca de la Palma to saber the Mexican gunners and begin the war against Mexico—but in July, 1918, the men were pea-green.

There were few improved roads around Charlotte, North Carolina, the political area where Cameron's men took their basic training. In the spring rains the roads disappeared. For a time, even drinking water was brought

158

in by pack trains to the fifty thousand men of the 3rd and 4th Divisions. As target ranges were the 3rd Division's priority, Cameron marched his regiments in full packs eight hours a day over terrain little changed since the squirrel hunters whipped the British at nearby Kings Mountain. They arrived in France for the Fourth of July parade, marching men to delight the Iron Commander's eye. One tour along those smart buttons, and Pershing hoped he had a future corps commander in their major general.

They were learning the murderous trade of trench war in a rear area with the British 16th Division when Foch asked for them in his quarrel with Haig. They knew something about Vickers machine guns, Lewis guns, and Stokes mortars. "What is this?" a British sergeant asked a Lewis gunner. "It's a monkey wrench." "That," said the limey instructor, "is a combination extension spanner wrench." That was their training. When they left the semantics of the British area, hastening toward the Marne, the 4th Division's 39th Infantry Regiment had never fired a rifle. Who needed a rifle in trench warfare? A soldier's duty was only to go forward and be murdered. In the 8th Field Signal Battalion they all had holsters, but none had a pistol or a revolver. Ashamed of the lack, they stuffed their holsters with toilet paper. Arriving behind Belleau Wood, Cameron offered to relieve troops there with those of his Doughboys who *had* fired a rifle, but Pershing would not release them to Foch at this stage. He gave them Hotchkiss and Chauchat. They got their Springfield rifles back, leaving the Enfields with the British, and somehow they mastered the French guns— as Private Bailey observed—in the four weeks Pershing gave them before Degoutte piecemealed them to strengthen his war-weary tatterdemalions.

When they attacked July 18, few battalions fighting side by side, their buddies five miles or so to their right or left, they not only carried their own objectives, but one outfit took the town of Noroy and presented it to the French, whose goal it was. They kept no records of their valor, and they gave their prisoners to the French.

The infantry—it did not yet have its own artillery—was scattered through Degoutte's III and II Corps, attacking due east across the center of the salient. After taking Noroy on the eighteenth, the next objective for one battalion of the 39th Infantry was the ravine two miles deeper into the cross section of the salient. H-hour was 4 A.M., and the battalion had the ravine by five-thirty, patching up wounded, chewing on field rations, veterans of twenty-five hours. But Degoutte had changed his timing without passing the word: five-thirty was to be the H-hour to shell the ravine before a "surprise" assault. The battalion now suffered horribly under the fire of German batteries which knew they had lost the ravine, and the fire of French gunners who did not know the Doughboys had won it. It was the severest initiation any American unit ever received. Two officers and 93 men were killed, 11 officers and 436 men wounded, 1 officer and 66 men missing. There were 609 out of 1,281 now answering adjutant's call. One company with fifty-nine men, and one officer surviving out of six, wondering how it might withstand the shock of a counterattack, was suddenly confronted by a buck private, a freckly-faced kid—and his name is not listed among the performers of such feats—who marched a group of survivors from various units, some of them sergeants, up to the only officer still on his feet. "Lieutenant, I got about fifty of 'em here. Where'll I put 'em?" The division historian said this nameless boy was made a sergeant.

On the far right, single companies soon fought along with the French. One battalion was so green it left its extra bandoliers in bivouac, and continued on imperturbably with bayonets when ammunition belts were exhausted. The French liaison officer reported: "Had I not seen it with my own eyes, I would never have believed green troops would advance under such fire." (Mr. Winston Churchill came to see them when they were relieved, much interested in pup tents, and the American mess kits and canteens, the latter items the only unique pieces of equipment the Republic supplied the Doughboys in quantity. The mess kit's two halves were joined by a folding handle, converting the lower half into a skillet. But for one fault, the canteen nesting in its cup was admirable. The Army genius who designed it had exhausted his talents before conceiving an effective catch for the cup's folding handle. When a man turned from the chow line, loaded with food, and his cup full of piping hot coffee, the catch usually slipped, and the aluminum cup seared the Doughboy's knuckles. Stooping gingerly and cursing, he would set his precious coffee on the ground and suck his burnt fingers.)

Cameron's battalions with blistered knuckles were soon dispersed everywhere. By the time the 42nd Rainbows had relieved the 26th Division and were following the retreating German Armies north of the Marne to the Ourcq River, toward the chalk hills around Sergy, two of the Ivy Leaf infantry battalions were fighting with them. It was only ten days after their baptism of fire at Noroy, and marked the first time any of Cameron's troops fought alongside Yanks. They were great in the use of the rifle as firepower. When one battalion exhausted its bandoliers, the men found Mauser rifles of Hamburg make and advanced with these, pulling the strings of grenades when they reached stubborn machine-gun nests. Lieutenant Gustav Brun came out of the Sergy fight commanding his battalion, 27 of its officers and 462 of its men having been lost there. When their artillery came up, Pershing had seen all he needed to know about Cameron. He would soon be given a corps and wear himself out.

Their artillery was hailed joyously by the infantry when the guns rolled up close. Lieutenants Lowell Riley and Peter Ebett, Infantry, took over a church steeple at the village of Ville-Savoye on the Vesle River, where they served as suicidal spotters for two days, when the Germans who were being butchered detected the source of the accurate fire and killed the two with a direct hit. When Pershing pulled the division out to rest in the Reynel area the third week in August, he deemed it a veteran outfit already. There were, of course, some unhappy officers who were sent to Blois when the men were relieved to delouse, to sleep, and to write the mothers of dead buddies. All such letters said, "He never knew what hit him," though he might have pleaded vainly with a buddy not to leave him there to die alone as the line swept on. They had lost 5,486 men on three fierce battlefields and they were ready for Saint-Mihiel. Shelled by French and Germans alike, knowing little of anything, and mainly led by green officers, the 4th Division, self-taught in battlefield skills, among men of an alien tongue, had never given up an inch of ground. One Marine officer, hearing the modest accounts of their wounded from the Ourcq and the Vesle, thought their qualities unsurpassed.

Dickman's 3rd Division, which had gone into Degoutte's Marne line in June as an untried outfit, had learned much in its great repulse of the grenadiers south of the river. Boehn knew of them and was wary. Ignoring Ludendorff's order of noon, July 18, to get out fast, von Boehn spent two days deploying and strengthening his Line of Resistance on every piece of high ground north of the Marne. Boehn would take his time getting back across the Vesle River, taking with him the guns and supplies he had brought for an assault on Paris; at the Vesle he could stand with the Aisne at his back, its chalk hills giving him artillery command of the Vesle crossings.

Following Foch's familiar plan, on July 21 the 3rd Division launched its counterattack across the Marne at Château-Thierry, from which a slender French division to its left had driven the Germans, its target Ronchères, eight miles to the northeast of the shattered town. The 5th Brigade of the 3rd crossed the railroad bridge it had defended the first of June, prowling through streets littered with dead, among whom was Lieutenant Bissell's fourteenth man. The 6th Brigade crossed the Marne in pontoon boats, many of which had been left behind by the surviving German grenadiers. With the French on either side, the division moved on in an ever-narrowing wedge through the apex of the salient where Foch, who abjured the classical pattern for a flurry of blows, would presently jam four more Yank divisions down the spine of the salient.

It was a race for the first three days. On the first day, Dickman's Rock of the Marne boys captured the disputed villages of Mont Saint-Père and Chartèves. A savage assault was needed to seize hilly Jaulgonne, where von Conta put them to the test of a frontal attack. It was against Jaulgonne that Captain Wooldridge enjoyed his finest five minutes. He was a solitary point, crawling along a drainage ditch beside the shell-swept road, happy at least to believe he was between his colonel and the enemy, when he bumped into Ulysses, crawling ahead of him. By July 24, McAlexander's 38th Infantry was at Le Charmel, two and a half miles farther north, the poorly led New Englanders to the left with a French division in between, gaining ground measured by yardsticks, so numerous were Boehn's machine-gun pockets some five miles into the salient. The cocky 3rd pressed on another three miles, a dagger in the German midriff, casualties contracting its front, fresh French divisions racing alongside.

On July 25, the 26th Division on the left of the vertebrae of the spine was relieved by the 42nd Rainbows. Father Duffy recalled that his joyous Irish regiment of the 42nd, when its Doughboys finally learned that they were to fight in the Champagne country, expected to find bottles of the Widow Cliquot's sparkling intoxicant hanging from every tree. This intelligence just about summed up a Rainbow's knowledge of the terrain Foch now decreed would be his battlefield: chalky hills, woods bristling with machine guns and one-inch cannon, and a network of small rivers which they thought of as creeks. They took over with great savagery, replacing the front of what would be three French divisions. Their artillery was phenomenal for its furious cadence. In two days they cleaned out two miles of machine guns and cannon to fight the Germans in the forested hills east of Fère-en-Tardenois, a railway town in the center of the salient which Foch now ruthlessly demanded. The weaker French on low ground were to enter it. The high ground above it was paid for with Doughboy blood.

Every man of the 42nd was saddened by the death of their poet, Sergeant Joyce Kilmer. He had asked to go forward with a regimental reconnaissance party on July 30, and a sniper shot him through the forehead. Father Duffy, when he first saw this *New York Times* journalist who had volunteered with the blessings of his wife and three children, said that the gentle Kilmer seemed to have the word *fated* written across his brow. The Rainbows buried him beside the Ourcq River, a purling little stream not deep enough to lap into a fisherman's waders.

The Rainbows knew that the German game was up long before Ludendorff did, however much fierce fighting might lie ahead. Their chief of staff, Douglas MacArthur, had issued a "Bulletin of Information" to them forty-eight hours after they had helped stop the German push around Reims July 15. MacArthur, always a dynamo, analyzed the Intelligence reports of division, corps, and army and by the night of July 16 summed up the situation as described by captured German officers. These men spoke as freely as captured Confederates conversed with Grant's staff officers after Lee's army stood before Petersburg.

It was an axiom of war that a great commander lost more men between the turning point and the final surrender than, say, from the first shot at Fort Sumter to the moment of truth at Gettysburg. The Germans feared the future. "We do not have enough artillery to mount two offensives at once," they complained, referring to the twin battles to the right and left of Reims. "One-third of our artillery is in the east, one-third in the west, and one-third up north." The last third was their desperate hope against Hazebrouck and the British.

They had suffered much from the raging epidemic of influenza that was sweeping the world. The German Reserves were ill-fed, thanks to the Royal Navy's blockade now heavily augmented with American warships; and influenza was a disease in which the physical strength of the patient, more than medication, raised the threshold against death. They had suffered heavy losses and bitter disappointment in their recent assault south of the Marne and east of Reims. The repulse, after their three great successes of the year, had taken all the spirit out of them. Having survived a potato winter, their victorious troops had gone forward the night of July 14-15 with hunger in their hearts, remembering the loot of wines and cheeses, kickshaws and comfits between the Aisne and the Marne. Officers of the German Quartermaster Corps were ordered to put sentries at all villages they planned to seize between Reims and Châlons. Troops were to by-pass the main streets and the loot was to be collected and distributed in shares to the several units after the battle, buccaneer fashion. Only the loot of the industrial town of Châlons was to be reserved for the national interest; special teams formed to organize this rapidly. And now all was lost.

Captured enlisted men were eager to talk to German-speaking Dough-boys, spontaneously correcting a comrade if he made errors in speaking of German troop dispositions. The men who had followed the well-fed shock troops were ravenous. They dipped their fingers hungrily into cans of corned-beef hash from Chicago or Des Moines, and told the Rainbows, "If there are more like you, then the game is up." They could only fight a delaying action and hope for a decent peace. They dreaded any last-ditch prolongation, American Civil War style. As the Rainbows swept on, they captured a position whose German enlisted men said they had been compelled to stand by their machine guns and field pieces by officers with drawn revolvers. But MacArthur warned the Doughboys that these same fellows, if permitted to withdraw, would fight on with consummate skill. And so they did. The cleaning out of the Aisne-Marne salient went on, fresh American divisions clawing into its shrinking center, side by side with skeleton French units once again teeming with guts. Numerically, the French were superior; but the sheer tactical shock of the big "square-shaped" Yank divisions made the difference between progress and delay, Yanks usually taking the most formidable of Boehn's complexes.

As July waned, and the dust of the Champagne country found Doughboys powdered white like flour millers, their thirsts making water-cart drivers shouting at their mules as welcome as a Good Humor man's tinkling tunes to children in the heat of a city's slums, Muir's Pennsylvanians swung into line in brigade strengths. The 28th Division sent one infantry brigade to flank the 3rd Division's movement to the Ronchères objective—just as it had buffered the Marne outfit's flank on the Rocq Plateau—the other brigade moving into the furious Rainbow front. And once again the German Seventh Army knew the stupendous shock of seventeen thousand Springfield riflemen and machine gunners with few orders and the greatest possible individual initiative.

The division's diarists were embarrassed by the richness of their valors. Grimpettes Woods, with seven hundred yards of wheatfields facing it, was an "instant" Belleau Wood, remembered only by those who fought there July 30. After the house-to-house town fighting in Ronchères, a less furious outfit than the 55th Infantry Brigade of Pennsylvanians might have learned discretion. But the sting of Belleau Wood's publicity was galling them, and two ferocious assaults against the wood were made that morning before artillery managed to come up. When the guns arrived at two-thirty that afternoon, the infantry refused to wait for guns to be registered. It carried the wood with steel. The key to the woods had been a church in the village of Courmont, and the Keystone Division's boys were shocked because the German had turned a House of God into a charnel house where Doughboys had to bomb snipers behind a beautiful altar, batter plaster saints to kill one-pounder cannoneers, and fight their way up fluted stairs to the belfry where only the sergeant leading the rush survived. (He killed the three gunners serving a 77 field piece in the belfry, and reported that the surviving lieutenant had "jumped" to his death.)

The devout Pennsylvanians took pride in their own chaplains, notably in the Rev. Mandeville Barker, an Episcopalian famous for his ability to spot snipers, four of such intermingled in a pile of grenaded arms and legs being known as "Barker's Boches." Then, too, there was Father Charlie Conaty, a Roman Catholic priest from Boston. He had a good tactical eye, and once when all officers were down, he led a company attack armed with nothing but his Rosary; but his dispositions were flawless, as the outflanked Germans discovered when they saw the bayonets.

The other brigade with the Rainbows contained a topkick, William G. Meighan, who was leading a platoon in gas masks when he did not get the word to withdraw. Alone in a shell hole, wearing his mask, he dug himself the deepest hole in Doughboy history, remaining fifteen hours there until once again his company tried to take the gunners ahead. Lieutenant Richard Stockton was the only one of five officers in Meighan's company who survived, and being shot through both legs, managed to crawl to Meighan's hole and pass the word before he was killed. The first sergeant then proceeded, by means of hand signals to his masked marvels, to take the position denied him the day before.

The Pennsylvanians had their share of miracles attending any war anywhere. Lieutenant Stuart Alexander of Altoona, regimental Intelligence officer in the fighting around the Ourcq, along with seventeen men of Headquarters Company was in a brick building, where he was questioning two German captains. Colonel Kemp, who had seen Degoutte butcher two of his companies on the Marne, was seated on the steps outside, talking to his lieutenant colonel, Wallace W. Fetzer. An eight-inch shell scored a direct hit on the building. Fetzer was killed outright, Kemp's jaw was fractured, the two prisoners and the seventeen headquarters Doughboys were killed. Alexander found himself standing on the opposite side of the street, his hair still combed and not a spot on his uniform. When the regiment again attacked, again a shell killed Alexander's prisoners. This time, Alexander's uniform was dusty, but he was unharmed. The division's diarist attested to the miracle of another Doughboy. Private Paul Helsel, among the 125 out of his 260-man company who returned after taking thirty machine guns in the ruins of the well-named Château du Diable, had six bullet holes in his shirt, two in his breeches, and one embedded in his first-aid pack. In the final rush, his bayonet was shot away.

A major general commanding a division could see little of his war, the old boy was unable to follow two infantry brigades of seventeen thousand riflemen and machine gunners; and Pershing's senior combat commanders suffered heartbreak because of it. In the fighting along the Ourcq, a company falling back after a repulse was astonished to see General Muir conversing with his chief of staff as a wave of infantry prepared to attack a clump of trees for a second time. A big man with iron curls, whose portrait resembled one of the Roman busts in the British Museum, as the first wave started forward, he suddenly blurted, "I think I'll command one of these outfits myself." The attack carried the woods, and the disheveled Muir came back to the line of support, breathing a little faster but, after this therapy, relieved of an anxiety. He was even a little apologetic, like some old hunting dog who suddenly breaks his point on quail to rush into the autumn brush and returns with a cottontail rabbit to lay at the hunter's feet. "Took me back to the old days in the Philippines," he said, and sheepishly went back wherever a major general belonged.

After the boys from the Keystone State gave Foch Courmont, Grimpettes, and the terrible Hill 192 behind the woods July 30, they were withdrawn for a well-earned seven days' rest.

By August 1, Boehn having lost the north bank of the Ourcq, the 3rd Division, after fifty-eight days in the front line, and having roughed up and defeated ten German divisions since July 15, was relieved by the 32nd Division. Boehn was glad to see the 3rd go, but he would soon find that these new Yanks, from around Milwaukee and Detroit, were German in their efficiency. At this point, for the first time since Johnson struck his colors to Sherman, Americans were in a solid corps front. Their line was an undulating one, bending from its western flank now beyond Fère-en-Tardenois, southeastward to a secondary road.

"Tell your men I like their spirit," Pershing ordered Major General William G. Haan of the 32nd Division when they moved toward the Vesle the last week in July after only twenty-five days of training in Alsace, where they had been subjected to the swooping descent of the Iron Commander from Chaumont. He rode horseback to inspect the artillery parks and engineer trains, but was on foot to walk miles between ranks, looking at every button on the blouses of seventeen thousand infantrymen and machine gunners. Many a proud battalion commander, having knocked out his brains to present a thousand gleaming men on that inspection day in Alsace, was crestfallen after the inevitable question: "How many venereal cases?" "Only one, sir." "One too many." And there were no compliments for officers. The hard eyes, the hard-bitten mouth, softened only when Pershing saw wound stripes like those won at Soissons. "Where were you wounded?" he might ask a lad from the Big Red One. "Third day at Soissons, sir." "Berzy-le-Sec?" "Yes, sir." "You have an enviable record, Corporal!" "Thank you, sir." The routine was changeless. So far, Pershing liked the new 32nd's buttons.

The National Guardsmen of the 32nd had never been in battle in France when they relieved the 3rd Division, but they derived from units which took a back seat to no other outfits of Civil War days. The Confederates venerated the Stonewall Brigade. On the Northern side, too, was a grand brigade which never lost its fame. The Iron Brigade of Michigan was so decimated by the time Gettysburg loomed ahead of Meade's marching corps that when a new regiment joined it the rookie regiment swallowed up veterans who had never lost an inch of ground. The 32nd was mainly composed of Michigan and Wisconsin units, with long records of friendly rivalry. Many of them spoke better German than English; though one of their best sergeant majors was a graduate of Haskell Indian Institute, a Chippewa with a trace of French *coureur de bois* in his blood. He stood five-feet-two, weighed 115 pounds, and became noted for his ferocity on patrols.

In pre-Civil War days, their companies preserved the spirit of the *Turnverein,* when militia privates from Detroit and Milwaukee, uniformed like the hussar tenor of a Viennese operetta, exchanged visits, bringing their oom-pah brass bands along to play the schmaltz songs of the German beer gardens. They were a close lot from the moment they began training at Camp MacArthur, though drawling Texans spoke of them as "Waco's Own." They were German in their military efficiency, and needed no inspector from Chaumont, no report from Liggett, to shake down their higher commanders when they reached France. They did this themselves. Haan, their West Pointer, forbade officers from the United States Military Academy, and other Regular officers in the regiments, to take part in the deliberations by which National Guard officers, not considered combat effectives, were sent to other posts. They had begun the process at Camp MacArthur, even screening personnel down to the rank of second lieutenant, and promoting sergeants to commissioned rank. They were the sixth division to arrive in France, and lesser men would have had their hearts broken by the first treatment they received in February, 1918. Someone at Chaumont, not so intelligent as Lieutenant von Buy, thought it best to break up so many German-American cadres, and the 32nd's Doughboys were told they would be cannibalized as replacements.

The first shock came when the 128th Infantry was ordered to send all its captains to the 1st Brigade of the Big Red One and all its privates to the 2nd Brigade. Sergeants appealed to General Haan for permission to rip off their chevrons and go with their buddies as buck privates; captains asked for demotion to shavetails. Seven thousand of the 32nd's men, the 127th and 128th Infantry regiments, were detailed as helpers in the Service of Supply, knowing nothing of that professional outfit's skills; and they slaved as coolies without protest. They never registered a protest anywhere at any time; they never asked a National Guard favor, and they kept their family failings to themselves.

Pershing managed to get them a brief period of training in Alsace trenches in the small corner of that region gained in the sluggish Joffre's foolish attack in 1914, where they lost 368 men while indoctrinating 12,000 replacements. Before the 12,000 arrived, Haan had been forced to spread his enlisted strength so thinly that 250-man infantry companies numbered less than 100.

The Alsatians in the corner of their province hated everybody; they were not French, and German was their language, but they hated Germans, too. No other Doughboys but the 32nd's ever held the upper hand with the mam'selles. They, too, were neither French nor German, and yet many spoke the *Deutsch* with fluency. On weekends, along the canal paths beneath the lime trees, there was standing room only in Lovers' Lane. Some of the Doughboys later jested about their German ancestry. "When a Boche goes after a Boche," one of their lieutenants said when stepping out to lead an assault, "there'll be plenty of hell to pay." On the Ourcq, corporals astonished German officer prisoners by lecturing them in the *Vaterland's* tongue, pointing out the disadvantages of living under Prussian rule. Once, stretcher-bearers bringing a wounded German officer back to Intelligence understood every word as he railed that the pigheaded American would lose the war. "Whatever happens, *Herr Oberst*," his bearers said in German as good as his, "you are not going to win anything." And without ceremony they rolled him out to the side of the road until he cried "uncle"—with his *"Bitte, bitte, bleiben sie mit mir,"* in chastened apologies.

After the men of the 32nd streamed into the battlefield to the right of the Pennsylvanians in the bitterly contested Grimpettes Woods, they pressed on north against heavy machine-gun fire to the village of Cierges. Here the *gemütlich* lads from Milwaukee sustained a midnight counterattack from Germans. Death was shooting from the hip, stabbing from the shoulder in those woods. Doughboys shouted in German to German troops. Cries of *"Heraus!" "Schrecklich!" "Himmel!"* resounded all night from different sides of a single tree. In the morning, the 32nd took Cierges and some troops crossed the Ourcq in pursuit of Boehn's men fighting a stubborn rear-guard action.

The 32nd and the Rainbows now held the line of the Ourcq. By the night of August 1, Douglas MacArthur could inform General Charles T. Menoher that the 42nd had cleared all the high ground east of Fère-en-Tardenois and that the French could set up headquarters in the billets from which Conta had directed his unsuccessful attempt to retake Belleau Wood and Bouresches and the high ground before Vaux. The Rainbows had one day of fighting left in them as they plowed due north along the backbone of the salient. By August 2, they were spent and Cameron's 4th Division, rested and revalued, came up to relieve them. (Eight colonels in the 4th were missing: one had been killed, one promoted, and six sent to noncombat assignments.)

The French command intended to fight the 32nd all the way to the Vesle, and the Milwaukee brigade pushed eighteen kilometers (pausing at Chamery, where they found Quentin Roosevelt's grave) to a climax at the village of Fismes, where they fought the Germans entrenched once more. Here the Milwaukee brigade was replaced by Detroit's. Mondésir was still their XXXVIII Corps commander, and he went forward to see the battalions assault enemy positions near Fismes. Watching them in action from his grandstand seat, he shuddered and cried, *"Oui! Oui! Les soldats terribles!"* and turning away, went back to Corps, muttering, *"Très bien, très bien."* When Mangin heard of this, he wanted the 32nd when they were relieved from Degoutte's command, in the middle of August. Bullard wanted them, too, to polish up their combat manners for fiercer fields than Champagne, but Mangin got them; and after they had rested two weeks, he gave them two bad days twenty miles northwest of Fismes, the 32nd moving around the western perimeter of the salient to get there.

Since the July 18 lightning bolt, Mangin's weary army had managed to drive only five miles north of Soissons, where the town of Juvigny and German gunners in steep, wooded hills were holding up his tired Frenchmen. There were two miles of heavy fighting with all infantry regiments deployed, before the 32nd gave the town to Mangin at the second sundown, having thrust due east just as the 1st Division had done two weeks before to seize the Dommiers plateaus. Their feat gave the French the road leading from Soissons north to Saint-Quentin. Mangin thanked them and immediately relieved them. The old flatterer issued an Army order, and recalling Mondésir's remark, referred to the 32nd as *"Les Terribles."*

Boehn had given the 32nd valuable lessons—notably that well-positioned machine gunners could survive any amount of bombardment and still come up for good shooting at the first wave of riflemen the instant an artillery barrage lifted, only men behind the steel plate of tanks being invulnerable to machine guns. The Mangin attack had cost "The Terribles" 485 killed or dead of wounds, 599 severely wounded, 19 missing, 5 captured—for a total casualty list of 1,108. This was the price of introducing a division to the political stupidity of attrition warfare and, by the standards of the hour, experience had been gained at small cost. Altogether, the division suffered fifteen thousand battlefield casualties in France and yet boasted only one distinction. "We are," they said, "the only division which did not claim to win the war." After Juvigny, recuperating men from Michigan's woods and Wisconsin's lakes saw the lovely country around Joinville, north of Chaumont, where they deloused their shirts and talked of home. They

were not much for the naïve Tin Pan Alley songs of the day. There were
key-of-C, eight-stop concertinas among some of them, and harmonicas.
There were *Heldentenors,* too, singing *"Täglich ging die Sultans tochter,"*
though no longer in the hussar-operetta uniforms. French villagers in the
Joinville country might hear songs in Heine's German to Mendelssohn's
tunes.

When they came up to relieve the Rainbows in the center of the dwindling
Marne salient, Cameron's half-rested Ivy Leafs were now a going concern,
with their own artillery, engineers, signal corps, and trains. They faced unpleasant country, a six-mile stretch of dry forest two miles wide running
almost due north to the Vesle River, closely contoured in small knolls and
verdant valleys where there were no roads. It was the region of the well-
named Bois de Dôle, and the doleful French on their left were still vexed
by the hill town of Mareuil-en-Dôle. Just as one of the 4th Division's green
battalions on July 18 had presented a French objective to the weary poilus,
so did a battalion—now not so green—take the hill and present it to the
French. It then proceeded back to its front, and the division began hewing
a way through the forests to the Vesle. Its right flank was now in place
along the 32nd's left flank.

The two divisions reached the Vesle by the night of August 4, the 32nd
storming into Fismes, the northbound 4th halting before the formidable
position of Bazoches, north of the river where the eastbound Big Red One
was spent three weeks before. The 32nd established bridgeheads across the
Vesle from Fismes in hand-to-hand fighting. In some instances, machine-
gun companies arched the pleasant little rivulet, infantry flankers covering
for them, and engineers going along to dig in for the gunners. Various
manuals on infantry tactics had been issued. But America had no tanks and
had not yet learned to make them; and U.S. generals had been forbidden
before April, 1917, even to think of warlike matters. The Doughboy
infantry had to make up for Mr. Wilson's coyness with fresh blood. Pershing
had thrown his men in piecemeal at times, but ultimately each division had
its own complex of infantry, machine guns, artillery, engineers, signal battalions, and trains. Their weight had been felt offensively in one-third of
its eventual force, some 350,000 Doughboys, and they had sustained fifty
thousand casualties in fighting from the Marne to the Vesle.

What a blunder it had all been when the French assured Dennis Nolan
on May 26 that Ludendorff would never strike at the Chemin des Dames!
Gouraud or Debeney would have given Boehn the Road of the Ladies after
sacrificing a few units, dug himself in behind a succession of lines with a

reserve body out of reach in the caves between the Aisne and the Vesle, and then, with a blackjack up his sleeve, invited Boehn to step into his parlor. As in any army in the world, the ultimate responsibility was Foch's; but elderly Duchêne was sacked, Franchet d'Esperey, Army Group Commander, and brightest of the French, made the goat and sent to the Balkans (where he won a marshal's baton), and the Doughboys, dedicated to the strong points of the line, received their education at Boehn's hands.

When the Second Battle of the Marne ended, the salient which Ludendorff had pushed through the laggard Duchêne's defense had been wiped out as far as the Vesle, Soissons was again in French hands, and the line from Soissons to Reims was nearly straight. It was not achieved in the classical pattern by pinching the flanks, but it was done. To accomplish this, Pershing had given Foch, in a magnificent gesture unparalleled in warfare, his 1st, 2nd, 3rd, 4th, 26th, 28th, 32nd, and 42nd, and was about to send in his 77th Division. But soon he would get them all back.

Chapter 10

BEHIND THE LINES

The spirit of the wounded is magnificent.

She can Sam Browne all over Paree.

Major James G. Harbord of the U.S. Cavalry had been astonished when Pershing, after his appointment to command the A.E.F., recalled him to Washington and said he was to be his first chief of staff in the American Expeditionary Force. He had been elated then at the promise of a combat command if he made good, and Pershing had kept his promise by giving him the Marine brigade at Belleau Wood. When Harbord told Pershing of a feat of valor there—and no Marine ever surpassed Harbord's yarns about his adopted corps—the Iron Commander grinned and said, "No wonder the Marines like you, when you can tell whoppers like that."

Two-star Harbord was again successful in the near-miracle of getting his brigades on the barrage line at Soissons, and his stock was high. When he was summoned to Chaumont on July 26 after his division was relieved from the fighting in the Second Battle of the Marne, it was not immodest of the ambitious Harbord to expect command of a corps. He was not in The Presence for long; he crossed the hall and slumped into a chair in Major Frederick Palmer's office. "Just see what my general has done to me," he groaned. Pershing had informed him that his fighting days were over; he was to command the Service of Supply. Pershing always said, when grievously wounding a friend, "You don't have to accept now; think it over until morning." Harbord was good at anything he tried. He thought it over for the length of time needed to say, "Yes, General. When do I take over?"

Pershing, in fact, was resolving a command crisis with Caesarean celerity. He had just received from Secretary of War Newton Baker the suggestion that Major General George W. Goethals come to France as Commander of the S.O.S., with an independent command, coequal with the Iron Commander. Goethals was a famous man, a great American who had cut a hemisphere in half at Panama; and he was possibly the only engineer of his day who could have cut it. Retiring to private practice, his prestige was monumental, bridges being named after him. He now wore the uniform of quartermaster general. He was distinguished by two marked characteristics: he could get anything done, and only the President of the United States could tell him what to do—even though a strong executive, Theodore Roosevelt, was not above getting a wigging from Goethals. (The great Teddy finally washed his hands of the civilian Panama Canal project; he had fathered it, but was happy to deposit his troublesome progeny on the doorstep of the West Point genius.) Pershing was in the habit of asking, on any given day, for corned-beef hash by the trainload, for acres of canned tomatoes, mountains of potatoes, from the great warehouses at Gièvres; for millions of shells, tens of thousands of horses; and Baker was letting him know that he was under heavy criticism. Baker's ominous letter did not say this, but "Such a plan," he wrote,

would place General Goethals in a coordinate rather than a subordinate relation to you . . . docks, railroads, storage houses, and all the other vast undertakings . . . the President and I will consider your reply together, and you may rely upon our being guided by confidence in your judgment and the deep desire to aid you.

It was the first command crisis Pershing had experienced. No other officer anywhere had anything like his independence—not even Ludendorff and the German admirals who ran the war and instituted unrestricted submarine warfare over the Emperor's angry opposition, thus causing Woodrow Wilson to throw his hat into the ring. Lloyd George ached to sack Douglas Haig, whom he hated; but knew if he did he might find himself sitting on an ex-prime minister's personal possessions waiting for the taxicab to turn from Whitehall into Downing Street. After Boehn's break-through to Château-Thierry, the profane Clemenceau thought of sacking Ferdinand Foch—whom he always distrusted because the pious Foch's brother was a Jesuit priest; but if he did, his own head might roll in the sand. Clemenceau also tried to make Foch demand that Wilson sack Pershing. Only Wilson, Commander in Chief of the Armed Forces by constitutional authority until March 4, 1920, was actually supreme commander anywhere on the globe, and neither he nor his smiling lieutenant, Newton Baker, ever considered replacing Pershing for a single day.

Harbord, in his autobiography, said that the Goethals move was an attempt by Peyton March, chief of staff at Washington, to rob the Iron Commander of his four-star autocracy. The matter was settled when Harbord came to Chaumont; the next day Pershing rushed off a cable to Baker, saying, "The man who fights the armies must control their supply through subordinates responsible to him alone." While Harbord was saying, "Here I had a first-class fighting division," Pershing followed up his cable with a long letter, at the end of which he mentioned that Harbord was now taking over the Service of Supply. He knew that Baker liked the genial Harbord's driving efficiency, his plowboy, schoolteacher, Kansas-State-Aggies, enlisted-man's simplicity. They knew each other, and Harbord had done Baker a favor.

On his March visit to France, Baker wanted his picture taken with a boy who lived across the street when Baker was mayor of Cleveland. He was just a "Look, Ma: no hands!" sort of boy, but the plaintive Baker said it would be "kind of nice" to send a snapshot of the two to the Cleveland *Plain Dealer*. He did not know for certain if the boy was in service, but somebody told him he thought the boy had been shipped to the Marine Barracks at Parris Island. It was late in the afternoon, somewhere in the Lunéville sector, when Harbord, then chief of staff, determined to find out if the boy who lived across the street was somewhere in France. No Yank could thread the Minotaurian labyrinth of rural French telephone exchanges to find some hearsay boy sleeping on a barn floor in a village of the 2nd Division area around Lorraine, or perhaps in one of the Marine replacement battalions in deeper Touraine. The French liaison lieutenant colonel angrily refused to doff his Saint-Cyr dignity and call five hundred crusty old women cranking side-winder telephone boxes, seeking the whereabouts of a simple *soldat*. It was almost *mano-a-mano* before Harbord bulled the Frenchman into a telephone booth for endless *allo-allo's* until midnight, when Harbord found the needle in the haystack. Harbord produced the boy around lunchtime in a rainy side car, swathed like a mummy in poncho wrappings. The snapshot was taken, and the boy sat by Baker for the novelty of ham and eggs to order.

Then came the moment of truth: *What did the Parris Islander think of the United States Army?* Ten West Point colonels held their breath. But the boy said the Army chow was epicurean, the stone floor he slept on luxurious, all division staff officers solicitous about his creature comforts, and General Pershing on his inspections as sweet and gentle as a Quakeress visiting an orphanage. The boy had told the biggest Leatherneck whopper since 1775; and when he arose to depart, ten colonels knocked over ten chairs to help the buck private with his overcoat. It was the only favor Newton Baker, Secretary of War, ever asked from two million Doughboys. And it had probably started Harbord on his unhappy way to Tours, for such were the infinite mutations of martial chance.

Meanwhile at Chaumont, Harbord, because of politics in an expanding army, proceeded to make something of it. With the Second Battle of the Marne reaching a climax, Pershing could spare him little time, but it was essential to tour the rear. The two friends started first for the Atlantic coast in Pershing's railway car, which was in continuous telephone hook-up with his corps commanders, whose green divisions were then still pouring into Foch's counteroffensive to drive Boehn back to the Vesle. The A.E.F. was now master of three ports in France: the great gantry-crane installations up the Loire from Saint-Nazaire with hundreds of miles of railway tracks, acres of sheds; the landlocked harbor at Brest where tens of thousands of Doughboys might come ashore in a single day; and the haven of the slow convoy freighters, the docks of the Garonne at Bordeaux. Brest was the liveliest port, and the scourge of the provost marshal. U.S. destroyers were there at ten-day intervals, and their boisterous crews were given short leave after days of chowing from spit-kids with one leg bent around a stanchion as their narrow-beamed ships knifed ahead of a following sea. Seamen had pockets full of money, and after days of crowding they were full of spirit. The Rue de Siam, with its regiment of streetwalkers and the often supercilious officers of the Royal Navy Reserve, saw times to try a Shore Patrolman's soul. Surgeons in U.S. Naval Hospital No. 1 there finally insisted that Shore Patrols cord their clubs to minimize scalp wounds. It made them bounce off a bluejacket's skull. "The only way," said a master-at-arms, "to save yourself now is to knock a knot on those Tin-Can heads and then knock the knot off." Doughboys rarely saw the Rue de Siam. They were marched away to Pontanezen Barracks.

There were other ports, such as the coaling docks at Marseille, all with strategic railways by-passing Paris and networked around the nexus of the Yanks at Chaumont. In addition, the British had docks at Le Havre, Boulogne, Calais, and other cross-Channel ports, where British transports delivered 52 percent of *all* Doughboys reaching France. Cannon and automatic weapons, tanks and airplanes were still matters of purchase from the well-nigh magical French plants. America had entered the war as the rich boy who had strayed across the tracks, got mixed up in a gang war, and had to buy his slingshot and zip gun from his more experienced pals.

Railway repair shops, sawmills, remount stations to disinfect the mangy horses purchased from Spain, depot divisions around central France, telephone and telegraph installations requiring thousands of technicians comprised an industrial empire created impromptu by sweating Americans in

1917-18. All work went on at a frenzied tempo; nothing like the measured 1941-44 preparations in America and England for the Allied landings in Normandy. The naval liaison and cooperation between British and Americans was always of a high order, but many chaotic situations arose once the Doughboys were ashore. Harbord, soon to be lieutenant general in deed but never in rank, would command nearly a million men; and to his credit he never ceased, in a futile war with Washington, in his efforts to gain some sort of token recognition for the great workers, technicians, and engineers among them. He pleaded for any sort of emolument: a button or an emblem he might bestow on some great black man from the Southern swamps who put in many a thirty-six-hour stretch at a back-breaking job because he knew his countrymen in the North would lose their war if he let them down. And so he sang:

> Oh, Doctor Cook's in town,
> Oh, Doctor Cook's in town,
> He say the North Pole
> Am too dam' cold,
> A'hm Alabama bound.

There was laughter later, when Black Jack Pershing, sometime captain in the 10th U.S. (Negro) Cavalry, spoke to Negro stevedores and machinists. Most of these men knew his soldier's reputation as a captain; the 10th Cavalry was the most exclusive of all U.S. regiments. Buck private troopers waited ten years to make lance corporal with yellow chevron and stripes, sleeves heavy with hash marks. (No noncom ever retired until he could no longer deceive Washington about his age.) Some of the Negro press, as venal as many of the white man's newspapers, had said that Pershing was using Negro troops as cannon fodder, killing them by the thousands while their white brothers caroused in Paris. Negroes grouped about Black Jack roared with laughter when he asked if they regretted he had not killed them according to these reports.

Pershing singled out one stevedore officer for inclusion in his memoirs, a Major John O'Neill at Bordeaux, who had unloaded forty lighters of troops in a single day. Asked his secret of success, the major said that after he had grown ashamed of bossing men around as he stood soldierly in his Sam Browne belt, he stripped to his shirt and worked like a navvy himself until he felt he was worthy to give orders. He pointed to two captains likewise slaving until he considered them worthy of a Sam Browne belt. When the train pulled out of Bordeaux, O'Neill was aboard; Pershing had named him Stevedore Instructor of the A.E.F., with a roving commission to sweat the lard off all officers who did not measure up to Major O'Neill.

The Sam Browne belt was a caste mark universally adopted by all Allied

countries. It was resented more, Frederick Palmer observed, by S.O.S. men
with a sociological turn of mind than by the combat Doughboys themselves.
A round-bellied British general originally designed the shoulder strap to
relieve pressure on his waist where his belt carried a sword, a pistol, binoculars, a map case, and, if he subsisted on the British ration, possibly a
separate pocket for his personal bottle of Eno Fruit Salts. To Pershing, it
was a delight: it made a man brace like a West Point cadet. The Doughboys
derided it, and General Peyton March at Washington hated it. He had
provost guards at port of disembarkation in America, ready to strip the belt
from any Pershing officer wearing it ashore. He even had men detailed in
New York theater lobbies to confiscate Sam Brownes. Some provosts were
informed by Pershing's Marine officers that General March cut no ice with
them. They were Navy again, within the Continental limits of the United
States, and the provosts were told, sometimes impolitely, to write a letter to
their congressman about it. "I wish March was more human," Pershing said.
"He would be happier."

Mainly the Doughboys jested about the belt, which gave a streetwalker
prima facie evidence that her victim was better heeled than the lad without
one. The Doughboy song ran:

> They say that love is a blessing,
> A blessing I never could see,
> For the only girl I ever loved
> Has gone and made a sucker out of me.
> She can Sam Browne out of Bordeaux,
> She can Sam Browne all over Paree,
> She can love herself to death in the A.E.F.,
> But she'll never find a sucker like me
>   [the word *love* being a euphemism].

Many officers detested the belt. Secretary Baker, homecoming on a transport
after the Armistice, was amused to witness a ceremony where the officers
gathered on the forecastle and, in a solemn ceremony led by their major
general, threw the belts overboard before General March could do it for
them. But the Iron Commander came home as General of the Armies of the
United States, and once again the Sam Browne found officers sucking in
their guts and bracing, West Point style. The man was changeless.

During their trip, the two friends, Pershing and Harbord, tramped around
a hundred installations, encouraging dejected colonels and brigadiers—
neglected in some measure since Haig's backs-to-the-wall order in April
forced Pershing to spend most of his time inspecting green combat divisions destined to learn their trade at Boehn's hands. Harbord saw a side of

Pershing seldom revealed. He visited the pension in Touraine where, in happier days, he had passed a summer with his wife and three little girls who later perished in the Presidio fire. Colonel Carl Boyd noted no emotion in the Iron Commander as he stood in the garden where the children once played, except that he reverted to his atrocious French, which he had once spoken to his little girls learning to *parlez* their *français,* most of it being misunderstood by the regional French, who boasted they spoke the only *vrai gaulois* of *La Belle France.*

Few understatements of naked misery could surpass the Iron Commander's allusion to his visiting Blois to inspect "the reclassification camp for the A.E.F., where officers found unfitted for a particular assignment were examined as to fitness for other duty and those recommended for discharge were assembled there until their cases could be disposed of." These thirty-seven words were all he had to say about Blois thirteen years after his visit there. . . . It was an interesting city. Touring its great château—climbing the architectural triumph of a columnar stairway so designed that those who were received by Henry III did not know on descending what informer was ascending a parallel flight of steps inside the column—many an American officer found unfit, not physically, must have stood miserably at the manhole cover in Catherine de Médicis' high boudoir into which her criminal son tossed such dignitaries as the Cardinal of Lorraine. Many officers had their hearts broken because of a cardiac weakness, and others because of high blood pressure, neither of which was disgraceful; but daily they were associated with those who, the Iron Commander ruled, did not possess the guts to drive men forward. The sick, the old, the inept, and the fainthearted all passed through the same channel. Even a general officer with an aorta the size of a fire hose, willing to lead a platoon against Maxims until he dropped dead of blood pressure, never cared to admit he had passed through Blois.

Many lightly wounded men went through Blois for reclassification, and these seemed as forlorn for their outfits as were the failures. They were barracked in a French casern, leaderless and sick for the sight of their buddies, praying that they might be reassigned to the old company, the old platoon, in the great exodus toward the fighting units.

An officer recalled picking up some Leatherneck casuals there to return to his brigade. A sergeant had them fall in, and they were dressed down for unsoldierliness, the officer threatening to leave all behind if, in three hours, they were not spit-shined to perfection. When they arrived at the railroad station to board the "40 & 8" the sergeant said, "Sir, there's a third-class carriage at the back of the train. You won't have to run a check on my outfit until we get to wherever we're getting to. They are so afraid of being left behind I'm going to have hell's own time getting them out along the line to piss them." A young Navy padre who had been a sprinter at one of the Catholic schools came along, and spent much time sprinting from boxcar to *estaminets,* and K. of C. and Y.M.C.A. huts, for beer and cigarettes. Not a man would take the chance at stops along the line.

Ladies of the Evening, quick to scent misery, flocked to Blois to exploit the sorrowing. But Hugh Hampton Young, Pershing's genitourinary officer, had preceded him to Blois and reported that he did not believe six street-walkers were left in the city. Colonel Young enlisted French mothers in his campaign to drive the ladies from discreet little houses in sedate neighborhoods. These informers were eager to join the French Housewives Auxiliary Corps of the U.S. Military Police Society for the Prevention of Fornication; and schoolchildren were given assorted reasons why old Monsieur Le Blanc had gone south after profitably renting his house, and why two Doughboys with fixed bayonets now stood at front gate and rear garden.

Hugh Young's real victory had been won in Saint-Nazaire, where the incidence of venereal disease had become particularly alarming. Here Private John Doe, having been ferried three thousand miles across the Atlantic, stepped upon French soil and went with his buddies to the nearest bar, where he had his first taste of alcohol, other than the bite of sherry in a Christmas syllabub, or the port wine his father poured down the hole in the center of the holiday fruitcake. After four two-ounce shots of *Rhum Negrito,* topped off with two fizzes made with a concoction the French labeled *Niger Gin,* he was drunk, and a steerer took him and his friends to one of the six major league brothels on the waterfront, where the girls worked forty to forty-five tricks each twenty-four hours before they were relegated after four weeks to the many minor leagues. Even here, they were too burned out to remain very long, being soon banished to the sand lots of the streetwalkers.

Private Doe and his friends bought tickets from the woman at the foot of the stairs, and surrendered them to a sixteen-year-old youth standing at the entrance to the upper hallway. The youth, the lover of the girl at whose door Private Doe took his place in line, was actively syphilitic. There were seven buddies ahead of him, with similar lines at five other doors along the hall. The boys at the head of the line were instructed to remove their shoes to facilitate the speed of the engagement, laces tied and shoes slung about their necks. The Martinique rum, the bathtub gin, the smell of the place sickened John Doe. But it was too late to back out. It was an axiom that a man who would not actively cooperate with one "f" verb would not fight, which was the complementary "f" verb. Private Doe, believing in this terrible heresy, which slandered many of the world's fighting men, reached the girl's room knowing he was in for it. She lay in an open robe upon an ineffably horrible bed, in a room where there was neither bowl nor washbasin nor anything else. The enterprise was soon over. Private Doe was the eighth Doughboy to whom she had, in succession, given syphilis. "What a hell of a way," said an old sergeant of his platoon, a fighting man who had avoided such cribs and brothels from Manila to the Mexican border, "for a nice kid to learn about the business!"

An aroused West Pointer had sent for his one-man task force against such enemies, the celebrated genitourinary surgeon from the Johns Hopkins at Baltimore. Hugh Hampton Young was a raffish, ghastly-humorous, garrulous scientist who detested only two things in the world of men and ideas: the microscopic, necklace-like chain of organisms known to Doughboys as The Clap; and the silver serpents, *Spirochaeta pallida*. Hugh Young had taken the train for Saint-Nazaire, where he examined Private Doe in the base hospital. Then he continued his research in other Allied headquarters. He knew that the English troops did nothing about prophylaxis, though the Canadians had imported a celebrated revivalist to implore the Maple Leaf killers to remain continent. The New Zealanders were a little better off, even though their chief medical officer thought that venereal disease was "a proper punishment for sin." The New Zealand High Commissioner, believing otherwise, organized a Venereal Prophylaxis Service on his own initiative in London, the office staffed by "a charming, curly-haired blonde."

"To each soldier on leave," she had told the inquiring Hugh Young, "I give a box of these prophylactic tubes." Young counted six tubes. "You give each one six?" he asked. The young lady replied, "Yes, every New Zealander needs at least six his first night in London. We have some particularly sturdy specimens." Young learned that conditions were deplorable among the British Armed Forces, and the French, since August, 1914, had registered 1,000,000 venereal casualties, 200,000 of them syphilitic.

The then Major Young had returned to Chaumont to find Black Jack Pershing boarding his private railway car for a journey to Paris. Young boarded the train, too, and made his report. The talkative, hard-headed doctor won his war before the train reached Paris. Pershing sent word to Allied leaders that his duties called him elsewhere, and caught the first train for Saint-Nazaire. Young said he was "like an enraged bull."

Pershing spared no one: headquarters staff, Medical Corps, billeting officers, commanders of troops aboard transports, Military Police, even the overworked doctors of the base hospital who, Young said, had almost given up the fight. Young did not give the name of the mayor of Saint-Nazaire, who had received the approval of the Premier of the Republic for the status quo in an earlier quarrel with Pershing. However, if His Honor the

Mayor walked abroad the next morning, foolishly believing he was master of his own bailiwick, he was promptly disillusioned. Armed Doughboys, in detachments, stood before brothel doors, before saloons, before pharmacies where cocaine was sold like candy. They were in side-street patrols before the lesser establishments, and where streetwalkers hustled, there were military police to trail them.

The Battle of Saint-Nazaire in November, 1917, unsung in military annals, set a pattern for the health of the A.E.F. Unlike so many victories, it was not a hollow one. As with any victory, there remained many outlying actions to be fought, in many French cities; but the bumptious surgeon no longer felt inadequate when he dropped in on a two-star divisional commander. That worthy had had the official word in black-and-white; he knew of the arena that day at Saint-Nazaire; he also knew he would be held accountable for such casualties. Young never again was bumped in the old buck-passing game. He was greeted at Division Headquarters by two-star officers who assured him, "There's no subject in which I am more interested. Please let me know in what way we can cooperate more effectively." The grinning Hugh Young always let the generals know. Even the Young Men's Christian Association got the word, agreeing to perform the services that the curly-haired blonde supplied the New Zealanders. As a result, the venereal rate fell to eleven new cases per year among a thousand Doughboys, an incidence never before known in any great army or civilian population in Western Christendom.

Historians gave this affair little significance. Actually, it was a declaration of independence, signifying the founding of a Doughboy Republic on foreign soil, henceforth free of interference by the President of the Republic of France or by any officer in its departments or prefectures. Pershing followed the Rockefeller study on prostitution in Europe by Abraham Flexner, which advocated its complete abolition. Pershing succeeded in abolishing in France—so far as Doughboys were concerned—an ancient French institution.

Young wrote a ghastly autobiography with illustrations that would make Jack the Ripper shudder. Only collectors know that, in order to make field medics read his twice-monthly circulars, he included two pages of smut, including such classics as Eugene Field's

> Now Francis Villon loved to sing,
> And Rabelais to treat,
> Of certain gross-grained Margots whom
> They rodgered in the street.

And again: James Whitcomb Riley's "Ballad of the Diabetic Dog": "His touch-hole shone like burnished gold, and smelled of bergamot." His office at Chaumont was a chamber of horrors from which Madame Tussaud would have fled screaming. This theater of operations was depicted on a huge, vividly colored mural of the genitourinary system, with each staffer's name lettered on some phase of that tract which was his particular field. Young himself claimed the prostate gland; and the unlucky young doc who edited the bulletin was represented by a wart on the penile head.

Young's triumph, supported savagely by Pershing, may have been the greatest single victory in the history of warfare—two million soldiers, three thousand miles from home, came home clean; though the French never gave up completely. When the Doughboys started streaming home, the mayor of Bordeaux, in a public appeal to Pershing, begged him to relax long enough to permit the Doughboys a *bon voyage* from the ladies of Bordeaux, who were in dire straits and who, he asserted, all had Paris medical certificates.

Pershing looked forward to inspecting the 41st Depot Division at Saint-Aignan below Touraine. The brigadier there had commanded one of his regiments in the Pancho Villa expedition. He was Robert Alexander, a Scotch-American who, lacking influence to reach West Point, enlisted to come up the hard way; he was an honor graduate of the Leavenworth Staff School. At Saint-Aignan, the commanding general was delighted; Alexander not only screened and sent forward replacements to the fighting brigades; he had set up provisional training regiments in the teeth of spirited stupidity from Chaumont inspectors who told him he was "Civil War style" in raising such cadres. He had a fabulous morale going for him: the French Mint made medals and trophies for his baseball league; Dr. Todd of the Y.M.C.A. provided funds; and he not only sought to correct the soldier faults he found in many men shipped overseas with little basic training, he also had such diversions as inter-Allied boxing matches. Sergeant Ray Williams of Headquarters Troop, under the urgings of Major E. C. Lowry, G-3, had been knocked out in one round by a sergeant-aviator of the French Army, a light heavyweight who would soon feel the terrible fist of the shipyard riveter, Jack Dempsey, in his short ribs. Sergeant Williams could always boast he was knocked out by Georges Carpentier.

Alexander's eldest son (he had two in France) was an instructor who chafed at the bit, but was satisfied when he got a battery in the 3rd Division where he was badly wounded and gassed. It had been the brigadier's unpleasant duty to break up and send as replacements to the 1st, 2nd, and 3rd Divisions the fine troops of Liggett's original 41st Division, the National Guardsmen from Oregon, Washington, California, Idaho, Wyoming, Colorado, the Dakotas. In his compulsory tour of the front, Alexander the Scot had spent his indoctrination period with the British 51st (Highland) Division, and knew that his kinsmen managed such things far better than the hard-pressed Yanks. The Highland Division's men never lost their identities: they were still Argyll-and-Sutherlands, Camerons, Black Watch, Seaforths, Gordons, with distinctive tartans and badges, kilted in the cold of early March, many only two weeks away from death in Ludendorff's March 21 offensive where they were an island of resistance.

Alexander's solicitude for all Doughboys was something to delight the Iron Commander's eye. Their embarkation for the front began at such towns as Thèze, Montrichard, and Selles-sur-Cher. Alexander had kitchens at railway stations there, and before a green boy entrained for combat under lieutenants he did not know, facing possible mutilation or death, Alexander fed him a rousing meal, filled his canteen with hot coffee, and put ham sandwiches in his mess kit.

Two years after the war a New Yorker, in his Hart-Schaffner-and-Marx best, accosted Alexander (the Private's General) in midtown Manhattan. "Remember me, General? I was the raggedyassed corporal you saw on the Vesle. You asked me where the supply officer could be found and I led you to him. And then you said, 'Why in the hell don't you give this man a decent pair of britches to go to war in?' I got them that same day." Alexander said he had never had "the advantages of West Point." He could not have cared less; nor could the Iron Commander, making his rounds with Harbord.

It was a near-miracle that Alexander ever broke away to follow his sons into battle, for he was well-nigh indispensable in his Saint-Aignan groove. But by the time he left Saint-Aignan, Pershing resolved, much to Harbord's disappointment, to give Alexander a fighting command. Brigadier General Eli K. Cole, the Marines' best artilleryman, was then positioned behind the Saint-Aignan 8-ball.

Pershing and Harbord made the rounds of hospitals that had been under heavy fire from ignorant American mothers back home. The fire was finally silenced by a newspaper story, the work of one woman. She was Mary Roberts Rinehart, herself a graduate nurse and married to a noted surgeon. She was also the most popular writer of detective fiction in America. She came to France, lunched at Chaumont, and then toured the wards scattered about the country. She reported that her own son was in one, and that the treatment could not have been better had his father been his doctor and his mother his nurse. Her overseas blast even silenced Colonel George Harvey, the loud home-front critic and self-appointed expert on all military affairs (the "Colonel" was politically earned), like some Long Tom French 155 rifle wiping out a German siege gun at Verdun.

Doughboys were connoisseurs of hospitals. All of them had a favorite nurse, and loved her starchy neatness, her clear, soft skin desperately, and not many had complaints. Private Bailey regretted he had only a few days in Base 27 at Angers, claimed to be the paradise of the wounded man by everyone who passed through there. It had been a French upper-class boarding school, L'Ecole Morgazon—staffed by a Roman Catholic order, with buildings in a Romanesque quadrangle, and a chapel turned into a lofty-ceilinged operating room; the priests had left their cutlery, their china, and their table linens behind. The staff was mainly from Mercy Hospital in Pittsburgh, with medics who had quit premed classes at Pitt to hustle bedpans. Patients on upper floors could see the white road winding through peaceful Anjou to the French School of Equitation at Saumur, where Doughboy artillerymen in classes of six hundred learned to jump barred gates bareback. (Those who knew their Balzac thought of old Grandet with his cart driving from Saumur to Angers on market days.) Base 27 saw many from "Collar-Bone Camp" checking in to have a scapula repaired or a clavicle wired after taking a cropper in the rousing exercises the French gave Doughboy gunners.

Over the years, ex-patients meeting at division reunions vied in asserting the superiority of this or that nurse. Miss Nell Brink, the little redhead, had the gentlest hands? "No, buddy, Miss Matilda Miller had 'em all beat." And then a disclaimer: "No. You guys are nuts. Miss McNair, the Scotch nurse, was the best, because she was as tough as a top sergeant. Guys who wanted a squad of men to lift 'em on a bedpan couldn't soldier on the morning job when she was around. 'Raise yoursel', mon.' And the guy arched his back if it killed him. Remember when she got the weekend leave for Cannes? When she came back I said to her, 'You must have had a good time in Cannes. I see where the Gordon Highlanders have retreated all the way back there.' She said, 'Mon, if there ha' been a single Gordon Hielander in Cannes, d'ye think I'd coom back here to a straggler like yoursel'?' " There was a quality about Miss Nelson, strawberry blonde from the Mercy Hospital, which made dying men ask for her. "Remember Lieutenant Norton, the aviator? The one they named a field for in California? When they put the screen around him, and he knew he was going to die, he said, 'I'm going to crash. Ask the Strawberry Roan to stand by my bed, please. . . .' "

After a few days in paradise, as an ambulatory wounded with permission to visit the Cheval Blanc and dine on stuffed quail, Private Bailey was moved on. Angers was filling with desperately wounded men from Fismes on the Vesle. Bailey was sent to Châteauroux, to an insane asylum the French gave the Yanks. There were few facilities left; the lunatics had been sent to some even less-favored place. Bailey, after Angers, found himself eating from wooden bowls with wooden spoons, standard for men with deranged minds. Food was almost inedible until some officers arrived from the 2nd Division brigades on a visit. Doctors and nurses there were grateful to them for the hell they raised at Tours about the fare their wounded men received. In fact, conditions improved everywhere after the jut-jawed Harbord began to crack the whip.

"Man, they put twenty-five ingredients in the stuffing." "Yeah, but why do they squeeze the chestnuts into milk? Why don't they put 'em in whole?" "Listen, buddy, the Frogs got to draw the line somewhere. They claim it's immoral to shove a chestnut into a quail's behind."

In the paradise at Angers, men whose legs were slung in Balkan frames were brought delicacies by ambulatory buddies. A rubber sheet under a pal's chin, a quail to eat finger-fashion, and a bottle of Château Belle Rive— the golden wine of Anjou: "Oh, burn my clothes, doctor. I don't want to go home." Many never reached home, dying in the quietness of the Angevin air. The Iron Commander ruled that every hospital fatality must receive the obsequies due a soldier. Every morning the stake-bodied trucks went by with flagged coffins, a weary band wailing its woodwinds in the *Marche Funèbre,* a firing squad of medics stepping behind the cortege, the bugler puckered to sound Taps. Gallows humor made the music bearable to those who awoke to find a buddy's bed empty beside them. Many sang lyrics to the funeral march to keep grief away. "Ten thousand dollars for the folks back home" was a reminder of the Doughboy insurance policy. Others sang: "Somebody hit me with a codfish ball."

Pershing visited Base 8 Hospital at Savenay, where stretcher cases were prepared for transit to the States. It was standard practice to encase broken legs and arms in plaster casts before transshipment. Since plaster needed two days' drying before a *fenêtre* could be cut into the shell above a suppurating wound, fever often rose to lofty notches on the thermometer. No one seemed to care. There was a song for that, too, based on "In the Good Old Summertime." Men with 104 Fahrenheit sang:

> In the base at Savenay,
> Where the sick and wounded lay,
> Running up their temperatures,
> More and more each day,
> Oh, they put them all in plaster casts,
> And that's a very good sign,
> That they will stay at Savenay,
> Till the good old summertime.

It might all be a blur at first. An officer badly wounded and being ferried back by German prisoners through woods littered with dead and dying, a

German officer walking beside the bearers, a buck private with fixed bayonet attending the procession, might find his best sergeant by the train, leaning on one elbow like the Dying Gaul, hand thrust into a rent in his breast. "Put me down, Oklahoma Red. Sling a blanket between two rifles for the sergeant. . . ." "It's no use, sir, I've got a hemorrhage beneath my heart and when I take my hand out I'm going to die. . . ." "But let's try, Sergeant. . . ." "There, Red, that's the ticket. Make the Boche officer take a hand. If he pulls the Geneva Convention on you, shoot him. . . ." "He's willing, sir. He's got the hind end." And a little later on: "It's no use, sir. The sergeant's done took his hand out." And the procession moved on, German batteries shelling the roads they knew led to dressing stations beneath culverts or in shattered farmhouses heavily blanketed against gas shells. "Give that squarehead officer some coffee, Oklahoma Red. He's been a good Heinie." Colonels were often around dressing stations after an attack. "The spirit of the wounded is excellent," they would message brigade. Morale as much as munitions won a war.

The tents of the field hospitals were not sights to attract the tenderhearted. There were no miracle drugs, no sulfa radicals and the antibiotics. There was only the Dakin-Carrel solution steadily dripping into wounds to liberate chlorine and destroy necrosed flesh. In the French Army hospital any orderly might stab a gangrene sufferer with a morphine needle. The Yanks kept to civilian practice; morphine needed an order from an M.D. Men sometimes cursed when a dying buddy anguished it out waiting for the merciful needle, only permissible when some surgeon stepped from an operating truck sick from ether fumes to clear his lungs and light a Camel or a Lucky. Major Cole, the Marine's "Harvard Man," the blue line of gangrene crossing his collarbone and nearing the red citadel of his heart, sat erect till the day he died and shaved himself one-handed with a straight razor. With some, discipline went on until the last gasp. The hardest trial was always that of the nurse who dressed the wounds of men destined to die. (Pershing noted, when with General the Honorable Sir Julian Byng behind Cambrai, that rows of Tommies were on stretchers against one wall of the collecting station. They were beyond hope and they knew it. Not one complained.)

Many men in hospitals were gas cases, particularly New Englanders of the 26th Division who had suffered much from it in and around Belleau Wood after relieving the 2nd Division. The Germans in their July 15 assaults against the 3rd Division attempted to neutralize the wooded patches around Lucy, Vaux, Bouresches, and the Woods, with heavy doses of toxic shells for three days. Mustard gas lingered longest, but Conta employed diphosgene, chlopicrin, yperite, diphenylchloroarsine, and ethyldichloroarsine.

There was no new kind of gas, yet gas discipline was always difficult. Gas officers there on the whole were efficient, promptly liming the low ground where mustard gas might hover several days, doing their best to keep men from heavily contaminated areas. But what gas sentry himself would not dive into a gully where leaves were yellowish with contamination if, as Private Bailey recorded, he heard one coming with his name on it? (A man would dive into anything, a standard classroom jest of friendly French instructors being the definition: "A latrine, Messieurs, is something you urinate in by night and dive into by day.")

The problem of malingerers who claimed to have been gassed was always a difficult one. Many badly wounded men, strapped into railway bunks, saw some fellow who had come aboard moaning, his face a vaseline mask, leap to his feet after the train got under way and begin scrounging for cigarettes. He would be moaning again when the wounded were unloaded at Paris on the concrete of the Gare du Nord, feverishly awaiting transshipment to the rapidly filling hospitals. He was a problem, this Doughboy. In justice to the thousands who were badly burned, and the tens of thousands who stuck with their buddies when they themselves were lobster-pink at armpit and groin, it must be said that gas malingerers were relatively few. But to gloss over the defection would be an injustice.

There was much humanity about the men who examined such cases. A shell-shocked man might honestly believe himself gassed. A neurotic would be sure of it. "The symptomology of gas poisoning is so complex," wrote Major William V. Somervell of the 3rd Division Engineers, and gas officer of the division, "and at the same time so indefinite" that any man claiming to be gassed had to be classed as a casualty and sent to the rear for further examinations. Surgeons there had traps to discover malingerers, such as the simple experiment of offering a "casualty" a cigarette impregnated with diphosgene. If he failed to detect this ruse with his first puff of smoke, he was a true gas casualty. If he complained of the curious taste, he was a dead beat. But then again, the frailty of human nerves, or the man shell-shocked by head-splitting bursts from eight-inch howitzer bombardment, could enter the case. And mustard gas often needed two or three days to begin its evident corrosion of the human flesh.

Much nonsense, both military and civilian, was written about the ineffectiveness of the American respirator patterned after a British model. It was not so effective as postwar changes made it, with the discomfort of the chestbox, the nose clamp, and mouthpiece, and the clouding of goggles in the face of the mask. But relatively few gas casualties were respiratory. Burns were commonplace, and many might have been avoided; but so could many gunshot wounds. As for the rumor that a gas mask might be worn only two or three hours before its wearer fainted, or the charcoal lost its efficiency, this was moonshine.

In April, 1918, two lieutenants, learning of heavy gas casualties—mainly from burns—to one of their battalions in a quiet sector, made a test run in gas masks while wearing heavy packs to learn how soon they fainted. They alternately jog-trotted and wind-sprinted from the village of Châtillon-sur-Cher to the bridge over the Cher at Saint-Aignan and return, a distance of about twelve miles. Their chin pieces were filled with mucus and their uniforms beslobbered, but neither youth was the worse for it, both immediately enjoying a hearty meal at the surgeon's suggestion. After that, the battalion commander announced that any platoon leader who suffered a man to remove his gas mask on any pretext whatsoever would be held accountable for this dereliction, and he was a hard soldier.

Nevertheless, all troops everywhere suffered needless gas casualties, and many a man saved his life when, stripped naked before surgeons, his burns found him relegated to a hospital for two weeks or more, his buddies meanwhile going forward to fight where the air zipped with small-arms fire and the earth shook from the roar of bursting shells. Paul Malone of the 23rd Infantry, always the analyst, reported that four thousand gas shells in his Château-Thierry lines caused more casualties than 200,000 high-explosive shells, machine-gun and rifle bullets, though only two of the 23rd Regiment's Doughboys died of gas poisoning on the field. Malone thought it the ideal offensive weapon, merciful in a war where the quality of mercy was not up to Shakespeare's standard.

After his tour of the rear areas Pershing returned to the wars and Harbord went to Tours, his loyal staff going with him into exile. Few went hungry after that, although there were some rations that only a bewildered peacetime army might provide. Someone in Hoboken had an erroneous notion of a multiplicity of sacred Jewish days and sent (presumably) a shipload of matzos to Bordeaux. The matzos were approximately ten inches square, packaged in glazed paper, with legends in Hebrew stamped in black. A battalion received a batch of these, with cans of monkey meat, for two days' field rations. When Jewish boys tried to apologize for some Gentile's miscalculations, they were waved aside. The matzos' crisp, unsalted freshness made a wonderful buffer to the embalming fluid of the monkey meat and enterprising amateur chefs secured strips of TNT from the gunners to kindle small fires beneath mess-kit pans and make matzo-monkey-meat hash, Father Frank Brady saying that Rome had overlooked a winner in the culinary department.

Pershing listed a few of the categories which Harbord, now that he had all the matzos he needed, would command as of July 29: foresters and general construction workers, laborers, carpenters, chauffeurs, checkers for docks and depots, watchmen, kitchen helpers, cooks, mechanics, stenographers, telephone installers, telephone operators, typists, warehousemen, quartermaster clerks, engineer clerks, ambulance drivers, bakers, blacksmiths, canvas workers, cable splicers, multiplex operators, photographers, punchers, sheetmetal workers, shoemakers, supervisors, tailors, toolmakers, and wheelwrights. America had them in God's plenty, but tens of thousands were still three thousand miles away, and shipping tonnage was always critical. By sundown August 8, an order received by Harbord that morning at 8 A.M. for three days' rations for 350,000 fighting men was on board a long line of freight trains moving from the great warehouse complex around Gièvres in central France, where twenty thousand men often worked around the clock.

Offensive,
First Phase

Chapter 11

LUDENDORFF'S "BLACK DAY"; ON TO THE AISNE

I have seen it too often before.

Pershing had given his friend Harbord three days to take in hand the Service of Supply. Now he had returned to the vicinity of La-Ferté-sous-Jouarre to wage his war against the Germans and conduct his second-ary conflict with his French colleagues, and the entire British cabinet, behind the lines. Foch had known by the evening of July 23, as Doughboys poured in by the tens of thousands and French observers reported them eager for hand-to-hand fighting, that the German superiority in rifles, de-cisive since the collapse of Russia, was disappearing. He now had his grand design for victory. He did not know whether this would come in 1918 or 1919, but he saw no harm in trying to win the war before the winter's lull. While both Haig and Pershing believed in the theory of Brusilov's Rus-sian break-through of 1916—a concentrated mass against a narrow front, ever widening as enemy wings gave way—Foch's formula for victory was, as always, *"Tout le monde à la bataille."*

Foch's strategy—and any grand design by a Supreme Commander must be called strategy—was to cut off all the tentacles of the German octopus holding the crown of northern France, artlessly and simultaneously. Never at any time did he think of crushing the heart of the octopus—the Saar coal fields and the Bricy iron mines, from whence was pumped the Ger-man's lifeblood. His grand design was not worthy of a great general, and

193

Foch for all his piety and patriotism, his flaming resolution, was never a great general. As for Pershing? He had no chance to prove his strategy, and so history must return a Scottish verdict on him: *"Not Proven."* To Doughboys, it is a tragic one.

Boehn could tell from the relentless pressure being put on him that it would be impossible to hold his Vesle line. By early August, the Second Battle of the Marne was ending, but Boehn knew Foch's lifelong passion for the attack well enough to understand that the latter would never cease to batter him senselessly until he fell back to the Aisne. And he knew that the operation called "The Aisne-Oise Offensive" would begin before he could brace to take the ceaseless punches bound to be thrown at him. On August 8, Boehn also knew that he could not hope for any succor whatsoever; for on this day, a date which Ludendorff called "The Black Day in the history of the German Army in the war," Sir Douglas Haig got into Foch's act around Amiens on the Northern front.

Ludendorff was late in realizing that his was a lost cause. Haig had to kick him in the teeth before he knew he was whipped. The German chancellor, von Hertling, was to write: "We expected grave events in Paris for the end of July. That was on the 15th. On the 18th even the most optimistic among us understood that all was lost. The history of the world was played out in three days."

It was the British view, never changed, that Hindenburg and Ludendorff both believed, before the dawn of fateful August 8 around Amiens, they could still win their war by crushing Haig before Hazebrouck. But Pershing was careful to quote Hindenburg on the matters of July 15-18:

We had been compelled to draw upon a large part of the reserves which we intended to use for the attack in Flanders. This meant the end of our hopes of dealing our long-planned decisive blow at the English army. . . . How many hopes, cherished during the last few months, had collapsed at one blow! How many calculations had been scattered to the winds!

Foch had wanted Haig to strike in Flanders, but the unimaginative Scot at last had had enough of its terrible terrain. He wanted a blow farther east at Amiens, and his wishes prevailed. Where the first great Allied assault of July 18 had been made by Foch, using a motley group consisting of his slender French and their magnificent artillery, his swarms of skilled and semiskilled Americans, and his handful of British veterans, the Scot at Amiens had an all-veteran team. Only his reserve division, the U.S. 33rd, Illinois National Guard, was new to combat. He had collected more than 450 tanks for his Cambrai-like attack with no preliminary bombardment, men and tanks springing forward to reach a surprise barrage line. Tanks were mainly thirty-six-tonners with eighteen-pounder field pieces in their snouts and galaxies of machine guns—augmented by some of the speedy new whippets. He used, with the French, about fifteen hundred airplanes to shepherd his attacks during the operation. He had Rawlinson's British Fourth Army, Debeney's French First Army, and portions of Humbert's French Third Army. Above all, he had the muscular Canadian Corps and the brawny Australians; the men of these all-volunteer divisions were the meat-eaters of two uncrowded Dominions, as big as the biggest of the Doughboys on the Marne, and skilled down to the newest sergeant. In addition to the daring lads from overseas, Haig had his customary anachronism, the Cavalry Corps, sitting on their prats ready for a dash into Never-Never Land.

Haig for once practiced every ruse and trick to deceive the Germans, who thought he might launch limited attacks in Flanders to keep them off balance. The effect of his surprise blow at Amiens—delivered by a general to whom the word *surprise* was a novelty—was stupefying. "Even more shocking to the German commanders," said *The West Point Atlas of American Wars* forty years later, "was the low morale, bordering on mutiny, shown by many retreating units. Still, between rallying stragglers and calling up reinforcements, they established a line."

The German was four days after August 8 turning his phantasmagoria of a shocking defeat into established order. According to von der Marwitz, whose army was first terrorized, he lost 700 officers and 27,000 men on the first day alone. Surprised that first day, the Germans must have minimized losses by the fourth day. But the French and the British claimed 30,000 prisoners before nightfall on August 8. Allied casualties that day were around 25,000 men. Haig's attack, in a boxer's parlance, was for the Canadians to deliver a bone-crushing left hook to the German's ribs, followed by Debeney's right cross to the jaw. After that, the German on the ropes would receipt for a flurry of combinations—British lefts and French rights—and the Kaiser would quickly throw in the sponge. It was not to be. The German character prevailed.

They were still tough, their officers still disciplined enough to come off the ropes and fight, and even though upcoming reinforcements were jeered by shattered retreating men who wanted an end to the slaughter. After four days, Haig called a halt to reorganize when his army commanders, on their own initiative, restrained corps commanders who, in the bulldog tradition, were ordering exploratory murders for the fifth day. Foch objected to the halt. A quarrel ensued whose grandeur was never exceeded in the history of the war, but the stubborn Scot dug in until ready for his next phase. After that, though Foch told Pershing and the French where to fight, Haig, who was not a strategist, called his own strategic shots. His success August 8 affected two million Doughboys in France and two million more back home.

No brief sketch of a great event could better show the state of the British mind that August dawn than an extract from the secret diary of young Captain Cyril Falls, later Criswell Professor of Military History at Oxford University, most even-tempered and generous of England's chroniclers. "Tonight the crowd on the roads was extraordinary," he wrote of the Canadians' stealthy transfer from Flanders to the Somme,

so thick that I was afraid the traffic would be caught by morning light. At times the flood hardly seemed to move for half an hour at a stretch . . . and so all the tricks are coming out of the conjuror's box. I have seen it too often before—the Somme, Messines, Ypres, Cambrai—to be fully confident of a great success on this occasion. But one thing is sure: if we take the knock this time after Ludendorff has shown us how it is done, we may as well give up. On the whole, I am hopeful. . . .

What tons of guts men like this young Dublin staff officer must have needed, to grope that first victorious evening between the Canadian right flank with its tanks seven miles deep into the German maze, and Major General Deville's French 42nd Division without heavy tanks still far in the rear. Farther in the rear were the sitting ducks on cavalry horses. Only the British lads were led by the steel plate of heavy tanks terrorizing the stoutest of German defenders; and Debeney had to delay until the enemy had panicked. Falls was liaison officer between Deville and the Canadians, and was one of thousands of staff officers who knew the terrible score of the last three years.

The U.S. 33rd Division sent one of its regiments forward August 9 to fight around Bray on the road to Péronne. Australians said they were fine fellows, but a little rough. Doughboys cited this as a tribute to their own ferocity, but it was difficult to believe that any fighters were even a little rougher than the Waltzing Matildas who shipped out of Melbourne. Perhaps the Australians meant by "fine fellows" that they fought with enterprise and spirit, the "roughness" being around the edges of new troops working in turn around the edges of machine-gun nests. They were little remembered in the fighting there, though Haig complimented them, notably the 167th U.S. Infantry. They had served, 983 falling there. The Argonne-Meuse would know well the skills of the 33rd Division around Forges Brook and Consenvoye.

Back home, newspapers were already saying that the Doughboys had won the war on the Marne, and few people understood the hot British resentment, with their four years of 750,000 battlefield murders, when their

"Black Day" troops were so informed. The blow at Amiens had indeed killed all German hopes; and by August 12 the Second Battle of the Marne had come to an end. The Kaiser told his Supreme Council that the time had come to seek a satisfactory peace with the Allies. The Germans counterattacked, hoping to hold out until such a peace was reached; but Haig was back at them August 21, and desolate place names famous in four years of fruitless attrition warfare began to appear in London papers again. Hindenburg ordered a gradual withdrawal, but the Australians wrested Péronne and Mont Saint Quentin, halfway east to the Belgian border, from him, the Canadians breaking through his strongest new position between Quéant and Drocourt. Hindenburg now fell far back to the "Hindenburg Line," into subterranean tenements four levels deep, where the austere British would soon find electric player pianos and beer machines, millions of men living years underground like Martians deprived of a planet's oxygen. Those British who survived the August attacks found unprecedented rewards. Soon after, there were not so many stragglers as there were drunks too unsteady to light captured cigars, Tommies, Maple Leafs, and Aussies going forward sometimes with horrendous hangovers. Disappointed Doughboys always complained that whenever they captured a position, someone else had drained all the bottles.

After the disaster at Amiens Ludendorff fell victim of panic and tried to resign. For reasons of national morale, he was retained as a figurehead, but Field Marshal Paul von Hindenburg had now grasped full command on the German side. His character was akin to Joffre's, phlegmatic beyond panic, though he did not have that old Frenchman's ponderous reserve of guts. But Ludendorff's loss of morale had infected many higher commanders of the line, and Haig would keep at the Germans, though he had no reserves to exploit his great success.

While Haig was pushing toward the Belgian border, Foch—no longer a major general, highest rank in the French Army, but a marshal of France—turned his attentions to Boehn in the Oise-Aisne area, hoping to prevent Hindenburg from sending troops to German Armies which were being battered by the British to the northwest.

On the Vesle, above Bazoches and Fismes, the 77th Division's New Yorkers went into the line on August 14 with the half-rested Pennsylvanians on their right, to push the Germans back to the Aisne.

Brigadier General Robert Alexander, escaping the S.O.S. after Pershing's visit to Saint-Aignan, took over a brigade of General Haan's 32nd Division before Fismes, replacing a fine officer, Brigadier General William H. Connor. Connor, astonished (he had not been notified of the change), remained at headquarters during the next attack to coach his successor, without rancor, in the characteristics of his old brigade, and then left for Blois, heartbreak, and reassignment. Harbord had asked for his engineer's talents to straighten out the tangles around the French Atlantic ports. (Pershing had the grace to route him through Chaumont for a drink.) When Connor reported at Tours bemoaning the loss of a combat brigade, Harbord probably said, "Hell, I lost a great division."

Alexander was with the 32nd only on trial; Pershing knew he could trust Hahn's report of his combat skills. Hahn could not have approved the loss of his own loyal officer, Connor, and he received Alexander with a scathing depreciation reflecting on the latter's depot assignment. But he kept his family affairs to himself and reported that Alexander was good. At Chaumont, the Iron Commander was being urged to replace Major General George B. Duncan of the 77th Division, and Alexander succeeded to his command in the midst of the fighting between the Vesle and the Aisne.

The 77th was called the Melting Pot Division, New York City's own. It spoke forty-two languages and among its gamblers could be found Chinese from Mott Street playing fan-tan, Jewish boys from Allen Street in stuss games, Italian boys from east of Union Square playing piquet, Germans from Yorkville on the Upper East Side. There were Turks who spoke a little Hebrew and Hebrews who spoke a bit of Arabic. Many could speak nothing but Brooklyn English; their accent was that of the Don Marquis ballad that ended:

> Prince, when you call on a Brookalyn goil,
> Say Poil for Pearl, and erl for oil.

There were even some Kentucky and Tennessee immigrants to New York City who referred to a dud shell as a "possum playin' daid." When it came time for Alexander to decorate three men with the Distinguished Service Cross, he thought they represented the warp and woof of the division's many-textured fabric. Sergeant Sing Kee's birth had been heralded with firecrackers in San Francisco; Captain Herman Stadie had seen his first light on the Rhine; Private Abraham Hirschkovitz had enjoyed the sanitary splendors of Ellis Island after early years in a Bessarabian ghetto. Little wonder the division, when it chose a shoulder patch, selected a white Statue of Liberty on a blue shield trimmed in red.

The 77th came into the Vesle fighting at its heaviest, going after entrenched enemy positions in the caves above the river at Fismette tooth-and-nail. One day when they found the going too heavy, alongside the now veteran Pennsylvanians on the left, Alexander issued a general order urging platoon chiefs to improve their "gang spirit" to reap the full benefit of the magnificent fighting qualities of the men; and their historian said there were many gangsters among them. Alexander told them they had barely beaten the Germans but could do a better job next time, and guaranteed he would send the enemy two shells to its one. Most of the lads in the 77th were conproof; they took in few wooden nickels. Alexander sent the Germans 400,000 shells between the Vesle and the Aisne, while his infantrymen in many quarters of the line counted the screams and counter-screams of the 75s and 77s to see if this new two-star bird at headquarters was trying to con them.

Alexander was their third commander in less than a month; he had to prove himself to everyone, and he did. No one could ever dislodge him from command of the 77th, though later he sacked a brigadier who, Malin Craig of Liggett's staff warned him, had many influential friends who would cause him trouble. They tried, but nothing could trouble this fierce mustang. Even an angry police dog guarding a German grave at the ancient Château de Fère, Alexander's first headquarters north of the Vesle, did not trouble him when he lunged ferociously at this American general who did not smell like a German general. Sergeant Glass, headquarters driver, was detailed to pacify this faithful brute; he did it with great patience, tidbits from the general's mess, and a mixture of Brooklynese and German with a little Yiddish thrown in. The dog was soon the pet of headquarters, riding beside Glass in the general's limousine.

By the time the division reached the Rhine, the dog had joined Lieutenant von Buy's category of German-born who regarded themselves unhesitatingly as American; and when the division came home, like any other Doughboy he was given freedom of opportunity to go his own way. Everyone wanted him for his own; but the immigrant chose Sergeant Glass instead of the general, and spent many happy years dodging trolley cars with the nimble children of Flatbush—probably soon addicted to banana ice cream licked from dishes below the many tables of that Brooklyn avenue which abounded with such neighborhood parlors.

The 77th embraced all the types of Doughboys found in other divisions, except for farm boys, cowpokes, and mountaineers. Bullard said that it lacked country boys able to find their way around in the dark, since most of its personnel had always been able to read a street sign beneath a lamp post, ask a solitary policeman his whereabouts, or inquire of the sleepy pharmacist at an all-night drugstore. Some of its elements did show a talent for getting lost. Nevertheless, one of its battalion runners across the Vesle gained fame by his speed in reaching Regimental on the road north of Bazoches. Then one dark night he was required to guide an Intelligence officer from regiment to battalion. It was discovered that the little runner had been crossing a half-mile of the German lines every night!

Sergeant Sing Kee of the 306th Infantry, one of thirty men operating the message center at the village of Mont Nôtre Dame, saw twenty-nine buddies knocked out. With the fatalism of his race, he thought this nothing worth reporting. Sergeant Sing remained at his post alone for twenty-four hours, all messages coming through.

The officers of the 77th were from many professional walks of life— perhaps many would now be classed as "The Fighting Eggheads." A quiet Princeton professor, Captain Wardlaw Miles, was fighting in the Aisne River Valley as late as September 14 while other troops were clashing with Saxon reserves at Saint-Mihiel, or rushing through darkness toward the Argonne.

Captain Miles cut the German wire ahead of his company, artillery having failed to blast a path. He did this at some cost, his legs broken by machine-gun fire and one arm fractured. He was not a glory hunter by nature, but a teacher by profession; so he had himself carried forward on a stretcher to tutor the ensuing attack once his men got through the wire to gain a mile of ground. It was difficult for those in a base hospital, observing the calm Miles as doctors and nurses daily dressed his multiple wounds with the painful techniques demanded in the use of Dakin-Carrel solution, to believe that here was a determination and a savagery beyond the hell-for-leather prototypes of swashbuckler fiction. No one in the ward knew that this middle-aged officer, quietly smoking with his free hand while a bevy of doc-tors and nurses gathered around the Agony Wagon with sponges and probes, had been awarded the Medal of Honor.

After a month of hard fighting, Foch relieved the New Yorkers, last of the Doughboy divisions to enter the Aisne-Marne counteroffensive, on Septem-ber 16, replacing them with the Italian Garibaldi Division, commanded by the famous liberator's grandson. City-bred, in bad moments of the fighting toward the Aisne late in August, the 77th had rallied with the spontaneous spirit of the tenement hive, without the slow deliberations of a town meeting in a Grange Hall. They produced leaders impromptu just as often as they missed directions. It was not an accident that they created the Argonne saga of the Lost Battalion, where leaders of sublime quality arose out of every squad.

Pershing made the most of Haig's great smash and visited Marshal Foch at Sarcus on August 9, pressing him on the plans for an "American First Army comprising the I, III, and V Corps, to undertake an offensive against Saint-Mihiel. On August 13, unable to restrain his exultation, he telephoned from Paris to his chief of staff at Chaumont, instructing him to announce to the American press that he now commanded the American First Army. Perhaps Haig's great victory of August 8 was as much a factor, as Pershing had calculated, in Foch's decision to give Pershing an independent command as was the work of the Doughboys on the Vesle. The Army was still scattered from the Swiss border to the English Channel; but it was American; and while Pershing, the soldier's soldier, would fight where his superior, Foch, told him to fight, he could command his own troops. Pershing's decision to press Foch at this moment must have been greatly provoked by such reports as one received at Chaumont from Bullard.

"I request the Commanding General be acquainted with these facts at Chaumont," Bullard's report had read. The facts were that Bullard had just witnessed the wanton slaughter of a Doughboy infantry company. The incident occurred in the first week of August. Bullard had just taken over the American III Corps from French Major General Mondésir, who had admired the green Doughboys and wherever possible been sparing of their lives; early in his experience with them he had understood and advocated the necessity of their serving as an independent homogeneous army with their own staffs.

Now Bullard was ordered by Degoutte to push out a patrol from bloody Fismes across the Vesle toward the village of Fismette. (In his memoirs, Bullard declined to name the unit, mindful of the bereaved at home.) The Germans were finely situated there, in the chalk hills of the treeless Champagne rising 150 meters above the bottom lands, their sides pitted with deep caves the French had dug before Bruchmüller's guns had driven them back to the Marne. The patrol, 150 strong, crossed the Vesle in darkness over a single-file footbridge. Morning found it pinned down in the river-side caves without food. It was hazardous to send out rations—even if sympathetic buddies could dash at intervals across a footbridge under fire to bring them. So Bullard himself got the 150 men out the following night, one at a time, between the methodical machine-gun bursts of the enemy, and brought them back where they belonged.

The angry chief of staff of the French Sixth Army informed Degoutte of Bullard's sensible action. Degoutte was incensed. He personally ordered Bullard to send the Doughboys back across the footbridge and into the trap again, a hopeless 150 knowing they were doomed. The Germans took their time; they held the high ground and could enfilade either side of the trap, maintaining a fire of interdiction against any attempt to bring up reinforcements. On the fourth night, Boehn's men came down the hill and wiped out the famished lads. Degoutte's communiqué the next day read, in part: "In the region of the Vesle, Bullard's American III Corps wiped out a counterattack." Degoutte was a warwise officer, a charming man who kept a sumptuous mess where American officers were always received with Gallic courtesy. Unlike Mangin and Gouraud, he simply had little regard for the lives of men.

Pershing came down on Bullard blazing. "Why did you not disobey the order of General Degoutte?" He shouted and pounded the table. Cadet-Lieutenant Bullard had been Cadet-Corporal Pershing's company commander in the plowboy's second year at West Point. He knew when it was his turn not to answer. Pershing understood that a corps commander, if a war was to be won, must be putty in the hands of an Army commander, even though hell-on-wheels to his own division commanders. And Bullard knew that Pershing would cool off. But the incident had an effect on Pershing's insistence upon an independent American Army.

Now he had it. Foch, elated by Haig's success, yielded to Pershing, agreeing in principle to his independence, with the reduction of the Saint-Mihiel salient as his first target. It was only a 50 percent vote of confidence, however. Foch proposed that the American Service of Supply be unified into a single Franco-American service under the French chief of staff. This would have been worse than Goethals's dominance, and Pershing turned down the old marshal hard.

The next day he visited Haig at his advanced headquarters and with many expressions of regret and reassurance requested that all but two of the Doughboy divisions in training with the British be released to American command. There was no quarrel, as there had been in July after Lieutenant General Launcelot Kiggell, Haig's chief of staff, had permitted the use of four green infantry companies of the U.S. 33rd Division in a local attack with Australians, a direct disregard of Haig's agreement never to employ green Americans training behind his lines in frontal attacks. Pershing had been enraged when he found out—no army ever had a commander more vitally concerned, not only with its buttons, but with its lifeblood—and the British never again broke their word. This time Haig said, "Of course you shall have them, Pershing." Then the latter went ahead with his plans for an offensive.

In Paris, the first week in September, when Eddie Rickenbacker went there on leave, even the taxi drivers told him that *les américains* were going to attack at Saint-Mihiel, and some of the rascals began to tick off the numerals of the divisions that were hastening there in the darkness.

Chapter **12**

SAINT-MIHIEL: THE BIRTH OF
AN ARMY

*It may succeed—but we must not be content with that;
for it must succeed.*

On August 30, a proud General Pershing took command of his American First Army on a forty-mile sector that bounded the Saint-Mihiel Salient, held four years by the Germans. He had sweated since 1883 for this day. There had been an over-all strategic purpose in his choice of General Headquarters and the network of communications he had built up around it. He had early declared for an American front facing the Saint-Mihiel salient, his aim being to drive into iron mines in the Briey Basin, after taking the German fortress town of Metz for a final victory in the spring of 1919.

The French generals were on hand for the change-over, clad in their dark blue coats and red breeches, making a fine courtesy of the day. They were glad to be leaving the unpleasant plain of the Woëvre with its dusty summers and swampy winters and the constant scrutiny of the German telescopes on Montsec. The chief of staff of the French Eighth Army presented Pershing with his plan for the reduction of the Saint-Mihiel salient, the size of a large telephone directory—a commentary on the techniques of trench warfare developed over the years—and his plans for defense, almost as bulky, in case the capricious Ludendorff had an offensive in mind. Pershing did not tell him that he had already issued his own plan—offense taking up eight

203

pages and defense six, the rest left to "initiative" and "individual" enterprise and improvisation.

Pershing had moved into French Army Headquarters at Ligny-en-Barrois, and when he returned from the ceremony he was immediately visited
by Marshal Foch and his alter ego, Major General Maxime Weygand.
Despite Pershing's generous gift of nine divisions—equal to about twenty
French—and Foch's agreement in principle to an American First Army, the
marshal's secret desires had not changed by so much as a single battalion. He
now presented Pershing with entirely new plans calculated to disperse the
American First Army.

The Doughboys were not to reduce the Saint-Mihiel salient. A few divisions were to execute a limited-objective attack on its south face—a minor
battle as a sop to the Iron Commander's pride. All the other Doughboy
divisions were to be split immediately into two armies, divided by the
Argonne Forest north of Verdun. One of them would be used to starch the
French Second Army, which was too limp to fight on its own, in an attack
between the Argonne Forest and the Meuse River to the east. The other
half of Pershing's forces would join in a French-American attack from
the Argonne Forest on the east to the Souain Road astride the Oise River
to the west under General Gouraud. Foch had chosen just the French
Army Group to take over the combined operation, and just the right general
—Degoutte—to take over, in the capacity of "adviser," the two widely
separated American forces. Stripped of its military malarkey, it was an order
for Pershing to give most of his 999,602 combat Doughboys to the general
whose brutal sacrifice of 150 of them on the Vesle Bullard had protested.
Again Foch was clipping off the tentacles of the octopus, ignoring its heart.

The quarrel began courteously, the way the great ones did between the
Allies and the Yanks. "Well, Marshal," said Pershing, hackles rising at the
word *Degoutte*, "this is a very sudden change."

Pershing should have reminded Foch that Woodrow Wilson had warned
all Allied embassies that the American Army would fight only as a unit—
just as Louis XVI had told George Washington the French before Yorktown must be a separate army. But acrimony grew and tempers soured,
until Foch's final "I must insist upon the arrangement" and Pershing's insolent "You may insist all you please, but I decline absolutely to agree to
your plan."

The marshal picked up his maps and papers at this remark and left the
house, his memorandum still on the table. He sweated out his exit line—
Pershing, after careful study, would agree to his plan. Foch was supplying
Pershing with all his artillery and shells, all his tanks, most of his airplanes;
and he had tried to weigh his scales with these gifts. Pershing sent him a

formal reply the next day, a mixture of the obedience a commanding general must display to a supreme commander and a refusal to give up the Dough-boys. There was no incompatibility in his position. He knew, for example, that the Canadians' Lieutenant General Sir Arthur Currie refused to split his great corps even into division piecemealing, a constant annoyance to Sir Douglas Haig, who nevertheless knew he must respect Currie's position. "In your capacity as Allied Commander in Chief, it is your province to decide the strategy of operations, and I abide by your decisions . . . how-ever, there is one thing that must not be done and that is to disperse the American forces among the Allied Armies. . . ." (Few even now realize that America was never a member of the Allies. Woodrow Wilson was so fiercely self-centered he would join with no one, not even his loyal opposition at home, in any of his dreams.)

Lord Reading, Ambassador and High Commissioner to Washington, and most adroit and deceitful of British pleaders, called on Pershing four days later at the behest of Haig to urge that the American Army move closer to Haig's forces and take part in a converging British-American attack in the classic style of Cannae, where Hannibal destroyed a Roman army, two claws meeting after seizing the German Armies in a death grip. It was un-likely, as Reading must have realized if Haig—never a strategist—did not, that even an old military booby like Hindenburg would not have been fooled by a Cannae trap. General Díaz of Italy also called and proposed that Pershing transfer two-thirds of all the troops Pershing had in France to the Italian front. To have complied would have more than somewhat depleted Pershing's forces.

The Allied quarrel continued in a series of strategy conferences and bickerings among Foch, Pétain, and Pershing. Foch argued that the French Army was exhausted and the British divisions, though still attacking with great skill and ferocity, were bled white and could sustain very few more casualties before losing their vigor. Pershing said the American Army would have 3,500,000 troops in battle by the summer of 1919 and it alone would be enough to whip the Germans into unconditional surrender. Eventually Foch compromised. When the round of quarrels was over, Pershing had accepted an undertaking as difficult as any in the whole history of war. He had contracted to reduce the Saint-Mihiel salient, with the Doughboys' First Army and a Johnny-come-lately staff, and immediately following this (abandoning the sound strategy of seizing Metz) to open an offensive in the Meuse-Argonne area for a drive on Sedan. In Pershing's word, "We had undertaken to launch, with the same army . . . two great attacks on battlefields sixty miles apart"—and within a period of two weeks.

The Woëvre Plain facing Saint-Mihiel had been an inactive sector of the line since 1915. It is hard to conceive the amount of labor required to prepare the bridges, roads, narrow-gauge railways and dumps, and transform it into an active sector. Only a captain as resolute as Pershing, with an army idealistic and fresh, could surmount the obstacles presented by the almost impossible twin missions assigned him. After back-breaking preparations were completed for the attack on Saint-Mihiel on September 12, a million tons of ammunition and supplies had to be transported sixty miles to the forts at Verdun on the inactive front extending from the Argonne Forest to the Meuse River for the next blow September 26. It meant that hundreds of thousands of the Doughboys fighting September 12 would have to hustle along three narrow roads dotted with spent and dying horses every hundred yards, moving by night and hiding in rain-soaked woods by day, fighting again at the first dawn after they reached their Argonne jump-off lines.

What opportunities there were for desertion! Yet comparatively few fled the scene. The Service of Supply, which embraced the genius of American civilization, was stripped half-naked of its matériel and manpower, of its engineers and technicians, telephone girls and linemen, railroad section gangs and bosses, chauffeurs, teamsters, hostlers, slide-rule professors, machinists, electricians, blacksmiths, cooks, doctors, and bottle-washers. Many were killed or crippled in the dark by accidents or collapsed and died of overwork, or shortened their lives. Allied Armies listed all the sick, the lame, the halt, and the dying among their service troops as casualties. Yanks did not list as casualties supply troops killed or injured behind the lines, nor sickness among combat troops beginning to be stricken with influenza. Only those felled at the hands of the organized enemy were "casualties."

No student of the Great War would fail to find Allied critics, particularly the staff hacks around war colleges, criticizing the disorder of American supply lines. Yet if there was confusion confounded in the twin mission, it was caused by rookie colonels who insisted on moving forward in staff cars; by officious majors bullying lieutenants into moving vehicles the wrong way on one-way lanes; by all the traffic jamming of a new army new to mobility on roads never seen before. Frederick Palmer, observing this chaos, thought of similar British jams along the Somme in 1916 contrasted with British perfection in their assaults August 8, 1918. Only in the field could soldiers learn logistics.

Early in September, Yanks were scattered from Switzerland to the English Channel. Two divisions were with the British near Ypres, the smell of corpses in their nostrils. Others were with the British along the

Somme. Six were on the French front between Reims and Soissons, the 77th still fighting toward the Aisne. Others had just come ashore at Brest and Cherbourg. Many were still training far behind the battle lines. Doughboys were scattered along 450 miles. Pershing managed to gather 450,000 of them to join the 110,000 French troops of the American First Army for Saint-Mihiel.

Unknown to the Allies, the Germans were preparing to pull out of the Saint-Mihiel salient by the same day scheduled for the attack, September 12. They expected the Doughboys to strike somewhere along the south face and Hindenburg wanted to shorten his lines and contract his front to thicken his last ditches of resistance while a suitable peace, giving Germany some sizable gains, could be made. The troops there were Austrians, Hungarians, Bavarians, and Saxons, who had become quite at home in restful villages with French mistresses and flaxen-haired, bilingual children. Though the Germans knew the Americans were coming, they did not, thanks to brilliant staff work and choice of route, expect 450,000 Yanks to face them so soon. There could be little surprise of place, but much of time and mass.

While preparations were moving forward for Saint-Mihiel, an elaborate ruse was put in motion. To confuse the German High Command, Major General Omar Bundy, commanding a paper-work VI Corps since he had been relieved of his 2nd Division command, was deluded into believing that he was to prepare an attack on the thirty-mile front between the Swiss border and Alsace's western face to force a passage through the Belfort Gap in the Rhine Valley beyond the Vosges Mountains. Commanders of divisions in that area were sent forward with reconnaissance parties to study terrain. As Saint-Mihiel drew closer, many became alarmed. Someone, they said, was making a tragic mistake at Chaumont; why was some idiot ordering their regiments westward toward the Woëvre Plain before Saint-Mihiel instead of eastward toward Belfort? Fox Conner, permanent G-3 for warfare movement at Chaumont, sent many new radio stations to the Belfort Gap that made the nights crackle with volumes of coded messages. The Germans began to wonder if Foch was now going to fight his Americans there. It seemed a fatuous thing to do; but fatuity had been a disease on either side for four years.

After all manner of activity, such as arranging for many poorly concealed tank tracks—made with two or three old tanks—for German aviators to photograph, Colonel A. C. Conger of the General Staff, a famous troubleshooter who sometimes led attack brigades, arrived in Belfort and engaged a room in the best hotel with a fine dash of cloak-and-dagger secrecy, preparing to light the fuse. He did nothing so obvious as to leave a "copy" of the forthcoming "operation" on his writing desk. This would not have fooled German G-2 for a moment. Instead, he chose a virgin sheet of carbon paper and made out a one-page carbon-duplicate report to Pershing on the status of the forthcoming operation. He then sent both the original and carbon copy off by courier, balled the carbon paper into a tight wad, tossed it into the waste basket, and went down to the bar for a five-minute drink. Spies, defeatists, and traitors were everywhere in Belfort, with easy access to the espionage bazaars of Geneva, and on returning to his room Conger found that his waste basket had been rifled during his five minutes' absence. He then left Belfort, but returned in a few days to explain to the duped Bundy, and the several divisions commanders, that the attack had been enlarged to embrace a *sixty*-mile front. American generals now knew that they had been the patsies of a *ruse de guerre,* but none dared say so; it could have meant Blois for them. Meanwhile, a French agent at Geneva, a gentleman named "G-78," who regularly corresponded with a German traitor, catalogued the effects of the ruse.

On the German side, villages around Altkirch were being evacuated, fortresses commanding the Rhine from Istein to Neuf-Brisach given heavier guns, Austrian artillery flooding the hinterland. The highly vulnerable Duchy of Baden was so panicked that burgomasters had to make public appeals for calmness. Munition dumps were moved rearward, hospitals evacuated, and three divisions brought in as reserves. The German Army commander said it was hard to believe the crazy Americans were going to try anything as difficult and unprofitable as forcing the Belfort Gap—but then, who could predict anything certain in the then state of *Weltpolitik?*

It was a small Doughboy joke enjoyed by four men at Chaumont, Pershing, James McAndrew, his chief of staff, Fox Conner, Conger, and by no one else in Europe, save possibly G-78 at Geneva. Surely it had given no pleasure to General Bundy, who was detached September 13, and given a one-way ticket to Blois. It had caused the German some annoyance, made him cinch his belt a little tighter; but it had not diverted his attention from Saint-Mihiel. In spite of the ruse, he had concluded that he was going to be attacked on the south face at Saint-Mihiel, and he was pulling out.

At first, Ludendorff had agreed with Lieutenant General von Fuchs's Group "C" (in General Max Carl Wilhelm von Gallwitz's Composite Army Group) that a prompt counterattack by his army around September 8 would upset the timetable. But after the British had panicked him August 8, Ludendorff was no longer in control. Hindenburg, the number of his rifles now little more than those of the Allies, and no more to be had anywhere, decided he could use his Saxons, Alsatians, Austrians, and Hungarians in

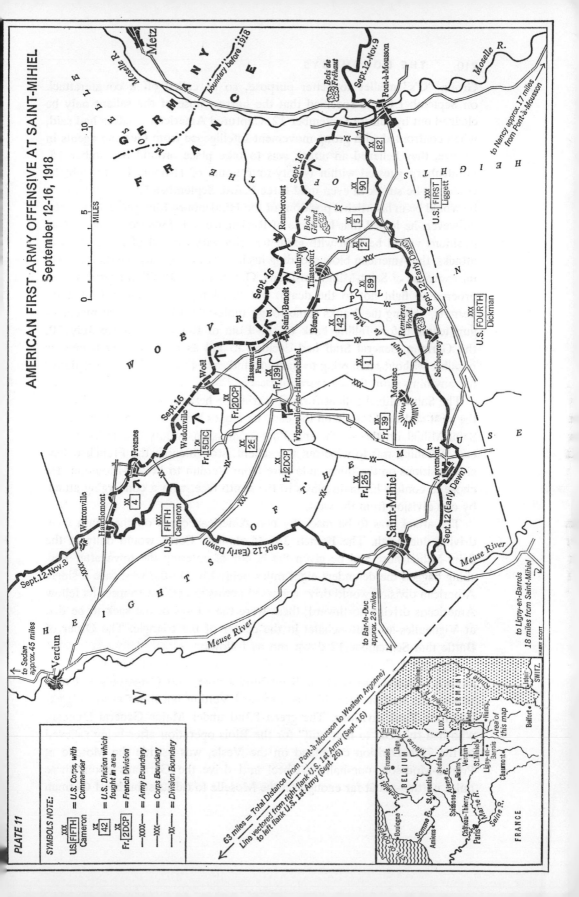

PLATE 11

AMERICAN FIRST ARMY OFFENSIVE AT SAINT-MIHIEL
September 12-16, 1918

SYMBOLS NOTE:

XXX
US|FIFTH| = U.S. Corps, with
Cameron   Commander

XX
42 = U.S. Division which
     fought in area

XX
Fr.|2DCP| = French Division

———— = Army Boundary

——— = Corps Boundary

—— = Division Boundary

63 miles = Total Distance (from Pont-à-Mousson to Western Argonne)

Line vectored from right flank U.S. 1st Army (Sept. 16)
to left flank U.S. 1st Army (Sept. 26)

HARRY SCOTT

Group "C's" medley to better purpose, so he called off a counterattack on September 8 and specified that the narrow nose of the salient only be cleaned out by sunrise September 12. Captured American aviators had said, when confronted with group movement intelligence from German agents in France, they believed an attack was to take place around September 15. Hindenburg guessed within twenty-four hours of H-hour. He thought he could not be struck in even mild force before September 13, by which time he would be in his Michel positions of the Hindenburg Line protecting Metz. However, he hoped that his Line of Resistance well forward of the Michel positions would be held with great tenacity with the aid of local counterattacks, the American blow spending itself after taking only the dangerously narrow nose of Saint-Mihiel positions. German First Position brigades were ordered to fight not to the death, but "as long as the tactical situation permits," giving the Yanks some rough molestation by sacrificial machine-gun teams before falling back to the Line of Resistance. Since July 20, the German General Staff had decided to kill as many enemy troops as possible without attempting to gain ground, and thus weaken Allied desire for anything more than a merciful peace.

The Saint-Mihiel salient formed a triangle between the Meuse River on the west and the Moselle on the east, its angles being Verdun on the north, Saint-Mihiel on the south, and Pont-à-Mousson twenty-five miles to the east. Pershing was to wipe out the salient, straightening the French defensive positions on the thirty-mile base from Verdun to Pont-à-Mousson. He chose to confine his main blows to the south face, with a converging attack by one division from the west.

The attack was to be made by two American corps on the south face, driving due north. The French 3rd (Colonial) Corps would dally at the Saint-Mihiel nose and be given the honor of entering the town after Pershing bagged the defenders eight miles behind it. On the west face a single American division would drive eastward across the salient to meet its fellow Americans driving northward; these were the strings of the sack to be tied at Vigneulles-les-Hattonchâtel in the center of the triangle. The Order of Battle that September 12 dawn ran as follows:

Liggett's I Corps was on the right, Dickman's IV on Liggett's left, a French Colonial Corps at the Saint-Mihiel nose, and Cameron's V Corps was on the western face, his back toward Verdun ten miles away. Liggett had four Yank divisions. The green 82nd under Major General Duncan, who had refused "to hold still" for the Blois operation after being relieved of the 77th Division command on the Vesle, was astride the Moselle at Pont-à-Mousson, one-half to wheel and drive the Germans about three miles north—about far enough on the Moselle to rid its suburbs of German field gun fire. The other half of the 82nd Division on the opposite bank of the Moselle would simply throw a flank block and hold. The green 90th Division on the 82nd's left would also strike northward, with about a five-mile fight to Foch's designated line. Pershing had also given Liggett another green division, the 5th, to tutor as it, too, struck for about five miles alongside and to the left of the 90th. (These divisions, of widely varying textures, would prove themselves in the Argonne.)

Liggett's trumps were the race-horse brigades of Doughboys and Marines in the 2nd Division. They were the left of his I Corps boundary, with a goal of about eight northward miles through woods which now, after Bouresches, Belleau Wood, Vaux, and Soissons, they were thoroughly qualified to exploit before reaching the town of Jaulny. The 2nd Division was fighting under its third commander, Major General John A. Lejeune of the Marines. He was a short, dark French Creole, his great-grandfather having migrated with Evangeline's people from Nova Scotia to the Bayou Teche country of Louisiana. Lejeune of Annapolis was no stranger to many on the field. He had attended the Army War College with Malin Craig. "If you make good at the college, as I am sure you will," the chief of staff had said to a younger Major Lejeune, "your future will be assured." Lejeune had booked so hard that his diploma read: "In case of a National Emergency, this officer should be given a division." Lejeune had brought two more Marine infantry regiments to France, all their men with rifleman's badges, in hopes of forming a U.S. Marine division; but these regiments were left in the mud around Brest. (It is not a part of this chronicle to enter into the question of interservice machinations.)

Dickman's new IV Corps had the green 89th on the right, to the left of Liggett's veteran 2nd Division. There was nothing green about the division in his center: it was the 42nd's ferocious Rainbows, also due to strike northward for about eight miles. On its left was Dickman's trump card, the Big Red One bound for Vigneulles-les-Hattonchâtel in the center of the salient. The French 3rd (Colonial) Corps, remaining at the tip of the Saint-Mihiel salient, with the lords on Montsec packed up and getting ready to run for it, would never have an easier assignment once the 1st, 2nd, and 42nd, and the green 5th, 82nd, 89th, and 90th began bagging von Fuchs's forward elements.

On the western face, Cameron had his V Corps of three divisions. His pivot for the left of Pershing's designated boundary at Haudiomont was given to his old 4th Division, conceived in the mud of Camp Greene and born on the Marne, and now commanded by an old 1st Division ex-colonel, Major General John L. Hines, who could have outlasted U. S. Grant in a taciturnity contest. Its task was simply a three-mile wheel north by west to push the Germans away from the hills around Haudiomont. In his center, Cameron had a poilu division which would swing along with Hines as a right-flank buffer.

Cameron's chief concern was the single division—Major General Edwards's 26th New Englanders—he must send forward due east to meet the Big Red One at Hattonchâtel and tie the strings of the sack. Its higher commanders were getting a chance to redeem themselves with troops Liggett had already admired. (He had said in his critique to Chaumont that he had nothing but praise from company level down to squad, and that its artillery was first-rate.) It was too much to expect Liggett, who had criticized the division, and Dickman, with whom General Edwards had failed to keep pace in the Château-Thierry push, would have been given the New Englanders. Their higher commanders were now something for the ascetic Cameron to worry about. And it was significant that Pershing was on the telephone to Cameron's corps after H-hour's guns roared into flame.

Both French and British had been generous. The French provided 267 light tanks, 113 of them crewed by poilus. There were 3,020 pieces of artillery of all calibers. Some of the trucks bringing up ammunition were made in Detroit, but not a gun had been fashioned by American hands. Almost half of them—1,329—had French gunners feeding French shells into the breech. Haig could not give the Yank any heavy tanks, greatest weapon of 1918, but he sent the best air arm then in being, the Independent Bombing Squadrons of the now Royal Air Force, under Major General Sir Hugh Trenchard, to plaster rear areas and matériel depots. General Pétain had sent his French Air Division, some six hundred airplanes. Together with the new Aviation Section of the U.S. Signal Corps, Pershing had (on paper) about thirteen hundred airplanes. (Trenchard's force was a strategic factor, and no tactical help.) To command the combined aerial tactical operations, the observant Pershing had found his own man. He was Colonel William Mitchell, a prophet whose head the Army's tactical toe dancers would later offer to President Coolidge on a platter.

George C. Marshall, Jr., now a chicken colonel and chief mover, recommended that artillery be in position to deliver, if necessary, a fourteen-hour bombardment. "There is no instance in this war where an attack has been made against a position as highly organized as this one without artillery preparation or the assistance of heavy tanks," he wrote to Chaumont. The British, to Pershing's chagrin, could spare him no tanks. (He had tried to buy 750 of them after 1917's Cambrai.) "To attack without heavy artillery preparation is taking a gambler's chance—it may succeed—but we must not be content with that; for it must succeed," Marshall wrote. Pershing settled for four hours' bombardment on the south face; from the standpoint of destroying enemy matériel, Marshall's fourteen would have been better. He assigned the French at the apex and the New Englanders on the west face longer periods of bombardment; they had fewer French tanks.

Saint-Mihiel presented a formidable barrier of permanent installations, rusty with broad belts of barbed wire and four years of deep dugouts. Four hours of bombardment would hardly suffice to clear them all. To topple the lords of the high ground, with the camel-back hump of Montsec, the Yanks had two innovations: giant-sized, two-handed, barbed-wire clippers of Spanish-American War vintage, and rolls of chicken wire eighteen feet in length to be thrown as footpaths over barbed wire still left pathless by a four-hour bombardment. The French were fascinated by the improvisations and Pétain sent captains and sergeants there to study them; but poilu officers said they were useful only to Doughboys, who had long legs and big feet.

Brigadier General S. D. Rockenback, USA, was tank commander that day, with mixed French and American crews in French light tanks. His staff officer was Colonel George S. Patton, Jr., who more than any other Doughboy had marveled at the tank smash at Cambrai. Somewhere in the German Armies were several young German officers who had shuddered over it—such as Reinhardt, Guderian, and Rommel. Hindenburg warned his Saxons and Austrians that troops soon to be confronted by enemy tanks should not be panic-stricken. Tanks could be dealt with if calmness prevailed. At Cambrai a German major, serving a single field piece by himself after a panic, had wrecked a tank wing before the Jocks of a Highland division got to him with the bayonet.

The Germans were on the move before dawn September 12 when the four-hour bombardment hit them and everything had to go underground. The 1st U.S. Gas Regiment had given the divisions attacking the south face forty minutes of a smoke screen, mixed with a little thermite for wooded areas, enabling all Doughboys to reach their jump-offs without molestation. By the time the bombardment lifted, Doughboys were chucking grenades into dugouts and their inhabitants were hurrying to get out with hands up. The French dallied about the nose of the salient, the exhausted Colonial Corps borrowing a regiment of three thousand rifles from the new 80th Division for stiffening. The 82nd, 89th, and 90th Divisions received their baptism in offensive warfare, the "Texas Brigade" of the 90th now led by U. G. McAlexander, who had won his star, and as usual reached his objective with the advance patrols. The 1st, 2nd, and 42nd veteran divisions for the only time in the war sustained only a few casualties. The veteran 3rd, the new 35th and 78th, the 80th less its borrowed regiment, and the 91st Divisions remained in various corps and Army reserve. The Saint-Mihiel salient was closed, victory easily won, when the 1st Division met the 26th at Hattonchâtel at sunrise September 13 after both outfits had pushed on all night. Brigadier General Cole had retained his star.

General von Fuchs was scolded for the unexpected beating his German divisions received, and though defeated in a single twenty-four hours, with Pershing master of the field on his fifty-seventh birthday, he continued feeble resistance until September 16, when Doughboys established the line Foch had outlined. Fuchs had no way of knowing Foch's intentions, though the long-range German guns around Metz would have made crossing the Moselle there a sanguinary enterprise for the Americans. Fuchs brought up another four divisions from reserve to aid the eleven there, and was shocked to learn that he had given up sixteen thousand prisoners and 450 cannon. American casualties were seven thousand, one-third of Medical Corps expectations, which had brought up sixty hospital trains in two routes and prepared fifteen thousand beds for south face casualties, and seven thousand from the Colonials for Cameron's corps. Fuchs delayed long enough to burn much matériel, and blow up some of his ammunition dumps. His counterattacks were ill-considered, it being the unfortunate privilege of his 31st Division, nine thousand strong, to try driving fifteen thousand Doughboy Regulars of the 2nd and eight thousand Marines and twenty-five thousand Rainbows from such dense places as the Bois de Rupt. Enemy wounded left on the field were put aboard their own hospital train captured at nearby Jaulny.

Saxons of the 123rd Division were brought into the Bois de Hanido on the afternoon of the first day to counterattack the next morning. Their field intelligence was good. They knew they were facing the green 5th Division and went forward in ignorance of Doughboy mettle. There were heavy casualties before the Saxons had enough. There was a bit of barbarism in some of Fuchs's acts, but the liberated French, four years after their countrymen broke off the 1914 folly of the Battle of Lorraine, said on the whole they had not been mistreated. They hardly knew there was an American Army in France. And new Doughboys discovered in their turn that *all French* women were sixty years old, and wine bottles cobwebbed from the inside.

The Doughboy was greatly beholden to the Allies for the air superiority he enjoyed by the time of Saint-Mihiel. Although the Wright Brothers had invented successful powered flight, their crass countrymen had made little of it, since there was no money in it. An aviator was looked upon as a barnstorming freak, something like a sword-swallower in a carnival. But the British, Germans, and Russians had, through various national physics foundations, extensively studied aerodynamics and the phenomenon of

Army Photographic Agency

Spring training, 1918, before the storm. Above, gas alarm at Verdun, 6th Regiment, Marines. Below, on the British front near Arras, 42nd Division troops with carrier pigeons.

National Archives

Cantigny, May 28, 1918, the first American attack. Top, the charge by the 28th Infantry, 1st Division. Center, French flame thrower in the village. Right, officers who took part: front row, left to right, Col. Hanson E. Ely, Lt. Gen. Robert L. Bullard, Maj. Campbell King; top row, Lt. Col. W. C. Sherman, Maj. R. H. Oglesby.

fter von Boehn's breakthrough on
e Chemin des Dames, May 27,
erman infantry (top) push south
ward Château-Thierry on the
larne (center), where U.S. 3rd
ivision machine gunners (right)
ver the retreating French and dig
on the south bank.

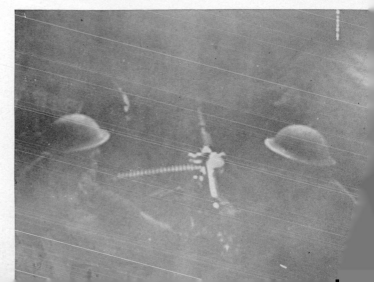

Army Photographic Agency

While the 3rd Division held the river line on the right, the U.S. 2nd Division, rushed up from Paris, took up positions in wheatfields to the left of Château-Thierry and attacked into the nightmare landscape of Belleau Wood (above), where the Germans were strongly entrenched (below). The struggle continued for three weeks before the Wood was captured by the Marine Brigade (above, right). Shortly after, the Doughboy Brigade stormed and captured the town of Vaux (below, right).

U.S. Signal Corps, National Archives

National Archives

While the 2nd Division fought to hold the left flank, behind the lines training and build-up continued. Above, the arrival of a Yank delousing machine at a French village. Below, Generals Pershing and Bullard arrive to inspect the 1st Division, now placed in support behind the defensive perimeter below the Marne. The 3rd Division, holding the river line east of Château-Thierry (opposite page), braced for von Boehn's next assault.

Army Photographic Agency

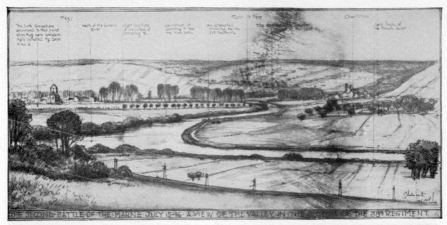

THE SECOND BATTLE OF THE MARNE · JULY 15-16 · A VIEW OF THE VALLEY IN THE SECTOR OF THE 38ᵗʰ REGIMENT

A BATTLE FIELD AT MÉZY

Aftermath of von Boehn's July 15 attack across the Marne on McAlexander's 38th Infantry Regiment positions; above, left, German dead and equipment in U.S. lines; above, right, two dead Doughboy machine gunners; below, captured German arms.

U.S. Signal Corps, National Archives

Foch's counterattack against the Marne bulge, launched July 18. Above, Germans abandoning positions near Soissons in face of the assault by 1st and 2nd divisions; below, field artillery on the move near Vaux, and (bottom) moving up from Château-Thierry.

Army Photographic Agency

U.S. Signal Corps, National Archives

Army Photographic Agency

Through August and September, Foch's assault continued. Men from the 77th Division fill canteens near the Vesle (above), advance through camouflaged German positions (below), and take a hillside (in background) near the Aisne River (bottom).

Army Photographic Agency

U.S. Signal Corps, National Archives

U.S. Signal Corps, National Archives

September 12: the first all-American Army offensive at Saint-Mihiel, supported by the "furious cadence" of its artillery (top). Above, men of the 3rd Division advance toward Montsec. Below, German front-line trenches and barbed wire.

Army Photographic Agency

U.S. Signal Corps, National Archives

The Saint-Mihiel attack rolled forward against dwindling resistance. Above, 42nd Division supply train moving up. Below, Rainbow infantrymen dig in near the Meuse River, while others rest on the battlefield (bottom). But there was little rest for the Doughboys; Pershing had committed them to a second major offensive only two weeks later and sixty miles to the northwest. This was against the Hindenburg Line in the very difficult Meuse-Argonne sector, shown on the opposite page. Top left, on the left flank, the maze of the Argonne Forest; right, in the center, a German trench on Hill 288; bottom, on the right flank, engineers struggling to repair a road in the marshes and woods near the Meuse.

U.S. Signal Corps, National Archives

Army Photographic Agency

Above, just before the attack on September 26, Doughboys of the 77th Division wait at the edge of the Argonne. Three of those shown were later killed in action. Below, later the same day, men from the 77th Division rest in a captured German trench.

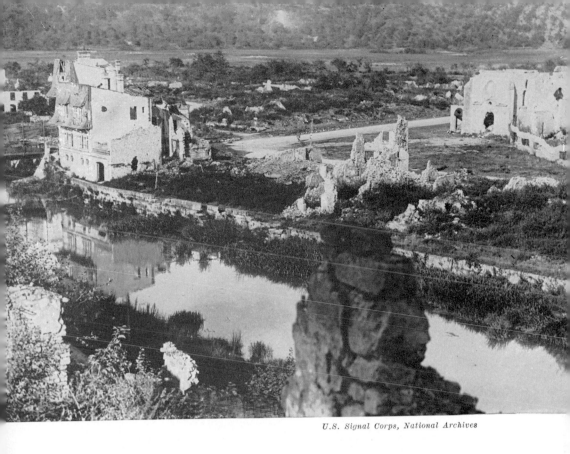

To the right of the 77th, the 28th and 35th divisions drove up the valley of the Aire River, their target Varennes (above), supported by field artillery (below, left) with their observers and spotters (below, right).

Army Photographic Agency

In the center of the American line, supply trains moved up to the front through such ruined towns as Esnes (above), while Doughboys stormed the towering hill of Montfaucon, captured September 27, and used its crest for artillery observation (left). A few days later they were marching through the town itself (opposite page, top). On the right flank near the Meuse, Doughboys slogged through the marshes of the Forges Brook (bottom, right).

U.S. Signal Corps, National Archives

Through October the advance continued all along the line: top, the attack on Hill 240, near Exermont; center, view of Cuisy, 4th Division Command Post; left, outpost on Hill 240. Opposite page, top, infantry charge, Romagne; center, some of the survivors of the "Lost Battalion," near Apremont; bottom, trench mortar battery near the Meuse.

Elsewhere on the front during October other American divisions were active. The 27th and 30th divisions supported the British in the capture of the Saint-Quentin Tunnel complex. Above, a view of the canal after capture; below, 27th Division horses at Bellicourt. Opposite page, top, entrance to tunnel; center, barges used by Germans as barracks; bottom, a short time later, the survivors were pushing on toward the Belgian border.

In the French sector to the left of the Argonne, Doughboys and Marines of the 2nd Division, supported by the 36th, stormed and captured the formidably defended heights of Blanc Mont: above, view of Essen Hook; below, looking north from Blanc Mont, the direction taken by the 36th Division. Toward the end of October, their buddies in the Argonne broke out of the forest at Mareq (opposite page, top), and pushed on to the key town of Grandpré (center). This town, strongly held by the entrenched defenders, as shown by this German machine-gun position (bottom), was captured by the 78th Division on October 27 after fierce fighting on its terraced slopes.

TO HELL
WITH THE
KAISER

The final assault of the American First Army in November met determined resistance at first, and then the Yanks broke through the Hindenburg Line and pushed on to Sedan. Opposite page, top, American trucks at Brabant-sur-Meuse; center, men of the 42nd Division rest on November 9 at the point of the farthest American advance; distant pines mark the site of the death of the leader of K Co., 166th Infantry; bottom, Doughboy entertainment interrupted by a German shell. Above, marching through Stenay; below, highest point of the Côte Saint-Germain, occupied by a smiling Doughboy after the Armistice— "Hell. You'd have thought I won the war."

U.S. Army Photograph

Some of those who won Pershing's accolade—"He is a fighter . . . a fighter . . . a fighter!"—pose with him and his staff at Chaumont. Those designated by an X are, left to right: Captain McMurtry of the "Lost Battalion"; Generals Summerall, James W. McAndrew, Chief of Staff, and Liggett; Capt. George H. Mallon, who used a right to the jaw; Generals Pershing and Bullard; Cpl. (now 2nd Lt.) Donald M. Call, tank driver at Varennes; Sgt. Johannes S. Anderson (front row), who preferred a sawed-off shotgun; Brig. Gen. Dennis Nolan (third row), Intelligence Chief; Lt. Sam Woodfill; Sgt. Sydney Gumpertz of Forges Brook fighting; Cpl. Frank T. Bart, whose short legs grew tired carrying messages.

Four who won their country's highest honor, the Medal of Honor. Above, left, Lt. Col. William (Wild Bill) Donovan; right, Sgt. Alvin C. York. Below, left, 2nd Lt. Frank Luke (posthumously); Pvt. John Joseph Kelly, USMC.

DISTINGUISHED FRIENDS . . .

Field Marshal Sir Douglas Haig

Marshal Ferdinand Foch

General Charles Mangin

General Henri Joseph Eugène Gouraud

Belgian Government Information Center

King Albert

. . . AND FOES

Belgian Government Information Center

Review of American troops, Brussels. Left to right, King Albert, Queen Elizabeth, Prince Leopold.

National Archives

General Erich Ludendorff

National Archives

General Paul von Hindenburg

SOME OUTSTANDING DOUGHBOY LEADERS

U.S. Signal Corps, National Archives

Lieutenant General Robert L. Bullard

National Archive

Major General Joseph T. Dickman

Major General Charles P. Summerall

U.S. Signal Corps, National Archives

Major General Hanson E. Ely

Major General
Ulysses Grant McAlexander

Major General John L. Hines

Lt. Col. Charles W. Whittlesey receives the Medal of Honor from Maj. Gen. Clarence Edwards on the Boston Common, December 24, 1918.

flight long before Washington diverted a few dollars from the pork barrel to examine this American phenomenon. By February, 1918, thus quite some time before Pearl Harbor, the British recognized air power as no longer an auxiliary arm but a separate force. The Royal Flying Corps had become the Royal Air Force under Hugh Trenchard, who won a great place in his country's military history.

At the beginning of the war American aviators had enlisted in the French Air Squadron, which became the Lafayette Escadrille, and some thirty-eight of them transferred to the Aviation Section of the U.S. Signal Corps after the United States entered the war. At that time America's air power consisted of the U.S. Army Signal Corps' Aviation Section—with only thirty-five men who could fly, and fifty-five planes, nearly all obsolete. American aviators were trained in France and England under French and British instructors with the help of the men from the Lafayette, and they flew French and British planes, since their own country was only beginning to produce the "Flaming Coffin" of the de Haviland 4.

The Yank airman won quicker glory than the ground soldier, thanks in part to the exploits of the Lafayette Escadrille. In other armies, they took a back seat the first two years of the war. But to Pershing the aviator was neither a freak nor a particular hero. He thought of fliers as Army officers no whit more privileged than platoon leaders dying in the shambles of a ground attack. He had asked Secretary Baker to abolish their 50 percent base-pay bonus. Baker agreed, but Congress, spellbound by spectacular feats and regarding aviators as supermen, refused.

Among the Americans who assisted at the birth of Yank air power in the sky that rainy morning at Saint-Mihiel was Second Lieutenant Roland H. Neel, aerial observer of the 99th Aero Squadron, who had, with his pilot, won the Distinguished Service Cross a month earlier for completing an observation mission and scattering an enemy infantry company around Saint-Dié after control wires had been shot away and Neel had pushed and pulled the severed cables with his hands.

On the ground beneath him east of Saint-Mihiel was his older brother, Acting Captain Joseph Neel, leading E Company of the 327th Infantry, as his 82nd Division held the pivot of the line at the Moselle River. Captain Neel had been seriously wounded that first day, but refused the battalion surgeon's invitation to retire with honors to a field hospital. Patched up and bandaged, the next morning, Friday, September 13, he led an exploratory attack of two companies to identify German reserves pouring into the stubborn "Metz group" of Hindenburg's left-flank guard, holding tenaciously, with fresh Regular troops, to their main Resistance Line. "The new troops behaved splendidly," Pershing, on the field that second day, observed.

Out of 6 officers and 252 men in Joe Neel's green company, only 2 officers and 70 men returned with their prisoners. They brought their bandaged captain back on a stretcher, a splinter of steel in his brain. A Johns Hopkins neurosurgeon could only chisel bone away to relieve brain pressure, and wait for the captain to die, which he did in Pont-à-Mousson two days later. It was beyond the Iron Commander's comprehension that Roland was ninety dollars base-pay braver than Joe. To him, all such brothers were equally valiant.

Pilots shot down in No-Man's Land or plummeted into friendly front lines were always sobered by the sight of the various private hells all were undergoing on the ground.

One of Rickenbacker's favorite pilots, a Lieutenant Sherry who, after the operetta of the day, was universally known as "Madam Sherry," had been shot down one Saint-Mihiel morning, as was his wing man, Lieutenant Nutt. Madam Sherry landed between the first and second American lines, and walked away from his wreckage unharmed. As he entered the friendly lines, a sergeant instantly shouted, "Hey, guy, where the hell's your gas mask?" After being identified, he was received with honor, and set out with some Doughboys to discover Lieutenant Nutt's fate. They found his crashed body shot through the heart. While they were digging a grave, an infiltrating sniper fired upon them. A detail set out to exterminate this ghoulish pest, and soon returned. Sherry had heard no shots from the clump of trees they had visited. Being curious about such an outlandish thing as earthbound warfare, when he started for the rear and a return to his squadron, the Madam made it a point to visit the woods. The sniper was there, his head a bloody sponge from the work of rifle butts.

Just north of Vigneulles-les-Hattonchâtel, where the Big Red One met the Yankees behind Saint-Mihiel, there was a body of water known to aviators as "Three Finger Lake," and above it the finest feat of any American aviator was performed September 18, while the Yanks were pulling out and moving along as much as sixty miles of choked roads. The performer was Lieutenant Frank Luke, the Texas Balloon Buster. If Major Raoul Lufbery from the Lafayette Escadrille was their best-loved pilot, and shrewd Rickenbacker their highest organized scorer, the Doughboys' ace of aces said that Luke was the bravest and most admired. He was an unbridled boy, as wild as a Comanche mustang when he took to the sky. Attempts to discipline him were fruitless; frequently he would land on a French field and spend the night there after some fabulous piece of recklessness, fearing he might be grounded for his impudence if he returned to his home field. His hatred of enemy balloons and of the havoc they might direct upon the Doughboys was a consuming passion. The remotest regard for his own safety was never present in Frank Luke.

Above Three Finger Lake that September morning, Luke set out alone to destroy two German gas bags. Approach was always perilous; the balloon company was surrounded by skillful machine gunners and antiaircraft cannon, often with pursuit planes ambushed in the sun. Sometimes a balloon failed to ignite because the velocity of a tracer bullet was so high it might pass through the bag harmlessly. Luke destroyed his first balloon on his first pass, and was immediately aware of three enemy aircraft hovering beyond, and waiting for him. He went for them head on, shooting down two Fokkers, while the third airplane took evasive action. When Luke turned to pursue he realized that by changing course slightly he could make a pass at the second balloon. This he made successfully, shooting it down in flames. He then pursued and destroyed the third German airplane, an A.V.G. observation craft, though six American Spads were moving on it.

He was a golden boy, with an unequaled record of fourteen victories in eight days, with five victories in eight minutes. The gods loved him; but he did not have to die young. He chose death himself after he disappeared from the sky as mysteriously as had Georges Guynemer, the consumptive youngling of fifty-six victories, who was the hero-genius of the French nation. Thin air seemed to have taken both these lads aloft to some other, and more benign, sky; but the inquisitive Captain Merian C. Cooper, armed with Frank Luke's engine number, returned from captivity after having been shot down, to discover Frank Luke's fate. He found the rusting engine, the skeleton of fuselage; and he found his friend's grave. The boy had been wounded and downed behind German lines, had leaped out and with his Colt 45 shot it out with a patrol seeking to take him prisoner, standing at bay and dying with his boots on, Texas style, taking others with him to eternity.

Historians rightly looked upon Saint-Mihiel not as a difficult victory, but as a skillful surprise of mass. Strategically, it was a great boon to Foch, a tremendous gain. Pursuit was engineered by troops who showed uncommon resources with so little experience, and the staff work of such a new army was surprisingly good. However, the Iron Commander, finger always on the French pulse, thought then, and all his long, useful life, that Saint-Mihiel was the strategic jolt that revived French morale—more than the stand at the Marne, or the far more bloody courage under French commanders on the Vesle and the Aisne, or Haig's great smash. After the initial Marne stand, there was scant mention of Americans in the French press. But Saint-Mihiel had been a four-year anguish. President Poincaré made the headlines prominently when he returned to his native heath.

The green Doughboy divisions were elated by their easy success; some of their staff officers were soon to suffer from overconfidence when they plunged the Doughboys into Argonne's lunar landscapes, where the enemy had no thought of withdrawal, or of anything but savagery from the last machine gunner. But after Saint-Mihiel fell, there were showers of congratulations to the Doughboys from the mannerly Haig, the half-convinced Foch, and the elated Woodrow Wilson; from the self-effacing Newton Baker present on the field that day trying to look like some hand-me-down civilian typist unaccountably peering over parapets at fighting men. "He scorned being treated like a guest," the commanding general reported.

Even the Tiger of France came up to Saint-Mihiel to offer congratulations, though angered because the Iron Commander put him under escort lest he stray too near the front. The 2nd Division's field artillery was still trading punches with Fuchs's gunners beyond Thiaucourt where the Tiger wanted to go. As a war leader, Gonfalon of France, Clemenceau was not expendable. Not so the gentle M. and Mme. Raymond Poincaré. They were permitted to visit their modest home near Saint-Mihiel, to find it a mass of rubble blown to bits by vindictive German gunners before they were captured. Diarists recorded that the French President, looking at the shards of his residence, simply said, *"C'est la guerre,"* and turned away dry-eyed.

Poincaré had recently awarded Pershing the Legion of Honor—the pie plate size—and had had difficulty bestowing the accolade of a kiss on each cheek. The Iron Commander stood six feet tall in his boots. M. Poincaré was five-feet-four in his pointed shoes. The ex-plowboy from Missouri cornfields was more embarrassed by the muffled guffaws of his staff than by the kisses he stooped to receive.

It was possible that Poincaré's attitude when he saw the cruel wreck of his home with its fine view of the Woëvre more than anything else in France moved the man from Missouri to tear the Germans to pieces. He recalled that two Doughboy gunners, sight-seeing, came up to them. Pershing formally presented them to the President of the French Republic; and the two buck privates then chummed along, crashing the high-brass party. M. Poincaré and his lady exchanged amused glances at this gaucherie, enjoying it amidst the wreckage of their home. Meanwhile, General Pétain, entering Saint-Mihiel, made a speech to local sashes, saying that its freedom had been the gift of *les américains*. Never was there greater *entente cordiale* among Allies and Americans anywhere. Foch and Pershing were unswerving in their conflicting resolutions, and Clemenceau was mercurial. Favorable winds could shift.

Meanwhile, the four original Doughboy divisions, the 1st, 2nd, 26th, and 42nd, were deep into the center of the Germans, eager to loot the German stores at Metz, which could have been theirs if the Iron Commander had been insubordinate enough to throw Foch's *"Tout le monde à la bataille"* out of plumb. The 3rd Division's famous Marne boys were in reserve. The Iron Commander, who had spent a year preparing to besiege Metz, said "the temptation was very great" to exploit the confusion of the shocked Germans in their disorder of September 13-16; but he had given his word to reach Sedan through the desperate Argonne-Meuse sector, the heights on the east bank of the Meuse, sixty miles away. Thus Saint-Mihiel became one of the great "ifs" of American history, a truly great one for hindsight strategists. Sleepless German Reservists, believing Foch to be a better general than that, wondered why the Yanks did not overwhelm them. To have forced Hindenburg to shift sixty miles east to defend Metz would have critically strained his lateral ganglia, forcing him to take many divisions away from Haig's pressure on his main railway running toward the Sedan-Mézières complex, his principal artery of withdrawal for a stand on German soil.

But the Paris-Nancy railroad was French again, affording the lateral movement the marshal's "tentacles" strategy must now employ. He could bide his time to enter the cathedral at Sedan where Roman Catholic priests would for once sing the Marseillaise, and Foch could at last find time to weep for his only son, dead in his lieutenant's uniform since 1914's Meuse.

Offensive, Second Phase

Chapter 13

MEUSE-ARGONNE: END IN SIGHT

The French gunners looked on smiling, as a middle-aged woman smiles over the enthusiasm of the debutante.

It wasn't a safe place for an out-of-work blacksmith.

In September 25's night sky above the Argonne Forest, a German aviator cut his engine and listened, gliding silently just above treetop level. He could see no lights below, but he could hear the bellow of mule skinners, the shouts of file-closers, the racket of light tank engines, and the crashing of truck gears. In daylight, there would have been little to photograph, but there was no mistaking the bedlam. *The Yanks were coming* —how many he could not discern, but perhaps his generals in their bombproofs at noon the next day knew there would soon be a million of them. His Fatherland could muster, in the final count, only about 450,000 combat troops to oppose them.

After losing the bastion of Saint-Mihiel, the Germans knew they were in a serious position. "We have suffered a severe defeat," Hindenburg scolded the unhappy commander of the German Composite Army Group "C," General von Gallwitz, who had fought on four fronts as Ludendorff's general utility man and had no great regard for Hindenburg's talents. "It has rendered the situation of the Group of Armies critical," Hindenburg continued. "I refuse to believe that two German divisions are not a match for an American division," adding that wherever German lines had been prepared for last-ditch resistance, American troops had been driven back in bloody

223

repulses. Perhaps Hindenburg—who was never very bright—was deluded into believing that Foch's termination of the Château-Thierry counterstroke at the Aisne River had been due to German defensive postures.

But it was soon to be a matter of last-ditch resistance, and the Germans were beginning to think of a peace based on Woodrow Wilson's Fourteen Points, a pattern of great nobility destined to go the way of most such appeals to the best in the nature of man. Just why the Germans, who never kept a covenant, should expect their enemies to hold the Fourteen Points inviolate was not a matter for German troops to ponder. Their orders were to hold the Hindenburg Line of the Argonne-Meuse sector, in the original German line of defense that reached from the North Sea to the Vosges Mountains, a network of barbed wire, trenches, machine-gun emplacements, and concrete shelters averaging seven miles in depth. It guarded the vital chain of the east-west railway whose most vulnerable link passed north to south between Mézières and Sedan, with their surrounding communication centers. Haig was clawing at the German's right flank in northern France; there they could fall back through thirty miles of mine-field desolation. But if the railroad center of Sedan was captured, the Germans would have no broad way of getting back to the Rhine for a last-ditch stand until a peace could be achieved, for the winter trails of the Ardennes Mountains were not easily passable.

Having vetoed Pershing's suggestion to continue the Saint-Mihiel attack northeast to Metz in favor of making Sedan the next goal, Foch at least—for once—gave him his choice of routes. Sedan was the apex of a triangle whose longer left side ran down to Reims in the west, whose right side followed the Meuse to Verdun in the southeast, and whose base was the Reims-Verdun front line. Thus the shortest route to Sedan, though still forty miles away, ran due north from where the front-line Reims-Verdun base crossed the north-flowing Aisne and Aire rivers, with the Argonne Forest between them.

Pershing's two choices were to attack over the valley of the Aire, with the Argonne his left flank; or he could shift westward and go forward through the valley of the Aisne with the Argonne on his right. Pershing chose the former, giving birth to an American legend—the Argonne Forest—which actually played only a flanking role, albeit a ferocious one, in what is known officially as the Meuse-Argonne operation, involving three great battles. His preference for the Meuse-Argonne front had originally been his idea, anyway, because the Doughboys were a fresh, muscular team and he was certain they could succeed over what was deemed more difficult terrain. (It is worth a conjecture that he also chose it because, between two great natural bastions, he thought he would be free of French staff meddling.

If so, events would soon prove he was pursuing a fallacy.) Actually, either side of the forest was equally forbidding; the French Fourth Army, which inherited the Aisne, and the U.S. 2nd Division, which fought on both fronts, would dispute any claim to the difficulty of one front over another down to the last platoon leader. And the German losers later said that either side of the forest was equally forbidding.

The first obstacle was the country itself. The forest was ten miles of jungle growth, rocky slopes, cliffs, ravines, innumerable brooks, its terrain shell-holed like the moon.

The course of the Aire River, twisting north till it turned left to join the Aisne after it outflanked the Argonne Forest below Grandpré, was just as difficult as the forest, with the extra hazard of open spaces offering no cover to the attackers. In addition, the Germans had had four years to prepare defenses, and they had gone at it with Teutonic thoroughness. The First Position was mainly barbed wire and sacrificial machine-gun units. Three miles behind it was the Intermediate Position, cannoned and fortified in depth from the Aisne River in the west to the fort on the heights of the Meuse.

Behind this outlying complex was the first of the three main Hindenburg barriers—the Giselher Stellung, with the hill of Montfaucon at the grim center of a promontory from which the Hohenzollern Crown Prince, in the safety of a bombproof, had watched the agony of one million men at Verdun in 1916, over half of them killed or wounded. Behind Montfaucon, five miles to the rear, were the whalebacks of the Romagne Heights—the second great barrier, the Kriemhilde Stellung, strongest natural line in France. Five miles back of those heights were the bristling eminences around Buzancy, the last-ditch barrier, the Freya Stellung. The Germans had named their three strong barriers after Wagnerian witches. ("What bitches they were," the Doughboys said later. "Every goddam German there who didn't have a machine gun had a cannon.")

While the roads had been permitted to fall into decay by a nation restricted in its access to oil and rubber, there was efficient transport on narrow-gauge railroads capable of shuttling guns and troops from one vantage to another, their toy locomotives burning coal from the Saar Basin. The defenders were able to wage almost push-button warfare; every road, bridge, and turn of the Aire's steep banks, ravines and cliffs, was registered exactly for lethal fire from three directions.

The first-ditch defenders themselves were mainly sedentary fellows, some men in the forty-year bracket, not like the youthful lads bled by the deathless British along the Somme. They had built comfortable dugouts and bombproofs; they had libraries and clubhouses. They were four-year professionals, their old skills habitual, and they would react more testily and cruelly to any attack than the younger generation whose mistakes at Amiens, Soissons, and Saint-Mihiel they freely criticized. They had inflicted shocking losses on the French poilu when the latter had attempted to dislodge them in 1915, and it was inconceivable to them that any new troops would so much as attempt to breach the first broad belts of rusty barbed wire now hidden in nature's undergrowth. They did not suspect the ardor of the amateurs about to attack them, even if they had heard of their valor; and their commanders, as Hindenburg's scolding of von Gallwitz proved, had not absorbed the lessons of their recent defeats. However, the German, secure in his four-year fastness between the Argonne and Verdun, knew better than any Doughboy the amount of effort it would take to dislodge him.

Preparation for the assault, unlike the long-considered, careful build-ups in a later war, was a matter of two weeks of frantic improvisation following the capture of Saint-Mihiel, sixty miles away. Troops and supplies began moving up by night over roads already drenched by fall rains, the newest and greenest divisions nearest the new front arriving first. Fox Conner at Chaumont, corps chiefs of staff like Malin Craig, and G-3s like George C. Marshall, Jr., had little choice in placing the divisions on any particular sector of the line. It was a matter of expedition effected in part by amateurs; whatever division was nearest a certain gap of the front was moved there by the closest available route at top speed under the rain-soaked blanket of night, a great movement rushing to achieve surprise of time, position, and mass. The result was bewildering to the Germans, and strengthened their self-confidence, for the Doughboy prisoners they captured during a few exploratory raids on the early arrivals on their right September 25 were mostly ignorant replacements who did not know the names of their colonels and had even lost track of time. If the Marines had confused Lieutenant von Buy in June with their ignorance of the United States Army and the names of the towns they had passed through, the average Doughboy prisoner captured in the wee hours of September 26 was enough to drive a Heinie Intelligence officer out of his mind.

Moving up the vital support for the infantry that would soon plunge into the tangle of undergrowth and barbed wire was perhaps the biggest undertaking of all under the impromptu circumstances. There were 3,980 guns of all calibers that had to be in place by September 25, the French crewing 1,464 of them, plus 40,000 tons of shells. Once they began firing, fourteen trainloads of shells must feed them daily from twenty-four ammunition depots established at nineteen railheads. The quartermaster needed nine more depots, the engineers demanded twelve for supplies, eight for water carts. Chemical Warfare required six. Trucks were going to transport 428,-000 Doughboys, twenty thousand at a time for an average haul of forty-eight miles, and these would need nine depots for gasoline and oil. Forage must come up for ninety thousand animals. Priority had to be given surgeons, who would need thirty-four evacuation hospitals. And greatest of all tasks for engineers was the rebuilding of the 164 miles of light railways out of the existing 215 miles. They needed to build only twelve miles of standard railways, and reconstruct some sixty-five miles of track. The greatest deficiency was in observation balloons. (Washington had sent none of these vulnerable bags since July.) As usual, Pershing said, we "had to sponge off the French."

In addition, Pershing was going to be without the services of three of his best divisions and another untested one. The 27th and 30th Divisions would never know the name Argonne; they were with Haig in the north, who had in mind just the spot for them at Saint-Quentin. Pétain had his eye on the other two divisions, the 2nd and the recently arrived 76th. Their assignment was formidable; a pillboxed massif behind the mutilated towers of the Reims Cathedral. Later, Pershing would lose two more divisions diverted to King Albert of the Belgians to help him break the Scheldt River line in distant Flanders.

From September 20 on, the American First Army, minus these 100,000 men, moved north and took over a stretch of front that extended over seventy-two miles, from the village of Beaumont northeast of Verdun in the east, to La Harazée on the French right flank at Binarville, La Harazée being an insignificant village halfway up the Argonne Forest in the west. The over-all plan was for the French corps on the eastern part of the line from Beaumont to the Meuse to hold by patrol actions, while in the west, 225,000 Doughboys in three full corps—each corps with three divisions—were to push north on a twenty-five-mile front. At the same time the French were to attack west of the Argonne in the Aisne Valley, and the British in the north were to drive east toward Valenciennes. It was, as usual, Foch's favorite plan—*"tout le monde à la bataille"*—and the over-all strategy was to close all the gateways to France, leaving the Germans without an avenue of retreat.

Colonel T. Bentley Mott, Pershing's old West Point classmate and the Doughboys' official representative at Supreme Command in the deserted town of Bombon, has left an unforgettable impression of Foch, the doughty Celtiberian, on the eve of this historic moment. Taking a constitutional through the silent streets, Mott came upon Foch returning from daily mass. His gilt-encrusted cap was cocked over his right ear, his back ramrod stiff, his artilleryman's barrel-stave legs fairly prancing as he walked along swinging his stick, invigorated by his Communion with Christ. Foch was a man of few words, unless in a heated argument. As Mott braced and saluted the most famous Allied soldier in the world, arbiter of Doughboy destiny, the marshal stopped and eyed him. Mott knew that being stared at by Foch was an invitation to speak. The colonel fumbled up something about how things were going rather well, weren't they? Foch's reply was pantomime, and prophetic. He seized Mott's belt with his left hand, dug a right fist into Mott's rib, then clipped him with a cross to the chin, and then a blow on the ear. Having demonstrated his victory combinations, the old fighter cock-a-hooped on without a word, carrying his stick at shoulder-arms.

Before dawn on September 26, Captain Eddie Rickenbacker took off on a sortie toward Dun-sur-Meuse. As he flew north through the blackness over the front lines, he looked down and saw flashes that reminded him of a switchboard in a giant telephone exchange, an aerial witness to the great artillery bombardment and the opening moments of the Meuse-Argonne offensive. Later he shot down a balloon in honor of his friend, the late Frank Luke, and returned the way he had come. Now it was after five-thirty in the morning, H-hour for the infantry, and when he looked down in the light of dawn he could see through the haze some ants swarming on gunned molehills. Having lived close to fiery death in the sky, Rickenbacker wondered why those ants on the ground "did not go absolutely mad with terror."

Had Rickenbacker had X-ray eyes able to pierce the concealing verdure of the forest, the smoke and haze created by four thousand guns, he would have had a magnificent bird's-eye view of American dispositions and the outcome of the first hours of that first day. He could have seen the left wing of Liggett's I Corps assigned to the American left flank beginning its attack in the depths of the Argonne Forest, hidden from the Germans until its forward patrols came into the sight rings of Spandau machine guns. Liggett's left hand was the 77th "Times Square" Division, fresh from Boehn's lessons north of the Vesle. His center was the 28th's Pennsylvanians under the erstwhile platoon leader, General Muir; only one-third of the 28th was masked by Argonne's trees, the other two-thirds were being gunned from left, center, and right as they fought their way toward the cliffs of Le Chêne Tondu, a forest promontory that pointed a rocky finger eastward toward Montfaucon. Liggett's right flank was new to war, the 35th Division of Kansas and Missouri National Guard whose carriage and jovial humor Pershing had admired. No Yank division anywhere ever had a rougher

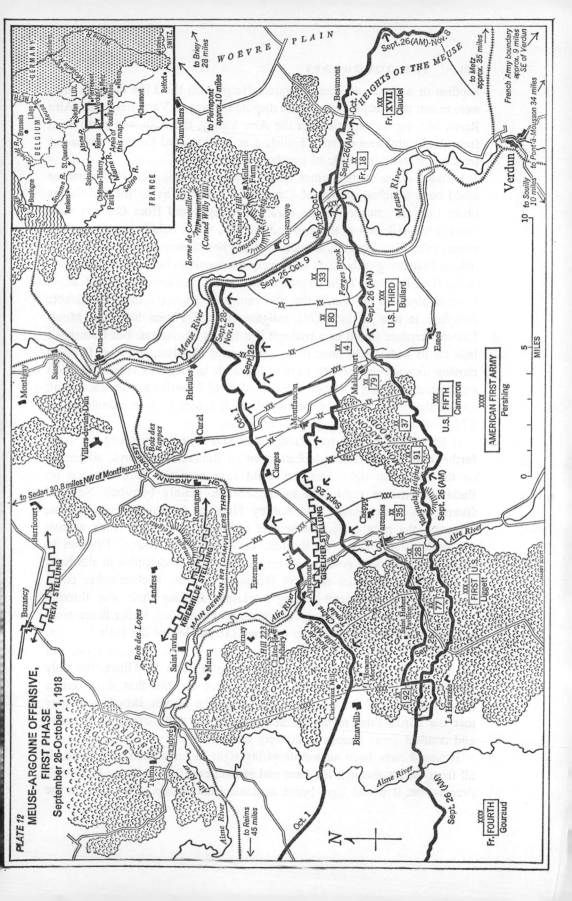

PLATE 12

MEUSE-ARGONNE OFFENSIVE,
FIRST PHASE
September 26-October 1, 1918

baptism or assignment—the Vauquois Heights on the Line of Resistance were meant to be held at all costs to dispute the way to Varennes on the Aire River. Moving forward through the Aire Valley, the 35th was easily seen from the heights and speedily punished as it scrambled through a maze of trenches as awry as a pile of toppled jackstraws.

Looking down on the center of the twenty-five-mile line, Rickenbacker could have watched groups of Cameron's V Corps as its three divisions broke through chicanes in the wire and disappeared from German view into the five-mile belt of saplings and thickets, thinly held by surviving Germans in the First Position. Cameron's Doughboys were mainly draftees, its officers Plattsburg enthusiasts and ninety-day wonders held together by wonderful West Pointers. Their target for the first day was towering Montfaucon, German since 1914, dominating the center of Europe's most formidable complex. It was an incredible assignment, and Pétain had said Montfaucon's capture would be a triumph if it fell by Christmas. But Cameron's lads set to with a will born of ignorance and idealism, the 91st Division moving forward on the left, next to the 35th in Liggett's corps, the 79th on the right, hoping to pinch the defenders of Montfaucon on each flank so that they might be compelled to fall back before a direct assault by the 37th National Guard Division in the center.

If Rickenbacker had had enough fuel and time to fly along the front farther east, he could have looked down on Bullard's III Corps, advancing on the American right. Here he could have seen the 33rd Division on Bullard's extreme right next to the Meuse, mainly corn-belt National Guardsmen from Illinois, blooded by Haig in August around Amiens, executing the only perfect movement of the day: a flank block against the banks of the river. To the left, the 80th "Blue Ridge" Division in Bullard's center was given as its target the town of Brieulles in the bend of the Meuse six miles north of the jump-off line. Rickenbacker could have watched its squirrel-hunting marksmen fighting their way through woods and marshes, wheeling right once past the 33rd, under fierce artillery fire from the heights across the river. To the left of the 80th Division, and next to the 79th in Cameron's V Corps, was Cameron's old 4th Division, now commanded by Major General John L. Hines, the only Regulars in line that morning. Their orders for the first day were a straight thrust and then a right turn across the Forges Brook until they met the 33rd's lines along the Meuse, with the 80th expected to retire and conduct some lessons in artillery liaison.

It would have been an awe-inspiring sight to have been able to see it all from the air through the haze and ground cover—a military historian's dream—but it would have borne no more relationship to the hell on the ground than Rickenbacker's switchboards, molehills, and ants bore to death-dealing artillery, hills bristling with machine guns, and the agony of flesh and blood.

The Germans, more annoyed than astonished when the four thousand guns began their roar in the darkness, had promptly gone underground, taking their newspapers, scientific journals, calabash pipes, and knitting needles with them. When in the dawn the shelling ceased and the first Doughboy began clawing at the first strands of wire, they were ready to meet him with all their accomplished deviltry, and each to fight like a cornered rat. The only consolation, as Hunter Liggett remarked, was that in such a situation the odds were always on the cat.

On the right, while Pershing's French corps menaced the German line east of the river, the 33rd Division pushed through the marshes of the Forges Brook, a nightmare of marshland, brooks, creeks, patches of high woods, bald stretches black with the stumps of slaughtered trees, pocked with shell holes the size of boxcars. The two years' undergrowth since the French attacked was laced with trenches behind belts of rusty barbed wire, here and there new pieces of wire glinting blue in the underbrush where the Germans continually added defense touches to their positions. Even if the Yanks crossed the first belt of wire, the Line of Resistance fronting the first Wagnerian Stellung was not to be relinquished under any conditions. The Germans had reckoned on everything save the youth, virility, and morale of the newcomers, three items listed as tangible assets in the ledger of war. The 33rd Division's infantry was through the belts by nine o'clock; then it wheeled ninety degrees right and attacked the banks of the Meuse.

Illinois men reached their fixed positions by noon, after falling upon the enemy in the Forges Woods in two claws. In the marshes, Doughboys sloughed through slime up to their ammunition belts; but mud was nothing new to lads from Cairo, "Little Egypt" of Illinois. By nightfall they had around fifteen hundred prisoners with all their arms and supplies, one piece of booty a narrow-gauge railway with cheeping locomotive and supply depots, delighting screwdriver mechanics and railroad buffs. They had suffered less than 50 killed and 250 wounded. No other outfit ever catalogued one day's fighting with such thoroughness. No other ever had time.

Mist clung so heavily to the Forges Brook that Captain George H. Mallon, moving on his timetable, could see only nine of his men that morning when he reached the first belt of wood. Mallon was a giant of a man with a bristling mustache, who could eat a six-pound porterhouse for breakfast—one of those human beings fortunate enough in middle years to retain the vigor and audacity of youth. He knew all others of his loyal company were moving forward. (The 33rd listed not a single man unaccounted for at the end of the day, a record in any war on earth.) And so Mallon with his nine picked up nine machine guns; one German gunner held out until Mallon, his pistol emptied, knocked the defender cold with a right to the jaw. Then they collected an antiaircraft gun of 110-caliber, and closed on the rear of a battery of 150 howitzers, taking all four with their astonished crews; none of the nine Doughboys was wounded in the exploit.

First Sergeant Sydney G. Gumpertz and others like him also kept to the timetable. When Gumpertz found his platoon checked by a stubborn gun, he took two men and jumped it. His buddies fell at the gun's muzzle but their topkick disposed in one way or another of its nine defenders. The 33rd's maneuver had been copybook style, flawless in its deportment. The division held the banks of the Meuse, and for a few days, aside from some bolstering operations, led a life under incessant shellfire and gas which other divisions might have considered idyllic in Argonne fighting. On its right across the Meuse was the great bastion of the Borne de Cornouiller. Pershing's French corps across the river, whose spirit would eventually need to be starched by three American divisions, was still weeks from reaching its concrete houses, its heavy guns.

One man's feast was another man's famine, as the Doughboys of the Blue Ridge Division were finding out as they plunged forward to the left of the men from Illinois, their target Brieulles on the Meuse River six miles north.

Some of the men of the 80th had to learn their three R's in training camp—"I done learned to write," said one of them, dictating a letter home to a Red Cross worker, "but I ain't learned yet to read what I wrote"— but few of them needed instruction in the use of the rifle, their prime weapon that September morning. After the 80th wheeled right toward Brieulles beyond the 33rd Division, they faced a beaten zone of lethal density across flat marshes as formidable as any Doughboys ever encountered. They had never known a day's rehearsal with artillery, which was now perplexed by the impassable marshes and rivulets of the extension of Forges Brook flowing toward Brieulles. Possum-hunting infantry was in the first belt of woods by noon, and the timetable called for it to attack again at three o'clock. Behind them, gunners brought up a few pieces of artillery over roads which engineers had improvised by filling thousands of sandbags by hand, dragging guns over sagging spots, hazing horses, swearing great oaths.

Staff was now learning that transport over muddy terrain where make-shift roads took pretzel turns around giant shellholes rarely went according to slide-rule plans. The British might have told them about the mud of Flanders, but a mere twenty-foot eminence in the Flemish landscape was a great prize. In the Argonne the great hills and whalebacks looked down upon them naked in the vale. The Blue Ridge men, "the last division in the Confederate Army," went along at three o'clock mainly with their rifles, woods echoing with yells which, their grandfathers said, could even move Stonewall Jackson's phlegmatic horse, Little Sorrel, to a gallop. However, by noon the German had perceived that he was being attacked in great mass. He proposed in classic style to prevent the enemy from advancing on his flanks. This would pinch the American progress in the Montfaucon center into a narrow salient which would be pounded to extinction from both sides.

The German had ideal positions to implement this posture. From the Consenvoye Heights east of the Meuse to lofty Montfaucon in the Dough-boy center, and Le Chêne Tondu to the west, his signals flashed from hill to hill. The riflemen of the 80th made five miles before facing a mile of gunned marshes, targets for the flanking Consenvoye Heights, and the gunners north of the Borne de Cornouiller—"Corned Willy Hill"—also east of the Meuse, who shelled 200,000 Doughboys in the Meuse-Argonne operation. The Germans in Brieulles, reinforced by units which scattered to avoid being bagged by the Illinois Guardsmen, were holding the bridges of the Meuse and the railroad that ran eastward to Damvillers. By nightfall, German gunners pouring in by rail were eager to turn their marshes into carpets of blood and khaki, but Bullard would have none of it. He halted his advance to exploit a better line, and the riflemen of the 80th were three days facing Brieulles marshes before Bullard diverted them, every squad sniped at, not by riflemen, but by heavy guns across their flanks and the sizzling 77s facing them.

Much had been learned about machine guns in the last summer. Now Yanks were being introduced to persecution by cannon crossfire in the kind of exchange the region had known between Montfaucon and l'Homme Mort in Verdun's 1916 days. It was a tribute to their woodsmanship that their casualties were only around a thousand men, and that they had nearly that number of prisoners when they finally faced the impassable marshes fronting Brieulles. They had accounted for nameless gray-backed Germans shot down in the woods, some as snipers in trees, where Blue Ridge boys would have considered a gray squirrel a good-sized target. There were disputes among claimants to a sniper's finger ring when he fell to earth from his sylvan perch.

The 80th's artillery had been assigned to the 4th, pushing forward on the left, third of the trio in Bullard's corps pivoting on Verdun that morning. It had to fight for each foot of ground the moment the First Army's heavy guns left off and the French 75s dropped their screaming curtain ahead of them. Enemy outposts quickened the air with the chatter of machine guns as khaki groups came out of the smoke. The target of its advance was to its right and away from Montfaucon, then a right turn to meet the 33rd along the Meuse. As each squad emerged from mists, it could be seen from Montfaucon, for the country was mainly treeless here. Targets which frontal German gunners there could not reach were assigned to flanking guns on lesser hills and bosks. Bullard counted only five thousand enemy shells sent them that first day. During the night the German moved his guns up. He multiplied five thousand by thirteen on the next day, so fluid was his system of support. The night of the twenty-sixth, he also sent up frantic units of enemy infantry and machine gunners to dispute every shell hole and half-vanished village. The 4th Division, latchstring of the gate Bullard was to swing from his hinge at Verdun, was going to be denied if humanly possible its attempt to join the men of Illinois on the banks of the Meuse. Tactics were easily read in such situations.

(Pershing's tactics in this first assault were going to be called obsolescent; of course they were, for his country had gone to war in Mr. Wilson's obsolete way, and Black Jack had no heavy tanks which his planner, George C. Marshall, Jr., had said were indispensable for a swift victory. Perhaps this first Argonne day, as much as anything that happened to five-star Marshall in a later war, led him to end his final report to the War Department with the 1945 conclusion: "We have tried since the birth of our nation to promote our love of peace by a display of weakness. This course has failed us utterly.")

The 4th Division proceeded to advance five miles the first day, breaking through the Line of Resistance protecting the first Stellung of the Hindenburg positions. Whatever Palmer's famous judgment of Regular officers—and he thought the National Guard and Reserve officers were four-to-one superior as battalion commanders (after culling the unfit), when military experience joined with the liberal arts education, their competitive lives—there were few narrow-minded Regulars left in the outfit Cameron turned over to Hines. This general, a Marine officer among them said, "ran a hell of a tight ship." Only the quick termination of the war saved some passed-over Regular colonels from serving under brigadiers who had spent their lives in law courts, countinghouses, and sales offices;

though the Regulars that Pershing finally screened into higher commands, —after sacking the narrow-minded—were superior to all other officers.

In the center of the twenty-five-mile line, all three of the divisions in Cameron's corps, the 79th on the right, the 37th in the center, and the 91st on the left, jumped off at five-thirty to see if they could capture Montfaucon in a single day.

The 79th Division was not in happy circumstances, for it had to share a single road with the 4th Division on its right, made by the 4th Engineers with forty thousand sandbags filled during the day under shellfire. It could not begin to accommodate the flow of traffic needed to feed ammunition and supplies and to evacuate wounded across brooks and shell holes for the two divisions, a body of fifty thousand men. (Hines knew in advance he would have to build his own road; to have asked Chaumont to build one might bring down a swarm of Parkinson's Law practitioners and there would have been no road.) Yet the 79th plunged into the five-mile belt of Montfaucon Woods facing Cameron's outfits to carry out its assignment to pinch the east flank of the towering fortress, while the 91st Division invested its west flank and the 37th assaulted it frontally. It was a sound pattern for attacking a strong point, whether machine gun or fortress. French troops had walked into Saint-Mihiel virtually unmolested when the New Englanders met the Big Red One at Vigneulles-les-Hattonchâtel behind the town. The Germans had no notion of agreeing to the same plan by permitting the 79th and the 91st to pull the strings of a sack behind them. They hoped to arrest all progress in the Montfaucon Woods. Von Conta at Fère-en-Tardenois had cautioned his divisions around Château-Thierry to give up no woods to Americans. It would make a bad impression on the troops.

The 37th Division, Tidewater lads from Maryland and Virginia, went forward to the left of the 79th that September 26, thrusting through the five miles of woods, committing all its infantry and hoping some of its guns could be up in time. By nightfall, its Doughboys crouched beneath the mountain's frowning guns, men dug into the sides of ravines, seeking any protection from all-night shelling by an enemy who had four years to plot every road and every gully on his maps. Ears were pricked for the ker-plop of green-cross shells carrying phosgene gas, a toxic projectile the Germans first introduced to French batteries at Verdun in 1916, almost winning a war when wheezing gunners could not read the markings on fuse settings. The rainy blackness was illuminated by the glare of bursting shells that revealed Doughboys struggling like pack mules under shoulder-loads of food and cartridges, here and there some hardy mess sergeant wrestling with his rolling kitchens among some artillery moving up, hoping to give his rain-soaked buddies, all 25,000 of them without blankets, enough hot coffee to ward off almost inevitable diarrhea.

At dawn on September 27, surviving riflemen were moving hungrily up Montfaucon's steep slope, but it was noon before their patrols were in the outskirts of the town, followed by patrols from the 79th on their right. The first arrivals were impressed by a house in the shattered center of the main street. Under its peaked roof was a powerful telescope in a cylinder of concrete with walls eight feet thick, property of Crown Prince Friedrich Wilhelm of Germany. Cameron, soon on the scene, bitterly regretted that he had not been able to peer through it the evening before. The achievement of the three divisions capturing Montfaucon in two days was tremendous. The work of the 37th alone disabused Hindenburg of his fallacy; two German divisions were not a match for a U.S. division, however formidably the Germans were emplaced!

Among those not able to peer through the telescope that second noon was Colonel George S. Patton, Jr., who had been given the honor of leading the 1st Tank Brigade—light French machines—in the frontal assault on Montfaucon. Toward the close of the previous day, the authors of *The West Point Atlas of American Wars* note in their dispassionate way, most of his tanks were used up; these little beetles were priority targets for Montfaucon gunners. Patton's leading tank being disabled, as were most others around him, the Germans now had their first sight—other than those in Hollywood films—of a bonafide two-gun man, the barrels of his ivory-handled pistols shiny in the afternoon sun, even though Patton was not in William S. Hart's faded homespun. He preferred glossy cavalry boots, a gleaming buckle on a Sam Browne belt, and buttons brassed to a high luster. While he was averse to walking, it was the only way to reach some German machine guns; and so he collected scattered drivers and their crews and anybody else thereabouts, descending upon the Germans with both pistols blazing, about as inconspicuous as a diamondback rattlesnake on a green velvet rug. Any man who attended war in that rig could not expect to remain on his feet all day, but Patton's disappointment was somewhat assuaged when his stretcher arrived back at Headquarters, where Pershing told him his conduct merited the Distinguished Service Cross.

The 75,000 men of Liggett's I Corps might well have claimed to have traveled a harder trail than all the six divisions to their right; and possibly the 35th Division of Kansas and Missouri National Guardsmen and draftees on Liggett's right wing, flanking Cameron's effort before Montfaucon, had the roughest road of any as it moved at dawn up the Aire River Valley east of the river's twisting course. Every feature there had been zoned for four years for defensive fire; no army was to be permitted to reach Varennes on the Aire—where the 35th was expected to go with all possible haste.

The 35th Division had been put together in time for reserve at Saint-Mihiel, moving up quickly from the Alps around Belfort. Their first big assignment was one to make an Allied veteran shudder, let alone river boys just come to grips with war. No U.S. division had faced more pestiferous terrain. Green troops made three shocking attacks among the jackstraws in the ten hours of daylight that first day; if Mondésir on the Vesle had shuddered at the *élan* of the green divisions there, he would have collapsed at the spectacle the 35th provided on Vauquois Heights and in its progress toward the town of Cheppy fronting Varennes. The heights had repulsed all attacks by the French in 1915; the ground was tunneled and cratered by mines and countermining operations. The new lads gave their best there, uninterested in the safety of their own heads, which were being counted by the enemy artillerists in a three-quarter circle around them. In the noon attack, Captain Alexander Skinker carried ammunition for his last Chauchat gunner until he was killed at the gun port of a barbedwire concrete pillbox. Private Nels Wold, a Chauchat gunner, with a lone carrier, got four machine guns that afternoon; when his buddy was wounded, he fetched him back to shelter, then proceeded alone against the fifth gun of the cluster until his luck ran out. The state of Missouri erected a monument there to such Medal of Honor men as these and the hundreds of other Doughboys left there and long since forgotten.

When the division was momentarily checked, light tanks came up and it proceeded to reorganize, attack again, and carry its first objective, the left of the division engaging in house-to-house fighting in Varennes, a specialty in which none of the men had been schooled. Hundreds of thousands of other Doughboys would pass through that bottleneck, engineers continually throwing up shaky bridges under shellfire, gunners frantically trying to support their infantry jammed to a snail's pace in the ruins of the once pretty village rising in tiers above the steep banks of the river. A weary Doughboy who knew his French history might have pointed out the house where Louis XVI and his queen, Marie Antoinette, were seized in their flight toward Luxemburg.

The 35th was on its way to becoming a first-class fighting outfit by September 30, having suffered six thousand casualties and some lineshattering repulses from cross machine-gun fire that wiped out its forward elements in several advances. That afternoon, one of the American balloonists whom Rickenbacker and his fellow pilots were defending against the red-nose Richthofen veterans and the yellow-bellies of Captain Loerser's 2nd Jägstaffel was shot up by a Fokker; but he had telephoned his intelligence to the 110th Field Signal Battalion of the 35th Division. Ahead of it an infantry battalion of the 35th was isolated facing a meadow, crouching against the base of a slope, with a German counterattack gathering in the woods to make an oblique strike at its left flank. The Signal Battalion selected its strongest runner to carry forward a message to a battery of field artillery ahead, telephone wires having been cut by enemy fire.

Runners were often among those neglected in regimental histories. They were chosen for strength and agility, for persistence. The 110th chose Paul Shaffer to thread the skein of shell-roaring death. Shaffer's own tale, recounted to the Elks Club in Whittier, California, reveals something of the quality and temper of the green 35th's personnel.

"I never did know my rating in the Army. I'd always wanted to be a cartoonist while apprenticed to a blacksmith in Topeka. I must have spent about five hundred dollars taking correspondence courses. All the teachers at the correspondence school wrote me that I was a budding genius each time I sent in another money order. Finally I sent the whole batch of my cartoons to a great editor, and he wrote me that I'd better stick to whatever I was doing, because my cartoons were the worst he'd seen in thirty years. So I stuck to shoeing mules. When I was twenty I got the White House greetings. I put my occupation down as a blacksmith and was attached to the Signal Corps, though I didn't know a dot from a dash, and had never seen a wireless set. It turned out that a field signal battalion was allowed three pack horses to carry wireless batteries and I was to go along and shoe them. I had a curious dingus on my sleeve, and my pay was something between corporal and sergeant. My buddies said I was a corporal sergeant, and the topkick said to take all my orders from him.

"We reached Le Havre on a British ship in April, 1918, and were sent to Flanders to learn trench-warfare signals from the British. General Pershing came down to inspect us, and took my horses for his artillery. I just carried a one-horse load of storage batteries on my back into the Flanders mud three times. The British were fighting all the time. They never stopped. And in the rear their signal outfits were teaching us.

"We had good chow for a time. Then something happened and they started feeding us British rations. Everyone admired the limeys for their guts, and there were few fights between us. We admired them even more when we ate the kind of chow they fought on. Every Doughboy in my outfit had shot a lot of rabbits, and had seen their mothers basting them with vinegar and prune juice. Most guys would say 'Do you want my share of the barn rat?' and pass it up. You could always have hard-boiled eggs. The eggs had been boiled in Melbourne in the fall of 1914. When you clawed one open, the yolk looked like the inside of a hand grenade, and if you ate one in a hurry you felt like you'd just swallowed a Mills bomb. Nobody complained. We were just lying around in two feet of mud while the British, their stomachs filled with barn rat and hen grenades, were always mud-fighting like a racoon in a creek filled with dogs.

"But we missed our coffee when the British started giving us their tea. All my buddies had tasted tea at one time or another—maybe when the preacher made you comb your hair and go to the old maids' church sociable, when you could put a scoop of sugar in the cup and squeeze half a lemon into it. Then it tasted like hot lemonade that somebody—well— had done something funny to. But the British tea was like soldering fluid. Our wireless boys said they could repair their sets with it. Then one day some of us were walking the duckboards by a battered old house and we smelled real coffee. We looked in, and there was a British senior noncom mess, the quartermaster beaming and about twenty noncoms grouped around platters of Kansas chow, with big pots of our coffee. After that, fights broke out every day.

"But we learned a lot from the limeys, and by the time Saint-Mihiel came the Doughboys gave the Germans hell. My job in reserve was mostly lifting heavy things when I wasn't running messages. I knew I ought to tell the major to send me back to a remount depot where I could do a lot of good. But, hell, when you get around buddies that have to have messages when enemy fire has torn up your wires, you can't tear yourself away. After Saint-Mihiel, we had trucks for the batteries, and I walked about a hundred miles in five nights in a seventy-two-pound pack as light as a feather, except my clothes were always dripping wet as I stood under trees during the day . . . and when they gave me the message that afternoon, it was for the Truman battery.

"I set out on the run, jumping into shell holes when I heard one with my name on it, or crashing myself against outcroppings when those big ones shrieked, 'Where are you, Corporal Sergeant Shatter?' I doubt any blacksmith ever ran so fast. I reached the battery in nothing flat, as muddy as an alligator, all the skin off my nose. Captain Harry S. Truman was standing there, his tin hat pushed on the back of his head, directing salvos into some spot toward the northeast. He was a banty officer in spectacles, and when he read my message he started runnin' and cussin' all at the same time, shouting for the guns to turn northwest. He ran about a hundred yards to a little knoll, and what he saw didn't need binoculars. I never heard a man cuss so well or so intelligently, and I'd shoed a million mules. He was shouting back ranges and giving bearings.

"The battery didn't say a word. They must have figured the cap'n could do the cussin' for the whole outfit. It was a great sight, like the center ring in Barnum and Bailey at the close of the show, everything clockwork, setting fuses, cutting fuses, slapping shells into breeches and jerking lanyards before the man hardly had time to bolt the door. Shell cases were flipping back like a juggler's act, clanging on tin hats of the ammunition passers, the guns just spitting fire—spit-spit-spit-spit.

"Then Captain Truman ran down the knoll and cussed 'em to fire even faster. When he ran back up the hill still cussin', I forgot how I didn't want to get killed and I ran with him, even though my bit tongue was hanging out and a tooth sticking through my lip. I couldn't see our infantry. It must have been driven back to the little knoll, trying to crawl around and change front. Beyond it was some mighty fine grazing land, and at the far end a clump of woods, pretty leaves still on the autumn trees. The leaves were falling fast, shells breaking into them. This time Captain Truman had his binoculars on them. I finally made out what he saw. There were groups of Germans at the edge of the woods, stooping low and coming on slowly with machine guns on their hips, held by shoulder straps. He shouted some cusswords filled with figures down to the battery, and shells started breaking into the enemy clumps. Whole legs were soon flying through the air. He really broke up that counterattack. He was still there being shot at when I came to my senses and got off the knoll.

"I went back to the sweating battery, but counterbatteries started ranging. They were looking for me and Captain Truman. I knew he had to move soon and I wished I could stay when he brought up the animals. Being from Topeka, I wanted to hear what a Missouri man had to say to his mules. But it wasn't a safe place for an out-of-work blacksmith. So I went back and told my major how Captain Truman and I had broken up a counterattack, and our infantry was now off the dime. I never saw the cussin' captain again until I voted for him in 1948. That night the First Division relieved us. 'What's the trouble around here?' some of their guys said. 'Anything need fixin'?' It sure was time."

Corporal Sergeant Shaffer did not say what needed fixing, but he knew his major's maps, with their close-curled contours of the Romagne Heights. The heart of the Hindenburg Line lay ahead. But there could be no fighting more valiant than that of the green 35th's. It had advanced six miles to the right of the Argonne Forest before losing cohesion in some of its decimated battalions.

The 35th was left in line too long for a green division before it was replaced by the 1st Division on October 1. Once its familiar officers and sage sergeants were lost in heavy fighting over desperate terrain it should have been quickly relieved to lick its wounds, and its higher officers given time to assess the lessons of combat, to reorganize its command and sack officers who were found wanting; to delouse and mourn their lost buddies and write letters home; but the veteran divisions were still on that sixty-mile transit. (At Cantigny, Ely's well-schooled 28th infantry was pulled out after two days of fighting that was mild compared to the 35th's baleful sector of the Argonne.) But wars are always fought that way. No army was ever ready for battle in all its echelons, let alone the army of a republic wary of garnishing many lances. Doughboys had no time for experimentation. Officers of many outfits, no matter how high their luster, were sacked on their first try if they were found not battleworthy, even though their fault was only inexperience and not lack of valor. A colonel who left the field lightly wounded was never recalled to combat; but he might be remembered longer than one who stayed in the line after he had received his mortal wound.

> Fight on, my men, I am hurt but I am not slaine.
> I will lie me down and bleed awhile; then I'll rise and fight againe

said Sir Andrew Barton. The 35th, like all the green divisions along the Allied front, had its full share of such men as the legendary Sir Andrew.

Their major general was Peter Traub, who had been the New Englanders' calm brigadier at the bitter surprise attack at Seicheprey. Before West Pointer Traub could fill his ranks, rekindle his fires, and put to shame behind-the-line carpers, the Armistice was upon him. The 35th had been tagged to fight again November 14 with Bullard's American Second Army on the Moselle. It never adopted a nickname, and it staged no big parades. It had simply fought itself out on a near-impossible assignment. Any general in Europe would have welcomed the survivors into his corps. Hindenburg warned his Chancellor that green troops had hurt him badly. Captured German lieutenants, witness to their valor and their inexperience, said to the corn-fed interrogators, "If only we could have met you in 1915 when we too were young!"

The Pennsylvanians of the 28th Division, in the center of Liggett's corps that first day, had been on the move since Degoutte left those forlorn four companies to perish beside the Marne. It had never had any real rest, many of its very good National Guardsmen, officers and noncoms, having fallen to be replaced by new officers from the A.E.F. schools, from training camps, with new lads from many states. Ahead of it, after long marching, on the morning of September 26 was a formidable landscape. Its troops must advance through the eastern hump of the Argonne Forest while its chief thrust followed the valley of the little Aire River to the east, one of its infantry brigades astride it. Something had to give, because its own right flank must shepherd the brand-new-to-combat 35th Division moving against the Vauquois Heights.

There was nothing green about the Pennsylvanians in the middle of Liggett's corps; they had learned the art of war. Their general was capable of telling Chaumont inspectors and troubleshooters to mind their own business. It was Muir's division, and its greatest motivation was state pride. Its troops may not have been so noisy as other state cadres about its wealth and its colleges, its mills, mines, and farms. It was not so showily prideful as the New Englanders, or some of the Southerners. Pennsylvania could swing the tide of national elections; it could also sway battlefields such as at Gettysburg. The Iron Division did not lack for guts, initiative, and savvy; it only lacked a fair chance to lick its wounds and get some sleep as it went forward at dawn, September 26.

Ahead of it were formidable belts of wire forming the German's First Position. Even if there had been three times as many cannon blasting this wire during the night, Frederick Palmer, on the field with Muir, observed, the belts would have remained largely intact. Hills and cliffs to the right and left, mutually interlocking in fire-control liaison, could shell intruders mercilessly; machine gunners were set in pattern to kill those platoon leaders who led through wire gaps. Yet the division was through the wire by nine o'clock in the morning, much Pennsylvania blood and flesh clinging to the rusty barbs. Observers wondered how these lads had any meat left on their legs. How truly great it could have become had the 28th Division been relieved the following night to bathe and doze around the red-tiled barns, the manure piles of village streets in redolent Lorraine! Other divisions of its veteran caliber, after savage mauling, had known a long respite, notably the 1st, 2nd, 3rd, 26th, 32nd, and 42nd being given a breathing spell.

Frederick Palmer, "Friend to Pershing" in the dramatis personae of September 26, was at every headquarters of the nine attacking divisions that day. What he wrote of them after a six-months study of the battlefield, tramping its still-shambled positions, was an apt description of the Pennsylvanians' start.

The ardor and ferocity of our youth in a furious offensive mood was never more compelling in its results. Caution was not in our lexicon. If strong points held out, the thing was to go through them. There was no time to lose. The first wave must go on according to schedule, leaving those who followed to do the mopping up of details. Our faith was in our valor and destiny. In our progress, the first-line fortifications were to be only another hurdle after the wire.

Carried away by the *élan* of the attack, Palmer was at one time three miles beyond the jumping-off place of the Pennsylvanians. He had been a Balkan War correspondent while still a youth before the turn of the century; had followed Lieutenant Summerall in Reilly's Battery at the 1900 relief of Peking, had watched the Japanese against the Russians in 1904; had known more Aegean wars after that; had been with the Old Contemptibles around Mons in 1914 and with the British at the Somme in 1916; and when Pershing arrived in Washington from the Mexican Border to receive A.E.F. command from Woodrow Wilson, Palmer had been waiting to brief him on the failure of Nivelle's 1917 offensive—where Palmer, walking the streets of Amiens with Sir Philip Gibbs, ace British journalist, heard his old friend ask, "Where will it all end, Palmer?"

Palmer could see the beginning of the end that misty Argonne morning before the sun burned through to show enemy guns their moving targets. He thought of the British, the French, and the Belgians as The Three Musketeers, the young Doughboy as a fiery d'Artagnan come to join them. It was a romantic concept, befitting the spirit of that day—and not conceivable in a later war with its great cartoons by Bill Mauldin, its sad-sack dispatches from the enduring Ernie Pyle, the masterful photographers of *Life* Magazine's corps. But it mirrored the innocent mood of Doughboy reflections. "The French gunners looked on smiling," Palmer wrote, "as a middle-aged woman smiles over the enthusiasm of the debutante."

The only hope for a quick advance in the forest rested, not upon the enthusiasm of the Pennsylvanians, but upon the attitude of the German Reservists holding Le Chêne Tondu, a rocky finger pointing east from the Argonne's fist toward the valley of the twisting Aire and the heights around Vauquois. Had the Pennsylvanians been able to advance in two days past Le Chêne Tondu, then blind Senator Thomas Gore of Kansas might never have visited the front after the war to clear the name of the 35th Division on the Pennsylvanians' right. (A phenomenal man, being told of the topography which he could not see, the senator excoriated the A.E.F.'s High Command. It was a loyal and understandable thing for Gore to do; it was unwarranted. His division needed no defense, any more than did the Pennsylvanians.) The German had had four professional years to fortify his positions, and he was the most indefatigable digger in Europe.

The Pennsylvanians were hardly through the wire and past the first field fortifications in the valley when they found themselves shelled and machine-gunned from their left. Had there been a thousand guns to back them up, and three hundred heavy tanks to clean out the banks of the Aire, they might have taken Le Chêne Tondu on the first day. As it was, they tried again and again in assaults on these verdant cliffs with their countless gun positions. The middle of the line, advancing along the twisting banks of the Aire, was shelled from other heights to their right with equal ferocity. Their tactical situation was such that they had to advance through a great pie-shaped crust of machine guns and cannon, with fire from all quadrants except that of the slice just cut from the barbed-wire pie.

Muir knew by nightfall of the second day that the positions could not be speedily taken with naked infantry backed up only by its division's artillery. He invited Pershing to send two Leavenworth staff-trained brigadiers to try their hand, with two Regular colonels to lead infantry assaults for them.

The two new brigadiers were to be Dennis Nolan, Chaumont Intelligence chief who had warned Duchêne that May morning on the Chemin des Dames, and Brigadier General Edward Sigerfoos; but the latter's limousine, hurrying toward death or glory, was spotted by a German battery and Sigerfoos died of shell wounds seven days later. His place was then taken by the ubiquitous Colonel Conger of the Belfort *ruse de guerre*. These two officers, Nolan and Conger, then planned twin attacks, with two Regular colonels leading. One of the colonels of the Regulars was wounded before he ever reached the infantry positions in the naked, fire-swept valley of the Aire. The second was killed leading an assault. Neither attack succeeded in gaining much ground. Conger and Nolan advised Muir to shorten his front and rest his tattered troops piecemeal; then they left Muir alone with his division's family problems and went back to Chaumont wiser men.

(Alone among Allied Commanders, Pershing saw to it that General Staff officers had a turn at experiencing what combat leaders had to undergo, what infantry must endure. One of the most celebrated utterances of the war came from Haig's chief of staff when he, after more than three years of hot meals and warm beds, ventured on a tour of inspection after the Passchendaele battle of November, 1917, in muddy Flanders. "My God," he cried, and broke into tears, "did we send men to fight in that?" There was no one around Chaumont or at the Iron Commander's First Army Headquarters in the town hall at Souilly who did not know the nature of the inferno General Staff sent men into.)

The Pennsylvanians inched forward for twelve days, constricting their front, and at last succeeded in taking, and mopping up, the accursed Taille l'Abbé, cannoned thorn beyond Le Chêne Tondu. Decimated infantry and engineers and sanitary trains were evacuated at last on October 7, having suffered 6,149 casualties, with another 1,200 carried out with influenza and pneumonia in sheer physical collapse. They had lived at times on raw meat and potatoes, sleeping on wet ground without blankets in the valley of death. Their artillery remained in place to assist the relieving division, exchanging their personal hells with the push-button gunners on heights beyond them for some days more. At last the Iron Division would know some rest, pick the seam squirrels from its undershirts, have baths and hot coffee—almost a novelty to these troops since they first heard the thunder along the Marne. They would now write letters to metropolitan dailies and country weeklies eulogizing the fallen and praising their outfits. Had not Muir told them on the Vesle to be of good heart and they would become veteran troops?

Many wrote of such lads as Corporal Donald M. Call, driving a French tank into the outskirts of Varennes around the noon of the first day, September 26, while some Kansas boys of the 35th Division were fighting tooth and nail for the eastern banks of that historic town. The tank's turret was torn off by a shell burst, and the corporal, choking on cordite fumes, did the only sensible thing to do. He crawled out, wheezing blindly, and found a fine, muddy shell hole twenty yards away. Then the corporal discovered something was missing. His wounded lieutenant was still in the tank. He went back and extricated him, carrying the young officer to a muddy shell hole's comforts, while a battery of field guns sniped at him. It was only a foretaste of the conduct of many in the twelve days required to clear all guns of Le Chêne Tondu and turn those cliffs over to Acting Corporal Alvin York's 82nd Division for safekeeping. The Germans would hear from it again.

The 77th Division, buried in the Argonne Forest on the extreme left of the American lines, made a brilliant rush through woods the first day of the attack on an east-west line running five miles. All four of its infantry regiments were widely deployed three miles from their jump-off points by evening, no relief in sight, facing the frowning cliffs of Le Chêne Tondu on the east, the hill of La Palette on the west. The 77th had been relieved on the Aisne in the middle of September to move in nine struggling days to its positions in the Argonne. It jumped off September 26, a sleepless, unrested outfit, having been given no chance to review its fighting experience, a serious omission in the school of combat. By now, it was below normal strength. A few companies had received replacements of green troops from the West, some of whom could not load a rifle or throw a hand grenade. Companies had come into the line with only two hundred men, shy fifty rifles.

After its initial success on the first day, the 77th was slowed, like every other division in the line, by furious German opposition. Still it pushed forward taking one fortified pavilion after another, harassed by German rear guards. These Argonne pavilions were not only fortresses; some were paradise camps for prime divisions which had earned rest and recreation in a French forest no Frenchman had entered in four years, the earth thereabouts a giant honeycomb after months of long-range bombardment. The 77th looted the Bagatelle Pavilion on the second day of the offensive, its scout platoons almost unable to believe the sight of the Aladdin-like caves which an astonished enemy had so wildly vacated.

Blockhouses with twenty-foot thickness of concrete roof were cloaked in log cabin husks, roofs gabled and fretted with the gingerbread of Swiss chalets, rooms paneled in walnut wainscot. Pantries were wonderfully stocked, gun rooms had sporting weapons and trophies of the chase. There were mirrored saloons stocked with schnapps and wines, *Danziger Goldwasser,* Havana cigars. There were electric power plants, pianos where music racks held the latest Tin Pan Alley hits. "I'm going back to the shack where the Black-Eyed Susans grow!" There was hot and cold water for blue-tiled bathtubs, summer gazebos and floral squares, artificial lakes, kitchen gardens, bowling alleys, and billiard rooms, poultry runs, and subterranean dormitories each with bunks for fifty enlisted men. Doughboys entered music rooms where string quartets had left instruments and Beethoven scores; they found libraries lined with science texts, and classics in many languages as eloquent testimony to the *Kultur* fostered by the Teutonic knights. It was undreamed of in a West Pointer's Army Post. These pavilions had everything but liberty.

A few lads carried off a *Sherlock Holmes* by Conan Doyle, or one of Sir Rider Haggard's African tales; but the skimpy pockets of the Doughboy's impractical blouse were not capable of receiving a tenth of the bottles a scout wanted to carry away. Scouts went forward with long-neckers of *Liebfraumilch* and *Johannisberger* peeping from their combat packs. Stretcher-bearers and their bullet-burdened men paused for *gesundheits* and *prosits* before reaching the surgeon's tweezers. No other Doughboys ever knew such a looter's paradise as that of the Bagatelle Pavilion, favorite haunt of German princes.

They soon became wary of German ruses around these pavilions. On September 28 a scout platoon learned the hard way. It captured outpost trenches of the Saint Hubert Pavilion, then was suddenly confronted by a group of old war dogs with hands skyward crying *"Kamerad."* The beguiled platoon accepted their surrender and lowered rifles as the decoys came forward. When they neared the position, a German assault team broke through the bush and, streaming through the line of bait, cut the platoon to pieces in a ghastly surprise. But the enemy had not reckoned on Lieutenant Dwight H. Schaffner, who, just coming up, stood upon a parapet with a Chauchat and cut down the attackers. He then charged with his pistol, gunning the German captain who had authored the ruse. Schaffner was God's angry man. He dragged his German back unaided, and obliged that treacherous officer to divulge the disposition of forces ahead, the names of units, and everything else the bleeder could not afford to remember. Schaffner's company was then faced on three sides by enemy troops for several hours, but the lieutenant now knew more about the enemy's positions than Saint Hubert's clubmen did of the Yanks, a rare circumstance in that forest. It was a Medal of Honor performance witnessed by wounded Doughboys littering the ground.

In three days, death and wounds had taken a heavy toll. In addition, hundreds of Doughboys got lost in the underbrush, where it was a lucky platoon leader who could see ten of his men in an attacking line. Bullard remarked, more prophetically than he realized, that the 77th, a division in which he took particular interest, had a penchant for getting lost.

"The assault of 26 September," Pershing caused to be written in his life work as Chairman of the Battlefields Monuments Commission,

surprised the Germans and disrupted their defense, but this situation was only momentary. From that day on the fighting was probably unsurpassed during the World War for dogged determination on both sides. Each foot of ground was stubbornly contested and hostile troops took advantage of every available spot from which to pour enfilade and crossfire into the advancing American troops. . . .

A lull in the battle of October 1 marked the virtual end of the first phase of the Meuse-Argonne operation. Green troops had given the Yanks a spectacular first round; they could be reformed and thrown in again, soldiers who had learned discretion, officers beginning to be familiar with staff work in a wooded terrain pocked with ravines and rushing rivulets.

Montfaucon had been the key to an American advance. If it had fallen the first day, it is possible that the Doughboys would have pushed beyond the Romagne Heights to breach the Kriemhilde Stellung, the second line of the Hindenburg defense system. By noon September 27, Cameron's men were fighting in the streets of Montfaucon, but the Germans had been given thirty hours to strengthen their forces with light railways, rushing divisions ot the bristling heights of Romagne. By evening that day, Pershing's idea of an uninterrupted advance until the Kriemhilde fell was beyond fulfilling. All hope of smashing through to the citadel of Grandpré and giving Gouraud's Fourth Army on his left a quick passage up the Aisne

Valley was now so many colored pins on staff maps that would hang for weeks on the walls of the town hall of Souilly, Pershing's headquarters.

If the veteran Big Red One, the 2nd's Doughboys and Marines, the 3rd's Marne troops and the quarrelsome fighters of the 42nd Rainbows had come up in time to hold the center that first morning, it is probable that Montfaucon would have fallen, but at a terrible cost; to judge from their hell-for-leather records, one would have to estimate five thousand casualties for each division in a single day—tantamount to a heavyweight boxer's breaking his right hand in the first round.

But the conjecture is hardly to the point. Pershing put in the fresh divisions he had available, and they acquitted themselves with more than honor. It was rather a matter of the overconfidence of battle planners whom the easy victory of Saint-Mihiel had made unwary of the enormous effort required by machines of war to support infantry where there were no roads, to cross lines where long-range German cannon were interlocked in a network of batteries that covered every inch of the line, with machine guns concealed everywhere and echeloned in depth.

By October 1, the American corps had advanced an average of four miles over the most bitter terrain fighting men had yet known. Colonel George C. Marshall, Jr., had secretly moved a million men in two weeks toward a quick victory. (So little remembered was the Doughboy's War that when General Marshall became Franklin D. Roosevelt's chief of staff before the next war, Major General Hugh [Iron Pants] Johnson, in an angry *Life* Magazine article, had to tell the people just who this soldier was.)

Pétain, who knew the ground, thought the first day was tremendous. Foch was displeased at the slowdown after September 27. Haig said he was not familiar with the ground but thought it needed staff planners more skilled in transport than the A.E.F. had had time to educate. Foch's displeasure was habitual. Pétain and Haig were closer to the mark. The fact remained that the Yanks had breached the Giselher Stellung that had thwarted the French for four years, and that the advance elements of the 77th Division on Liggett's far left had pushed into the Argonne Forest, where they would soon present their republic a saga that rivals that of the Texas Alamo.

Chapter **14**

FLYING THE FLAMING COFFINS

I hope he roasted all the way down.

The first morning of the Argonne-Meuse offensive was memorable for another outfit that took to the sky at dawn only a few hours after the lonely Rickenbacker in his Spad. Colonel William Mitchell was making his first essay in independent bombing with eight de Haviland 4s, two airplanes from each of four other squadrons. (Mitchell himself was in a Spad that day, in a prodigious dogfight he has described with a clarity few aviators—who rely mainly on hand pantomime and rat-a-tat-tat gibberish—have ever achieved in print.) The executive of the bomber group, which hoped to bomb the supply depots at Dun-sur-Meuse, was the then First Lieutenant Merian C. Cooper; but he did not lead the element, for his Liberty engine began bugging along the taxi strip. When airborne, Cooper had to full-throttle to join his flight as Tail-End Charlie. Only seven of the eight de Havilands climbed aloft, one airplane crashing on the strip, killing both pilot and observer. Lieutenant Sidney Howard, later a Pulitzer Prize playwright, led the way in what he called "the very worst airplane between the North Sea and the Swiss border," the flaming coffin of Captain Eddie Rickenbacker's vitriolic postwar denunciations. It was the most vulnerable airplane ever built, its gas tank between pilot and observer, its Liberty engine a product of American wartime improvisations. An incendiary bullet into its gas tank created a bonfire between its two occupants, or a tracer into the twelve-cylinder, V-type plant, with its individual cylinders clasped in welded water jackets, usually set the engine afire.

249

Some blamed the de Haviland's faults on American modifications that had made the landing gear too small and too weak; some attributed its engine failures to spark plugs from war profiteers who shaved costs. Others felt—and may have been nearer the mark—that it was because any new engine had a hundred bugs. Less pessimistic pilots said the Liberty only had seventy-five bugs. It was an all-purpose power plant also designed for tanks that were never produced, and such was the state of necessity that both French and British clamored for it. (Actually, it is to the credit of America that the Liberty turned out as well as it did.)

Americans tutored by headlines—in their customary way of "thinking big"—read early in the war that Congress had appropriated a hundred million dollars for airplanes, and not knowing any better dismissed the airplane situation as a mission just as good as accomplished by the passage of the bill. The airplane itself, despite its terrible hazards, was also a product of thinking in terms of future bigness along the right lines.

By the time the Doughboys were fighting on the Argonne-Meuse front in September of 1918 the Franco-British team had won the air with the Spads and Sopwith Camels, and the Yanks were not subject to the horrors of 1917's aerial ground strafing, when sometimes whole divisions were broken and dispersed by savagery from the skies. Few Yanks ever knew what their comparative security had cost both sides; in the fall of 1917, when the early arrivals were streaming toward their training areas in boxcars, many of the great aces were already gone. For some of the others the handwriting was on the wall.

The nineteen-year-old Captain Albert Ball of the R.F.C., a Sunday school boy who had done so much to give the English foot-sloggers in Flanders security from air attack, had forty-three victories when he was shot down in May, 1917. He had made a habit, when returning from German skies, of buzzing the Flemish village of Annoeullin to read the hands of the clock on the church tower, captive villagers waving to him from the privacy of walled gardens. Some German G-2, noting this custom, got Ball with a machine gun secretly placed in the belfry. (Baron von Richthofen tried to claim the credit for his brother Lothar.)

The great Captain Georges Guynemer, hero-consumptive of French skies, with fifty-three well-confirmed victories to his credit, disappeared in Flanders September 11, 1917. Again the Germans tried to claim credit, but the chances are Guynemer had hemorrhaged and fainted, splintering his Spad and himself into a giant hole.

Captain Werner Voss, "the greatest pilot any of us ever encountered"— according to Captain James McCudden of the R.F.C., no amateur himself with fifty-eight confirmed victories before he was killed by engine failure on take-off—was killed on September 23, 1917. The Jewish genius dove his red-and-white-checkered triplane straight into a twenty-plane mass of British SE-5s, and for twenty minutes kept the wheel of fortune spinning in his favor, with his plane as the axle in a wheel of enemy aircraft, until Lieutenant Albert Rhys-Davids, like Voss a nineteen-year-old, shot him down.

The legendary Richthofen was killed in the spring of 1918. A great birdman—though his eighty claimed victories, inflated by himself and the Hohenzollerns, do not bear postwar examination— it was in his concept of airpower as a disciplined mass both strategically and tactically, taken over from the great Boelcke, that he proved himself a superior leader. Although he was reportedly shot down and killed by a British pilot, there are some who believe he made a successful dead-stick landing in No-Man's Land only to be shot through the head by a British sniper. Richthofen was not popular with the opposition, as was Voss, the gay Ernst Udet, Captain Wisseman and most of the others, because of his Prussian haughtiness and his many untruthful claims. "I hope he roasted all the way down," said Major Edward Mannock, the great English killer with seventy-three victories to his credit, when apprised of Richthofen's death. Mannock himself was killed a few days later in his twenty-first year.

There are others who survived to protect the Doughboys as 1918 drew to a close: Captain René Fonck, highest French scorer with seventy-five victories; Captain William Bishop, the Canadian with seventy victories who was so miserly with his ammunition. Sidney Howard, Merian Cooper, and the Doughboys below had many obligations to such as these, living and dead, who preceded them.

But Howard, leading the flight that day, and Cooper, flying rear guard, obscure pilots in the sky famed only for its pursuit artists, were not just then dwelling on the past, nor on any future extending more than sixty minutes toward the chord of their horizon. They were among the first Americans to cross the air lines in a home product. None of them had any familiarity with bombardment craft. They had been trained as two-seater fighters in British machines, and none knew what to expect, if he reached Dun-sur-Meuse, when he released his bombs and the airplane leaped skyward.

The seven airplanes were over the Argonne Forest when five yellow-and-black Fokkers, sharks of the ocean sky, knifed into them. One Fokker— or perhaps two, for one rarely knew an accurate score in the days before camera verification—spun out to death below, the others breaking off. The seven Yank machines continued on. Unknown to the other six, the observer in Howard's leading plane had been killed in this encounter, his death throes causing his legs to stretch outward and jam Howard's controls.

Presently, the Yanks saw a flight of Fokkers, sixteen or twenty alerted by the first encounter, coming head on. It was now etiquette, just as in old naval days when a squadron of swift frigates turned away from Ships-of-the-Line, for the Yank bombers to break off at full throttle and attempt to re-enter the Dun sector from another quarter. But Howard, with his jammed controls, could do nothing but fly a straight course heading into the enemy. The seven DH-4s had fourteen machine guns among them, minus Howard's aftergun. The Fokkers, far more maneuverable, each with three guns, probably outgunned Howard's element by a three-to-one superiority. The other Americans followed him as the Fokkers flew in among the American planes, above and below them the sky garish with a flock of many-colored birds. It became impossible to distinguish casualties. Howard thought (correctly) he saw his wing man and best friend, Phil Rhinelander, with his observer, spinning down to fiery cremation. Cooper saw one Yank observer, his Lewis ammunition gone, stand in the cockpit and throw the steel drum at a Fokker twenty feet away. Howard under compulsion flew on, his observer still jamming the controls. The world was all red and yellow and black paint, streams of tracers, bundles of bonfires, as friend and enemy plummeted in pinwheels of acrobatics. Lt. Clarkson Potter could not see that Howard's observer was dead, but he held his course, giving the leader rear protection.

After proceeding some twenty miles over enemy country, Howard's observer changed his posture—the sky was cold and rigor mortis an early attendant upon death—and the controls were freed. Howard, with the faithful Potter, who had a few days of life to live still backing him up, then turned. He came back to American lines, landing on a field where he greeted his friend Gilbert Wynant—schoolmaster to Thomas Hitchcock, who had also gone to war—then a pilot in Major Carl Spaatz's Pursuit Squadron. Only Howard, Potter, and his observer had made it back, three live men and a dead observer of the sixteen who proposed to bomb Dun-sur-Meuse. It was months before Cooper, called by Howard "The Perfect Adventurer," returned from captivity to post the score and write his father of his experience.

I had never been able to understand why men jumped from a burning plane to their certain death below, but I knew then that death did not seem to matter at all. The only thing in the world that I wanted to do was to get out of that pain, so I jerked off my belt and started to hop out when it flashed through my mind that I was leaving Eddie to burn up while I died easy; so I thought I would take one crack at it instead of doing him a yellow trick. I pulled out of a spin and dived vertically, opening the throttle up wide, and taking the one chance of burning out the gas in the motor, though I did not believe there was any chance at all; but to my surprise the fire did go out. Meanwhile, I had fallen partially on my back, and had an awful job keeping from falling from the plane, because I had no belt.

So wrote Captain Merian C. Cooper to his father, using his left hand, his right still burned too badly for penmanship, of events attending Colonel William Mitchell's first essay in independent bombing on the opening day of the Meuse-Argonne offensive. (Lufbery had jumped near Pont-à-Mousson, trying to hurl his flaming body into a lake.)

While Howard flew on, Cooper had made a three-point landing in a fallow field by controlling the stick between his knees, hands and feet seared from the fire in his engine. Edward C. Leonard, his observer, opened his eyes and smiled. He had been shot through the neck, had bled a while, and regained consciousness. Immediately a victor flew over the field at fifty feet, hand-signaling for the Americans to step away from their airplane. He kicked over and came back, landing beside the two, Leonard lying upon the ground, Cooper helpless in fiery agony. The German saluted, extended his hand for their pistols, and claimed them prisoner, an ace wearing the Iron Cross of the First Class. German garrison troops were running across the field, and the ace, who did not reveal his name, had field medics attending them at once.

The following afternoon an elegant Lieutenant Goertz called upon Cooper, who had been isolated from Leonard. Goertz had *Intelligence* written all over him. After the traits of his calling, he also had cigarettes and a bedside manner. He exchanged a few pleasantries, saying he too had been shot down, prisoner in Russia until the Soviets released him, and then proceeded to business: how many troops did America have in training at home?

Cooper knew there were around two million, and so he promptly said twenty-five million. Lieutenant Goertz gave up on Cooper's patent falsehoods and in turn made the Yank with bandaged hands and feet his confidant. He said Germany could no longer hope to win the war, but it could obtain a good peace, this despite the French, who were fighting for revenge.

While Goertz was shoring up his own morale, in a field nearby three little French girls, by special dispensation of a German major billeted in the house of one of them in the village of Hani, a mile from Pierrepont, were mourners at the funeral of Phil Rhinelander and three friends. "Here lie four Americans," said the German Army chaplain to the sentimental little girls. "One of them had a fiancée. He wouldn't have been here if he had stayed at home. She would not be sad." Paul Demage, a twenty-year-old woodcutter who heard the tale from the little girls, remarked that a German pilot, probably killed by Cooper, was also being buried nearby. He would not have been there either, Paul thought, if he had stayed at home. The little girls received permission to decorate the graves, an even rarer dispensation. They wove pine-bough wreaths and made an American flag, or at least fashioned their notion of Old Glory. The flag had four white stars on a blue Union, the four stripes of red and white running vertically. Children of occupied countries, more sensitive to enemy reactions than adults, seemed to have a little ammeter in their hearts. As the chaplain droned his saws, the needle in the dial swung to "charge." They knew *les américains* would soon be there, just as clearly as Lieutenant Goertz did.

The diarist of Howard's squadron sometimes carped about conditions in Argonne's rear areas. The squadron spent four weeks in one small town where the hangar was drafty, the feather beds provided in the honest little bourgeois houses none too comfortable, the laundresses not too prompt returning linen. The shops were spare of souvenirs. A few embroidered pillow slips and bead purses just about completed their tally, and these were nothing to impress young war widows in neighboring châteaux. The mess tent was some distance from the hangar, a pilot sometimes wearing gum boots to reach a piping-hot meal. There were only a Red Cross hut with some nice girls quick to serve hot chocolate and a Y.M.C.A. canteen with well-to-do American ladies selling chewing gum and cigarettes. In fact, it would have been a paradise to any of the foot-sloggers these aviators frequently died to serve; but none of the Y.M.C.A. matrons or the Red Cross workers wanted to drink champagne out of a slipper, or even so much as dance barefoot on a table to an orchestra accompaniment of soup-plate cymbals.

On leave, even the auxiliaries around Paris were no help at all. Who among them wanted to help at midnight with a cold chisel to cut the chains anchoring captured field guns grouped about the Étoile and then race them from the Arc de Triomphe down the Champs Élysées as far as Fouquet's? And once in Fouquet's, the ladies would even threaten to leave the party when aviators stuffed hard French rolls with cherry preserves and surreptitiously bombed the ear of every staff major guzzling in the place. The mere thought of removing the trousers from the gorilla-like *commissionnaire* at the Hotel Continental filled them with horror. In an aviator's vocabulary, these women were not *women*. It remained for two young Marine officers, in the company of some women of absolutely no reputation they had met, to visit the Continental and peel this officious bouncer as clean as a banana, a Leatherneck affront to an aviator's priority on such patent devices.

What an earth-spurning fraternity they were, these aviators! Even the hardy French families maintaining restaurants under long-range fire behind Amiens, risking their lives to serve a *pintade rôti* surrounded by *pâtes* and earn a few hundred thousand honest francs, banned English aviators from the premises. A crystal chandelier could stand just so many skin-the-cats. And as for an Australian pilot or a Canadian observer? *Mon Dieu, Monsieur, quel dommage!*

Theirs was a grim humor, impossible to suppress on flying field or in hospital, one escaping a ward at Angers in bandages, drainage tubes, and pajamas, hiring two French youths to push him to the Cheval Blanc in a hand cart. He returned at two A.M., as drunk as a lord and twice as happy, pish-tushing an infuriated surgeon, bussing the cheeks of a head nurse who had the temper, when needed, to rival a regimental sergeant major's scorn. He bore presents for everyone in the ward, one of the wounded in heavy plaster and pulleyed in a Balkan frame receiving a tennis racquet and a child's jump-rope with painted handles.

Seeing him then, and meeting him later on, it seemed impossible that here was the same man. Major Corliss C. Moseley came home from Argonne's heavens to fight the battle of General Mitchell in his sacrificial goading of the General Staff—Mitchell conscientiously had to get himself sacked, and Coolidge constitutionally had to sack him—but it was difficult to reconcile the aviator with the airfield executive of a later war who trained fifty thousand pilots. Moseley shortly after the war, while a prize-winning test pilot at Wright Field, landed an airplane on West Point's parade ground, saying to the first tactical officer who approached, "I would like to introduce you gentlemen to a new weapon of war, of which you have doubtless never heard."

To see the later Moseley, in his Beverly Hills home, discussing Canada's nickel deposits with Captain William Bishop—who might guess that Bishop wore the Victoria Cross for seventy fabulous victories in a fiery sky? He stood rather stoutish and balding, holding a dry Martini in his hand, just another financier enjoying an *apéritif* after a hard day at the office. Or conceive of Ted Curtis, the Amherst freshman whose first kill over Château-Thierry delighted the 3rd Division, as being anything but the conservative Eastman official, Edward P. Curtis, who explained that he "couldn't take the gamble" on some independent producer's wildcat project? Or could visualize Cooper, a producer on the set of *Little Women* timidly advising Miss Katharine Hepburn about her hair-do, as a boy upside down without a belt in a bonfire DH-4, controlling the stick between his knees? Or Sidney Howard at Harry's Bar in Paris telling the black-garbed man of affairs, Captain René Fonck, highest of French scorers, that a Spanish olive, unpressed, smoothed the taste of Gordon's gin? What a taste of courage had once been theirs! And how quickly it returned when hundreds escaped the Pentagon in a later war: Cooper, Curtis, Hitchcock—endless the list, from Madam Sherry, Rickenbacker's decoy, to the ace of aces himself. Many were killed with a new generation—such as the favorite Lieutenant General Millard F. Harmon, the Miff Harmon of Argonne's heavens. "Just one of those things," they all said, unchanging through the years.

Young pilots, until they too were being shot at, did not understand their attitude. Then the new ones knew the Retreads well. A staff officer, returning from England, was asked by Air Secretary Robert Lovett—himself a Navy Cross aviator of Doughboy days—what he thought of the new pilots. "They are twice as smart as our fellows were, Mr. Secretary, but only half as mean and nothing like so gay." And again, one of General "Hap" Arnold's observers, returning from Casablanca's first week, repeated to the Pentagon troops: "In the rear, all is confusion. When you near the forward fields, the situation begins to clear, and when you reach the boys who fly and fight, you find they know the score. Never since 1918 were so few commanded by so many from so far away. It's the mixture as before."

Among the tortured hills and ravines below, no Argonne Doughboy ever begrudged them their heralded fame. He envied them and admired them, though many of his generals, never airborne, bitched because observers could not achieve the impossible. They had become by Armistice Day a force as skilled as any in French skies, but the rains, the haze of early fall, found them unable to render anything like the services summer weather had afforded the great aces of the past. Below them, as Cooper fobbed off Goertz's queries, the fighting was just beginning. . . .

Chapter **15**

SAINT-QUENTIN TUNNEL

The bravest man in our company is that little Wop lying
behind you.

On September 29, three days after Pershing sent his American
First Army—minus a few key divisions—smashing against the German's
Meuse-Argonne defenses, Haig launched his assault against the formidable
Saint-Quentin Tunnel complex 125 miles to the northwest. Two of Haig's
trumps were the U.S. 27th and 30th Divisions. They were there because
King George V, and later Haig, had personally asked Pershing to leave
some American troops with his forces, and because a U.S. Army Corps
was the minimum return Pershing could have made after Haig's contributions to an American Army. Haig had been magnificent in his generosity,
however badly his countrymen shredded his reputation after the war.

The 27th troops were from all over the Empire State. Farm lads from
the Chautauqua watershed, woodsmen of the Adirondacks, and slum-bred
city boys shared billets with representatives from the ballroom armories
of blue-blood regiments. Only one of its original National Guard cadres
was missing; New York's "Fighting Sixty-Ninth" Infantry of Civil War
days was now the 165th U.S. Infantry of the 42nd Rainbows—where
they were known as "The New Yorkers." Haig liked the rank-and-file and
the younger officers with their quick responses, but he thought some of the
colonels too far along in years to undergo the physical rigors of leading
troops in attrition warfare. "Could be quicker" was not a term of opprobrium, however, any more than was the phrase, "a bit of a subversive in-

257

fluence in his platoon." This might be another way of saying "a born leader," as Wooldridge on the Marne had learned about the forever bitching Corporal Enright.

Their major general was unique; the 27th's commanding officer was a National Guardsman who was a full-time soldier in the pay of his state, a graduate of the War College and the Staff School. He was a National Guard buff, a lawyer who had no time to practice law. John F. O'Ryan, whose troops had been the best behaved on the Mexican border, also had literary gifts, as his two-volume history of his division, the most detailed of the roster of the A.E.F., will testify.

The 30th Division was made up of National Guard troops from South Carolina, North Carolina, and Tennessee, and—a rarity among Doughboy cadres—95 percent of its original troops were sons of American-born parents. Since Andrew Jackson had been born in the first state, mixed his law studies with cock-fighting, drinking and gambling in the second, and won immortality in the third, they called themselves "The Old Hickory Division" —though they were soon augmented by a few draftees from Indiana, Illinois, Iowa, Minnesota, and North Dakota, plus others from Jackson's three states. Their major general was Edward M. Lewis, who had commanded the Doughboys' brigade at Belleau Wood.

Haig thought the 30th Division was quick-witted, and it became the apple of his eye, though no U.S. division was ever as brawny as the Australians, with their sombrero brims pinned to the left against the band, their refusal to maintain a military bearing behind the lines, their easy, almost insolent way with officers, who fought alongside the "Old Hickories." The Australian New Zealand Corps was all volunteer, out-of-doors men from thinly populated dominions. Some of their brigadiers had enlisted as privates. An unfettered, hell-busting lot, they were capable of unsurpassed cohesion and style in the attack. On the other hand, every Yank division had its peewees—each commander in training camps saw to that, when orders came to supply embarking divisions, by sending those judged least likely to succeed in combat and reserving the cream for his own summons to France. The National Guardsmen of the 27th and 30th had their share of peewees drafted from tenement alleys and the cotton fields of Dixie. Yet when the time came to total up Medals of Honor, it was found that the 30th Division had won more than any other division in France, confirming the mystery that physique and parade-ground carriage are no test of courage under fire against a savage enemy.

The two divisions had undergone all their training with the British since their arrival in France, an experience that had had its advantages in care and thoroughness, and some disadvantages.

Major General O'Ryan left testimony of the difficulties of training with friends who presumably spoke the same language as the Doughboys. Yanks training with French cadres had interpreters: they also had the benefit of Gallic gestures in pantomime where one picture was worth a thousand words. With the British, they only *thought* they spoke the same language. The Englishman's four-year habit of secrecy, combined with his characteristic of saying few words, miserliness with gestures, dependence more upon voice inflection than vocabulary, caused misunderstandings with the American arrivals. Above all, the English reticence was at first taken to be an assumption of superiority, an insularity amounting to condescension. A Yank battalion commander, invited to a British mess to have "tea or something," did not understand that the "something" could mean a fifth of Johnny Walker Red Label if he so desired. When he introduced himself by saying, "I'm Major Joe Doakes of the Umpteenth Infantry," his host merely said, "Quite so," and let it go at that. In wartime, when the ears of the enemy were always listening, an Englishman did not say who he was.

There was ill-will at first, until someone higher up alerted the British to this situation, ordering them to loosen up a bit with the Americans. Even so, it still went like this: "I'm Major Joe Doakes, etc." and the answer came back: "Quite so. This is Dados." Whereupon the Yank said, "Pleased to meet you, Mr. Dados." This made things worse. Did not the American bloke know that Dados meant Deputy Assistant Director of Ordinance Service? How could the colonel have said, "This is Major the honorable Buff-Orpington-Traxle of the Tins? That is, of the Queen's Bays, officially the Second Dragoon Guards—Household Cavalry and all that sort of thing, old boy." The British did their best to unwind. "This is Captain Jones," a colonel of Dragoons would say. "He is the one, ought, five American infantry of one of the American regiments. He is of the 27th Division, you know, and he is here with us, and all that sort of thing." Then, after a sip of tea, the colonel said, "Oh, yes, Captain Jones, this is Dados of our 41st Division." The British waged their war by initials.

In technical matters, it was even worse. Many a Doughboy platoon leader, relieving a Frenchman in the dark of night, had a far better idea of his situation when the Frenchman eager to escape his private hell, if only temporarily, simply said, *"Les boches* [he pointed] *sont là. Beaucoup mitrailleuses là."* He uttered a child's "rat-a-a-a-rat" sound of imaginary machine guns, pointing to a high spot against his right flank. *"Prenez la garde, Monsieur! Boom-boom! Terrible! Là!"* He made a sweeping movement with his arm, and then squatted and imitated the short, ugly bark of trench mortars, ending with a "whoom" to indicate a bay in the trenches where a wise soldier would not throw his shadow in daylight hours. Having thus communicated to the Yanks a precise estimate of the situation, he simply said, *"Bon secteur. Au'voir, M'sieu,"* and hustled back to whatever was awaiting him behind the lines.

This clarity, unmistakable to the Yank lieutenant, could be contrasted with the following passage set down by O'Ryan in an exchange between a British officer, still miraculously alive, who was a wizard in trench mortars and a Yank who was hoping to achieve the English proficiency:

Yes, I've been out here for quite a bit. I came over as a subaltern in the 6th Don Aac. Directly I got here, I was given a rather cushy job. I visited a lot of places of the R.A.M.C., but hardly was I on the way with this work when I got a chit from the G.O.C., R.F.A., of the 40th Don Aac, who asked me if I would care for a billet with him. You see, he knew I was a gunner. As a matter of fact, what I was really interested in was the Tock Emmas, with the Emma G's as second choice, but I felt I did not know enough about them and dreaded the school work. You are not with the Tock Emmas by any chance, are you?

There was no interpreter present to explain that the speaker was an artilleryman; that his first assignment was with the Royal Army Medical Corps; that the General Officer Commanding, Royal Field Artillery, of the 40th Division's field artillery, needed a second lieutenant who had been trained as a gunner; that the speaker was afraid he was needed as a machine gunner, about which weapon he knew nothing; that he dreaded more schooling; and that he had been lucky enough to be assigned to trench mortars, about which he knew a great deal. The question he addressed Captain Jones, "You are not with the Tock Emmas by any chance, are you?" might have been couched in Sanskrit.

Men of the 30th and 27th eventually learned—they had not been briefed by the British—that auditory similarities between letters such as "M" and "N," and "T" and "P," had converted the alphabet into words: "Tock" for "T," "Emma" for "M," and so forth. As for the rest—R.A.M.C., G.O.C., R.F.A., and expressions like "Dados"—eventually the Doughboys learned the limey military lingo and knew it to be superior to their own.

In late August, during the latter part of their training in Flanders under a seventy-year-old lieutenant general whose pukka-sahib, cheerio chipperness and horsemanship made them marvel, the Yanks had been blooded in small fights. The New Yorkers of the 27th Division went forward to flank the British at Mont Kemmel, a tragic place-name in British history, on August 27. Corps order forbade the use of a barrage or a general attack; it was to be done in the pattern of cautious patrols advancing ahead of skirmishers, ferreting out strong points of a weak line, and then working their flanks in turn. Only the men who fought there recall this skirmish to seize Vierstraat Ridge. Here and there both junior officers and men, new to the business, threw away their British-taught caution and rushed gun positions frontally, leaving some forty dead Doughboys at gun muzzles. The few German machine gunners posted there sacrificially were loyal stuff; many died in their tracks rather than surrender when offered a chance.

There was too much fire in the hearts of the Empire Staters. They suffered 349 casualties in this exploit against Saxons who had yielded a first line hoping to retake it, with many American prisoners rushing into their trap. After two days, the New Yorkers still held it, their major general, the National Guard buff, being touched by the loss of men to whom he had a sentimental attachment. He was deeply moved the first day when, arriving at an advanced dressing station, he stopped by a blanketed private. Wanting to decorate some of the wounded, he asked, "Who is the bravest among you?" Whereupon, a lad sat up and said, "General, the bravest man in our company is that little Wop lying behind you." O'Ryan pivoted and saw a boy bled blue-white. "I feel-a fine," said the bravest of the brave.

The 30th Division had known a similar small Flanders attack, the British thinking they had followed the book more faithfully in their wariness. Their target that August day was the town of Voormezele, beyond Lock No. 8 of its canal. Having spent a long July digging trenches and stringing wire, with not a jug of corn whiskey within three thousand miles that July Fourth, they were eager to leave off hard labor and drive the enemy back fifteen hundred yards and take some prisoners, doing it copybook fashion. North Dakota Swedes among them knew enough German to identify the enemy as members of the 236th Division, an average outfit the British were happy to interrogate—inasmuch as it had just arrived in the vicinity of Ypres from Rupprecht's dwindling pool of reserves.

After these exercises, the two divisions had been moved eastward from Flanders to the Somme. They were beginning to look British; most were wearing British uniforms, their own having worn out, fastened with American Eagle buttons rushed to them by the ubiquitous Harbord. They had traded in thirty thousand American Enfields for the true British models, varying by a hairline difference in caliber. They spoke the English military lingo—earning criticism from Chaumont inspectors for their "foreign" manners—but they were expert with Vickers machine guns, Stokes mortars, and Lewis guns, and they were ready. Haig wanted them to help break a formidable complex in the Hindenburg Line final positions, the Saint-Quentin Tunnel maze, and they were attached to General Sir Henry Rawlinson's British Fourth Army as the U. S. II Corps.

The Hindenburg Line curved in front of the Saint-Quentin Tunnel of a canal system the Emperor Napoleon had designed. At first glance it looked like a drainage ditch cut through a garbage dump. The steep canal cut itself was festooned with shacks and shanties resembling a hobo jungle, but dug into the shambles were concrete cubicles with steel casemates baring the fangs of machine guns. The tunnel was filled with barges capable of housing a German division. Its mouth was shark-toothed with a three-deep trench system, each faced with belts of barbed wire fantastically woven about concrete pillboxes placed on every mound of high ground. The tunnel itself was terra incognita; not even the enemy knew where other passages had been tunneled laterally into bombproofs beneath the three trench lines, hideouts so deep that thirty wooden steps led down to them. It was an underground city, with electric lights and telephone systems, the Germans having learned, as Robert E. Lee had long ago known, that strong works, properly linked, could be manned by relatively few small arms. The complex was about four thousand yards in depth.

The attack was scheduled for six o'clock in the morning on September 29, with the 27th Division on the left, the 30th Division in the center, and the British 46th Division on the right. The assault on the three-thousand-yard front of the 30th Division, carried by three infantry regiments with one in reserve, accompanied by the neighboring British 46th, went off like clockwork. The former fought through three belts of wire, overran the three trench systems, blocked both ends of the tunnel in concert with the U.S. 27th and the British, and seized the towns with which subsidiary tunnels were connected. By nightfall, they had captured 47 German officers and 1,434 men. But things went badly from the start—and even before—for the 27th Division, facing even rougher ground, and with no expert British division on its flank.

First of all, the British division it relieved had been unable to seize the jump-off lines, so the 27th sent a regiment through the British two days before the attack to try to take them. After a day of furious fighting, in which nearly all the officers were killed or wounded, the Germans were still in possession of the lines except for a few patches of isolated New Yorkers.

The fighting could be best described by the conduct of Second Lieutenant William B. Turner in the early part of the evening. He had a section of nine men left. When a machine gunner discovered him, he went into the trench bay alone and pistoled its gunners to death. He had killed one gunner of the second echelon when his nine men arrived and finished the rest. He was now bearing three wounds, but moved on to the zigzag, where all engaged in hand-to-hand combat. Now out of ammunition, he used a German rifle and bayonet on the fourth position, which he with his men captured in a blind fury of rifle bullets and bayonet. This was his objective.

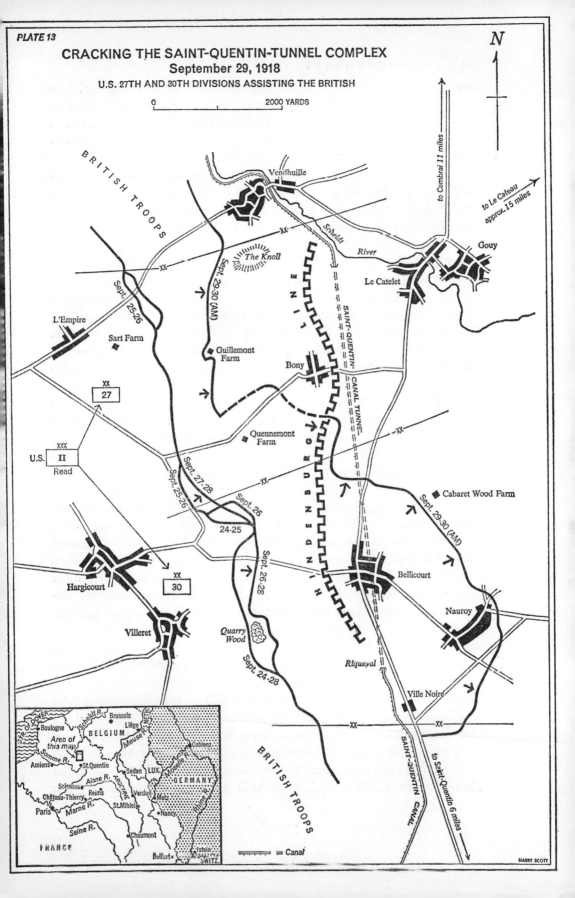

CRACKING THE SAINT-QUENTIN-TUNNEL COMPLEX
September 29, 1918
U.S. 27TH AND 30TH DIVISIONS ASSISTING THE BRITISH

PLATE 13

N

0   2000 YARDS

BRITISH TROOPS

Vendhuille

to Cambrai 11 miles

to Le Cateau approx. 15 miles

Gouy

The Knoll

Sept. 29-30 (AM)

Scheldt River

Le Catelet

SAINT-QUENTIN-CANAL TUNNEL

L'Empire

Sept. 25-26

Sart Farm

Guillemont Farm

Bony

HINDENBURG LINE

XX
27

Quennemont Farm

U.S. XXX
II
Read

Sept. 27-28

Sept. 25-26

Sept. 26

24-25

XX

Cabaret Wood Farm

Sept. 29-30 (AM)

Hargicourt

XX
30

Sept. 26-28

Bellicourt

Villeret

Quarry Wood

Nauroy

Riqueval

Ville Noire

SAINT-QUENTIN CANAL

to Saint-Quentin 6 miles

Sept. 24-28

BRITISH TROOPS

XX   XX

▬▬▬▬ = Canal

HARRY SCOTT

Inset map (FRANCE)

STR. OF DOVER

Boulogne

Scheldt R.

Brussels

Liège

BELGIUM

Meuse R.

Area of this map

Somme R.

Amiens

St.Quentin

Soissons

Aisne R.

Aisne R.

Argonne

Château-Thierry

Reims

Marne R.

Paris

Seine R.

Sedan

LUX.

Moselle R.

Verdun

Metz

St.Mihiel

Nancy

GERMANY

Coblenz

Rhine R.

FRANCE

Chaumont

Belfort

Rstein

SWITZ.

Like the British of the day before, he was not long in possession. The enemy came in force at the Yanks and killed Turner, taking prisoner those wounded who remained. On the following day, September 28, British orders forbade an attack, and thus the full division now faced three strong points without jump-off lines—the principal one being simply "The Knoll."

The Orions—they wore this constellation as a shoulder patch in honor of their general—spent thirty minutes in a berserk fight to seize their own parallel of departure long after the creeping barrage had lifted a thousand yards beyond them, fighting Germans who now appeared in bulletproof vests, some of which were soon worn for snapshot enthusiasts among Doughboy looters, many of the vests bloodstained from the bodies of those who put too much reliance upon them. By the time they had seized their own jump-off positions, corps artillery, concerted for the 27th, 30th, and British 46th, had swept on ahead with its lifepreserving barrages, and the New Yorkers had no choice but to go forward without its protection. They had asked for a renewal of the barrage to gain their jump-off line but the British refused to provide it on grounds that some of the New Yorkers might be cut off in the area where Turner had been killed. It was an international foul-up—one of the instances cited by Pershing in support of his reluctance to amalgamate Doughboys into foreign cadres. By that time, the enemy had reappeared from unshelled depths to dispute the way. Many New York Guardsmen gave their lives in fifteen hundred yards that morning, after years of more preparation than the average A.E.F. leader ever knew.

The 107th U.S. Infantry had 227 officers and men killed and 658 wounded by sunset. The Australians had come up at noon to plug serious gaps with orders to pass through the stricken regiment. Things really went awry then, as at Missionary Ridge in the Civil War when regiments attacked without waiting for orders. The survivors of the 107th, along with other elements who were ordered to hold fast, refused to do so. Doughboy platoons went forward in a body as cadres in broad-hat companies, single Doughboys joined Australian squads, until the attacking lines were a quilting of Aussies and Yanks following the orders of Australian captains. Their conduct delighted the men from down under. Pukka-sahibs in comfortable staff billets were shocked.

Lieutenant General Sir John Monash, writing of the free lances who joined his Australians, said: "It was found to be a matter of some difficulty to induce these men to withdraw from the fighting and to rejoin their own units, so keen were they to continue their advance." Some were still with the Australians two days later. Monash was somewhat put out, for he found himself in an ambiguous situation with so many Yanks among the broad-hats of his own corps. Rawlinson's British Fourth Army had taken heavy knocks; it needed American blood to blast the Saint-Quentin complex, and his decision to send the Australians through the New Yorkers was a fine example of the improvisations that led Haig to call him his best general, an opinion shared by few of his countrymen. But it was up to Monash to send the Yanks back where they belonged, which he finally managed to do. There was irony in his letter to the Yank corps commander two days later. The Jewish general, who wore every brave ribbon in the royal book, used such nouns as *gallantry, devotion, admiration,* but the phrase some Doughboys of the 27th liked best was his "great pleasure it has been to me and to the troops of the Australian Army Corps to have been so closely allied to you in the recent very important battle operations which have resulted in the breaking through of the Main Hindenburg Line." "So closely allied" was the phrase the truants liked. It needed class to travel with the Southern Cross.

In a division that wore more Medals of Honor than any other, and in the 27th which showed such guts in the face of adversity, there were bound to be many illustrious individual performances. In the fog of that attacking morning, many concealed positions were overrun and passed, empty ones then being manned by enemy soldiers emerging from lateral tunnels of the main bore. From one of these positions a machine gun opened fire, holding up the 30th Division's Sergeant Joseph B. Adkinson's second-wave platoon at fifty yards. This so enraged the sergeant that he ran the distance in the wide-open, miraculously unscathed. Arriving at the mouth of the inferno from a flanking angle, armed with rifle and bayonet, he used neither. He simply kicked the machine gun into the faces of the gunners, who then called it a day. His platoon arrived to find three Germans busily turning the gun to face their own men, under the sergeant's directions. They then continued on, the sergeant still angry and still taking many prisoners. Sergeant Milo Lemert also won a Medal of Honor that day, but this one was sent to his wife. His luck ran out at his fourth gun similar to the one Adkinson had kicked around.

The British had been generous with supporting tanks, some of them crewed by Yanks. In open country, where the enemy had learned to concentrate upon these primitive monsters, they were a mortal risk. Sergeant John C. Latham, Corporals Alan L. Eggers and Thomas E. O'Shea, fighting in isolation on the summit of the tunnel, saw a British tank disabled by a direct hit, and heard cries from its crew. O'Shea stopped a mortal one before he reached the tank, but Latham and Eggers made it to the lee side. They pulled out a wounded officer and two wounded sergeants, all Americans. After getting them into a shell hole, one of the crew, Sergeant Frank J. Williams, hobbled back to the tank because he was the only one able to operate its six-pounder cannon. He served the gun for some time, keeping counterattackers at bay until an armor-piercing shell disabled it. When he rejoined his new friends, all agreed they were goners unless they had more firepower. Accordingly, the two rescuers, the firm of Latham & Eggers, together with Williams—who knew how to dismantle the Hotchkiss machine gun still in the tank—again ran the gantlet of enemy fire to secure it, returning to the shell hole to rejoin the disabled officer and the wounded sergeant. They were now in business, and tended the store until darkness, when Sergeant Latham and Corporal Eggers then brought the officer and the wounded sergeant, the weakened gunner, Sergeant Williams, hobbling along, back to the stabilized line. They also brought the Hotchkiss gun.

The 27th Division fought small battles like the Latham operation all day, its left flank exposed to Germans who, until the Australians arrived, were free to attack in detail. Latham, Eggers, and the dying O'Shea were all awarded Medals of Honor. It was difficult to understand the Board of Awards when multiple examples of devotion beyond the call of duty were weighed on headquarters scales. Williams, the wounded sergeant who had driven the tank, manned the cannon, and operated the Hotchkiss, making three trips in the exploit, was awarded the Distinguished Service Cross.

Both divisions, after resting, continued on with Rawlinson's British Fourth Army into October, driving to the Selle River south of Le Cateau, taking ground the Germans could ill afford to lose, in a magnificent demonstration of skill and courage. They never received the publicity back home that was heaped on their brothers in the Argonne, but they suffered about the same number of casualties: the 30th 7,455 officers and men, the 27th 8,088—the variance in figures attributable to that fatal jump-off line. The 30th especially won the praise of British critics for its performance; the 27th was never quite forgiven by the rule-book-minded English for its impetuosity, and its difficulties in the jump-off at Saint-Quentin, though Pershing himself wrote that their inability to keep pace with the protective barrage was "due to no fault of their own." In any case, Pershing would have been delighted to have them both, and could have used them almost anywhere on his Meuse-Argonne line, especially to help the 77th Division, deep in the forest on his extreme left.

Chapter **16**

"THE LOST BATTALION"

He is quite a soldier. We envy you.

By October 1, the 77th Division, deep in the Argonne, on the First Army's left flank, had reached within striking distance of the Palette Pavilion, more austere than the Bagatelle Pavilion it captured earlier, but much prized by the enemy. He had entrenched and barb-wired it years before, for it commanded not only the dense south forests of the Argonne, but the spur valley from the Aisne where French troops, flanking the New Yorkers, must attempt to advance through its patches of green fields. The cliffs there were as formidable as those confronting the 28th Pennsylvanians on the right. Woods defended the pavilion's approaches, with chicken-wire nets suspended and hidden amidst underbrush and saplings to snare Doughboys like birds, and light trenches were dug into its southern slopes where fire teams of machine gunners might discourage even the most determined to gain bayonet range with the main defenders on the heights beyond. On the night of October 1, corps orders were given to attack these positions at 6:30 A.M. the next day.

Charles W. Whittlesey's 1st Battalion of the 308th Infantry was in the front line the next morning, having with other elements captured a great German supply base, the *Dépôt des Machines*. As was always the case in the Argonne-Meuse operations, each difficult position, when captured, only led attacking troops to face an even more difficult one in the vast maze of traps and caves, machine guns and cannon, the enemy had been four years

267

in devising. Whittlesey's battalion had for its leapfrogging support the 2nd Battalion of his regiment, commanded by Captain George G. McMurtry, an old Rough Rider and Harvard lawyer, also a Plattsburg graduate in days when such civilians were laughingstock play-soldiers derided by the ideological die-hards of Woodrow Wilson's day.

Because of the attrition of the preceding six days, instead of sixteen hundred men Whittlesey and McMurtry had between them a little less than half that number. Ahead of them, a diagonal across their front, was a major ravine splitting their battalion strengths. Whittlesey had three companies (A, B, C) to the east of this tortuous ravine, D Company of his front on the west side virtually isolated from its battalion commander. That was the way of the Argonne Forest. Captain McMurtry's supporting battalion was also divided, his isolated F Company backing up Whittlesey's D Company, his others in support of Whittlesey's A, B, and C. The 3rd battalion, 308th Infantry (Colonel Cromwell Stacy), was in Brigade Reserve, subject only to the brigadier's orders. And no matter how soundly the Leavenworth staff professors drummed "unity of command" into its graduates, in the A.E.F. this was—through fault of divisional organization, according to Major General Alexander—rarely respected. Colonel Stacy did not have a regiment to work with; he had only two-thirds of his command to execute an assignment on a regimental front split by a ravine.

After a barrage from a regiment of supporting field artillery Whittlesey plunged forward at 6:30 A.M., McMurtry following, two machine-gun companies going along. The attack failed everywhere on a corps front in a shocking repulse. The 77th's 153rd Brigade found the going impossible, Whittlesey's 154th doing little better. The French could not move to the left up the valley of the Aisne, so forbidding was German gunfire from the Palette Pavilion. On the right of the New Yorkers, the Pennsylvanians had found the cliffs of Le Chêne Tondu just as formidable, and could not move. By ten o'clock in the morning things were little changed from dawn, stretcher-bearers and groaning wounded everywhere.

Pershing's orders, fully explained to divisions by their Corps Commanders Bullard, Liggett, and Cameron, were for each division to press forward looking after its own flanks, heedless of the divisions on either side. And so Major General Robert Alexander ordered the 77th to resume its attack at one-thirty in the afternoon. This gave Whittlesey and McMurtry time to regroup their men and chew on field rations. Promptly at 1:30 P.M. on October 2, Whittlesey broke through, crossing wide bands of rusty barbed wire, overrunning German trenches, with McMurtry on his heels, elements of C and D Companies of the 306th Machine Gun Battalion killing flankers with their Hotchkiss heavy tripod gear. They had gone forward after lunch with about 675 men, and they lost 90 in their advance. They had killed or wounded an unknown number of the enemy, and had taken only two officers and twenty-eight men prisoners, capturing two machine guns. The Germans fell back to stronger positions, taking their guns with them, leaving a mile of trenches unmanned. Whittlesey now had his emaciated A, B, and C Companies, McMurtry his E, G, and H outfits, in a ravine just south of his brigade objective for the day, which was the Charlevaux Mill. They had crossed the fearsome ravine, and were digging into the road which ran along the side of a hill, the road a rough, benchlike cut hugging a steep contour where enemy guns above could not depress upon them.

Whittlesey now assumed a posture of defense to await the counterattack, setting up his lifesaving machine gunners on his flanks. The major was in good shape with McMurtry to back him up, his line of runner posts extending back to his regiment's other battalion which Brigade held in reserve. It was now up to Brigade to bring this battalion to the line of Whittlesey's flank along with D and F Companies—for there were no French on his left flank as yet—and take the Charlevaux Mill position. The French division, right flank of Gouraud's French Fourth Army, was a long gap away, and still fifteen hundred yards to the rear around Binarville.

As the afternoon waned, Alexander ordered his brigadier to close the gap with the battalion of the 308th, plus the reserve battalion of the other brigade's 307th. He was not too concerned; such things happened every day, especially in woods fighting. But as night came on, so did confusion; the two battalions never reached the gap. Morning found one of them dazedly facing the French flank in the Aisne Valley, minus one company. Captain Nelson M. Holderman, of K Company, in Whittlesey's brigade twin, the 307th Infantry, had the eyes of a lynx and the heart of a leopard. He brought his stealthy company of ninety-seven survivors up to Whittlesey's bench that morning, October 3, the only one of the captains to do so.

In the meantime, Whittlesey had dispatched one of McMurtry's officers, Lieutenant Wilhelm, with a force to backtrail in hopes of bringing up D Company and F Company from their far side of the ravine. Wilhelm never made it; for early that morning the old German pros had begun examining the new American positions. They had dispersed the runner posts and reoccupied the mile of empty trenches on Whittlesey's flank in the yawning gap of the absent French. They had infiltrated machine gunners, mortarmen, and infantry support into the positions—which they had dug in long ago. Wilhelm was surrounded, but ordered Lieutenant Lenke back to Whittlesey's command, while he covered for him. Lenke reached the bench road with nineteen men, reporting that the runner posts had been scattered. Wilhelm eventually retreated across the ravine with a few survivors.

Whittlesey now knew he was bagged with elements of three infantry battalions and his machine gunners—650 American soldiers trapped in a slender oval, with fourteen elements of a fresh German division, including riflemen, machine gunners, shock companies, flame throwers and mortarmen, skillfully positioned in a full circle around them at a radius of about two hundred yards. At this point, Whittlesey sent two of his eight carrier pigeons to Alexander, asking for ammunition, rations and support, giving his approximate whereabouts, an obscure road he occupied in a depth of 70 yards on a 350-yard line.

Alexander made his second move to rescue Whittlesey's battalion at dawn October 3, again attacking with both brigades, and gaining nothing. A company commander of the 307th Infantry, now about to attempt a relief of Whittlesey, described the dawn of his first Argonne attack:

The heavy fog had kept the powder smoke down and as morning dawned I found myself with two runners adrift in a blind world of whiteness and noise, groping over something like the surface of the moon. One literally could not see two yards and everywhere the ground rose into bare pinnacles and ridges or descended into bottomless chasms, half-filled with rusty tangles of wire. . . . At the end of two hours I had collected two squads of infantry with a few engineers and so, with forces joined, we pushed on into the thickest jungle I have ever seen and it seemed to go on forever. And by one o'clock, in a fifteen-foot trench with unscalable walls of mud and a stream along its bottom, I knew where nothing was except the guide, my Company Headquarters and half a platoon.

The 2nd Battalion of the 305th Infantry, with elements of the 3rd, tried again to reach Whittlesey around four o'clock that afternoon, the 2nd having five officers down, two hundred men casualties, runners down everywhere. There was always difficulty in preserving clarity among relays of runners carrying word-of-mouth messages under fire. Platoon leaders labored in the fields of France to perfect systems. Some made running games of it, with squad prizes weekends free of all rake-and-broom duty. The relay race began, runners passing the whispered message instead of a baton, each team timed for speed wearing full packs and bayonet-fixed rifles. When the anchor man came racing in, the message might be gibberish. A wise chief of platoon then left the immediate vicinity while the losing squad disciplined the nonconductor. It was difficult enough when everyone spoke with the same accent; it was doubly so with the dialects of the 77th. Six runners might speak six different varieties of English, one valorous immigrant becoming a nonconductor in the chain—like a short circuit on a power line. General Alexander recalled one such garbled message. "Watch out for shell holes," a captain sent word in darkness to inform his support officer that machine guns were thereabouts. "The captain says to go wash yer clothes," the support officer was told.

Everywhere the advance now had been stopped cold by the furious Germans, desperate because green Doughboys had progressed for six days into what the German Staff considered impregnable positions. They placed their forest reliance mainly on heavy machine guns echeloned in depth, each gun with traverse pins set to cover its captured neighbor. Outflanking such gun nests was beyond the capabilities of any but sacrificial units expert with grenades and Stokes mortars. Many Doughboys died as soon as they had overrun one of these chattering assassins with its stovepipe water jacket, seven-point-six millimeter nose protruding through its flash screen and feed-belt cartridges glittering like a rattlesnake's back. No sooner had an attacker thrust his bayonet through the breast of the surviving gunner than a flanking gun, until then silent on the checkerboard of dense underbrush, killed him mercilessly in turn. Any man badly wounded and bleeding at its captured muzzle lost his life, too, unless he lay still. It could mean death to grope toward his cartridge belt for a first-aid pack. Nothing but an attack of tanks could overrun these nests—and primeval tanks were useless in ravine terrain.

Following the morning's failure, Hunter Liggett summoned his division commanders to corps headquarters: Muir of the Pennsylvanians, Alexander of the New York's own 77th, Duncan of Acting Corporal York's brawling, blasphemous 82nd Division now coming up to take over part of Muir's front, and Summerall who had arrived with the 1st Division. Alexander's chief concern was Whittlesey, but Liggett's was the American First Army's reputation; after Pershing's struggle for an independent command, it was at stake all along the line. The Allies were carping about Pershing's check after the second day; it was the kind of criticism newcomers had to expect. Fresh German brigades were pouring in along the forest line, under desperate orders to hold. Whittlesey's surrender would be a feather in the German's war bonnet, and a shock to Doughboy morale.

To counter such a disgrace, Liggett changed his tactics. The Big Red One would replace the green 35th, which had been rendered battleworthy at a terrible cost, and drive a flanking gap into the German lines beyond Exermont east of the Argonne Forest. At 5:30 A.M. on October 4, the general onslaught of the American First Army would be renewed. Back at 77th Division headquarters, Alexander gave Brigadier General Evan M. Johnson *carte blanche* to strike mainly on the left, driving through the hole Whittlesey had torn in German wire.

On Liggett's far right, the 1st Division proceeded in its customary manner to carve a wide gap in the Hindenburg Line beyond Exermont. However, its success did not immediately affect Whittlesey's situation and on Liggett's far left Johnson did not make any sizable gains against the tenacious Germans.

By October 5, Whittlesey on his bench was beginning to suffer severely. He had been there three nights now. His medical supplies were exhausted, about half of his men wounded, many dying. He had no food and little water, but he still commanded the respect of the German, who began to starve him out. McMurtry was hobbling about with a knee the size of a football, where shrapnel fragments were festering. Holderman had three wounds thus far, one of them a piece of the wooden stick from a potato-masher grenade lodged in his back. Their chief torment was the avalanche of grenades hurled from the hill above. The German was engaged in psychological warfare. Men on the bench below could hear the roll call of German sergeants ticking off the names of grenadiers above and the slow count: *ein, zwei, drei* . . . and then the avalanche. Men dug in everywhere, too feeble to bury their own dead. Field medics, when a man's body began to stiffen, crawled to cadavers and unwound the stiffened bandages, applying these blood-soaked gauzes to freshly wounded men, while other wounded rifled the pockets of the dead in hopes of finding a morsel of chocolate, a few shreds of tobacco.

French artillery, replying to the challenge on Charlevaux Mill's hill, shelled Whittlesey's outfit. Some American shells fell among them, too. Allied artillery's problem in punishing Whittlesey's besiegers was that, say, of a battery in the Hollywood hills striving to shell the unseen spectators in the Los Angeles Coliseum without injuring two football teams playing between the fifteen-yard lines on the field. Whittlesey sent more of his pigeons, urgently asking all artillery counterfire to cease.

Airplanes from the 50th Aero Squadron, assigned to locate Whittlesey's slender oval—seventy yards in depth—to drop him food and ammunition, were unable to spot his small white ground panels through the autumn haze and smoke. Some of the squadron's aviators still tell their grandsons that Whittlesey had put out no panels—at least none they could see. Nevertheless, many of them, flying DH-4s, the "Flaming Coffins" of Sidney Howard's recent experience, courted death to drop food and ammunition onto the forlorn bench, and not one bundle ever fell there. On the morning of October 5, Lieutenants Harold Goettler and Erwin Blackley, pilot and observer, made several passes at two hundred feet over the ravine without discovering Whittlesey's position, while the Germans withheld fire to avoid revealing it. When the plane came by for another pass, the Germans on hills above opened downward fire on it, shooting its fabric into sievelike patterns while the two Yanks dropped packets of medical supplies and food as best they could and miraculously got away. Arriving back at Squadron, they patched their ship for another sortie while other planes kept trying, two of which were shot down in No-Man's Land. In the afternoon, Goettler and

Blackley set out again. As they came to treetop level, Germans above poured heavy machine-gun and rifle fire down upon them. Both were mortally wounded, but Goettler lived long enough to pull back on his stick, clear the trees and land his plane in French front lines; two dead men among one of Gouraud's divisions in the valley of the Aisne, their feat unremembered until the Board of Awards at Washington gave them posthumous Medals of Honor.

On the same day, October 5, the French pushed up the Aisne Valley to the left in a fine advance, and for a few minutes they held the Palette Pavilion beyond the Charlevaux Mill, where Whittlesey one thousand yards below still clung to his desperate position. It was a golden opportunity that came to nought when the brigade seeking to relieve Whittlesey was repulsed again, and the naked French flank was driven out by German counterattacks from Whittlesey's front. General Alexander blamed the colonel on the far left, an officer of twenty years' service in the Regular Army who, his brigade commander reported, declined "to assume responsibility for the attack." The colonel thought it a lunatic enterprise. When Johnson was told to sack him and appoint the next in rank to regimental command, the brigadier protested. He had no lieutenant colonels or majors left. Alexander angrily gave the regiment to Captain Lucien Breckenridge, noted for his guts and his ginger. Breckenridge never bothered to move back to Regimental Headquarters; instead, the headquarters mountain moved up to Mohammed. But the opportunity had passed.

It was the same story on October 6. Liggett, hearing that the Germans were talking about an armistice on the basis of Woodrow Wilson's Fourteen Points, ordered another attack along his corps front to keep the German on the hook. No man could hear his own voice in the deafening fire fight that roared through the valley of the Aire that morning, yet lines were unchanged around Whittlesey when it was over. Again the French asked permission to shell the Mill positions, but Brigadier General Johnson was quick to protest that Whittlesey was still in situation there. Somehow, it was a foregone conclusion, never once changed, that he would never surrender.

However, this day brought a ray of hope to those trying to rescue the beleaguered group. A lieutenant and two privates from Whittlesey's outfits managed to filter through German lines, having spent three stealthy hours the night before in the midst of sleeping Germans in a Moulin de Charlevaux bivouac and then shooting their way out. Their information was invaluable, and Lieutenant Colonel Eugene H. Houghton, most European warwise of Alexander's commanders, a Minnesota lumberman who had joined the Canadian Army in 1915 and had had three years of fighting before transferring to American ranks, told Alexander he believed he could get his

307th Infantry to Whittlesey through a gap in the German wire. The attempt would be made in the general attack scheduled the next day. (As the two officers discussed their plans in a forward dressing station, the body of Captain Edward Grant was brought in. John McGraw's Giants would miss that fine pair of hands.)

At daybreak of October 7, an insubordinate private in McMurtry's H Company, with eight buddies, slipped through the forest hoping to retrieve a package of rations aviators had dropped nearby. The nine famished lads were ambushed by a German patrol setting a lure. Five were killed, the other four wounded and taken prisoner. One of their captors was Lieutenant Fritz Printz, a platoon commander in the 67th Reserve Division, who had spent six years in Spokane as German representative for a tungsten company. Thinking it suicide for the Americans to sustain another attack, and alarmed at the discouragement creeping over his own men at the buoyancy of the Americans, he suggested to his major that a plea to surrender be sent back to Whittlesey. The major agreed, and a prisoner was selected to carry it. The prisoner refused, and was entreated to do so in the name of humanity. He demanded that the note, if he was forced to deliver it, must clear his name with his commanding officer. The note was written, the prisoner was blindfolded and released near the machine-gun flank of the bench road. Major Julius Ochs Adler, of the *New York Times* family, was an infantry captain in the relief that day, and later division historian. He blanked out the private's name in the note. He understood the plight of this hungry, insubordinate, and yet honorable boy; and he thought censorship was humane. The isolated company admired this crippled boy, and was proud to name him. He was Private Lowell R. Hollingshead, H Company, McMurtry's battalion. The note the boy handed to Whittlesey at four o'clock that same afternoon was published as follows:

To the Commanding Officer—Infantry, 77th American Division.
Sir: The bearer of this present, Private [Blank], has been taken prisoner by us. He refused to give the German Intelligence Officer any answer to his questions, and is quite an honorable fellow, doing honor to his Fatherland in the strictest sense of the word.

He has been charged against his will, believing that he is doing wrong to his country to carry forward this present letter to the officer in charge of the battalion of the 77th Division, with the purpose to recommend this commander to surrender with his forces, as it would be quite useless to resist anymore, in view of present conditions.

The suffering of your wounded men can be heard over here in the German lines, and we are appealing to your humane sentiments to stop. A white flag shown by one of your men will tell us that you agree with these conditions.

Please treat Private [Blank] as an honorable man. He is quite a soldier. We envy you.

THE GERMAN COMMANDING OFFICER

Whittlesey of the 1st Battalion, crippled McMurtry of the 2nd, and the much-wounded Holderman of the other regiment read the note—McMurtry now on a single tree-branch crutch, the shrapnel in his knee festering for four days, a bullet lodged in his shoulder from when he had moved some wounded men, making even a crab's gait an effort. They sent a bold lieutenant to take in the white ground panels, fearing the Germans might mistake them for a sign of surrender.

Whittlesey sent no reply to the note, but grapevine carried news of it along the foxholes of the bench road above the little brook feeding the Aisne, and a chorus began when a wounded man rose on one elbow and shouted down the valley, "You Heinie bastards, come and get us!" It was the German commander's first news of the unknown Doughboy commander's reaction. Scores joined in, and wounded trees on the torn slope soon rocked with obscenities. Lieutenant William Cullen recalled forty years later that he knew enough German to call the enemy sons-of-bitches in its own tongue. *"Windbetreben"* was a favorite term of opprobrium with those Doughboys. It meant, literally, "Wind-bag Circle"—denoting armchair strategists—but there were other, and more vulgar, connotations; it also meant the noise made by a horse with the bots. The German's humane sentiments now changed. He attacked with flame throwers on the right flank where there was the one remaining Hotchkiss gunner, who fired pointblank on the assault teams, kindling the *Flamenwerfer* men into human torches.

Forty years afterward, Walter Baldwin, who was a corporal on the bench road that day, could recall the figure of his captain, Holderman, where he stood erect using a pair of rifles as crutches, giving the gunner fire cover with his Colt .45. The captain, suffering from his four previous wounds, the stick of a potato-masher grenade still in his back, got his fifth wound about the time he got his fifth German.

Houghton's Canadian-tutored sagacity was confirmed in the general attack of October 7. Patrols got through the gap in the wire he had discovered, and Kenney's battalion of the 307th Infantry poured in to turn the German flank. Brigadier General Evan Malbone Johnson, USA, an old Apache fighter who first learned mathematics at Brooklyn's Polytechnic Institute, his tactics in both the Infantry and Cavalry Schools at Leavenworth, his strategy at the Army War College at Washington, threw away his textbooks that day and attacked like a private soldier in the first wave on his fifty-seventh birthday, thirty-six years after his enlistment as a private in the 10th U.S. Infantry. (Having quarreled over Alexander's sacking of the colonel, he had to "request transfer" to another combat brigade when the bloody day was finished.) The division's whole front swarmed through behind Johnson's brigade.

The machine gunner on Whittlesey's right, with McMurtry giving pistol support, was still at it in sporadic bursts when, far away, Doughboys heard the familiar chatter of Hotchkiss guns, the curious, racking coughs of the Chauchats, and soon, nearby, the Springfield's high-pitched whine. Presently a new Doughboy arrived, one never seen before. He was carrying on his bayonet a sack with a few cans of corned beef. Then many others flooded the valley and others killed the recently arrived *Stosstruppen* on the fatal hill. "Look at 'em run, the Heinie bastards!" shouted the wounded as an officer went the rounds of festering men with an eight-cent mess-kit spoon wanting every man to share a first taste of food in five days, the two surviving field medics too weak to do more than crawl to their patients. Many of the unwounded were too weak to walk, let alone risk nightly fire fights and dig a grave; some had cramps from eating the bark of trees, others had racking coughs from smoking aspen leaves. The survivors told of the enemy's taunts; the shouts in English; the avalanches of potato-masher grenades and mortar shells from the hill above the bench road; of flank attacks, frontal assaults, ruses; of a Yank aviator (still unknown) who succeeded in directing a bombardment of the hill above by hovering over it and signaling *"Fire on me"*; the shouts of joy when German corpses were blown sky-high above them, hunks of human cadavers hurtling down upon the road.

Many of them wanted to know the fate of their eighth, and last, carrier pigeon, *Cher Ami*. The little bird had been released that morning, after friendly shells again fell among them, but he perched in a treetop with his leg-band message, not wishing to brave the shrapnel coursing through the skies. He was sent on his way when the pigeon man, Omer Richards, climbed the tree under fire and scolded him. Yes, *Cher Ami* was back at the pigeon wagon, minus an eye and a leg, the division veterinary surgeon in attendance; and he would recover. The men back there were carving a wooden leg or two for *Cher Ami,* who was going to be retired and, some-day, be mounted in a glass case at the Smithsonian Institution. "These men," said their historian about those asking for news of *Cher Ami,* "who had only recently been subjected to the pogroms of Russia . . . gunmen and gangsters . . . Italians, Chinamen, the Jews and the Irish . . . [were] truly representative of the varied human flotsam and the sturdy American manhood which comprise the civil population of New York City. . . ." The survivors marched out next morning to the collecting station with their wounded, McMurtry still on his crutch, the last man to leave the bench.

Major Kenney had reached Whittlesey with rations and ammunition—and cigarettes—while there was still an afterglow on the hills of torture above the bench. Major General Alexander reached the position on foot at next daybreak, walking along the bench road swinging his malacca walking stick, a captured German cigar stuck in his big Scots face.

A gaunt Whittlesey was distributing rations to his wounded. Alexander did not stay long and he did not say much. What were his thoughts? He recalled that a sentence from Lord Napier's *History of the Peninsular War* ran through his memory. It was from the description of the aftermath at Albuera: "The enemy rolled backward down the slope, the rain followed after in torrents stained with blood and fifteen hundred unwounded men, the remnant of six thousand unconquerable British soldiers, stood triumphant on the fatal hill." One hundred ninety-five stood unwounded on Whittlesey's bench, the remnant of the unconquerable 550 who first gained it. American morale, half of war anywhere, had soared sky-high. Alexander hurried back to Division, telephoned Liggett, and then telephoned Whittlesey that he was now a lieutenant colonel, McMurtry a major and that both would wear the baby-blue ribbon of the Medal of Honor, as would Holderman. Kenney's battalion, giving away all its rations, emptying its pockets of treasured cigarettes and Hershey bars, the more frugal from the Bagatelle Pavilion passing canteens filled with schnapps, now heard the tale.

Alexander carried the surrender message back to Division as Medal of Honor data, but not until Kenney's Doughboys had looked upon it with heart-warming profanity. By this time, a legend had begun to grow up around "The Lost Battalion"—first misnamed by a news editor cabling his correspondent for more copy on it. Damon Runyon, brightest reporter of his time, enriched the legend by quoting Whittlesey as saying "Go to hell" in reply to the German officer's demand for surrender. Runyon is supposed to have scrambled through shellfire to reach Alexander, and asked him what the commander of the Lost Battalion had replied to the surrender note; and Alexander is supposed to have answered in Army lingo, "Why he told him to go to hell, of course." Runyon, who was an accurate reporter, was writing in good faith when he told his breathless readers back home of this reply; it made headlines all over America.

Major Whittlesey was a slender, bespectacled New Englander, a man of manners, a practicing lawyer in New York, and "Go to hell" was as far from his idea of an appropriate riposte to the enemy officer as it would have been if addressed to the prosecuting attorney in the New York Court of Appeals.

No other legend was ever so fascinating, or so warmly human and heroic, as the facts that nurtured this one: "The Lost Battalion" was not a battalion, nor was it ever lost. No commander ever knew his whereabouts better than Whittlesey, senior among officers from seven companies of three infantry battalions and the machine-gun elements of a fourth. He had been cut off short of his objective for the day, a French division on his left flank and his own brigade failing to keep pace. He sent his position back by carrier pigeon, and he was not out of line by more than ten feet.

According to legend, Whittlesey had advanced precipitately with a single battalion, and while he might have been court-martialed for his impetuous act, his conduct after his initial blunder merited a Medal of Honor. Actually, Whittlesey had advanced strictly under orders.

Much has been written of Whittlesey's character, many chroniclers seeking contradictions and complexities in his makeup; but there is nothing recondite about a New England conscience. He was a man who despised war and yet thought it his duty to take the Plattsburg courses on the art of war. There are few assets in our national reserves better evaluated than such a New England conscience. Doubtless he was always angry, always lonely, and always hated his role. Who puzzles over the late Mr. Justice Holmes, who, alluding to his Civil War wounds, could say, "We were touched with fire"?

Then, too, there is the grapevine that Alexander had issued orders, not only that no man was to withdraw, but that such conduct would be regarded as traitorous, which would give the Military Police the right to shoot such defectors. It is difficult to believe that "The Private's General" who saw that a green boy leaving Saint-Aignan had his mess kit filled with ham sandwiches, his canteen filled with hot coffee, would have issued such an illegal ultimatum. Yet the unofficial cackles still continue that Whittlesey heard of such an order, and in his dedicated way sought to save his command from being shot by pushing forward.

War is in the province of conjectures, and armchair strategy is usually festooned with them. As for the speculation that Whittlesey should have attempted to fight a withdrawing action, crossing a mile of trenches occupied by the enemy after learning that his runner posts had been overrun—this would have been madness. Had Whittlesey surrendered, or been totally destroyed, the recriminations might have reached the inflated heights of Custer's defeat, and doubtless a goat would have been found; much as the United States Army, to its everlasting shame, eventually saw to it that Major Reno, madman Custer's second-in-command and a superb officer on the Little Big Horn, died a derelict in a Washington alley and now lies by the Potomac in Potter's Field. But Whittlesey, having left his country a legacy of unsurpassed leadership, doubtless heard whispers, or received blackguardly letters he never mentioned, which eventually drove him to leap into the sea from a Havana-bound liner. It is difficult to think of Whittlesey with his pinched features, his spectacles, and sloping shoulders as Leonidas combing his long hair with his Spartans at Thermopylae; but the two men were of equal heart, for there is something Spartan about the New Englanders, such as Whittlesey, at their best.

What was left of Whittlesey's command immediately volunteered to remain in the line. The Argonne was a New York forest now, and the Wall Streeters intended to keep advancing until they owned 100 percent of the common stock.

Chapter **17**

BLANC MONT

Yes, the general got the Croix de Guerre,
But the sonofabitch wasn't even there;
Hinky-dinky, parley-voo.

What the Saint-Quentin Tunnel represented to Haig, and in a lesser way the Palette Pavilion to Whittlesey, Blanc Mont, midway on the Hindenburg Line between Reims and the citadel of Grandpré just north of the Argonne, meant to General Gouraud commanding the French Fourth Army on Pershing's left flank. As October came, Gouraud faced the ridges to the east of Reims from where Germans had looked south upon the Chemin des Dames, the chalky hills and vineyards of the Champagne, since 1914. In the general offensive of September 26, French troops, no longer stout enough to take such positions, had gotten nowhere with these heights dominated by the "White Mountain" about fifteen miles north by east of Reims. (It was a situation Foch, who had a fine eye for ground, had foreseen in his violent quarrel with Pershing at Ligny-en-Barrois August 30.) If Gouraud could bring his 155s to the summit of Blanc Mont's woods and pockets, the enemy battle lines would be withdrawn toward the Aisne, and the sacred Reims Cathedral's mutilated towers would no longer be subject to the vile Boche's artillery whims. As the old battle-ax with his flapping sleeve, his leg gnarled as Sir Harry Lauder's blackthorn cane, stared at the heights, he could think only of Mangin's "You rushed into the fight as to a fete," that first morning at
280

Soissons; of the Rainbows who had shown him their lustrous wares standing before the Marne. The U.S. 1st Division was committed on the Exermont Road in the valley of the Aire, the 42nd's Rainbows moving up, but the 1st's Corps brother of that July day, the Marines and Doughboys of the U.S. 2nd Division, were not yet in the line. Gouraud asked Pétain to use his influence with Foch.

Foch asked Pershing for the division, pointing out that it would actually be in support of his own left flank, fighting just west of the Aisne as an accompaniment to the American First Army's Argonne-Meuse operations and Pershing gave it to Gouraud, though it was one of his first-flight four. Until Blanc Mont fell, Gouraud had no hope of advancing northward to join hands with the Doughboys on the Grandpré Road. In order to have Yank reserves, he sent with it the infantry of the 36th Lone Star Division of Texas and Oklahoma National Guard, bringing it up from Amant-Saint-Ronde.

This latter outfit, liberally textured with Cherokees, Apaches, and boys of Mexican descent, had never even been in a dummy trench. It had no trains as yet, no hospital services; nor had its artillery or engineers joined it; but as subsequent events would prove, its men probably had the finest legs in France. The Iron Commander almost dared hope it would not be used, save as a holding force after the race-horse brigades had carried the hills. Although he had passed little time in Gouraud's company, Pershing knew him; and he did not think it necessary to send an American corps commander to safeguard the interests of his two divisions—a tribute to the humanity of that unconquerable *mutilé de la guerre* who had withheld the 42nd's Rainbows from the First Position those July days when he checked von Einem and von Mudra.

Accordingly, the 2nd Division arrived to relieve the stalled French the night of October 1-2, breathless as usual because some chance of war always found it receiving orders when it was too late to study the battleground it must conquer. There had been *noblesse oblige* among its commanders. When Bundy commanded it, the Marine brigade got the hot end of the stick in Belleau Wood. When Harbord took over, he gave the infantry brigade the roughest assignment at Soissons, even hoping the 6th Marine Regiment, chief sufferer in the Château-Thierry sector, might not be deployed—a courteous piece of wishful thinking.

As usual, everyone hoped the feisty 2nd Engineers would not have to fight as riflemen; their lieutenant colonels were still scolding brigadiers like Hanson Ely and Wendell Neville. "All the digging they usually did," their lieutenant colonels said, "was in their own foxholes." Even the 2nd's three fine artillery regiments had known open-sights situations, since the

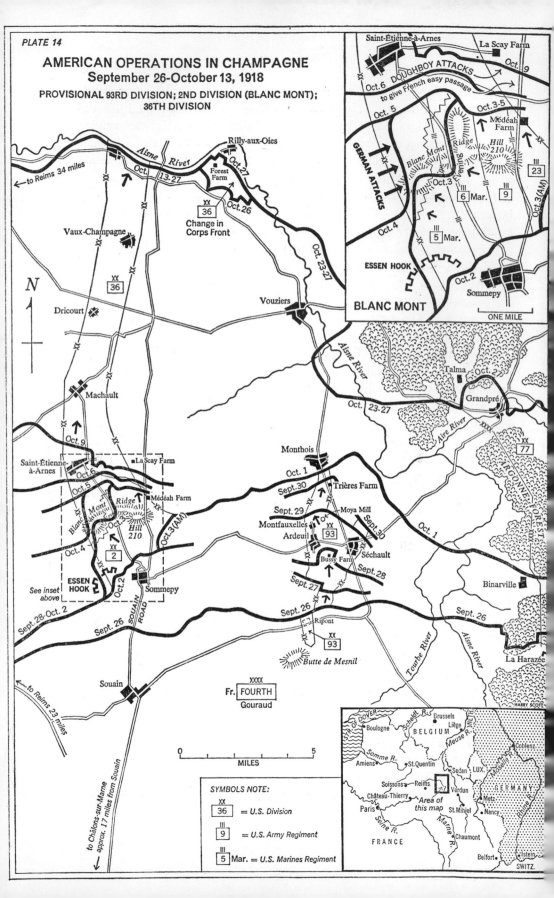

PLATE 14

AMERICAN OPERATIONS IN CHAMPAGNE
September 26-October 13, 1918
PROVISIONAL 93RD DIVISION; 2ND DIVISION (BLANC MONT); 36TH DIVISION

to Reims 34 miles

Aisne River

Rilly-aux-Oies

Oct. 13-27

Forest Farm

Oct. 27

Oct. 26

Change in Corps Front

Vaux-Champagne

Oct. 23-27

Vouziers

N

Dricourt

Machault

Oct. 9

La Scay Farm

Saint-Étienne-à-Arnes

Oct. 6

Oct. 5

Médéah Farm

Ridge

Oct. 3

Hill 210

Blanc Mont

Oct. 4

ESSEN HOOK

Oct. 3 (AM)

Oct. 2

Sommepy

Souain Road

See inset above

Sept. 28-Oct. 2

Sept. 26

Souain

to Reims 23 miles

Aisne River

Talma

Oct. 2

Grandpré

Oct. 23-27

Aire River

Monthois

Oct. 1

Sept. 30

Trières Farm

Sept. 29

Moya Mill

Sept. 30

Montfauxelles

Ardeuil

Séchault

Bussy Farm

Sept. 28

Oct. 1

ARGONNE FOREST

77

Binarville

Sept. 27

Sept. 26

Sept. 26

La Harazée

Tourbe River

Aisne River

Ripont

93

Butte de Mesnil

Fr. FOURTH
Gouraud

HARRY SCOTT

0   5
MILES

SYMBOLS NOTE:

36 = U.S. Division

9 = U.S. Army Regiment

5 Mar. = U.S. Marines Regiment

to Châlons-sur-Marne approx. 17 miles from Souain

BLANC MONT (inset)

Saint-Étienne-à-Arnes

La Scay Farm

Oct. 9

Oct. 6   DOUGHBOY ATTACKS
to give French easy passage

Oct. 5

Oct. 3-5

Médéah Farm

GERMAN ATTACKS

Blanc Mont

Ridge

Hill 210

Oct. 3 Evening

Oct. 3

6 Mar.

9

23

Oct. 3 (AM)

Oct. 4

5 Mar.

ESSEN HOOK

Oct. 2

Sommepy

ONE MILE

(France locator inset)

STR. OF DOVER

Boulogne

BELGIUM

Brussels

Liège

Coblenz

Amiens

Schelot R.

Somme R.

St.Quentin

Soissons

Reims

Sedan

LUX.

Verdun

Meuse R.

Moselle R.

GERMANY

Metz

Château-Thierry

Paris

Area of this map

St.Mihiel

Nancy

Rhine R.

Seine R.

Marne R.

Chaumont

FRANCE

Belfort

SWITZ.

division always seemed to be on a moving belt. Mess sergeants of the brigades often debated among themselves as to which rolling kitchen "got there fustest" with the strongest coffee. And now that Lejeune, a Marine, was the 2nd's chief, he believed the left face of Blanc Mont's summit would present the roughest problem, so he gave a high mound in the right face, a French objective, to the infantry brigade. This, too, was a piece of wishful thinking; whenever the French asked for that Yank division, it meant that there were no easy approaches to the enemy positions. The poilus were either retreating, exhausted, or stalled.

The Germans occupied a position which, when viewed from the air, resembled a starfish holding a cocklebur in each of its tentacles. Each bur was crowned with concrete pillboxes, looking on the horizon like half-filled tanks of a city's gaslight service.

On the morning of October 2, the Marine brigade that disliked the position the stalled French had turned over to their two veteran regiments noisily jumped the gun and took the German advanced line, mopping up grenadiers and machine gunners with the customary shouts and cries. They were now in a suitable jumping-off place, ready to follow the next morning's barrage. On the far right, the French assured the veteran Doughboy brigade that the 9th and 23rd Regiments had nothing in front of them except French whom they could leapfrog through the next morning. Unfortunately, during the night the Germans drove out the French, who failed to notify Brigadier General Hanson E. Ely of this critical withdrawal. In the center, Lejeune left a gap. He had no intention of making frontal assaults on the giant pillboxes, the deep cuts in the chalky hills and forest patches. He would leave the 36th Division's four new infantry regiments with its Field Signal Battalion facing this gap, in reserve lines.

The plan to capture Blanc Mont was a good one. Marines would seize the left flank, a position something like Little Round Top, from its western face. The Doughboy brigade would take the eastern flank of the ridge facing Médéah Farm, almost a copy of Blanc Mont's knoll. Then the two would meet across the chalky summits, exploiting the many wooded slopes interwoven with open strong points. Lejeune's tactics of uniting two wings in the center of a fight would have attracted the attention of another Frenchman, Napoleon Bonaparte. It was that simple—provided the French on either flank, attacking in concert along lower and easier ground, kept pace with the objectives. Frederick Palmer said of this brilliant division that each brigade thought itself the best in the American Expeditionary Force, and each agreed that the only brigade capable of holding a candle to its reputation was the other brigade. Theirs was a mutual admiration society, with something like the ferocity of the Army-Navy game.

At dawn, the 75s and 155s of their division's cannoneers, the 12th, 15th, and 17th U.S. Field Artillery, laid down a perfect barrage after French Corps Artillery had given the Germans a deafening four hours, and the Yanks went forward to seize the ridge that had stalled Gouraud for seven frustrating days. East of him, between the Aisne and the Meuse, the Yanks had gone six miles. Gouraud had made only three, his army around Sommepy unable to put any push against the Line of Resistance the Germans manned below the crests of the ridge. (Foch had been correct when he asked Pershing, at Bombon, to put some Yanks astride the Souain Road at Sommepy.)

The Marines got there first, being on the crest of the Blanc Mont knoll in three hours, after traversing three miles in naked ferocity assisted by a battalion of tanks. The French to their left attempted to move, but a rocky amphitheater called the Essen Hook held them up before they had gone two hundred yards. The Marines had seized the hook and presented it to the French, whom the German promptly drove out in a counterattack. The rest of the French infantry went little beyond the jump-off lines. No German captain had to be told that he now had the Marines enfiladed naked on their left flank. The Leathernecks not only had an enemy facing them; they had to wheel two battalions to the left, at a ninety-degree angle to their main line, and fight for life in the gap left by the tardy French. All day there were intricate little battles of maneuver, the enemy quick to exploit a trap, working savagely to regain the lost crest. Twice he failed, each time withdrawing to reform and try again. When night fell, the Yanks still held the ridge.

On the far right, the Doughboys' brigade had no flank support. Undaunted at finding Germans instead of Frenchmen in the jump-off line, they killed the defenders, having no time to take prisoners as they raced to gain their barrage, which their artillery quickly readjusted. For a distance of three thousand yards on their right the French line moved tardily. By noon, Hanson E. Ely's outfit was a little farther advanced than the now beleaguered Marine battalions. Around three o'clock in the afternoon he again attacked to the left of Médéah Farm, a French objective. That night he had Germans in front of him, on his right flank, swarms of them in woods to his left. But the enemy had better pickings on the Marines' left flank, and turned his tactical savagery to this more favorable and higher ground. Also, Ely had made a deeper penetration than the outflanked Marines, a feat which a man like Ely was not likely to overlook. Colonels like Logan Feland of the Marines and Paul Malone of the Doughboys agreed that October 3, 1918, was their bloodiest day of the war, in the bloodiest division of the A.E.F., even after Feland crossed the fire-raked pontoons of the Meuse before Sedan five weeks later.

The next morning, October 4, the Marines left two battalions to face the French gap and attacked again. By noon, they had come up to Ely's line far across the ridge. That afternoon they tried to outdo Ely's first day. They won some ground, but advance patrols had to relinquish much of it. Meanwhile, Ely attacked both morning and afternoon, having to give up his afternoon gains. The Germans had devoted much savage attention to Ely's brigade, repeatedly counterattacking.

Hindenburg knew he would never recover the position which, eighteen miles south of the Aisne, was his ace of trumps in his contest with Gouraud. The Argonne, Saint-Quentin, and now Blanc Mont had finally convinced him that he could not withstand the American divisions. He gave orders to fall back toward the Aisne and stand before that river. But he could not afford to give up any rifles, or his ten-million-dollar storehouses.

By nightfall October 4, the Marines had driven all enemy troops off Blanc Mont knoll. Lejeune then halted the race-horse brigades, and they sat on their haunches the next day, in order that the French might now proceed lightly molested up to the 2nd Division's line. Lejeune, in an angry telegram, informed Chaumont he would resign his commission rather than fight with French liaison again, and Lejeune was a Bayou Teche Frenchman, noted for his Creole courtesy.

The French arrived in the afternoon and the Marines, as if to taunt the French, then drove another three hundred yards. The tired French—and no Yank ever thought they needed any excuses for their weariness (Wooldridge had noted at Château-Thierry that no poilu had strength to join in a friendly boxing contest, a wrestling match, a tug of war) attacked alongside the Marines and brought their own line up to the three hundred yards. Ely spent the afternoon regrouping, driving a few hornets from nearby nests. The next morning, October 6, both brigades slammed into the Germans, the French on both flanks now keeping pace. Wherever French saw Doughboys take objectives considered impregnable, it kindled new fires. The enemy had begun to fight in sacrificial groups to gain time, the ground no longer so favorable.

That night the 71st Infantry Brigade of the Lone Stars arrived to take over the center, the two brigades of the 2nd Division meeting to examine one another's claims. Two battalions of its Marines and two of its Doughboys remained to shepherd attacks of the newcomers October 8, battalions of Leathernecks and Doughboys bird-dogging into Saint-Étienne-à-Arnes just to show how such things are done. On the right of the line, the Doughboys' battalions had snuffed out all opposition in the approaches to La Scay Farm, giving another French corps new blood.

On the night of October 10, the two brigades were relieved. The 2nd Division had broken through five miles of Hindenburg's strongest position in the center of the French Armies, had taken about two thousand prisoners, killed or wounded countless others, and had suffered casualties of 6,300 officers and men. The Germans now had to get back fifteen miles to the Aisne. They were going to step lively to keep out of the Lone Stars' clutches. Lejeune gave the cowboys and Indians his 2nd Engineers, his 12th, 15th, and 17th Field Artillery. These four regiments were going to step lively, too, for Bill Smith, the new major general, was not a man to lose contact with a retreating enemy. And once more the 2nd Engineers knew they would fight as rifle companies again, losing many college boys who knew triangulation meant

$$S\ A/2\sqrt{\frac{(s\text{-}a)}{(s\text{-}b)\ \ \ (s\text{-}c)}}.$$

The days had been distinguished by countless gallantries. Marines mourned the death of a celebrated character. He had entered Belleau Wood a warrant gunner already wearing a Medal of Honor ribbon. He had picked up a Navy Cross. After Soissons, Harbord named him for a D.S.C. and promotion—as if a warrant gunner could attain any higher rank, short of two-star general, that could impress a Marine. When he learned that the Iron Commander had come down to the Marne to decorate men from the 1st and 2nd Divisions, he swam the river to stand dripping wet before Pershing to receive the Cross; one of the rare times Pershing was ever vain of the regard of any man. He was killed while reorganizing a company to meet one of the counterattacks on Blanc Mont's flank. He was Lieutenant Henry L. Hurlbutt of the 5th Marines, Medal of Honor, Navy Cross, Distinguished Service Cross, Croix de Guerre (with palm).

On the right of the line Hanson E. Ely was still alive, and soon to receive the D.S.C. The last sound some Germans thereabouts heard was the roar of his voice above the bellow of his pistol as he led his brigade; though Marines could show him maps to prove they had advanced about seventy-five inches farther than he had in the five-mile race. The Doughboy brigade never forgot a little runner named Frank T. Bart. He was supposed to carry a message back to battalion to say that his company was held up by machine gunners near Médéah Farm. Instead, he picked up a Chauchat and ran ahead of the stalled line, killing the gunners. Frank's short legs had grown tired of carrying messages. When a similar situation occurred an hour later, he duplicated his exploit. Lejeune asked Pershing to give this lively boy the Medal of Honor, as well as a similar medal to the mother of Corporal John H. Pruitt; and to Buck Private John Joseph Kelly of the Marines.

Back at Pétain's Group of Armies Headquarters, a résumé of the Blanc Mont operation mentioned that, "In the course of the first day's advance, the 5th Regiment of Marines sent a detachment to the [French] XI Corps to help it clean out the German trenches." Inasmuch as the French were two kilometers from those German trenches at the time, wits of the 3rd Battalion, 5th Marines, devised a new series of verses for the immortal "Mademoiselle from Armentières," one of which ran like this:

> Oh, the general got the Croix de Guerre,
> Parley-voo.
> Oh, the general got the Croix de Guerre,
> Parley-voo.
> Yes, the general got the Croix de Guerre,
> But the sonofabitch wasn't even there;
> Hinky-dinky, parley-voo.

Hanson E. Ely, who was sometimes given to laughter, had his greatest laugh of the war when he and Neville were holding a council in a captured pillbox. The day was warm, and Neville hung his green overcoat with the elaborate foliations of a Marine brigadier's sleeves on a nail outside the door. A mule skinner, driving by, spotted it as a piece of German booty. When the two generals emerged from their council, the Army mule was wearing a new bonnet, his earpieces having promoted him to honorary brigadier general in the U.S. Marine Corps, highest rank any Army mule ever attained. Ely had enough presence of mind to blister the mule skinner for looting, and then retired to the pillbox where he could laugh without being heard by the enraged Marine.

The cowboys and the Indians, the Mexicans and the Okies from the wide-open spaces were not the kind to be fenced in. No sooner had the veterans left than they sallied from Saint-Étienne-à-Arnes, a name no one could pronounce, and improved their position considerably. The French of the XXI Corps, which now controlled their fate, sent liaison officers to say that aviators saw retreating columns of the enemy, and Gouraud desired a speedy pursuit. There was nothing the newcomers liked better than a chase, but first they had to fight a hardy mile or two to break through some determined Germans ordered to stand by machine guns to the last man. Their target was the town of Machault. By nightfall, they were beyond it, and the race began.

They went thirteen miles in a single day. They were committed to a night attack tough enough for veterans, and were successful in the black confusion of a ravine—the Indians among them said that nighttime was the only time for fighting. No one, not even their company officers, ever understood how their swift units held together. Frantic adjutants usually found most present or accounted for at morning's muster. Some of them would run through barrages provided by the 2nd Division's artillery, which generously followed to give them support, if they saw a convenient gap. No secrecy was needed by telephone talkers. Who among the enemy understood the Choctaw tongue? More than any other Yank infantry they defied the maxims of warfare. Their prisoner count varied in every history. They were not interested in taking as prisoners those furious Germans angered by the 2nd Division's breaking of their four-year stranglehold on Blanc Mont. They saw no reason why they should use the bayonet either. Bayonets were for broiling stolen chickens. A rifle bullet struck a two-ton blow. When they reached the canal that paralleled the Aisne River, William R. Smith halted them so that he, not they, might draw a few deep breaths.

What dusty country it was! Some of them now had a chance to wash their feet (with snipers covering for them) in the canal. Gouraud was delighted with them and gave them the front of his XI Corps, and they set out from places like Dricourt and Vaux-Champagne, having first ascertained that there was no champagne in the latter town. They swept past the canal, and by October 17 were facing the Germans south of the Aisne, having captured Hindenburg's ten million dollars' worth of supplies, none of them drinkable. Ludendorff had no intention of retreating over the Aisne. It made him too vulnerable where the river bent around Rilly-aux-Oies—"Riley's Nose," as the Texans called it. The French had been brutally repulsed there the day before. Bill Smith spent several days perfecting his liaison with the engineers and artillerists before October 27. On that day he loosed them again, and by nightfall they had driven every German to the far side of the Aisne.

Open warfare infantry had staged a masterly pursuit, never losing contact with a retreating enemy diabolical in its defensive checks. It had then mounted an attack against fixed positions. Moreover, it had learned its arts by employing some men who had never stripped a Chauchat when the flimsy, half-moon magazine had jammed its crudeness. They had lost around fifteen hundred infantrymen; this low curve of casualties was a tribute to their native intelligence, their adaptability, and their excellent West Point commanders, their National Guard battalion, and Training Camp junior officers. They were relieved after the Aisne fight, and were never in battle again; though Bullard knew of them and wanted them for his American Second Army in the projected November 14 attack which the Armistice forestalled. He had in mind a spot on the Moselle he knew they would swim to if the engineers took too much time building bridges.

Many diaries and histories mention feats by private soldiers. The Lone Stars included in their ranks a private first class who would have delighted those that said born soldiers would leap to arms overnight. He was a freckle-faced kid, Harold M. Turner, who was suddenly born to leadership in his first attack. His company had suffered heavily, his own platoon badly hurt. He organized and led half a platoon of headquarters noncoms, clerks, and signalers, and proceeded until he flanked a concrete emplacement with four machine guns interlocking their fire and holding up his company. By now, Harold had only four buddies left. He led these to cover and waited his time, twenty-five yards from the gun. The enemy, now believing it had wiped out Private Turner's little army, changed its traverses. Turner was on them alone in a few seconds, his bayonet at their backs. His four buddies arrived to help him supervise the work of prisoners in refacing the guns. They were the first machine guns, friendly or enemy, the Lone Star quintet had ever operated. His work enabled his battalion moving out from Saint-Etienne-à-Arnes to take its objective. Nameless others like him fell.

Bullard always regretted that foul-ups in railway transportation had kept this division stateside so long. In a Texas training camp they had read the German bulletin put out by Berlin wireless in April of that year: "The Americans recently captured—are strong young fellows but do not seem to have much desire to fight . . . the war . . . to them is an enterprise undertaken by New York financiers." (Possibly Berlin was thinking of such as Captain McMurtry of the Lost Battalion. He had made a million dollars before he stood on Whittlesey's bench.)

Before the cowboys were relieved on the Aisne, company commanders had to restrain men who wished to swim the river and carry the Lone Star flag into Hindenburg's last line. They seem to have embodied the qualities of a Marathon runner and a beaver, still lively after penetrating sixteen miles into the enemy's heart. There was a marble shaft erected on Blanc Mont Ridge, and the Lone Stars for all their brief service were remembered there as the equals of the race horses. What a lightning corps the 2nd and the 36th might have made under a pursuit artist like Bill Smith!

Offensive, Final Phase

Chapter **18**

MEUSE-ARGONNE: ACT TWO

I hear you have captured the whole damned German Army.
Nossir, I only have one hundred and thirty-two.

The lull in the Meuse-Argonne fighting on Ocotber 1 had marked the end of the first phase of the general offensive of September 26. The quiet—if such it can be called—was short-lived, for it was shattered the next morning when Whittlesey went forward, and in the ensuing days the assault was renewed between Reims and the Argonne by Gouraud's French First Army, with the 2nd Division leading the attack on Blanc Mont, and all along the American First Army front. On the morning of October 3, this front stretched in an uneven line from the western edge of the Argonne to just below Brieulles on the Meuse. Roughly only six miles had been gained in the preceding seven days, but the German First Position had fallen, and the Doughboys had taken Varennes and Apremont on the American left, powerful Montfaucon and the village of Cierges in the center, key positions in the Giselher Stellung, and a large piece of useless but necessary swampland on the right.*

As of October 3, the 77th and 28th Divisions were still in line in Liggett's I Corps on the left, the 35th Division having been replaced by the veterans of the Big Red One. The 91st Division still held the left flank of Cameron's V Corps in the center, but its companion divisions in the capture of Montfaucon, the 37th and 79th, had been relieved by the 32nd National Guard and the 3rd Regulars. In Bullard's III Corps on the

* See Plate 12, page 229, and Plate 16, following page 328.

right only two divisions, the 4th and 33rd, were tending the store, both still in the line as the Meuse-Argonne operation went into its second week. From now until the end, a little over five weeks away, many of Pershing's divisions would shuttle in and out of action whenever the opportunity and/or need arose to rest one that had been sorely tried or—temporarily —found wanting. It was to be five weeks of unremitting pressure all along the front, and for the Doughboys in the line, of "one damn machine gun after another."

To Clemenceau, the fall of Montfaucon was an event to rival the capture of Saint-Mihiel. On Sunday, September 29, two days later, he had arrived at Souilly and demanded passage in his limousine to visit the desolation. At Saint-Mihiel, Pershing had fettered him; but on this morning there was no restraining the elated Premier of France. He wanted to look through the hated Crown Prince's telescope, for he was a magnificent hater. He had set out on the single road now choking with the full panoply of the 1st Division beginning its move up to relieve the eighteen thousand survivors of the exhausted 35th Division moving back. Clemenceau's idea of a military road had been formed from his memories of the Sacred Way from Bar-le-Duc to 1916's Verdun, a Napoleonic artery where the great French of that year saw a camion passing a kilometer marker every five seconds.

On the road to Montfaucon he saw field guns fall into shakily bridged craters, and fifty pairs of arms lift them to level road again; exhausted horses dropping dead, replaced by men manning tug ropes; broken-down trucks lifted by cordons of Doughboys to any level spot off the road and instantly swarmed upon by mechanics; forage trains intermingled with life-or-death ammunition trucks, water cart loads of corned beef, and ambulances with ambulatory wounded perched on roofs. Clemenceau had never seen the Doughboys in action, believing many were still interspersed by battalions into the trained fabric of the French Army, and he never recovered from his shock at this seemingly endless pandemonium. He knew little of armies and had distrusted them since the Dreyfus days. (As a reporter, he said—and it is not proved—he had followed Abraham Lincoln around the streets of captured Richmond.) Mangin would have rejoiced at the Doughboys' eagerness to reach the enemy's throat; Haig would have bemoaned the lack of seasoned staff officers, and in the same breath congratulated Pershing on the *élan* of his men.

Clemenceau never did get to Montfaucon. To Doughboys, he was "just another goddam politician blocking a lifeline with a black limousine." He sat for hours chivvying his chauffeur until, somewhere in the heart of the six-mile congestion, Doughboys lifted his car high in the air at his request and faced it to the rear, some of them recognizing the bald pate, the straggly mustache, the Neanderthaler brow behind which clicked the quickest mind in Europe. He arrived back at Souilly in a dark mood. Always a familiar figure to chefs in Allied kitchens, he often carried the principal article of his frugal diet wrapped in a newspaper tucked into his left armpit. "I am Clemenceau. Here are my noodles. They are all I want to eat." That night at Pershing's dinner table, probably over chicken and noodles, he began to consider asking Foch to demand that Woodrow Wilson sack a commander whose army seemed to move like a plague of locusts.

The German High Command was also upset, but for different reasons. Hindenburg appreciated what had happened the preceding week and what it presaged for the future, if Clemenceau did not, and the same day as the latter's unsuccessful visit he had informed the German Chancellor that he must immediately sue for a quick peace. Two days later, October 1, he had reiterated the demand, this time saying he might have to make a terrible decision himself if peace was not quickly made.

Had Clemenceau asked for a seat on a caisson, and witnessed the work of the Big Red One and its fellow divisions, he would have understood why Hindenburg had been so demanding. The German's divisions had not only been unable to retake Montfaucon; they were giving ground everywhere between the Argonne and the Meuse; grudgingly and bitterly, but they were yielding it. Sixteen divisions had now been defeated. There were few replacements. German battalions were being cannibalized; and every division taken from those facing Gouraud around Reims, from the resistance to Mangin beyond Soissons, made careful French progress easier. Taking more than two divisions from Rupprecht's Army Group facing the British killers was out of the question. And one had to be sent there, in turn.

After the first week of the offensive, the American First Army was discovering that the hardest fighting always came with the second assault on a series of natural strongholds such as the Germans were now reinforcing in the Meuse-Argonne complex. The first phase of the attack might have been compared to a fullback's breaking through a thinly held scrimmage line when the defensive team had expected an end run. The fullback would now bull into line-backers from the secondary defense rushing up to plug the hole, and it was this second effort that counted. By October 8 the fighting resembled a football game where both sides had cleared the bench and the two squads from coach to cheerleaders swarmed in a mid-field fist fight. When the 82nd Division moved up the night of October 6-7 to take over a wide section of the front where the 28th Division had been making slow gains for eleven days, the combatants were locked in savage disarray.

The 82nd was a medley of backwoodsmen and cotton pickers from Dixie alongside city boys reared in gangways between tenements and bartenders from neighborhood saloons. Discretion never became a word in its lexicon, despite the caution urged by its commander, the unsinkable Major General George B. Duncan, once commanding officer of the melting-pot 77th Division, which he had lost on the Vesle when his "physical fitness" was questioned. Called to Blois for the test, Duncan raised the roof with the examining board. If Chaumont wanted to send him home, it could have his resignation on the spot; he would enlist as a private in the army, any damned army, to fight the Germans. His anger was so great, his insolence so dauntless, that the Iron Commander himself stepped in. Whatever Chaumont inspectors might have said about his dispositions, this man was *a fighter . . . a fighter . . . a fighter!* If he had not dropped dead from his choleric outbursts at Blois, he never would. So Pershing gave him the 82nd, and in the Argonne he was hell on wheels.

About the time the Lost Battalion was hearing again the familiar whine of Springfields, the 82nd moved west across the Aire River on an engineer's bridge to the right of the Argonne Forest. Its leading battalion had carried what was left of enemy positions on Hill 223 beyond the village of Châtel-Chéhéry north of Le Chêne Tondu, after the Pennsylvanians had swarmed through its western positions, and was now dug in, two companies having lost two-thirds of their rifles. The leading battalion was holding for the arrival of the next leapfrog battalion, their attacks bent on cutting the Decauville railroad, north-south supply line for the Germans in the Argonne Forest to the left.

Captain E. C. B. Danforth, Jr.'s company of the leapfrogs, its flank in the air, had pushed forward through the night over shell-torn hill country sporadically wooded, under a continual rainfall. The enemy, to deny passage to the battalion on Hill 223, was shelling the route of the Americans between the town of the Châtel-Chéhéry and the hill, and the road back to shattered Varennes. The left flank moved through mud and rain, all ranks wearing gas masks in country saturated with mustard fumes. In order to keep his company together, Danforth had to move in column of squads shouting and calling—removing his mouthpiece and lifting the chin fold of his mask from time to time—to hold his floundering company in one piece in the darkness. He was behind time, and he knew it; the country was so forbidding, the night so dark, that shepherding lieutenants and sergeants were exhausted by midnight.

By 5:30 A.M. on the morning of October 8, Danforth was on his jump-off line. He then went along his files, explaining his objective, the railroad more than two miles ahead whose capture would lead to a German withdrawal. He emphasized its strategic importance, and did not minimize the savagery of the work that lay ahead. Sleepless men were briefed in the little detail available. Lieutenant Stewart, the platoon leader on the left, and his noncoms such as Acting Corporal Alvin York, who commanded the squad on the extreme left of Stewart's line, were given their objective. Farther to York's left, unseen and beyond a wide gap, the exhausted Pennsylvanians of the 28th Division tidied up some remaining enemy posts beyond the crests of Le Chêne Tondu—wanting to leave a clean house for the next American tenants. Tactically, the Pennsylvanians were at right angles to York's squad, turning their backs to it as their surviving infantry clawed into the flank of the Argonne's cliff.

Danforth explained that his H-hour was ten minutes past six of a gaseous morning, when the battalion would be given a protective barrage. Danforth chose to attack in two waves, a two-platoon front leading in thin lines of skirmishers, his other two staggered about a hundred yards behind them. Corporal York's half-platoon was in its second wave, led by a Brooklyn boy, Sergeant Harry M. Parsons, Lieutenant Stewart taking first-wave honors with the other half of the platoon. The Germans had seen them at daybreak and enemy artillery forced them time and again to disperse, one shell wiping out a squad. At six-ten the barrage failed to materialize; staff officers had allotted frantic gunners, still threading the shelled roads intermingled with the Pennsylvanians' supply trains and ambulances, too little time to come up. Only a giant lieutenant whom Corporal York had never seen before appeared with a trench mortar to lob his toy shells into the continent of Europe and that was the barrage. No heavy tanks, no long artillery preparation on gun redoubts solidly manned ahead—York's company now undertook the kind of assignment which Colonel George C. Marshall, Jr., had said before Saint-Mihiel would have little chance of success. Nevertheless, Captain Danforth kept his commitments. He attacked.

Lieutenant Stewart did not get very far; the battalion that had taken Hill 223 the day before had found it impossible to mop up the beehive of machine guns on the hill, and enemy gunners had filtered through in the darkness. The lieutenant was soon down with a shattered thigh: but he managed to gain his feet and hop a few yards forward until a sniper shot him through the head. The dying Stewart's half of the platoon was now pinned down and digging for life, ground shaking from hostile mortar fire, the morning alive with bullets. It was now Sergeant Parsons's turn to do something about these beleaguered men with his half-platoon.

After reconnoitering the situation, the sergeant knew his best chance —Marshall had said it would be a gambler's choice—was to outflank the hill beyond him by moving a force through dense cover to his own left to get behind the hostile nests directly ahead. No infantryman in the history of warfare ever wanted to do what Sergeant Parsons must do. It was not evolved out of the formal fruitless French and British instructions in war of attrition. Sergeant Parsons fanned out, sending his three left squads even farther left in the charge of Sergeant Bernard Early, a song-and-dance man from vaudeville, with their three junior noncoms: Corporals Murray Savage, William Cutting, and Alvin York. Among them were thirteen private soldiers. Alvin York never forgot their names, listing them in this order: Dymowski, Weiler, Waring, Wins, Swanson, Muzzi, Beardsley, Konotski, Sok, Johnson, Saccina, Donohue, and Wills.

Sergeant Early commanded a force of sixteen men against the right flank of a German division. Somewhere to the right, separated from him by a gunned hillock, was Captain Danforth having his own troubles, and somewhere behind him Sergeant Parsons's handful holding the pivot. There was nothing suicidal or ill-timed about Sergeant Early's essay in minor tactics; it was not only classic; it was as native American as the Republic itself. The many-tongued little force was stylish. He committed it to single-file silence and thus it stalked the far flank of the German nests, only Early exposing himself from time to time to scout the hell ahead by flitting from brush to brush, loyal men then following.

When the detachment reached a position where the guns were now firing to their right, Early held a council of war. Most of his Doughboys, knowing they were three hundred yards in advance of the Brooklyn sergeant's pinned-down men, wanted to surge forward in a flank attack, but Sergeant Early overruled them. He wanted to attack from the rear. The little column filtered on another three hundred yards. The seventeen were now in position to attack the rear of the gunners opposing Sergeant Parsons and their buddies. Again here was style; if it had to be done at all, it could not have had better execution. And it had to be done.

The sergeant advanced in three combat teams, Early himself boldly leading, Corporal Savage's squad behind him, Acting Corporal York echeloned following Savage, with Corporal Cutting taking the rear guard, all seventeen still alive. The first Germans they saw were Red Cross men. When called upon to surrender, they turned and fled into a wood, the riflemen in Savage's squad missing them in a fusillade of shots, a situation which would have been resolved instanter had Acting Corporal York been leading the van. Sergeant Early presently leaped a little brook, the sixteen following, and found himself in a battalion commander's breakfast circle: about fifteen housekeeping troops with bread, jelly, and steaks, unbuttoned and unarmed. In his own little world that morning, Sergeant Early had now repeated Chancellorville's classic surprise, an obscure Stonewall Jackson in the midst of an enemy campfire. Only the German major was armed, and he reached for the sky on command, calling for his headquarters detachment to do likewise. He had no notion of Early's strength.

As the major surrendered, the alarm sounded by the Red Cross fugitives became evident and the glade was swept by whining steel. Early went down with six slugs in his tough frame, Corporal Savage was shot dead, Corporal Cutting went down with wounds, and six others were bleeding, five of them dying on the ground. Corporal York was now in command of eight unwounded men. These eight huddled against their Germans, all dropping to deep brush, unarmed prisoners ahead of them for protection, steaks and coffee pots flying. York, now the rear guard, wanted to get to his feet, his favorite shooting posture being off-hand.

About twenty-five yards to his right, on a small eminence, were clusters of machine guns, consolidating to face this rearward surprise. The corporal had outflanked the pool of German reserve gunners who now sought to depress upon his eight buddies flattened behind their prisoners unable to raise an elbow. Rarely had a superlative marksman well concealed in high brush behind a tree trunk been presented with so many targets so close at hand. Where there were steel-bucketed heads sighting down the barrels of machine guns, Corporal York, in his own words, said, "Every time a head done come up, I knocked it down." A Tennessee mountaineer, he could "drive the cross" of a half-inch penciled "X" on a scrap of paper pinned to a tree at a hundred feet, the usual target of the long hunters who had killed so many British officers at New Orleans.

The enemy was now shouting orders, bellowing above the din where their gunners were falling with the viscous gray of brains spilling into helmets the instant they seized the spade grips of a gun. It was difficult for York's Germans to discern whence came this murderous fire. What ear could distinguish the well-aimed single shots of an American-modified Enfield rifle amidst the chatter of twenty magpies of approximately the same caliber firing bursts of a hundred shots, holding off a moment and then resuming—a hundred being the standard approximate of a Spandau gunner's cadences? Meanwhile, the backwoods corporal did not know if he had any army left. Between him and the gunners there was only under-brush being sheared away by the many-toothed crosscuts of machine-gun clippers. In time, the enemy located the approximate source of this aston-ishing musketry and resolved to do the only thing that could dry it up, a counterattack by infantry in a bayonet assault. Anyone attempting to rise and throw a potato-masher grenade would be instantly hoisted by his own petard. Six of the enemy, led by an officer, leaped from a trench and, single-file, began a rush at the mountaineer's position.

York's tactics in meeting this team were in the style of a meat hunter who had built a turkey blind, baited it with a trail of sweet acorns, and then shot down a file of birds—wild turkey, the most methodical of game. Rather than alarm the leader of the German flock, York began by killing the hindmost man first, then the next in line and so on up to the leader, his rifle barrel so hot, his rifle magazine so depleted, that the little finger of his trigger hand was dangling his cocked Colt .45 automatic in readiness. He needed it before he had killed his sixth, and leading, man, the German officer; having in turkey-hunter fashion avoided alerting that courageous fellow until the split second the latter had time to feel the pistol bullet enter his face. The corporal had not given them a chance to drop in alarm as the leader fell, and then to fire sporadically into his brush, a tactic which would have doomed him.

York now holstered his pistol and thumbed a fresh clip into his Enfield. He was still in command of his situation, the six Germans having miscalculated that the sniper was firing from a five-clip magazine. By any ordinary odds, at least one of the six should have survived to reach York as he tried to thumb a fresh clip past the cartridge guide of the Enfield's magazine or jerk the Colt, never a weapon for a fast draw, from its holster. They had been devoted but not dexterous.

The Germans were not convinced. York then began to split skulls above the barrels of the Spandau gunners, and call upon the survivors to surrender. He was not too long at this brace-of-birds tactic. Possibly he had killed some fourteen more when, in a lull between firing, the captured German major heard his demand to surrender. He stood up. Corporal York said he would kill no more if they would surrender. The major blew his command whistle and, in the discipline of their kind, about thirty men came off the blood-soaked knoll with their hands up, one of them concealing a grenade in his fist. "So I had to tetch him off," York reported to his brigadier. The major, who may have had some experience in the days of the Old Contemptibles with their fifteen-well-aimed-shots-a-minute, first asked York if he were English. "American," said York. "Good Lord," said the major, who had worked in Chicago and now had the corporal's automatic pistol at his head. He heard the Doughboy demand that he order all his remaining men on the lethal hill to come down with their hands up or the major would suffer irreparable consequences. The rest of the enemy came down. The corporal now had about eighty prisoners.

His buddies, no longer flattened beneath the fire, stood up and reported for duty.

York evacuated his wounded, collecting more prisoners as he went along, avoiding the Chicago major's attempt to lead him into entrapment by holding the Colt .45 against the back of his head; ordering him to blow the whistle as fresh positions came into view. Corporal York collected more and more en route, and these were now bearing Sergeant Early with his five body wounds, his broken arm, and Corporal Savage and his surviving wounded men. The best thing York said all day was uttered after his battalion commander ordered him to report back to his brigadier, General Lindsay, with his prisoners. "Well, York," said the brigadier, "I hear you have captured the whole damned German Army." . . . "Nossir," said York, "I only have one hundred and thirty-two."

Cornay was the place-name the 82nd's old Doughboys recalled best in after years. It was their hill town, and they took it October 10, scaling eroded cliffs where attackers moved by handholds on bare roots to gain approaches from the valley below. It needed four days of fighting to take it, in a series of house-to-house rushes, the slopes below it littered with dead in cross-piles of feldgrau and khaki.

The men of the 82nd came from everywhere; it had no special state pride, nor did it vaunt its regional variety like the Rainbows. It had promptly called itself "The All-American Division," and felt entitled to all the connotations that Walter Camp had conferred upon this designation in picking football players. Its engineers were riflemen by day, bridge builders when darkness fell. Sergeant York in his memoirs said that his platoon would drink anything in bottles and always hankered to break things, even each other's heads if nothing else was handy.

The sergeant himself was a teetotaler, a nonsmoker, and a nonwencher. Until his officers persuaded him that he was justified in breaking the Commandment against killing, he observed all Ten. A conscientious objector, he responded to the draft call and did his duty as a soldier in doubt and despair, making his beliefs known to his commanding officers, who were compelled to respect his sincerity. His battalion commander in a Georgia training camp quoted Scripture—like the Devil, to his own purpose—and won the debate by citing the first six verses of Ezekiel, Chapter 33, ending, "But if the watchman see the sword come, and blow not the trumpet, and the people be not warned; if the sword come, and take any person from among them, he is taken away in his iniquity; but his blood will I require at the watchman's hands." York also said that he had never known the meaning of love until he fought alongside his buddies. It is a commentary on the spirit of civilian officers who handled Doughboy draftees that a new major, who might easily have sent York to prison as a conscientious objector, worked so manfully not to. (Baron von Steuben, writing from Valley Forge to his friend, Baron von Gaudy, complained that he always had to tell Washington's troops *why* they had to do something. He called it the "genius of this nation" that a private soldier always wanted to know the score.)

York was promptly made a D.S.C. sergeant by Division, but the Iron Commander added to this. Nothing but the Medal of Honor would suffice for the mountaineer whom Pershing named the outstanding civilian soldier of the A.E.F. and Marshal Foch called the outstanding one of the war.

On October 8, about the same time Alvin York leaped the little brook in the Argonne, Bullard ordered the 33rd Division to cross the Meuse that ran across its front and right flank above the stubborn village of Brieulles. Its target was the detested Borne de Cornouiller that loomed high on the Consenvoye Heights, its guns dominating the Meuse Valley, firing into the right flank of every Doughboy advance. The 4th Division, for example, corps brother to the 33rd, was living in gas-soaked forests beneath the Meuse Heights under continual fire from the Borne de Cornouiller on the right. Frederick Palmer, frequently visiting the 4th, said its Doughboys were as accustomed to pulling on gas masks as a baseball catcher was used to putting on his mask when the other side came to bat. The Ivy Leafs lost about six thousand officers and men in their twenty-three days, taking about half that many prisoners and around fifty guns. They moved forward about five hundred yards a day, the total advance being about eight miles. Toward the end of their tenure, when the 33rd and 29th had drawn some of the Borne's fire, the Big Red One and the 3rd Division's Marne boys now attracting the attention of the Romagne Heights, the Ivy Leafs thought their lot a little less irksome.

The 33rd's companions in the attack, all east of the Meuse holding the line north of Verdun since September 26, were to be the "Blue and the Gray" 29th Division, mainly National Guardsmen from New Jersey, Maryland, and Virginia, the 26th New Englanders on the 29th's right, and two French divisions. These were to advance frontally and seize the approaches to the heights, and the ground on the east side of the river, so that the 33rd's engineers might connect their bridgeheads.

There was trouble from the start. The French failed to make any progress and the 29th Division had to be piecemealed for their support, one of its brigades strengthening the left of the French 18th Division, the other assisting the right of the same poilu outfit and another French division alongside of it. Then, while the pontoons had been thrown across during the night by the 33rd's engineers, for reasons never explained the division's Doughboys swarmed across the two narrow bridges in broad daylight. There was no urgency in the crossing. Midnight or foggy dawn would have served just as well, and with few casualties, the 33rd being perfectly coordinated for crossing a river in the dark. But daylight it was, and the Austrian and Württemberg gunners on the Borne de Cornouiller had prime targets.

While the 33rd's Doughboys struggled across the fire-raked bridges, the men of the 29th bore the brunt of the first day's assault, fighting like savages to gain the woods facing the approaches to the Borne, the French having decided that they would rather let the Americans take the accursed hill, the New Englanders confined to putative gains around Molleville Farm fronting the heights. The Germans, alerted to the fact that Doughboys were now fighting east of the Meuse, brought up two more divisions and dared the Yanks to try a frontal attack. The resistance was as severe as anything west of the river. The Germans were extremely quick for three days, particularly against the leading brigade of the Blue and the Gray boys which had to draw fire away from the 33rd's pontoons.

For sheer virtuosity, Sergeant Earl D. Gregory of the Blue and the Grays must have been at concert pitch when he earned the baby-blue ribbon with its twinkle of thirteen white stars. He entered a wooded patch guarding Richène Hill, one of the barriers fronting the Borne de Cornouiller, well ahead of his own patrol. He carried a rifle and bayonet for protection, but relied mainly upon a mortar shell, which he toted like a log of wood, as his prime weapon. Three of the enemy were left alive after the sergeant threw this pineapple into a machine-gun nest, and they surrendered. He then proceeded, using the German trio as a shield, to seize a mountain howitzer from some Württembergers. With this as a weapon, he then invited its crew of nineteen to emerge from their dugout or swallow some of their own medicine. The sergeant had performed his feat well in advance of his company, which needed his twenty-two prisoners for stretcher-bearers. The brigade had gone three miles into some Austrians when it discovered that the French divisions it beefed up had only progressed two. It had some difficulty falling back to the French line.

There was no rule of the book for a force without heavy tanks in the taking of a nest where there was a multiplicity of machine guns concealed in woods. Such a position had no flanks; other guns saw to that, and unless an advance was to be held up all day, it was a question of losing as few lives as possible. Such a dilemma was presented to Second Lieutenant Patrick Regan in the second day's fighting for the approaches to the Consenvoye positions. His platoon was faced by an Austrian platoon with four guns in a well-positioned corner of a ravine near Molleville Farm. Regan split his platoon into three sections, taking the center with three volunteers, sending his two main forces to the flanks. Then the rush began. Two Dough-boys of Regan's team in the frontal rush were killed outright. Regan with his Chauchat, an unusual weapon for a shavetail, and Private Henry G. Costin were still on their feet when they began to feel the blast of the gun on their ear drums. Costin was then mortally wounded, but he gave Regan as much cover as possible, using a rifle until he blacked out. Regan was now seriously wounded in the belly, but he dashed with an empty pistol into the nest, figuring that he might as well stage a bluff there before he bled to death. This piece of audacity led thirty Austrians to surrender. Regan's company commander then came up. He had to order Regan to lie upon a stretcher and call it a day. Regan survived.

A lone corporal of the 33rd was the first Doughboy of that division to cross the Meuse, and he got a Medal of Honor for it. He was Corporal Raglin Hill, who saw a French Nieuport shot down on the opposite bank, its wounded pilot crawling from the wreckage. The corporal ran across a footbridge and beat the Württembergers to him, bringing the Frenchman piggyback to safety in an acrobatic feat. Hill was soon followed by thousands of his buddies, who survived the perilous crossing only to find themselves in a hornet's nest of defensive positions guarding the right flank of the heights.

Here fighting for position and exploiting of the woods at the base of Cornouiller was distinguished by the same versatility and daring of Dough-boy sergeants and officers that was displayed by men of the 29th, both divisions demonstrating various ways of taking machine-gun nests from veterans that had nothing to do with classroom lectures or textbook tactics. One of the 33rd's Medal of Honor performers was First Sergeant Johannes S. Anderson. First Sergeants were armed with the Army's brutal Colt .45 automatic, which left an exit hole in a man's back the size of a derby hat; but the Chicago sergeant, undergoing much hostile fire to reach a concrete pillbox, made his entrance through the stage door of the pestiferous ma-chine-gun nest bearing a sawed-off shotgun. Two buckshot blasts and the twenty-three performers left on their feet surrendered. Like Sergeant Gregory, a mile to his right, Anderson was scornful of conventional weap-ons, and there were others who felt the same. Without tanks or close ar-tillery support, infantry had to have ingenuity against such positions. This was called obsolescence.

For two successive days the 33rd tried to flank the crest of Corned Willy Hill, but even ingenuity and courage were not enough. Having learned professional discretion by now, on October 12 the division dug permanent lines at its base. They would bide their time until they could swing farther

east and go after the Borne from other country. This sensible halt, imperative upon any troops not bent upon suicide, particularly irked Foch. He
wanted Major General Claudel's XVII Corps of Liggett's Army to be given
about five divisions to kill off.

It was during the fight for Consenvoye that there occurred the only *cause
célèbre* of the war. The 26th New Englanders were fighting alongside the
29th when Brigadier General Frank E. Bamford, a tough colonel from
the 1st Division, relieved Major General Clarence Edwards of command
at Division Headquarters. If the Germans had bombed the White House
to ashes from a transatlantic Zeppelin, the event would have been put on
the back page of New England weeklies along with the church notices the
following Saturday. *Pershing had fired Clarence Edwards!* The controversy
raged for ten years, and all three histories of the 26th Division remind a
reader of the caustic solutions in which Civil War commanders were
dipped by the editors of that day. It is possible that it was not Pershing who
relieved Edwards of his command; he was too much a soldier's soldier
to have undermined Liggett's authority; Liggett probably sacked Edwards
and Pershing dutifully had to assume the role of villain from Eastport to
Bridgeport. Pershing in his memoirs twelve years later referred to the
incident only in a one-line footnote: "Brig. Gen. Bamford took command
of the 26th Division on Oct. 25th."

In justice to Liggett, it is worth noting that Brigadier General Cole of
the 26th, whom he censured so severely after Château-Thierry, was now
leading his old brigade with skill and savvy; it was one of the few times
that an officer under such harsh criticism caused his commander to change
his views. Lieutenant Colonel Shelton, whose regiment had hell licked
out of them when Germans occupied abandoned trenches at Seicheprey,
had now won his star and was leading the New Englanders' other infantry
brigade. Apparently in Liggett's view many in the New England National
Guardsmen's higher command could master the art of war, but the charming West Pointer Edwards could not. But only a foolhardy critic would
take up the cudgels for Hunter Liggett in an American Legion post in
that area. As for Pershing, it was one of the episodes which inspired hostile
critics to cut his reputation to shreds after the war.

Yankee division chroniclers say that the 26th's Doughboys were so dispirited by the loss of their "beloved leader" that they had hardly any fight
left in them. But the facts do not bear this out. Under Edwards they had
not made noticeable headway in the attempt on the Consenvoye Heights.
Within two days Bamford had them on the line with the 29th's Blue and
Grays, fighting like leopards in the woods.

Chapter **19**

FROM THE SCHELDT TO THE VOSGES —THESE ALSO SERVED

Greet Them Ever With Grateful Hearts.
God Dam, Le's Go!

It was an axiom of the war that no private soldier ever wished to be where he was; any other hole would be a better one. Two divisions got their wish before the worst Argonne fighting was over. These were the 37th and 91st Divisions—the former National Guardsmen from man-packed Ohio who called themselves the Buckeye Division and who had Montfaucon on the second day. The latter were mainly draftees from California, Idaho, Montana, Oregon, Utah, Washington, and Wyoming, a roll call of states with beautiful names. The 91st called itself the Wild West Division, and its Doughboys spoke almost as many languages as the Bowery Backwoodsmen. A wild, broad-shouldered lot were they—so the enemy routed from woods around Montfaucon had discovered in the first two days of fighting the Westerners. The Buckeyes and the Wild Wests found themselves in boxcars in the chill of a rainy October 18, happy to loll on the wall-to-wall carpeting of trampled horse manure which characterized these vehicles. As they whistled at sixty-year-old women cranking the barrier arms at railroad crossings, at old farmers in fields turning fallow, they did not know where they were going but at least the boxcars afforded a change of air.

They were on their way to the fields of Flanders. Marshal Foch had made a peremptory demand upon Pershing. He wanted two veteran American divisions—the equivalent now of five exhausted French—sent to the Franco-Belgian Armies to pursue the Germans who were trying to break contact beyond Ypres and Ostend and hold a line at the Scheldt River.

No one ever knew why the Iron Commander agreed to disperse two of his best divisions to a faraway Army Group whose chief of staff was now General Degoutte, notorious for being prodigal of American blood. Although Pershing knew that Clemenceau still wanted Wilson to sack him, he also had his own counterintelligence in rear areas of his Allied enemies— thanks to General Bliss—and knew that Newton Baker, alerted to the Clemenceau quarrel, had said the day would never come when a French premier could fire an American general. He did not have to obey Foch and send two fine divisions to Belgium. It may be that he did it out of admiration for the King of the Belgians, who like Wilson had constitutional authority and had twice put Degoutte in his place with royal rebukes. King Albert was *a fighter . . . a fighter . . . a fighter!*

Nevertheless, it was a costly gesture. Because of it, in the Argonne new regiments of four divisions just off the transports and filled with stateside divisional pride would be cannibalized as replacements. Some of the green lads, robbed of their regional morale, not even knowing the names of their lieutenants, would see as much as thirty seconds of war amidst strangers — about the time needed to make a fatal mistake in the bright danger of these bloody ravines.

The Belgian First Army was a refugee army, most of its men having rallied to their hero-king after Ludendorff forced the Liège gate in 1914. The Belgians were a brave lot, as Julius Caesar had remarked two thousand years before, but now as then they were a one-shot army, with no replacements. King Albert had saved his 175,000 men for the last brave shot.

Degoutte had made his plans to deprive the Wild West major general, a good one named William H. Johnston, of all but the administrative command—and the Buckeyes' commander, Major General Charles S. Farnsworth, who also knew his profession, of many tactical responsibilities. Degoutte managed this by leaving the 37th and the 91st side by side, as they had been in the Argonne fighting, and yet attaching each division to a French division on their flanks in separate corps. Thus the two Doughboy outfits would be under the eyes of French divisional commanders. It was like attaching two big, ferocious dogs to two very weary tails.

Like all Doughboy divisions entering a foreign army, everybody wanted to show his wares. Degoutte unleashed them October 30, the 37th Division as a part of the French XXX Corps, the 91st reinforcing the French VII Corps. They wanted the railway north of the town of Waereghem, in a roll-

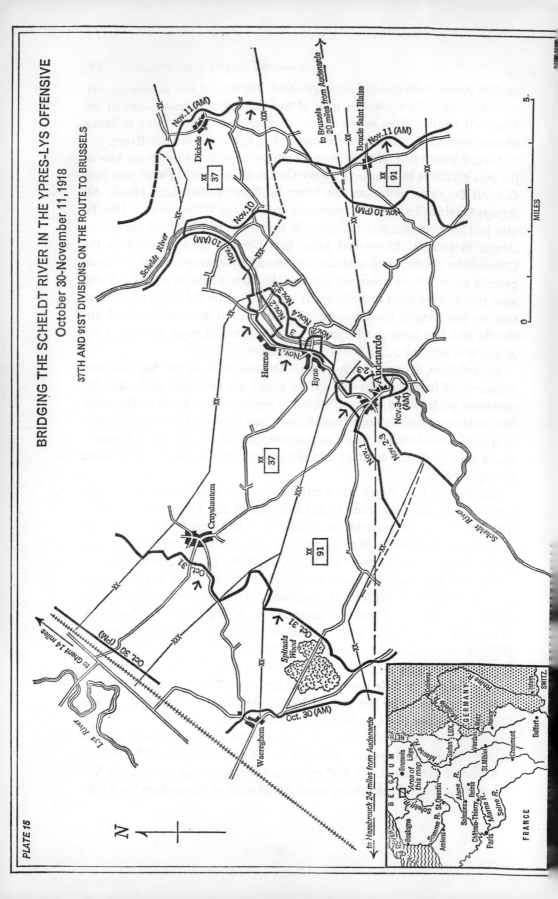

PLATE 15

BRIDGING THE SCHELDT RIVER IN THE YPRES-LYS OFFENSIVE

October 30-November 11, 1918

37TH AND 91ST DIVISIONS ON THE ROUTE TO BRUSSELS

ing countryside where the Germans had been living high on the hog since 1914 in villages little damaged by war. The Buckeyes, emulating their Illini brethren of Forges Brook's 33rd Division, went about three flawless miles the first day, killing the enemy in last posts of resistance with a violence, brutality, and rapidity the Germans there had not seen since the Jocks and the Canadians pulled out for the Somme. Belgian villagers emerged from earth to greet the Yanks joyously. The newcomers consolidated their lines that night, dug the shallow holes which were about as deep as Doughboys ever went into earth, and waited for their buddies of the 91st to come up.

The Wild Wests had no such luck. They had needed all day to break through the Spitaals Wood looming a few hundred yards ahead of their jump-off lines; for the stalled French on their right had no intention of moving until these tricky forests were captured by the Yanks. There was a great deal of cursing in the 91st ranks, oaths in Finnish, Swedish, Norwegian, Danish, German, Portuguese, Basque, Spanish, and just plain "podner" profanity, not all of them directed at the men in *feldgrau*. Battalions on the right-flank gap had to wheel and kill off enfilading gunners all day. By nightfall, the Germans had seen enough of the new arrivals. They began withdrawing as stealthily as possible. The following day the Wild Wests caught up with the Buckeyes and together they raced six miles due east toward Brussels killing rearguards as marching outposts seized the railroad, arriving at the Scheldt River around nightfall beside such weird little Gothic towns as Eyne, Heurne, and Audenarde. Degoutte had known he could not cross the river without them.

The Germans did not wish to relinquish Audenarde to the Wild Wests. Yet patrols were in it by the third day, and by the fourth all Germans there were either dead or prisoners after fierce fighting. Buildings, such as the *hôtel de ville,* were always troublesome places from which to dislodge snipers. Narrow Gothic windows in three stories, a high-pitched roof with two levels of dormers, were always rough on patrols until mortarmen and grenadiers could lob explosives into the hideaways.

Among the Wild Wests the Iron Commander remembered with a Distinguished Service Cross was Sergeant Charles E. Reilly of the 91st's Engineers. Under the pretext of examining possible bridgeheads of the Scheldt, the sergeant joined an infantry captain leading the first patrol into Audenarde and had himself a fine day with a Springfield rifle among the Gothic twists and turns. Among other deeds, he winged a nearby sniper who was drawing a bead on the captain; and, rarest of all Doughboy exploits, he captured a German spy in a Doughboy uniform and turned him over to the French. Just how Reilly's Irish ears could distinguish a difference in the spy's English and that of the many accents in his own outfit was never explained; but the captive was a spy and the French disposed of him.

The Yank engineers bridged the wide, rain-swollen Scheldt in several places, infantry rushing across to fight off some counterattacks before they were relieved after five days of savagery. By November 10, while the German delegation stalled in Marshal Foch's Armistice railway car and the Kaiser had spent his first night in Dutch exile, most enemy cadres were in headlong flight, wishing to avoid the certain hard labor the French and Belgians would have in store for prisoners. The Yank divisions then came back to their bridgeheads, not one of which had been expanded or supplemented by the French in four tired days. There was still hard fighting for the Buckeyes November 10 before the full division was on the north bank of the Scheldt. The enemy had left field guns and machine gunners there.

The Buckeyes had paid a price of sixteen hundred casualties in Flanders, the 91st receiving about a thousand. Few American tourists ever knew that, had they driven their cars forty minutes south of Brussels, they would have come upon a brick-walled cemetery where 368 Doughboys lay in Flanders Fields, a tiny fraction of the English-speaking hosts who slept forever thereabouts, fifty thousand of them sunk without a trace of recovery in the Flanders mud. *"Greet Them Ever with Grateful Hearts"* was the line carved above their chapel door. The Americans lay not far from a monument erected to a Belgian volunteer regiment which had fought with Maximilian in an effort to bring the Hapsburgs and their beribboned lackeys to power in Mexico City in the days of their own Civil War grandfathers.

The 37th's poet was a national figure, the sports writer Grantland Rice. At the age of thirty-nine he had enlisted in New York City as a private in the United States Army, converting his $75,000 assets into cash and entrusting it to a New York lawyer to invest for his pretty wife and their baby daughter. Rice had then been trained as an artillery lieutenant (using a sawed-off tree trunk as a dummy cannon) by a remarkable artillerist, known from Mindinao to Mexicali as "Good God Gus" Gately, who later spent his war as the Rainbow Division's feisty artillery brigadier. Lieutenant Rice had been dragooned into being a reporter for the Doughboy newspaper, *The Stars and Stripes,* the week his outfit arrived in France, but he managed to break away in time to join his regiment for the Flanders fighting, having missed the Argonne, where he lost many friends. (Among them was Captain Edward L. Grant of the 307th Infantry.) Rice came home from the war to find that the lawyer had lost the fortune and then shot himself. Once again he began carrying his typewriter to the windy levels of football stadium press boxes. To Granny Rice the war had been an annoying interlude a sportsman must endure; he deplored it and wrote verses honoring his lost buddies. Like most Doughboys, he was glad to forget it, though of course it was unforgettable. When the Yankees met the Giants in the Polo Grounds wars, the figure of Eddie Grant was always there, ghostly in the outfield.

The late October nights were cold on the Vosges front at the four-thousand-foot level. There, in the opposite direction from where Pershing had agreed to send the 37th and 91st Divisions, could be found the 369th Infantry Regiment of the provisional U.S. 93rd Division.

The 369th was one of four Negro regiments that were never constituted into a division. These lads from New York City, Connecticut, Illinois, Maryland, Massachusetts, Ohio, Tennessee, Arkansas, and South Carolina were the only American regiments that became French regiments. Brigaded with the French after Ludendorff's blows crippled the thin British divisions along the Somme, the 369th, 370th, 371st, and 372nd Infantry of the provisional U.S. 93rd Division never received their own artillery, engineers, signalers, or trains from the States. Pershing, wanting his big Negro regiments back, repeatedly asked Washington to send these elements, and his requests were met with silence. The chief of staff back in the States never gave them a regular sergeant from the 24th or 25th (Negro) Regulars. Sergeant majors were chevroned on the spot. These troops were eventually among the "all that I have" which Pershing told Foch "are yours." When the Iron Commander inspected them, he remarked on their carriage, physique, and appearance, writing to Colonel Perry Miles of the 371st that he was confident their conduct would be a cause for pride.

The only true chronicles of these soldiers were in the battalion memoirs written by their admiring officers. In three of the regiments these were mainly white. The fourth regiment was New York National Guard recruited from scratch at the request of Governor Whitman by a remarkable colonel, the dashing William Hayward of New York's upper crust, who had been a good officer in early years with the Nebraska National Guard. Originally the New York 15th National Guards, they became by Army designation the 369th Infantry. Their armory had been a cigar store in Harlem and a dance hall above it, their recruiting surgeon Dr. George Bolling Lee, whose grandfather had given up the military persuasion at Appomattox. This regiment had both white and Negro officers from the outset. The former were mainly Ivy Leaguers from Harvard, Yale, and Princeton, the latter their equals from the intellectuals of a minority group in Northern cities.

The "15th Heavy Foot," as its soldiers liked to call themselves, was to folklore connoisseurs the most colorful regiment in France. The regiment's two great figures were Hayward, a handsome man whom James Montgomery

Flagg delighted to paint, and Jim Europe, the great Negro band leader. First Lieutenant James Europe was actually a line officer in a combat unit; the band was his relaxation. He secured for a band sergeant the illustrious Noble Sissle; his first trumpet Frank de Broit was imported from Chicago.

When Hayward approached Jim Europe about forming the regiment's band—the world knew Europe as arranger and leader for Vernon and Irene Castle—the scholarly lieutenant was diffident. Army regulation called for twenty-eight instruments in a regiment's tables. What sort of band was that? Certainly the colonel should know, sir, that anything less than forty-eight pieces was not going to blow up any storm. Only sixty men could give a composition tonal finality. Besides, the American Negro of that day was not much on reeds, liking brass and percussion and strings. But you could not have violins and bull fiddles in a marching band; reeds had to make up for strings, or it was not worthwhile writing arrangements. The only good Negro reed men were all in Puerto Rico—flutes, saxes, clarinets. Then again, you could not ask family men and virtuosos like Noble Sissle and Frank de Broit to enlist on a sergeant's pay. A sergeant's pay would not buy the wax for Frank de Broit's Kaiser-like mustaches, his trademark when he lifted that shining horn into melody.

Hayward told Europe he could have the forty-eight pieces, and any Puerto Rican instrumentalists he wanted if he would give a little attention to the band. Hayward would soak the rich, and have an unofficial contingency fund for families of the virtuosos. He wanted to recruit the cream of the Harlem team for his riflemen. The colonel asked Mr. Daniel Reid, the tin-can king of American industry, to write to forty wealthy friends for contributions to a ten-thousand-dollar fund. Reid made out a check for the ten thousand dollars. "That's a damn sight easier than writing a lot of letters," he said. Others, such as John D. Rockefeller, Jr., began sending checks for five hundred dollars, asking Colonel Hayward to "buy another musician." He did, and the result was catnip to the cats of the day; he got his volunteer fighters, and *bons soldats* they were, the French said.

It was a miracle that they survived the indignities heaped upon them when the War Department idiotically sent the outfit to Spartanburg, South Carolina, to train. The mayor made a vicious speech of nonwelcome at the chamber of commerce that was duly reported in the *New York Times* of August 31, 1917. Captain N. B. Marshall of the New York bar was soon called "a dirty nigger" and thrown off a streetcar. Privates were knocked down when they tried to use the sidewalks. Hayward, some years ahead of Gandhi, demanded that no New Yorker in his command, white or black, strike back, though Hayward had difficulty restraining his white officers, many of these from silk-stocking outfits like New York's old 7th

Infantry, from retaliating upon the mayor's paranoiacs. Frank de Broit, walking with Jim Europe, asked if he might dare enter a hotel and buy a newspaper from the lobby stand. Lieutenant Europe said he might try. The desk clerk knocked Sergeant de Broit down, with the usual obscene adjectives prefixed to n-i-g-g-e-r. There were about fifty white Doughboys of the 27th Division's Orions in the lobby at the time. The future Hindenburg Line outfit was closing in to pluck the desk clerk's legs from his body when they heard the cry: *"Attention!"* When they faced about and saluted the uniform they discovered a tall, bespectacled Negro lieutenant. Lieutenant Europe said that he wanted all there to leave the lobby two by two. All marched out silently. The desk clerk then called Jim Europe a "black son-of-a-bitch." The gentlemanly Europe was undeniably dark-skinned. He quietly left the premises of the white s.o.b.

The other three Negro outfits, then under all-white officers, such as the 371st training at nearby Columbia, South Carolina, met no stupid indignities. There the citizens cheered them when they paraded to trains headed for shipside and France. The different attitude toward Negroes still under white masters was one for psychologists, not soldiers, to ponder. One of the 15th Heavy Foot's officers, when bundled into a hospital bed alongside a Marine officer, was asked where his outfit had trained. "We trained in Rectum, South Carolina," said the purist from the Harvard Yard.

As the backbones of French divisions, the men of all four regiments wore the poilu's blue helmet and they carried the Lebel rifle, little more than a musket with its three-cartridge clip, fusils used mainly since Vauban's day as a pike for a bayonet point as the soldier went forward with his bag of grenades. Their food was the French ration, a difficult one to digest with its principal commodity of bread and dried vegetables with no French chef to work miracles in soup kettles by adding a few scraps of meat. French gastric processes took care of so much starchiness nicely with a daily issue of red wine. The Negro Doughboy was denied this digestive boon. Many on the home front would have demanded Pershing's head if "our boys in France" were given the same issue. And so the Doughboys with the French each received a daily ration of one and one-fourth ounces of barley sugar in compensation.

"Something is crooked and should be adjusted," a Negro Captain Ryan wrote a white Major Greenough of the 2nd Battalion, 371st Infantry, after receiving one day's rations for 220 hungry fighting men. The captain inventoried his larder: "1½ goats (deduct 30 pounds for skin and bones); 1 leg of beef, 40 pounds; 2 pieces of fat, 15 pounds; 6 pounds of rice; 10 pounds of salt; 96 loaves of bread." It was a far cry from hominy grits.

The only French equipment any liked was the gas mask. The English chest respirator required, if the wearer was not to be tortured by the clamp, an aquiline adenoidal nose. Most of the brawny boys from the rice fields and the cotton patches had the African septum. "The Pig Nose" respirator of the French had a snout which required no nose clamp. The men were often lonely in rest billets after their fights alongside the French. Irvin S. Cobb, humorist turned war correspondent, had heard them at night, singing "Little David, Play on Your Harp" and "He Never Said a Mumbling Word." They never grumbled either. How strong was the American dream, that they would fight for a liberty they did not fully share.

General Gouraud had served most of his long career overseas in French possessions among many racial strains, and the 15th Heavy Foot fascinated him. He could not hear enough of Lieutenant Europe's band; and he sent his personal photographer to make battle studies of the New York City's 15th. He wrote the captions and sent a sheaf of pictures to Major Arthur W. Little, who told their story. Little, a publisher, whose son was in another combat outfit, spoke of his battalion as "men of bronze." The regiment underwent harder fighting than its three brother outfits, leaving 367 men in French earth. It began its fighting beside the Marne just after Ulysses Grant McAlexander's 38th Infantry put on its great show. As *La 369ème R.I.U.S.* of the French 16th Division, it had received its training under a fine taskmaster, Major General Le Gallais; but he was not to witness the results of his patience. The 15th Heavy Foots were detached, and brigaded into the French 161st Division under Major General Lebouc, who used them defensively behind the Marne between a regiment of Blue Devils (Chasseurs Alpins) on their left, and a regiment of Moroccans on their right. The official slogan of the Harlem boys, never printed on official documents, was *"God Dam, Le's Go!"* They needed this spirit before Lebouc finished shuffling his deck, supporting the French on July 18 in their counterattack against the seven German divisions holding a bridgehead five miles deep on the south bank of the Marne—to the right of the Doughboy 3rd Division.

The Harlem boys were in three battalions, no two contiguous, each under a different French colonel. They had been in ceaseless night movement the first three days as reserves, moving as often and as swiftly as had Stonewall Jackson's "foot cavalry" in his Valley campaign. Regimental identity was gone. Major Little's 1st Battalion, 369th U.S. Infantry, was now simply the Batallion Little, sandwiched between the French Bataillon Salerou and the Batallion Moretteau. No one knew where the other *"God Dam, Le's Go!"* boys were fighting, but all were in for some tough going. Gas was heavy. The enemy could throw toxic shells in massive corrosion as a barrier against

French attacks on their troops across the Marne. There were instances of near-panic in the rushing darkness until officers, to assure the men that gas was not necessarily fatal, removed their masks from time to time. Many were nauseated by this show of *sang-froid,* but were not evacuated.

Major Little said that, while there were isolated instances of misunderstandings between white and colored officers, the question of whether American Negroes would fight Germans was settled forever those days beside the Marne. Little said one of his captains was convinced that any dressing down the battalion commander gave him—which was routine in any outfit anywhere—was that of a white man hazing a Negro because of his color. The Negro captain transferred to another outfit. Later, when he had been decorated because of a citation written by Little, the captain came forward and, without a word, took the major's hand.

The general impression of Americans was that the colored soldier was mainly a comic figure, incapable of undergoing danger over long intervals. The Harlem boys were the first to wipe out that impression. As for being comics, they were natural humorists gifted by God Almighty, deliberately sending their officers into gales of laughter; but the loss of fifteen hundred men in 191 days in the zone of fire was not a laughing matter. The erstwhile brigade twin of the 369th Harlemites was the 370th U.S. Infantry. It was much like the outfit Pershing commended to his West Point friend Colonel Perry Miles, but it did not see as much fighting as the others. It was interwoven into the French 59th Division, whose general began to use his Dixie poilus cautiously, piecemealing them in company strengths at first. Dixie poilus in their blue helmets, carrying their Lebels, were the last of 330,000 Doughboys who fought von Boehn from the Marne to the Aisne. In his battlefield survey the Iron Commander said the Dixie poilus in the French 59th Division made a fine advance in five days of fighting before the division was relieved. They were back at it in early November when American guns throwing shells onto the Sedan-Mézières railroad had all Germans—save those facing the Doughboys on the Meuse—scuttling back everywhere. The regiment had lost five hundred men, only a third as many as its brigade twin in the provisional 93rd U.S. Division.

All four regiments had been in fighting lines September 26 when the green U.S. divisions set out on Foch's great offensive.* The 371st and 372nd had been on the Verdun front for several weeks before the scheduled assault, exchanging nightly patrols and bickerings with the Germans across the lines, and their men were looking forward to the big show when their French division was relieved the third week in September. Now they were moving to fight on another front. They were placed under Le General Goy-

* See Plate 14, page 282.

bet, whose outfit had suffered a terrible mauling on the Vesle. He had rounded up what was left of one infantry regiment of his 33rd Poilu Division; had found broken pieces of his engineers and gunners to reform the division, his other infantry elements having dissolved. And now he had a good division again, his infantry one-half great dark-skinned men from Dixie. Their white officers were 90 percent Southern college boys from the First Officer's Training Camp. Most of these had been downcast at being assigned Negro draftees, among whom, in one day's batch of fifteen hundred, there had been only two educated men. Now they were converts to the brotherhood of man; even colonels like Hayward could not have restrained these whites had they just then walked the streets of Spartanburg. They hated leaving as the white Doughboys came up to face Montfaucon. They wanted their men to vie with men of lighter skin.

Captain Chester Heywood of the 371st, who understood their culture, their psychology, wrote their story. One night on the Verdun front, a company runner sent to the four platoons with messages returned to ask Captain Heywood to take charge of 2,250 francs (about $600), producing a prodigious bankroll. "Of course, Cap'n," said the runner, "I was off duty at the time." He had made a fast killing in the dice games that whiled away front line's daylight hours. Given safety razors, they put little reliance upon them; a safety razor could not be regarded "as a social weapon," they said, in enterprises against the Germans. All of them had put a razor's edge on mess-kit knives. The regiment was now *La 371er R.I.U.S. de la 157ème Division Goybet,* the "Red Hand" division. Their French buddies referred to the Germans as Boches, even in official orders. Many of the baseball players among the French Doughboys simply referred to the enemy as "them bushers." They, too, with their Dixie buddies of the 273rd, had a crack at the Hindenburg Line.

Goybet's Dixie Poilu Division was in support the morning of September 26. Ahead of it to the left of Liggett's corps, General Gouraud was opening his French Fourth Army's sector of the general attack with his Moroccans and poilus, keeping Goybet's division in IX Corps reserve. The blue helmets from Dixie could not see the Argonne Forest far on their right, or ahead of them the chalky hills of the Champagne. All day they sat tight and heard the thunder rolling over the hills ahead. By nightfall, Gouraud wanted them to come up; there were going to be gaps along the line Butte du Mesnil–Ripont—Les Petites Rossières, and these had to be seized and exploited.* For a long day the two Negro regiments, taking up a corps front, moved warily in French fashion—their colonels under orders, French style, of a French colonel who commanded all divisional infantry. The slopes and swales

* See Plate 15, page 308.

were strewn with dead and dying French of blue poilu and tan Moroccan; of enemy gray. On the morning of September 28, about the time patrols were moving in force from captured Montfaucon on the far side of the
Argonne, the 371st hit the Germans in battalion strengths, this too in French
style, Captain Ryan of the goat-meat company leading Major Greenough's
outfit.

Early in the attack, a German noncom came forward with a white flag
and asked to surrender his thirty-five-man platoon, which had been left to
hold at all costs on a crossroad. The *Feldwebel* said he no longer cared to
die for a lost cause. The wily Germans, quick to notice green troops opposing them, profited by the *Feldwebel's* defection. A little farther on,
as Doughboys cut wire left intact by the bombardment, and cleaned out
nests, one company soon encountered a fierce resistance near a hillock and
prepared to flank it. Suddenly fire ceased from the position ahead, and many
Germans leaped from the trenches with their hands up. The two leading
platoons started forward, leaders ordering a cease-fire, to accept the
prisoners. The Germans, however, remained on the lip of the trench. More
experienced lieutenants would have ordered them to approach hands up,
and had they refused, shot them down. But the trusting platoons went forward a hundred yards. The Germans then leaped backward into the
trenches, and their machine guns opened again. The two platoons were cut
to pieces in the "*Kamerad* trap." After that, there were no deceptions, and
short mercy. The Germans were teaching the Dixie poilus.

On the third day, the regiments were in open warfare, missing many
fleeing targets where a Lebel could not achieve a Springfield's accuracy.
By the fifth day, the regiments were where Gouraud wanted them to be,
unable to advance farther because French artillery had not come up. Some
battalions had lost fifteen out of twenty officers, one-third of their men. As
they rested in sunken roads and ruins, they could see the Aisne River four
miles ahead, and they offered to fight some more; but Major General Goybet would want to use them later, and he passed French infantry through
them. He wrote letters to the colonels of the 371st and 372nd. Goybet's
letters, after the formal encomiums about courage and honor, said his
division had shown the lead to others in the IX Corps. He added a sentence
that was particularly apposite: "The bravery and the dash of your regiments
are the admiration of the Moroccan division and they are good judges."

When payday came around, the French poilus shared the red fez admiration for the Dixie poilus. French money looked like soap wrappers, anyway,
no matter how patiently the lieutenant insisted that a franc note was a two-
bit piece in any man's army. The poorly paid poilu, who had seen physical
bravery for four years, now saw financial daring beyond the call of duty.

When a pile of franc notes the equivalent to two riotous weeks in Paris was heaped in the middle of a blanket, a Dixie poilu blew on the dice, saying, "Step up and fade any or all of it, gen'lemen, and get ready to read 'em and weep." Even André Simonet, linguist extraordinary, was unable to find idioms for such terms as *Big Dick from Boston, Ada from Decatur, Snake Eyes,* and *Little Joe the Hard Way.* By nightfall, when fifty-seven men of a fifty-eight-man platoon eyed the plutocratic fifty-eighth man and said they had been "sent to the cleaner's," Simonet was nonplused. Sergeant Major Simonet was an elderly man doing his bit for France as a front-line interpreter, keeping up with American infantry forty years younger. When he was killed later, the wound was only that of a small pebble entering his temple, a bit of gravel flying from the hole a bursting shell had made. Everyone noted the serenity that now graced the old Frenchman's often worried face.

Each of the two regiments, the 371st and 372nd, lost about fifty white officers, many of them with brave Confederate names. The Dixie poilus of *La 371er R.I.U.S.* suffered 997 casualties, or a third of their number. They were a hardy lot. Only 113 were killed outright, 25 dying of wounds. The other 859 were durable men, patients who won the esteem of nurses and surgeons in French hospitals where at last they dispensed with 1¼ ounces of barley sugar; though some never learned to like the harsh *pinard noir* of the poilu. It did not have the kick of Tennessee whiskey. . . .

The French gave their greatest ribbon, the Médaille Militaire, to Private Junius Diggs for an exploit of September 30 near the village of Ardeuil. Private Diggs seemed convinced that he was invulnerable, and he gave a demonstration that afternoon when his company encountered a cluster of machine guns there. The company was withdrawn immediately for a pause, French style, to study the situation, leaving many wounded under the heat of the guns. Private Diggs went back five or six times to retrieve buddies unable to walk. He also wore the Distinguished Service Cross and the Croix de Guerre (*avec palme*) when he returned to Columbia, South Carolina. The day before, Corporal Sandy E. Jones, after all his officers had been knocked out, and most of his sergeants, put a company together and led it for two days against a hill position. Corporal Jones was the Iron Commander's idea of *a fighter . . . a fighter . . . a fighter.* Pershing pinned the D.S.C. on his left breast.

Two of the regiment's soldiers bore famous names. These were the much-decorated Robert E. Lee and Burton Holmes, the latter known to three generations as a lecturer with magic lantern slides. Both were killed after serious wounds found them unwilling to lie down. Robert E. Lee particularly was persistent. He had been blasted and his Chauchat broken. Lee was carried back, but soon showed up again with a new one, and was killed while attacking the second of two machine guns holding his company at bay in a crossfire. Someone in Tin Pan Alley wrote a popular song about such lads, with its "Instead of picking melons off the vine, you'll find 'em picking Germans off the Rhine." One officer recalled that, when the heat of August caught them, many wished just for once they could find a watermelon and cool it in a creek where the catfish were jumping. These were the tenant farmers and day laborers who, six weeks later, the infantry commander of a French division said, had shown "in their first engagement, the very best qualities of bravery and audacity which are characteristic of shock troops."

During the September 26 offensive, the 369th Regiment was in the line nine consecutive days as a regiment in a French division. They never lost a foot on defense, and they failed in only one attack, this their final one when they went forward against concrete naked of any barrage, the French artillery having failed to come up. French artillery had tried, over roads that were sometimes a butchery of exploded caissons, gunners and postilions in pools of death amidst lead horses, swing horses, wheelers. This failure, of course, gave rear-area critics a chance to carp.

If there was any common fault among the white officers in the twelve lost battalions, it was their belief that they could reproduce the various Negro dialects. There was no Mark Twain among them; though their anecdotes, never condescending, were hilariously funny or tragically moving. When their French division was relieved and sent to the Vosges front, the 369th went with it. By this time they had lost most of their equipment, there being one blanket left for every four men to keep out the cold night air. "They laughed to keep themselves warm," their chronicler said.

The Vosges sector was a quiet one, mainly a matter of nightly patrols through wire, with an occasional *coup de main,* or full-dress raid. The enemy soon discovered there were Negro regiments facing him and, with characteristic misguidance, hoped to encourage desertion. On mountaintops such as the Tête des Vaux where front lines were within range, he removed the detonators from hand grenades, thrust messages into the threading, and tossed them into Negro trenches. "You would be better fighting the money trust at home instead of fighting your fellow soldiers in gray over here where it doesn't really matter two sticks to you how the war goes. . . . You better come over while the going is good." The Doughboys sent the messages back to headquarters. They wondered who the German writer might have been, with his "you better come over" lingo.

Some Doughboys were still coming over the night before the Armistice, but they were brandishing bolo knives and throwing live grenades.

Most regiments thought of their famous personnel as the great medalists. The most celebrated man in the 15th Heavy Foot was the wearer of a modest Croix de Guerre. Lincoln Eyre of the New York *World* wrote the story of what became known as "The Battle of Henry Johnson." In an April tour in a quiet sector, Private Johnson, in a listening post with his friend, Private Needham Roberts, would have preferred a straight razor to a Lebel rifle for the work in progress. Having only a Gillette, he secured a bolo knife and a whetstone some time before he entered the lines. He honed double edges upon the weapon capable of splitting a cat's whiskers with a feather's blow. Before the Harlem regiment began its fighting it had known front-line training in the southern cage of the Argonne Forest, in an exchange of patrols and ambushes there during the dark of the moon. Old positions there in the shadow of l'Homme Mort were poorly linked, and Colonel Hayward began to improve them. He used a maze of combat posts, all lightly garrisoned, setting them as traps to invite enemy patrols into his net. It was an exciting week for the Harlemites; it was like the child's play of rival kinds around tenement lanes. Nothing happened for three nights, and then ensued the battle of Henry Johnson.

An enemy patrol made its way to the wire flanking the No. 28 post, a half-platoon commanded by Lieutenant Richardson Platt of Brooklyn, to raid the subpost, No. 29, commanded by a corporal and a guard of four men. Privates Johnson and Roberts were on watch, the corporal and the off-relief two privates sleeping peacefully. Roberts heard a clinking, as if someone were cutting wire. He led Johnson toward the spot. Again came the sound of clippers on barbed wire. Before they could rush back to alert the corporal and his men, rockets lighted the sky and the Germans were on them, throwing grenades. The corporal and his two men were isolated.

Johnson and Roberts went down, both crippled for life. Roberts began firing from a sitting position, but Johnson with broken fibulae got to his feet. He fired the three cartridges of his Lebel clip, the third German powder-burned by the last one, which killed him. Johnson now wanted to draw his eight-inch, three-pound bolo knife, but a fourth enemy leaped over the third dead man, pistol in hand. Johnson clubbed him down. No remark he ever heard was more astounding than the clubbed German's cry in English: "The little black son-of-a-bitch has got me." Henry Johnson shouted for the corporal of the guard and then made the retort courteous: "Yes, and this lil' black son-of-a-bitch is going to git you again if you git up."

The German faked death. Johnson looked around for his buddy, and saw two Germans carrying him back prisoner. Private Johnson now had time to unsheathe his bolo. The rear man was carrying Roberts by head and shoulders. The bolo went through the pillbox cap the German raiders always wore, through the skull and into his throat. The German carrying Roberts' feet fled. As Johnson turned, the clubbed German came at him, firing a Luger pistol. When Johnson was hit, the bullets drove him to his hands and knees. Johnson came up between the German's legs and disemboweled him. By this time, the whole sector was in arms and Johnson began throwing grenades, his face a bloody cascade from the German's aorta, hobbling after Germans to the gaps in the wire with his terrible knife. The next morning, Major Little and his party cautiously explored the trail a half-mile to the banks of the Aire through the wire—*la chicane,* as the French had taught him to say. There were plots of blood, of bandages, of flesh clinging to barbs. The battle of Henry Johnson was history.

Major General Le Gallais, chief of training, asked for the pillbox cap, and framed it as a souvenir, Private Johnson being his idea of a *bon soldat.* When the regiment was relieved, Major Little visited Henry Johnson in a French hospital. Whence had come his skill with the bolo? Had he, in his career as a redcap at the Albany depot, ever been involved in a fight with razors? Private Johnson buried his face in the pillow to smother his laughter. All his wounded buddies in nearby beds smothered their laughter, too. They admired and respected Little as their battalion commander. In this case, he was just another fool white man asking silly questions.

Johnson soon escaped the French hospital and arrived at Hayward's headquarters hobbling on heavy sticks. He did not want to go home. Hayward made him a headquarters sergeant and Johnson hobbled through to the Rhine, wearing his Croix de Guerre ribbon at the peak of his overseas cap, the bronze cross dangling as an ornament over his left eye. Major Little always remembered Private Johnson's remark when the ambulance team arrived. He had been wounded from head to foot, so many bones broken, so much blood drained, that death seemed imminent. "Suh," said Private Johnson, "you-all doan want to worry about me. I've been shot before."

Major Little never forgot the thrill of seeing his Harlem boys loosen the bolos in their sheaths the first day of the Argonne-Meuse offensive. Jumping off that afternoon to pass through poilus into the hell they had heard all morning, wags among them were crying: "All out for Custer's last stand!" When the regiment was detached, and at last joined its white buddies on the Rhine, General Lebouc wrote to say that it rivaled any of his French regiments in attitude and discipline. He had always called it "my Black Watch." He was coming to decorate its colors with the Croix de Guerre.

"I shall have great joy in kissing you in front of your regiment," he wrote Colonel Hayward. The general had a fighter's face, bisected by a mustache like a Gay Nineties barber's.

Not even the giant sergeant major, who was color-bearer, laughed that day. It was a sacred occasion for the 15th Heavy Foot; though the color-bearer had unique ideas about the preservation of the colors. In a rear area while marching in column, he had refused to take cover when strafed by an enemy airplane, explaining he had promised Governor Whitman that he would never droop its folds in the dust. He had continued marching. He had also, when passing General Gouraud in review, dipped the National Standard to the Gallipoli veteran, saying that George Washington would have done the same.

Irvin Cobb, Kentucky son of an illustrious Confederate family and conscious of the faults of his prejudices, was a great admirer of these regiments. He fallaciously thought the word n-i-g-g-e-r would soon mean "American." The war they fought failed to end any war but that of 1918.

The most rousing military show New York City ever witnessed was the homecoming when Jim Europe's band came back to Harlem with sixty bandsmen, plus forty drummer and buglers, no more than two pieces with the same arrangement. Hayward had moved his 15th Heavy Foot up Fifth Avenue in French blocs with sergeants, lieutenants, and captains taking center intervals in single file, rigorously military with such airs as "Stars and Stripes Forever" and "Madelon." He changed to regulation Doughboy column of squads after clearing Central Park's flank, turning left and marching to such tunes as "That Old Girl of Mine" until he neared upper Broadway. Then the 15th Heavy Foot switched to its third style, a front of half-platoons, each rank gapped by five paces to provide lodgment within the parade for sweethearts and wives. The column hit the heart of Harlem to the tune of "Won't You Come Home, Bill Bailey," a sea of laughing soldiers and weeping sweethearts, alongside the band many volunteer sidemen in purple-and-fine-linen contributing myriad breaks and bridges in brass unisons to whatever Europe chose to play. Colonel Hayward, a soldier and psychologist, a combination any good regimental commander might strive to achieve, was also a showman, and in the 15th Heavy Foot he had the talent to take Broadway by storm with the same dash that his Men of Bronze had taken the Germans.

Chapter 20

BREAKING THE KRIEMHILDE STELLUNG

Tell her I have fallen on the Field of Honor.

On the morning of October 12, four days after Sergeant York's turkey shoot in the valley of the Aire, an important courier came to Souilly to see the Iron Commander. He was Major General Maxime Weygand, Foch's alter ego, a small man of delicate mien, with the porcelained features of a Chinese doll and an almost Mongolian inscrutability. In the immediate future he would know the supreme triumph of standing behind Foch when the latter compelled the German Matthias Erzberger, hat in hand, to ask for an armistice. His ultimate fate would be to follow poor old Pétain into Hitler's Vichy satrapy twenty-two years later after having surrendered the French Armies to the Nazis.

On this particular morning, while the Doughboys were grinding out bloody advances yard by yard, Weygand's errand was to deliver to Pershing a letter from Foch proposing that the American commander limit his control of his brawny divisions to those which were storming the beetling fortresses in the center of the Meuse-Argonne front, giving up two-thirds of his men to French generals on the right and the left to beef up their riddled divisions. It was the final attempt to take Pershing's army away from him, and under the circumstances it was understandable. General von der Marwitz's German Fifth Army, holding on desperately with twenty-six divisions in action and eleven in reserve, the fate of his nation at stake if Sedan fell, had inflicted 75,000 casualties on the Yanks (11,000 more were being felled each week by influenza and pneumonia). But the French,

323

by comparison, had suffered 175,000 casualties since mid-August, and this in their fourth year of slaughter. They were so physically drained that as at Blanc Mont and before the Consenvoye Heights, and at the Amiens "Black Day," they now waited for the Americans or British to take the most formidable positions before they put any real push into their attacks.

Although Weygand did not say so, Clemenceau had been urging Foch for weeks to ask Woodrow Wilson to sack the Iron Commander. Pershing knew of this; grapevine had alerted him. "They are at it again," he told Frederick Palmer. And now the Tiger had written Foch that he wanted no more arguments about it; this was an order. The French soldier must demand that Wilson recall Pershing in disgrace! It was the ugliest situation in Pershing's career, and the undercurrents of the conflict might have washed away everything the American command had struggled to achieve.

Pershing understood politics as well as Foch, and he realized that, the American First Army now being the equal of any in Europe, Clemenceau might try to deprive Woodrow Wilson of his blue chips at the peace conference by removing its commander, thus ridiculing the Doughboy effort by placing the American divisions under French control. But the West Pointer also knew administrative processes, and all their background chicanery, having served since his lieutenancy under some of his country's great administrators—Theodore Roosevelt, Elihu Root, Henry L. Stimson, William Howard Taft, and Woodrow Wilson. Pershing knew nothing short of a cerebral accident at Souilly would cause Wilson to recall him; but then too he was aware that the Tiger, in Château-Thierry days, had hinted that he might send Ferdinand Foch to Limoges, the French Army's equivalent of Blois. Accordingly, the West Pointer met attack with counterattack.

When Weygand left Souilly, he carried a letter from Pershing announcing the latter's proposal, already communicated to Liggett and Bullard, and to General Pétain, that his forces would now be divided into two armies, with Bullard and Liggett lieutenant generals commanding corps commanders he had found worthy after some battlefield testing. Pershing was a weary man. Impeccable Weygand could see the slackness of posture, the tallow skin and drooping folds of the once-iron jaw. The American had done too much too long, refusing to relinquish detail of all operations until he was certain the officers he promoted would do all things *his* way. (He had even made a personal project of seeing to it that Dr. Walter Damrosch, of the New York Symphony, improved the music of the regimental bands.) The time had come to be an overlord, rather than a driver. He demanded of Foch that he no longer receive orders through Pétain's Group of Armies;

he desired an independent chain-of-command, coequal of Haig and Pétain. He may have looked ten years older than the day he stepped ashore at Boulogne-sur-Mer, but he was *a fighter . . . a fighter . . . a fighter!* Pershing was summoned the same day to report to the marshal at Bombon.

There followed a scene in the drawing room of an abandoned town house at Bombon, the principals being Foch and his alter ego, Weygand, on one side of a table littered with maps and plans, and Pershing with his aide and interpreter, Colonel Carl Boyd, on the other. The Army's Historical Division in 1948 published the colonel's *aide-mémoire* of the exchanges between Foch and the obdurate Yank, most of its text in indirect discourse. After military courtesies were disposed of, the dialogue in a free adaptation ran about as follows:

Foch tried to be nonchalant in his first sally when he asked, "What do you think President Wilson expects to do under present conditions?"

John Joseph Pershing had worn his country's livery as a servant of his Republic too long for him to venture an opinion on his Commander-in-Chief's state of mind or his future plans. "I have received no communication whatsoever from President Wilson," Pershing said.

This seemed to relieve Foch's anxiety somewhat, as it assured him that Clemenceau had not yet written Wilson asking him to sack Pershing, a shocking impropriety that Foch, always a staff paragon, would have abhorred. Foch then said politely, "I hope he will not presume to speak for the Allies. I am afraid the President will allow himself to become involved . . ." He broke off for a few seconds before uttering the phrase most hateful to him. ". . . Involved in *long conversations.*"

Here again Pershing had to refuse a direct answer. "Newspapers at home," Pershing said, "find everyone resolved to push the war to a definite conclusion."

This did not satisfy Foch. Suspicious of orators and politicians, he distrusted the idealistic Wilson. He began to gesture emphatically. "I have no confidence in the Germans. *A long conversation* would give them an opportunity to withdraw and reform their armies."

Pershing smiled faintly and answered obliquely. "The talk around the White House is," he said, as Foch leaned forward, "that Mr. Wilson will not become involved in long conversations."

"*Eh bien,*" said the old marshal. "And now—" he looked long at the Orders of Battle on the wall map and girded his loins for the struggle— "how are matters progressing on the American front?"

"We have met with very hard fighting," Pershing said quietly. "The Germans are putting up a very determined resistance."

Foch answered this with his first querulous remark. "On all other parts of the front," he said acidly, "the advances are very marked. The Americans are not progressing as rapidly."

Pershing controlled his temper, saying nothing about the 100,000 fresh Doughboys who had contributed to breaking some strong points in these progresses. Instead he said, "Our fighting facilitates the advance of the other armies. We are drawing enemy divisions away from the other fronts." The point was not too well taken. Only two divisions were diverted from the German forces facing the British, and one was sent there to replace them, making about 11,500 fewer hostile troops for Haig to conquer.

Foch got down to business. "I would like to see the Americans advance more rapidly."

The room grew chilly with Pershing's sharp answer: "No army in our place would have advanced farther than the Americans."

Foch became waspish: "Every general is disposed to say the fighting on his front is the hardest." Again he waved toward the wall map. "I myself," the old marshal said pointedly, "only consider results."

Pershing met this slur with scorn. "Results? In seventeen days we have engaged twenty-six German divisions."

"Shall I show you *my* figures on this?" Foch asked.

"No." Pershing was brusque.

There must have been a pause while the two old soldiers measured one another until Foch said, "I want the Americans to come up to the level of the other Armies in the direction of Mézières."

Again Pershing was cool. "I will continue my attacks until the Germans give way," he answered, and then changed to sarcasm with a final ". . . provided, of course, that this is Marshal Foch's desire."

"By all means," Foch said emphatically, and then infuriated the West Pointer by suddenly changing to a classroom lecturer. "In order to have an attack succeed," he began professorially, "a commander must go considerably into details, so far as corps, division, brigade, even regimental commanders are concerned. Subordinates should be required to bring their orders in writing, so that they can be examined and operations of different units coordinated. If they are not in writing, how will the commander know they are ever written?"

"It has always been done that way in the American First Army," Pershing answered.

"Yes?" said Foch with a shrug.

Pershing must have thought of the hell of confusing orders that would result if he agreed to Weygand's proposal of that morning to piecemeal

600,000 Doughboys under French commanders, inevitably pouring single Yank battalions into shattered poilu regiments. He replied, "How else would I know the difficulties of ground and the savage resistance of the enemy if I did not receive written orders? We are not advancing rapidly because the Germans are fighting by echeloning machine guns in depth." He had grown angry at last. "The Germans could hold up any troops Marshal Foch has at his command."

"Ah," said Foch coldly, "I judge only by results."

"Nothing any French general could say," the Iron Commander said harshly, "will put more goodwill, energy, or coordination into our operations. I have done all in my power, as have the officers under me."

Foch reverted to his professorial demeanor. "If an attack is well planned and executed, it succeeds with small losses. If not, the losses are heavy and there is no advance."

Pershing received this Grandmaison gabble drily. "True only to a certain extent. Much depends upon what your enemy does." He became testy. "Why bring all this up? I am speaking of conditions that actually exist on my front. *No other troops could overcome them!* I would like to call your particular attention to the terrain."

"I am aware of the terrain," Foch said coldly. "You chose the ground of the Argonne, and I allowed you to attack there."

Pershing recalled the red-trousered travesty that had preceded Saint-Mihiel. "I had not understood it that way," he said. "In the first place, you proposed to split my army in half, fighting one force west of the Argonne, the other in the east, with the French in between the two halves. I said I was obliged to fight them as a whole and wherever the marshal indicated."

Foch had no desire to repeat the frustration of his Saint-Mihiel quarrel, and he knew he had lost game, set, and match in his great fifteen months' tourney with the Yank. "Oh, well," he replied wearily, "it is a matter of no consequence now. The only thing that matters is results."

At this point Maxime Weygand who, everyone said, was Foch's mind reader, spoke his only line. "Here is General Pershing's plan for the formation of two armies." Foch did not even look at the plans Weygand placed on the table.

"Ah, yes," the marshal said cheerfully, "I am inclined to grant your request." He still preserved his supreme authority with an unnecessary admonition: "However, you are not to construe this as a plan for you to withdraw to Chaumont."

"As usual," Pershing said drily, "my headquarters train will remain in the woods at Souilly. I will visit Army, Corps, Division, and Brigade as often as possible." (Many Doughboys had seen Pershing around Brigade Headquarters—from Harbord's shell-rocked shambles at Lucy-le-Bocage behind Belleau Wood to the advanced posts of Pennsylvania's harassed brigadiers trying to claw their way into Argonne's Le Chêne Tondu, his person sometimes in danger.)

"*C'est bon*," said Foch, standing to end the long conversation. "General Pétain is agreeable to your plan."

Pershing must have left Bombon believing the whole thing a dodge by Foch, who knew the Iron Commander was intractable, to report to Clemenceau that he had given Pershing a scolding. One month later in a Paris drunk with victory, the old Tiger fell into the arms of Black Jack Pershing and wept. And some years later, Marshal Foch recalled the scene at Bombon in his *Conversations* with M. Raymond Recouly. Bullard, then in happy retirement in his New York apartment, reading the marshal's account of how he had had to goad Pershing into keeping pace with the French, leaped in anger from his chair to write on the margin of the passage, "The hell you say! I was there. The French just went through the motions." Bullard's judgment was not entirely accurate; the French had fought until their nation was murdered in Nivelle's tragedy in 1917 and victory was a mirage.

But there were no perfunctory motions on the part of the Doughboys who now faced the Kriemhilde Stellung. They were new.

As a result of the meeting at Bombon there was a new look to the Doughboy staff setup and its personnel. Pershing was now an Army Group commander coequal with Haig and Pétain, responsible only to Foch. Liggett took over command of Pershing's old First Army. Bullard was promoted to command the newly created American Second Army, with a front stretching forty miles from Pont-à-Mousson in the east above Verdun, his target Pershing's original plan to seize Metz, and push on to the Briey iron mines, the Saar's coal basin. Dickman then inherited command of Liggett's I Corps on the First Army's left, Summerall took Command of Cameron's V Corps in the center, for Cameron had worn himself out, and in an unusual staff change, had been returned to command his original 4th Division. (Who knows what transpired between Pershing and Cameron on this change-over? Suffice it to say that Pershing, when he chose his Hall of Fame photographs of persons he admired, did not include Cameron; though Cameron's 4th Division, always loyal, gave *him* the place of honor in its official history.) Hines left the 4th Division and took over Bullard's III Corps on the right.

Pershing had wanted to fight again on a general line October 15, but the French at his left were ready to begin a cautious advance sooner, now that the Bowery Backwoodsmen of the 77th had taken the punishing Argonne pavilions and broken into the clear to secure the French right flank. So Pershing moved up by a full day the H-hour for what was now Liggett's First Army.

The front that October 14 ran from just south of Grandpré on the west, across the face of the Hindenburg Line's strongest positions in France, the Romagne Heights and Cunel in the center, to the western banks of the Meuse. It was a wriggling serpent of a line, winding southeast from Grandpré, and falling away from Sedan until it curved almost due south where Yanks still faced the bloody marshes south of Brieulles, that tremendous thorn in the Doughboy side still protected by the Borne de Cornouiller on the eastern heights of the Meuse. Liggett's French corps under General Claudel was still baffled by the Consenvoye Heights there, the approach to the Borne.

The divisions in line, all of which had pushed on regardless of flank situations, could be ticked off left to right, as follows: the Bowery boys of the 77th, Robert E. Lee's 80th Division, the ferocious Rainbows of the 42nd, the *Gemütlichkeit* boys of the 32nd, the Red Diamonds of the 5th's Regulars—and straddling the Meuse below Brieulles was the 33rd Illini. East of the Meuse the 29th's Blue and Grays of the National Guard were beefing up the French XVII Corps, who were also buffered by the Yankees of the 26th Division. The line was as crooked as the coast of Maine, and every position in the Kriemhilde Stellung was difficult. . . .

In after years, many reunionists at division jamborees claimed to have taken some point which they, as flank patrols, may have been in at one period of fighting, but there would be other divisions which rightly claimed that their mass, their tactical shock, had actually carried the day. Liggett's attack on October 14 defies description in detail other than a series of maps only a professional eye can comprehend. There were eight divisions in the line. From the moment the first Yank barrages fell on advanced lines, the Germans were as violent and as savage as in their best years. Along other fronts in France they were beginning to pull back, but against the Doughboys they never gave up.

When the Meuse-Argonne operation was launched September 26, the American First Army's objective on the extreme left of its line had been to seize the citadel of Grandpré east of the confluence of the Aire and Aisne rivers, and make a junction with Gouraud's French Army moving up on the left of the forest. The 77th Division's Bowery Backwoodsmen finally got a toehold at Grandpré's approaches on October 9-10 as it emerged from the

Argonne blinking in unaccustomed sunlight. The key to Grandpré was Saint-Juvin, an ugly piece of fieldworks on a hillside that had resisted the best efforts of the infantry of the tired 82nd Division on the right.

General Alexander ordered an assault on Saint-Juvin from both flanks by the 77th Division in battalion strengths on October 13. The left-flank battalion began first and was hard at it and suffering when the leading element of the other battalion wove through the forest to begin its attack. That element consisted of Captain Julius Ochs Adler, of the *New York Times* family, his personal Chauchat gunner, and the ammunition carrier. Adler came upon a left-flank guard of the 82nd's units still in the line to assist the refreshed divisions moving up again, the guard consisting of a major with three Hotchkiss teams. When Adler told him that he and his two friends were now going to capture the deafening town on the hill beyond, the major was dubious but said that he would come up behind him with his Hotchkiss gunners.

Adler and his two buddies gained the eastern outskirts of the town unobserved, the German garrison concentrating on the left-flank Doughboy battalion. The three then began to shoot up the town like a bunch of cowboy drunks at the end of a cattle drive, giving the impression that a larger force than three isolated Doughboys was advancing. A Chauchat team of the 77th came up and one of the guns was instantly placed on the far side of a house, the gunner shooting through the windows on both sides, the parlor itself a baffle that muffled the chatter of the gun. Bewildered Germans, trying to change front, ran into a stream of soundless steel, and Adler and his buddies now had clay pigeons for targets. Parts of other companies heavily reduced by casualties came up and Adler reorganized them, sending back word to the skeptical major of the 82nd and his Hotchkiss teams, who kept his promise. The division was relieved that same night. . . . It was difficult in later years for anyone invited to lunch in the paneled room high above Times Square to see in the quiet, self-effacing Major Adler a soldier with the effrontery of a con man and the ferocity of a bear.

After the fall of Saint-Juvin, Major General Dickman of the Marne assigned an unenviable task to the 78th Division, green I Corps brother to the 77th, which it had just relieved, and the 82nd. The 78th, composed of drafted lads from the mountainous hinterlands of New York and New Jersey, called themselves "The White Lightnings." The sobriquet had nothing to do with thunderstorms, but with creeks where revenue officers sniffed for the smell of sour mash from moonshine stills; and the lads wore a white lightning flash on a field of whiskey red for a shoulder patch.

Their objective across the Aire River was Grandpré, a citadel town storied up slopes suitable for goat pasture—the Bois de Bourgogne beyond it, a forest like a giant flatiron, the point of it shod with granite, and the Bois des Loges flanking the point. The modest Aire River, growing strong under increasing freshets, made a sharp turn to the west after it cleared the flank of the Argonne, passing through the narrow valley which separated this forest's tangles from the equally difficult Bois de Bourgogne ahead. Where it flowed into the Aisne it split into two beds, marshy islands of saplings dividing the two courses. The left brigade of the 78th, new to combat, found itself looking on a muddy valley between them and the hills that still kept the armies of Gouraud and Liggett apart. No one, corps or army commander (except Foch), expected the 78th to capture the German positions before them. Their assignment was to exert flank pressure by exposing themselves in a series of attacks to contain an enemy seeking to sideslip toward the center, where brigades such as MacArthur's and Winans's, of the 42nd and 32nd Divisions, were ripping into his heart.

The French had done their fiercest to reach the 78th's flank as early as the day—October 13—the Lightnings relieved the Lost Battalion outfit. The poilus had swept into the village of Talma to their own right, along easier ground, but the hills beyond made it rough for them to hold their position, the Germans driving them out the next day. A day later, October 15, the 78th's left brigade captured the farm guarding Talma, and finally, after nine days of continuous infantry maneuver in a series of tactical exploitations which needed a staff bureau to detail, they took the town of Talma and all ground about it on October 25.

The Germans had no thought of giving up the Bourgogne Woods that October. It was their wedge between the Doughboys and Gouraud, and the town of Grandpré was the bastion they must hold. Its loss would signal the collapse of their right flank, and they brought up gunners of exceptional skill to defend it. But Major General James H. McRae, a modest, quiet fellow, had other ideas. He had no intention of sacrificing his troops for barren gains. He decided to capture Grandpré, the front of the Bourgogne Woods, and the Loges Woods flanking them. He would do it with his mountain-goat infantry, keeping each infantry brigade intact, fighting his division as a corps. He was good.

Germans and Doughboys soon wrestled hand to hand on Grandpré's terraced roofs after the Lightnings had captured the house beneath. German field pieces fanged the town, many of them rigged with block and tackle to appear, fire, then disappear into hiding places until some gutty Doughboys with a cluster of Mills bombs found them and wiped them out. The Grandpré fight could have been led by Richard the Lion-Hearted with a battle-ax.

It was like storming a castle. The Lightnings, who possessed the mountaineering qualities suitable for such a *dégringolade,* captured it by nightfall of October 27 after two furious days.

By the time all the Germans in Grandpré were prisoners or corpses, the 78th Division had around five thousand casualties. It had been mainly a holding force, a flank detail, but McRae and his men had fought with the skill and persistence of veterans. Like the Germans in 1914, who had also astonished the military world by boldly committing untried Reservists not as piecemeal units, but as full-fledged corps, to fight alongside Regulars, the 78th Division's commanders had known that newness and fresh bravery would cover many minor blunders as they hacked away at their objectives. Less than any other division with a similar experience did they single out individuals for valor. They thought all their men valiant. For their troops, it was mainly a matter of showing the Lost Battalion veterans they had seen stumbling back to rest that they, too, had the wherewithal to crack the strongest line in Europe, crossing a river's double channel to scale granite cliffs.

McRae asked that a buck private named Parker F. Dunn be awarded the Medal of Honor. His battalion was pinned down October 23 facing extinction beneath the hill that had rebuffed the French at Talma. The open crossings were swept from three sides, bullets kicking up muddy divots from three directions. The battalion commander refused to send any of his runners back, knowing it would be a fatal enterprise. Private Dunn was in his Intelligence Section, and he insisted upon trying. All watched him set out, darting like a quail. He was down with a wound and then up again. Once more he was down, and then on his feet staggering toward Regimental. When he reached the third crossfire, Private Dunn did not get up again. When word came that night for the battalion to withdraw to a less exposed position, troops disputed their officers. To withdraw, it seemed to them, was like letting Parkey down. So it was reinforced, machine gunners gaining some high ground. "Any youse guys from Joisey?" were the whispers in the night.

In later years as Commandant at the Citadel Academy at Charleston, Major General Charles Summerall achieved national recognition by his fame as an educator, his ability to rip the air with his warnings about American softness, but in the Argonne he had won command of the V Corps by a display of driving force, of personal daring, that was news to no one on the roster of the Regular Army. (Legend had it that, when with Reilly's Battery in the relief of Peking, he had dashed forward heedless of fire from the defenders on the walls, to chalk-mark pinpoint targets for his gunners to shell and make a breach.) At Cantigny, he had opened the artillery ball. At Soissons, he had led the brilliant 3rd Brigade of the 2nd Division. And given command of the Big Red One on October 1, he had proceeded to carve a four-mile hole in the German positions in Liggett's effort to out-flank the Argonne. Now he had the V Corps.

In the fighting of Liggett's first phase—October 14-25—honors must go by all odds to two National Guard divisions, the 32nd and 42nd. These two divisions in Summerall's V Corps, in line October 14 to the right of the 77th and 78th Divisions in Dickman's I Corps, faced, respectively, the forested cliffs, the gunned fortresses, and the hideous terrain of a wooded whaleback called the Côte Dame Marie, which guarded Landres, the Romagne Heights, and the pendant town Romagne. Pershing and his staff planners had hoped to reach these unscalable bastions in an uninterrupted advance if Mont-faucon had fallen on the afternoon of September 26. Now, three weeks later, with no tanks, with no chance for the four brigades of these two divisions to flank the strong points before them, there was no other solution to breaching what any military topographer would call the strongest positions on the Western Front than naked frontal assault by infantry—or by what Pershing liked to call "superior determination."

If there was bitter rivalry throughout the Doughboys' War between the Regulars of the 1st and 2nd Divisions, spiced of course by the presence of the "goddam" Marines in the latter outfit, the rivalry between the Guards-men was even more intense. The 32nd's *Gemütlichkeit* boys, still holding to their national characteristics despite some fifteen thousand replacements from many states, were now side by side with the 42nd's Rainbows, from twenty states. Supported by fierce artillery, these four brilliant infantry brigades were led by West Pointers who were imbued not only with their Long Gray Line traditions, but were now indoctrinated by the savagery of competitive civilians who had risen to regimental commands.

The 64th Brigade of the 32nd Division was led by a brigadier general who hated the itchy Doughboy shirt of coarse flannel and was resolved, if he survived the war, to go home and compel the Army to switch to poplin. Brigadier General Edwin B. Winans knew that there would be no doves in the mountain-goat country of the Côte Dame Marie—only holes cooing with machine guns, one-inch cannon, mine throwers, and field guns which would meet any company advancing with murderous crossfire. Nevertheless he had taken it with his brigade about the time Ochs Adler of the 77th Division to his left was blazing away like a cowboy drunk, and that night

Winans's companion brigade had the town of Romagne and a piece of the woods flanking it.

Winans himself was flanked that day by an officer just as ambitious as he was, a flamboyant fellow who was the perfect example of the maxim that you cannot tell a West Pointer by his uniform. Where Winans looked like a tailor's specifications of what a West Point graduate should look like, his rival's uniform was too green to delight an Army tailor, and there was no grommet to stiffen his cap. Douglas MacArthur's 84th Brigade of the 42nd Rainbows, having relieved the Big Red One on October 13, went forward in a blinding rainstorm, yet by nightfall they had the other half of Winans's woods, as well as the fiendish and well-nigh unscalable heights of the Côte de Châtillon. It was like a battle royal among teams of homicidal wrestlers armed with lethal weapons where there was no split in the purse. After this the two center divisions gained about a mile in two more days of furious fighting—at the cost of three thousand men in MacArthur's brigade alone, the ground carpeted with *feldgrau* uniforms, bayonets stabbed in earth as headstones for dead Yanks. Pershing cited Winans and MacArthur as deserving of "unstinted praise."

Liggett's tactical dispositions had been sound, his orders clear in concept and execution, but, as Pershing had told Foch, much depended on what the enemy did. It was October 17 before MacArthur's brigade held the razorback of Châtillon's deep defense system, possessors of a great chunk of the Kriemhilde Stellung. In three days of unexcelled fighting, flanks making one-mile advances, the center only half that distance, the Rainbows had wrested the heights before Landres from the enemy, they had captured now-forgotten farms, fortress strong, with names like la Musarde Farm, la Tuilerie Farm, the Côte de Châtillon's razorback heights a mile east of where the Aire River hastened toward its junction with the Aisne.

These positions, with Winans fighting just as strongly to the left of the Rainbows, were the aces of the German's trump cards. Now they had lost them and were struggling to find any strong points they might hold. On October 17 Liggett pulled out the 42nd and 32nd Divisions to rest, refit and absorb replacements for his final grand attack. Staff had vainly hoped that the 42nd and the 32nd, with the 5th converging from the right, could push past the Kriemhilde into the final positions of the Freya Stellung; but the target was beyond human capabilities for divisions which had made supreme efforts for three successive days. In their place Liggett threw in the Doughboys and Marines of the 2nd Division, whose brigades had recently taken Blanc Mont, and on their right flank the 89th Division, new to war, but resolved to show the boastful 2nd Division that they, too, could whip any man in the saloon.

To the right of the 32nd, the 90th Division between them by October 15, General John E. McMahon of the 5th Division was told by his new corps commander, the granite-like Hines, on the same day as the latter's appointment—October 12—that he would like a reconnaissance to find out what was ahead of the Red Diamonds for the October 14 attack.

Such matters were always costly. It was possibly at this time that Pershing told his friend Palmer how much he admired the young civilian soldiers, how good they had become, and how he hated to send so many forward to death while armistice talk was buzzing the chancelleries of the world. McMahon's orders to Major Davis were to take his full battalion the next morning, with heavy machine-gun elements, and have a look at the railway around Cunel and scout the German defenses there.

Major Davis had in his ranks the man whom Pershing was to name the outstanding "Old Army" soldier of the war. York and Whittlesey had won their niches in the Iron Commander's pantheon. Samuel A. Woodfill, Doughboy of Doughboys, now first lieutenant and acting captain, was actually the eternal sergeant of Black Jack Pershing's esteem. (He had been fighting on Leyte forty-five years before MacArthur returned there in 1945.) After a Kentucky boyhood spent listening to the great yarns of his grandfather, late sergeant of 5th Indiana Volunteers in Mr. Lincoln's war, a few years of schooling and a term as a woodchopper in Indiana, he had enlisted in the Army. Like Sergeant York, he had learned musketry with a muzzleloader. Woodfill liked the snows of Alaska so much, and the winter stalking of big game along with Eskimo friends, that he served four hitches there, the only Doughboy able to outshoot the champions of the Canadian Mounties. York was a great draftee and Whittlesey a great Reservist, but Sam Woodfill had six hash marks on his sleeve when he was commissioned, and the wreath-and-rifles of his expert's badge dangled from a long ladder of qualifying bars. Since 1886, Pershing had known that sergeants like Woodfill had given West Point lieutenants the first courses in their postgraduate education. Sam himself had made corporal in only thirteen years and, a sergeant when the United States entered the war, he was commissioned a first lieutenant and acting captain. This great increase in pay enabled him to return to the Wabash country and marry his boyhood sweetheart, who had promised to wait.

Spandau machine gunners protecting Cunel's heights, artillerymen with German 77s, had detected the 5th's movement into the lines October 10 and immediately punished it. Woodfill saw friends dropping all around him, others finding deep cover. The eternal sergeant could only find a shallow depression, the Spandaus cutting his pack to pieces. Valiant Sam Woodfill tasted death then and there. Lying prone, he took the picture of his wife in her wedding dress from a breast pocket and wrote:

October 10, 1918. In case of accident or death it is my last and fondest desire that the finder shall please do me a last and everlasting favor to please forward this picture to my Darling Wife, and tell her that I have fallen on the Field of Honor, and departed to a better land which knows no sorrow and feels no pain. I will prepair [sic] a place and be waiting at the Golden Gait [sic] of Heaven for my Darling Blossom. The address Mrs. Samuel Woodfill, 167 Alexandria Pike, Fort Thomas, Kentucky.

The acting captain did not need long to rid himself of death's taste; an outfit on his right was making an exploratory racket in some woods fronting Cunel, diverting the 77s, and fog closed down on gunners sighting down the barrels of the wicked little Spandaus. Sam Woodfill was permitted to live to fight another day.

On the morning of October 13, Woodfill first had to fight his company through to the Bois de la Pultière. Fog gave them some cover at six o'clock that morning until the company began crossing turnip patches near a shelled church. Enemy forward posts passed the word to the Spandaus. Where York had faced a cluster of guns from one direction, Woodfill, in the lead, could hear them from three sides. His top sergeant lay dead beside him, his company was being ripped to pieces, men flattened out behind any furrows they could find. Had Captain Woodfill been willing to call off his exploration, he would have arrived back at his original line with his company decimated and discredited. To move in any direction was to invite extinction. Woodfill tried to run forward, but the air was screaming with bullets. He chose the nearest shell hole and took stock of his situation, a little sick from the gas that lingered there.

There were three guns firing across the patch. The one on the right was in the shattered church tower. The second gun, on the left, was in the loft of an old barn. The gun ahead was in a pit concealed by brush. For a man to sight down the barrel of a Spandau, as York had found out, he must place his eye to the sight, hunch his shoulders forward, and seize the spade grips with both hands. Where York had been able to see his targets, Sam could only see the flash from the gun's screen in the tower. He had to consider the inches from the eye to the hairline of the gunner, a four-inch bull's-eye unseen at about two hundred yards. He put five Springfield shots into what he hoped was the center of the ring. After each shot the gun was silent for a moment. It was finally silenced after the fifth shot. His next target was his easiest. He could see the flash from the barn roof where some tiles had been removed; a favorite haunt for single-shot snipers on both sides with telescopic rifles, but not a shrewd place for a chattering gun. The fellow in the loft was a single bird with a light automatic. Woodfill had no trouble killing him on his first shot. There remained the one ahead in the brush.

Woodfill took some time to reach the muzzle of this gun, but was relieved to know that nothing was alive in the church or the stable as he advanced by shell holes. Five different gunners took turns trying to kill Woodfill from the brush ahead. Like York, whose exploit Woodfill knew about, he had placed his automatic where he could use it in a flash. With a five-cartridge clip, Woodfill killed in succession the five Germans as each in his turn served the gun. When a sixth fellow reared with a bayonet, Woodfill pistoled him. The clearing was now quiet. Woodfill reloaded and strode forward to count his bag. He had shot six men in the head. Beyond him lay a German first lieutenant, seemingly dead. As Woodfill bent over to discover how five Springfield bullets and one Colt's slug could have killed a *seventh* man, this brave officer leaped up and seized Woodfill's rifle, at the same time reaching for his own Luger pistol. He got a bullet from the Colt in his heart. Woodfill moved on until he sighted a fourth gun, echeloned in proper depth.

For once the German, noted digger that he was, had not gone deep enough to give his team headcover. Woodfill had the high ground now, and one by one killed the five men of its crew. Meanwhile, his loyal men, as the guns no longer pinned them down, were coming forward in patrols. He then encountered three German boys of the class of 1919, downy-cheeked kids, carrying boxes of ammunition toward gunners who would never need them. A new lad would have killed them. Cool Sam Woodfill disarmed them and sent them toward his own patrols as prisoners.

His men were now trying to negotiate a muddy ravine, but there was a fifth Spandau enfilading them and they took cover again. Woodfill ruined his uniform then, crawling through foot-deep mud for thirty yards to reduce deflection on the fifth team. As usual, there were five of them—gunner, helper, belt-feeder, and two grenadiers. He killed the five of them with his Springfield. When crossfire opened on him, Woodfill jumped into a deep, elaborately wickered trench, and there did the only bad shooting of the day, shooting a German lieutenant through the abdomen with his pistol. The German fell, and Woodfill turned to find a man rushing at him with the bayonet. The Colt was now jammed, mud from the thirty-foot crawl in its slide. Woodfill seized an enemy pickax and poled the fellow like an ox, turning in time to see that the gut-shot lieutenant was sitting up, unconquerable, and weakly raising his Luger. Woodfill split his head with the pickax, and began to free his Colt of the mud. Of the enemy opposing him, only one had any thought for his own skin, the fifth fellow at the third gun whom Woodfill had killed when he tried to squirm away. It was eloquent of the fighting capacity of the troops of General von der Marwitz, once the Doughboys reached the critical positions. (York's prisoners from the forward lines were less stern stuff.)

Sam could not understand at first why, wherever his shadow fell across bays of the deep, revetted entrenchment, Germans in the open were firing at him. Then he knew: *he was inside the Kriemhilde Stellung, and they wanted it back.* By now his company was in the Stellung with him—what was left of it. They had counted the unseen gunners in the church. Yes, there had been five of them, all shot through the head. He sent back his runners, and the battalion recalled him. The regimental surgeon said that Woodfill's bronchial tubes were so heavily corroded from the lingering mustard gas of the shell holes he had occupied—it was American gas—that pneumonia was just around the corner. He finally came out of surgery, and anesthesia, at Bordeaux.

Sometime after the war, a reporter found that the once-again Sergeant Samuel Woodfill, home on three months' leave, was digging ditches for a pipe-line company on his leave time to help with the mortgage on the farm Blossom Woodfill worked while he was on duty at Fort Thomas. Woodfill had reverted to his sergeancy to preserve his tenure of service; as a Reserve officer he would have lost his benefit. The mortgage was for about eight thousand dollars. This was in the heyday of vaudeville. The Keith-Albee circuit made a ten-cent campaign, and the great hoofers and comedians paid it off in a few days. Woodfill was a rifle range major in a later war, retiring with that rank in a more enlightened service procedure. In 1951 he followed Pershing into Arlington's earth, in a comradeship the Iron Commander must have welcomed.

Reading of Woodfill's exploit, it is difficult to understand why a full battalion with supporting elements was sent to reconnoiter strong positions it could not possibly hold. A quiet man, McMahon had done a first-class job of organizing the division and training it, yet he was relieved after his division took Cunel three days later. Division Headquarters never forgot the day a big fellow appeared to take McMahon's place, much black braid on the sleeves of his trench coat. "I am Major General Ely, your new commander," he said, grinding his teeth, and soon had everyone moving in leaps and bounds. Hanson E. Ely had got his second star, and if the war had continued until the spring of 1919 he would have bitched a little had he not got a third.

For McMahon, there remained the agony of Blois and a slow boat to Baltimore. Perhaps he was ill, or tired too easily; or was a victim of that human injustice which it is impossible to eradicate in armies. Pershing's derogatory estimates of the commanders he fired never saw the light of day; and it would be unfair to infer that orders sending a full-dress battalion on an errand a smart young Intelligence Section might have performed at less cost was a factor in McMahon's dismissal. In a later war, Pershing's great disciple George Marshall followed this example in "refusing to hurt anybody." For history's sake it is regrettable.

"Young man," said an old general to John W. Thomason, Jr., when he asked for secret files on Union Army operations for his study of the Confederate J. E. B. Stuart, "there are certain operations in the Revolutionary War we are not ready to reveal yet."

By the end of October, the lines from Grandpré east had been straightened, and Hanson E. Ely, driving the 5th Division's Red Diamond boys, had finally taken the Bois des Rappes in the junction of the center and the right-hand corps of Liggett's First Army. For three successive days Ely's Doughboys had been driven out of its southern face whenever they tried to secure a hold there. Then Ely, roaring out of Sam Woodfill's old town of Cunel, had the six miles of forests for keeps on the fourth day, bringing up his supplies from the 3rd Division's old stamping ground of Madeleine Farm. The American First Army had cracked the main positions of the Hindenburg Line, though part of the Kriemhilde Stellung was still held in force by the enemy. Even the old marshal broke his reserve, and Pershing received a telegram from Ferdinand Foch which spoke of "the valor of the command."

Dickman's corps on the left was five miles farther into the defenses, and Summerall's center corps was about three miles farther advanced than was Hines with his III Corps. His line, if Summerall's outfits were pointed at twelve o'clock, would be more like an hour hand at five o'clock, his battle bent so strongly southward because he could not submit his III Corps to the cannonades on his right flank. Liggett had serious problems everywhere for the last great attacks on a scale of grandeur the United States Army had never known.

There have been various cacklings about tactics in the Meuse-Argonne series of battles, some commentators going so far as to class them with Grant's battering of Lee before Petersburg. Both points are poorly taken.

Grant was fixing the attention of Lee, the cream of the Confederate team; but Liggett had no General the Honorable Sir William Tecumseh Sherman ripping out the guts of the Rhineland. For Liggett would now be head to head, with locked horns, to break the Freya Stellung, last great natural barrier of the four-year invaders holding the crowning heights of northern France.

Chapter **21**

BREAKING THE FREYA STELLUNG

Buddies, you didn't miss anything.

Lieutenant General Hunter Liggett, USA, who had no fat above his collar, stood before the last defenses of the Hindenburg Line at daybreak November 1. He was commanding the American First Army and his tactical plan was threefold. First, he wanted to seize the great fortifications of the line Buzancy-Barricourt running west to east, at his center. Second, he would then outflank the Bois de Bourgogne on his left by hard fighting into the village of Boult-aux-Bois some six miles northwest of Buzancy and thus join hands on the Grandpré Road, literally, with Gouraud's French Army in the Aisne Valley, Doughboys and poilus all bearded and muddy as swamp rats. Third, he wanted to seize the stubborn mile of death fronting the galling town of Brieulles on the Meuse to his right, still in enemy hands after more than a stubborn month; and he could only do that by outflanking the Germans on the Borne de Cornouiller, the shotgun duenna frowning from her steel jalousies on all the Doughboy advances toward the hussy of Brieulles, and then killing the garrisons there.

Liggett had wanted to fight October 28, but Gouraud said he could not possibly gather his weary French for a concerted drive until November 1. Meanwhile, Marshal Foch sent Major General Paul de Maistre, the most courteous of Frenchmen, to the Iron Commander's headquarters to meddle with Liggett's tactics. Liggett, said de Maistre, was to forget about seizing Buzancy in the center as his main effort. He must attack beyond the citadel of Grandpré—which he now held—diverting his main force to his left against the eastern edges of the Bois de Bourgogne in an operation which could be as bloody and as confusing as the Argonne Forest. Under such a plan, Liggett would actually be subordinate to the French Gouraud—showing that Foch was a hard man to convince. Pershing promptly told Liggett and his chief of staff, Brigadier General Hugh Drum, to ignore Foch's orders; Yankee tactical dispositions were none of the old professor's business. He then gave Liggett his final command: Liggett must end all his orders to all his divisions and corps commanders with "There can be no conclusion to this war until Germany is brought to her knees."

Foch's strategic goal was now unchanged from the day the nine Yank divisions hustled into line September 26. Liggett had to reach the heights ten miles north of Buzancy and throw heavy shells into the railroad yards at Sedan, where German forces were still attempting to move guns and supplies northeast to Mézières. It was the only plausible strategic aim between the Channel and the Swiss Alps. Haig was still about two hundred miles from the Belgian gate at Liège; Pétain in the center still far from Luxembourg. Ligget alone had a real chance for a massive break-through before Christmas. If the November 1 offensive succeeded, he had drawn his order for battle for his next phase, scheduled for November 14, its strategy formally detailed and far more complex than Pershing's for Saint-Mihiel, tactics infinitely more sanguinary in their intricacies. (No historian has cared to map it.) As for his tactical concept of November 1, Captain B. H. Liddell Hart, who devoted a lifetime to studying such matters, thought of Liggett's staff team as the equal of English Sir Herbert Plumer's; he considered no Allied team superior.

Liggett had been presented with an army second to none, accomplished in all its parts, as polished as the U.S. Army of the Potomac Grant had inherited when Lincoln sent him down to the Rapidan to see what he could do about beating Robert E. Lee. The difference was that Liggett had no Lee opposing him. Ludendorff had resigned October 27 rather than be unceremoniously sacked. His field successor was, significantly, Colonel General Wilhelm Groener, Director of Railways, and a wizard in transportation. The ten miles of track from Sedan to Mézières was Groener's jugular, and Liggett had just the weapon to slit it. He was attacking with 650,000 men of all arms, 100,000 French among them. His army was, as Foch observed, fresh and growing in effectiveness every day.

Foch had everything going for him. In Italy, the Italian Armies, stabilizing a line on the Piave after their massive defeat at Caporetto the year before, had repulsed the last Austro-German bid for victory in June, then had given the Austrians a decisive beating in the Battle of Vittorio Veneto, collapsing the Hapsburg Empire by the end of October.

In France, Foch had everything he needed. The Doughboys near Auden-arde were giving bridgeheads to Ghent and Brussels to the Belgians. North of the Somme, the British had just relieved for the last time their two fine Yank divisions, and, with extraordinary persistence for armies so depleted after four years under generals apparently still gloating over the senseless Charge of the Light Brigade at Balaklava, were pressing the armies of Crown Prince Rupprecht everywhere, their prisoner count nearing 150,000. In the center of the vast line, the French had taken nearly as many prisoners as the British, and in the midst of the poilus Bullard's American Second Army was giving battle north of Saint-Mihiel astride the Moselle.

Liggett had everything he needed except heavy tanks, the greatest of 1918 weapons. An America boastful of its prowess in the Age of Steel had never succeeded in making even one of these simple monsters, although one of its citizens had invented the Holt caterpillar tractions which made the British tank feasible. Despite Secretary Baker's best efforts, the Detroit auto makers were more interested in dealers who sold passenger cars than in Doughboys fighting for their lives. Liggett did have nineteen French Whip-pets, about one light tank per 35,000 Doughboys.

He had another innovation: The United States Navy had sent up four fourteen-inch rifles on railway mounts to work on the communications at Dun-sur-Meuse. Doughboys were elated to see the first artillery of any caliber from their ignorant homeland, and exchanged pleasant ribaldries with bluejackets in peacoats, swapping tin hats for flat hats when no M.P.s were around. The guns had difficulty hitting a small target twenty miles away, but this was overcome when someone ferreted out an infantry captain who was a wizard in the mathematics of curved space and time. This Doughboy, as Dr. Edwin P. Hubble, later won a Nobel Prize and built the 200-inch telescope on Mount Palomar.

So Liggett, without the premier weapon, the heavy tank, prepared for his attack that November dawn in good weather, with three corps plus his "French" corps east of the Meuse, now augmented by three Doughboy divisions. Claudel's XVII Corps, that had begun the attack September 26, had been relieved by a Colonial corps and was now four miles beyond the boundaries that Colonel Marshall had designated for that operation. Over-head, Liggett's aviators were now devoted to tactical support entirely; on the ground his captains and sergeants had mastered not only the business but the art of war. With *"Tout le monde à la bataille,"* according to Foch's formula, only where Liggett stood before Buzancy was there a strategic concept worthy of the art of a general.

While the American First Army clawed for better positions in the jump-off for November 1, Pershing sent the Allied Supreme War Council his

protest against the granting of an armistice. The council was composed of
Prime Minister Lloyd George, Premier Clemenceau, and Premier Orlando,
with General Tasker H. Bliss as Woodrow Wilson's alternate. After pointing out the numerical superiority of the Allies—1,563,000 rifles against
1,134,000, with 22,413 guns against the German 16,495—he said that the
great German victories of the past four years could only be erased by the
unconditional surrender of the Hohenzollern Armies. The gist of the matter
lay in his Paragraph 11:

By agreeing to an Armistice under the present favorable military situation
of the Allies and accepting the principle of a negotiated peace rather than a
dictated peace the Allies would jeopardize the moral position they now hold
and possibly lose the chance actually to secure world peace on terms that
would insure its permanence.

Some said this protest was prompted by Pershing's ambition to become
the dominant military figure in the spring of 1919 with eighty divisions
promised him by Baker. In conversations with Foch, Haig, and Pétain, he
had proposed a demand for unconditional surrender—in a spirit of humility
voicing his views last because of his relatively few casualties, his comparatively brief service in the four years of the holocaust. He knew that his
authority, with victory in sight and his Doughboys soon no longer wanted,
would count for nothing in Europe. He also knew that Woodrow Wilson
had even objected to Allied determination to occupy the German bridgeheads on the Rhine. Mr. Wilson thought this might "constitute an invasion
of German territory."

Woodrow Wilson had been superficially courteous to inquire as to Pershing's views from the day the Germans began proposing an armistice conversation on the basis of Wilson's Fourteen Points. Colonel Edward M.
House of Texas, his roving leg man, was detailed to learn the Iron Commander's views. "Colonel" House—Pershing, in his rigid etiquette, address-
ing him as Mr. House, unconsciously revealed what he thought of his
military capabilities—had sent a junior staff officer to inquire as to the
Iron Commander's disposition. The "colonel," in a peace vanguard at Paris,
did not come to Souilly in person. He offered as an excuse an apology which
would have turned the Alamo Division—steel-swept in Liggett's gassy foxholes—into laughing hyenas. House said, in justifying his slur, he could
not come up to the Argonne Forest because he was afraid he might catch
influenza.

"Victorious armies are never fresh," Foch had told his three paladins
when warning them to increase pressure on the Germans despite British
divisions now bled white, any Frenchman understandably eager not to be
the last man killed. Only the Americans were unsatiated, but they were still

relying on their comrades for everything martial except the new Browning machine guns now arriving, pistols at their belts, and the rifles on their shoulders. Haig lacked 250,000 riflemen, Pétain an equal number. Haig, who owed his position to royal favoritism, feared Red revolution in Germany, the collapse of monarchy in Europe. Pétain was tougher than the British in his views; but Clemenceau was disposed—and he was Foch's background superior—to accept Wilson's Fourteen Points for a new world order. He would then blithely ignore such points as high-minded rigmarole.

Foch made the top decision: he wanted the Germans on the ropes when he, as referee, would stop the bout, but Pershing wanted the German champion stretched cold on the canvas for the count of ten. Only M. Poincaré, President of the French Republic, later agreed (privately) with him, though history afterward revealed that the Germans would have accepted Pershing's terms. Old Doughboys who sent their sons, frequently joining in with them, to a later, far more complex war, should not censure Woodrow Wilson because the Armistice gave Adolf Hitler powers to revive in Germans a militarism Pershing knew would still be latent in their culture. They should recall their own early 1918 days when they, too, were green and ignorant. President Wilson was the last rookie ashore, his own staff nothing like the tough colonels that Pershing brought with him. At Paris, there was a meeting of the Allied Supreme War Council, three members keeping it secret from the fourth. Clemenceau and Lloyd George and Orlando quietly steamed the stamp from a fresh deck and began to mark the cards.

General Bliss had become the "grand old boy" of the American Expeditionary Forces. Never a soldier's soldier, his term as acting chief of staff at Washington marked by confusion in directives and dispositions along the Mexican border of 1916, he was noted for his skill as an administrator and arbiter. When Woodrow Wilson first dispatched him to the Supreme War Council, he had soon found himself in a hearty dispute with Pershing. (Bliss favored piecemealing into British Forces.) At a point in the argument when he suggested they submit their differences to the President, the Iron Commander retorted that two generals in the field who piled their troubles on the White House doorstep both deserved to be fired. From that moment, Bliss was Pershing's loyal pleader in all his causes, whether the old arbiter believed in them or not. His was a witty devotion. "It seems to us somewhat evident that the European Allies will attempt to minimize the American effort as much as possible," Bliss wrote Baker after Saint-Mihiel.

They think they have got the Germans on the run and they now do not need as much help as they were crying for a little while ago. . . .

I think I told you sometime ago that I had heard a gentleman in high position here say that the United States was building a bridge for the Allies to pass over; that the time for the United States to secure acquiescence in its wishes was while the bridge was building; that after the Allies had crossed over the bridge they would have no further use for it or for its builders.

Bliss had great prescience. The Doughboys had built the bridge, the Allies had crossed it, and already Foch was making foolish plans to turn American soldiers into coolies to rebuild shattered French villages.

The Iron Commander went back to the business at hand, his total strength 76,800 officers, 1,790,823 enlisted men. Batteries were on the line, ammunition trains in sequence, firing data in proper registration. The gunners had become veterans, many regiments such as those of the 1st Division at Soissons, the 2nd at Blanc Mont, dozens in the Argonne, had remained in line to support unfamiliar infantry brigades as their own buddies came through them to refit and refresh. They had become precisionists, with the steadfastness of the French and English, and the ardor of the marvelous Canadian batteries. Above all, they had learned to defend a flank with massive saturation of mustard gas; they had always been quick in cadence and now they were swift to exploit targets their infantry wanted them to shell. Their aviators were acquainted with the difficult business of reconnaissance, many of them having been given tours of indoctrination with the guns. Their engineers had become superlative. Gunners were always saddened to learn that some infantry buddy they had waved to as he went through them to and from the firing line would no longer be coming back.

One of the most moving of loyalties in the war was the steadfastness on both sides of the line. The English could cite an example against Ludendorff's April smash where five officers of a battery, miraculously alive when all enlisted men were dead, one gun still functioning, continued to serve the piece until four were dead, the fifth a sieve of bloody wounds and the gun knocked out, when the German infantry arrived. The Germans could point to their lone major at Cambrai waiting for Scottish bayonets as he, singlehanded, knocked out nineteen tanks.

Such was the eagerness of the new Doughboys to share in this last battle that the 6th Division, largely without transportation, began towing its artillery by hand, men in the wagon trains hitching themselves in improvised dogharness to follow, in a hopeless effort to take one crack at the Germans. This division was the last to arrive on the front. It comprised the 11th and 12th Infantry Brigades of the 51st, 52nd, 53rd, and 54th Infantry Regiments; the 3rd, 11th, and 79th Field Artillery; and the 318th Engineers. It lost three prisoners and captured twelve in *petits coups de main* while training in the Schlucht Pass of the Vosges Mountains. One of its platoons, boxed by a barrage and attacked by three hundred Germans with supporting flame throwers in early October, had repulsed an inquisitive enemy. It had suffered only 380 casualties in forty-three days there. In the parable of the Argonne, the 6th Division was the last to arrive, but the laborer was worthy of his hire. "Buddies," said the ambulatory wounded streaming by these eager Doughboys when the guns of Europe fell silent for twenty-one years, "you didn't miss anything!"

And so on November 1, at five-thirty of a chill dawn, his tactical positions ideal for his attack, Hunter Liggett heard the faraway popping of the Springfields, the distant barking of the 75s and the chatter of the machine guns, here and there a 155 exploding an ammunition dump to paint a crimson geyser on the gray backdrop. He sat down to his deck of double solitaire. He could not follow his twenty-mile-spread infantry of his three-pronged corps, his persistent gunners. It would be at least an hour before Colonel Willey Howell, his G-2, began changing the flags on his maps. He had done all he could, as had all under him down to the veteran corporals, to teach the Doughboys the art of war; it was too late to add any finishing touches; the last assault was on. The lieutenant general began playing his cards, curtaining his mind against the horrors he knew brave men were undergoing against the wounded hills, the open spaces between the two great spines of the Meuse-Argonne sector. Desperately he sought to find an open space himself so that he might lift the black king off the fattest pile, hoping he would turn up a red queen for the next card.

Liggett struck the Germans that November dawn with prodigal violence in the Napoleonic tradition, breaking the enemy's center with a powerful vanguard and then maneuvering. The weather had turned fair, his aviators presenting him with photographs showing where von der Marwitz had been fortifying his last desperate center—the line Buzancy-Barricourt—since the fall of Montfaucon. Liggett wanted to break through the enemy infantry and swarm upon his artillery, brushing machine gunners aside. He had been given five weeks to study the ground and mass his artillery, a trifling boon no other Yank commander ever knew. Behind his center V Corps he also had riches in veteran reserves no Allied commander possessed—among them the rejuvenated Rainbows of the 42nd, and sixteen thousand veterans of the Big Red One now absorbing eight thousand new lads just off the boat. The ordeal of capturing Barricourt's main ridges had been assigned Bullard's old gunner, who had brought his single gun up to Captain Bullard's Philippine line. Major General Summerall's V Corps had a few light tanks, but he had his "thank God he's *our* son-of-a-bitch" gunners; and wherever his infantrymen jumped that morning, they were interlaced with singleton 75s, Philippine style, to relieve Detroit's money madness among Belle Isle's *soignée* matrons.

Summerall made his first attack on a two-division front, the race horses of the 2nd Division on his left, the 89th on his right. They wanted the woods and ravines of Barricourt's spiny ridges, these all gunned now to precise register in von der Marwitz's desperate last-ditch effort. If Liggett could bring his heavy guns to Barricourt's eastern ridges, he would command the crossings of the Meuse to his right, and the Germans in the great supply complex of Dun-sur-Meuse would be goners.

The 89th Division called itself the "Middle Wests" and was filled with men from the Canadian border to the Rio Grande, mountain men and trappers, cowboys from the plains, farm lads from the prairies and cornfields and sundry characters from the ranches and deserts, again in a roll call of states with beautiful names. The Middle Wests even brought some Mississippi gamblers along ready to offer odds on anything from a carrier pigeon's first flight to how long they could safely hold a Mills bomb after pulling the cotter pin. They chose for a shoulder patch a dark "W" on a brown circle, with no artlessness about the device; because it was known (privately) as "Wood's Division." The indiscreet godfather of all "Ninety-Day Wonders," and author of the Plattsburg Plan, Leonard Wood, had bidden it good-bye in tears; and Pershing, on a spot, had schooled the best general available to take over command in France. He was Major General William M. Wright, whose tour of the front had been under the tutelage of the Iron Commander himself and who had turned his own great 30th Division over to Haig. The Middle Wests, trained by a master, were probably the best-schooled relatively green division on September 26 that ever entered a major Doughboy fight. Sons of the Doughboys may be interested to learn that its stylish chief of staff was Colonel John C. H. "Courthouse" Lee, who later set up a quartermaster's plush satrapy in Italy and was ridiculed by the combat sad sacks who survived Anzio.

The Middle Wests went into the business of seizing Barricourt's ridges with all the aplomb of the 2nd Division on their left, determined not to be outdone. What an example it was of how the Old Breed can germinate its valor and skill much as bees pollinate the air, the unfathomable *mystique* of the fighting man. By nightfall November 1, the Middle Wests, keeping pace with the 2nd's veterans, had torn their way five miles through Barricourt's saw-toothed positions, breaking the German infantry line. They were hand-fighting among von der Marwitz's heavy artillery positions when darkness fell. Buzancy on the left of the Marine brigade was just outside Summerall's corps boundary line.

Frowning Buzancy was a matter for Dickman's I Corps to settle. Dickman, no longer plagued by faraway Degoutte, had inherited Liggett's old corps chief of staff, the brilliant Malin Craig, and they had assigned the urgency of Buzancy, six miles distant, to the last division in the Confederate Army. By nightfall, squirrel-hunting patrols of the 80th Division were pot-shooting wherever a bucketed head appeared on Buzancy's southern approaches, and by noon of November 2 the garrison there—what was left of it—heard the yells which could move even Stonewall Jackson's little horse into a gallop. Buzancy-Barricourt in the center was now Liggett's. He had broken through the German center, enemy infantry there no longer capable of establishing a line. The ten miles he wanted north of Buzancy were his—provided a dogged pursuit never let the enemy break off contact. He immediately began his westward wheel toward Boult-aux-Bois to show Ferdinand Foch that his tactics were superior—wanting no part of the suggested assault through the Boulogne Woods to create another Argonne Forest. It was up to Dickman's Doughboys of the I Corps to scramble now for five relentless days and outflank this death trap.

In Dickman's corps center, to the left of Robert E. Lee's last division now whooping around Buzancy, the Bowery Backwoodsmen, who were convinced that the line around Grandpré had remained unaltered while they were changing fungoid socks and delousing animated shirts, began a rapid advance due north toward Sedan. Theirs was the best chance of spearheading into Sedan, and Marshal Foch, who secretly wanted French troops to receive that honor, became so alarmed by their progress that he began changing army boundaries almost daily before the week was out. (It would be the fate of the 77th Division's motley patrols to lie anguished in the suburbs of Sedan, those nearest the railroad station wincing every time an American shell burst nearby, rattling the bottles of wines and liqueurs they knew would stock the station's buffet.)

On their left, and on Dickman's left boundary, the 78th Division began its hard-fighting oblique across the Aisne's twin courses, leg-weary now, but determined to seize Boult-aux-Bois before being relieved. They had brutal fighting ahead of them; for von der Marwitz knew what they were up to, and sent what he could to fringe the eastern verdure of the Bois de Bourgogne and make the White Lightnings pay dearly on their left flank for the privilege of shaking hands with Gouraud's Fourth French Army poilus, still fighting after four tragic years.

On the far right that November dawn, the III Corps of the tough ex-colonel from the 1st Division, Major General John Hines, had a two-pronged mission. His failure would be inexcusable if he did not seize Barricourt's easternmost ridges. (The Middle Wests to the left would then find themselves butchered by flanking enemy howitzers.) He had about fourteen hours of daylight to confront these German gunners with the steel of American bayonets.

He had been given the 90th Division for his left flank task. Its Doughboys called themselves the Alamo Division, hence no further description of its personnel is necessary, save to mention that many of them had been taught the art of the fast draw by their pioneer grandmothers, their shoulder patch of a large red "T" surmounting a rather small "O," an acknowledgment that thousands of killers from the old Cherokee Strip had infiltrated their ranks. They had the weapons for the task, the principal one being their leg power when at dawn they sallied forth to scale terrain an Andes llama would have shunned.

Pershing had seen to it that their commander was Major General Henry T. Allen, a timber-topper able to look any of the Texans in the eye. Their 180th Infantry (Texas) Brigade was still being led—not just directed—by the North Dakota brigadier whom the Texans adopted, Ulysses Grant McAlexander, the hydrant-legged colonel of the Marne. To show what the Alamos thought of his work in the next ten days, it is only necessary to view his portrait at Austin. (Two wars later a remarkable Reserve officer, Brigadier General S. L. A. Marshall, shocked the High Command by his survey of the diminishing leg power of the American soldier. Marshall, a Doughboy lieutenant somewhere in France the morning the Alamos jumped for Barricourt's spine, may have had a yardstick by surveying the five miles these Texas-Oklahoma lads covered by nightfall. They stood in triumph on the ridges, the howitzers now shared with the Middle Wests.)

On the Alamo right, Hines had the Red Diamonds of the 5th's Regulars, the professional designation no longer needing quotes since Hanson E. Ely first informed his brigadiers that he was going to cross the Meuse on his eastward way to the Moselle. Tactically, Ely's division had the trickiest of assignments that November morning. His was an oblique attack, moving northeast to tie the strings of the sack north of Brieulles. He too had brought along a new brigadier, Paul Malone, ex-23rd Infantry Regiment, who like Caesar thought it unwise to check the spirit of fight in ardent youth.

By the night of November 2, Liggett had no more use for his solitaire cards. He could move forward to his corps and division commanders, and listen on field telephones to the bold patrols. On his far right across the Meuse, Liggett had ordered his Yank divisions in the French II Colonial Corps mainly to maintain pressure. He could soon devote his tactical attention to the pinwheel warfare around the Borne de Cornouiller.

In Berlin, after Buzancy-Barricourt was broken asunder, the Hohenzollerns soon began throwing things into overnight bags, their main interest now one of house-hunting in neutral Holland.

Among the higher commanders, Ely had finally made adjustments in his 165th Artillery Brigade, once giving interim command to an officer who wore the gold oak leaves of a major, Ralph B. Fairchild. He must have been hell-on-a-handcar to keep his guns to Ely's furious pace across the congestion of stubborn German withdrawals in his progress toward Villers-devant-Dun on the Meuse, Fairchild the only major ever temporarily to command one of the Iron Commander's combat brigades. Because of Washington's intransigence, and unable to create major generals of temporary rank lest the sedentary generals at home have to fight to keep their wartime rank when confronted by homecoming combat temporaries, Pershing had unhesitatingly given brigadiers such as Parker and Bamford and Brown—and in the last days Douglas MacArthur—two-star commands.

Higher commanders of superior concepts, even though deprived of proper rank, were no longer in short supply; but straggling had become a serious problem in the bitterness of Argonne's third week when the brave brigades, such as Winans's and MacArthur's, broke into the Kriemhilde Stellung. In his memoirs, Pershing mentions the problem in his diary, but fails to say in his text how many tough fighting men were detached from forward units to M.P. companies to round up the faint-of-heart and return them to the line. It was a serious omission and Allied chroniclers never ceased to belabor him for this lapse—Captain Cyril Falls as late as 1958 giving the Iron Commander a posthumous scolding which he deserved.

The French had their four-year *cordon sanitaire* difficulties with stragglers and the panic-stricken, unofficial chroniclers describing panics around Verdun in 1916 when many human beings could no longer nerve themselves to endure its horrors. . . . Even Pétain had known bad moments when he wanted to fall back, his Field Commander Nivelle and his superiors in Paris needing to cajole (or to threaten) him to stand fast. . . .

The British made no bones about their "Straggler's Posts," any corps commander empowered to try officer or man after breakfast and shoot him before lunch. Sir Philip Gibbs gives instances of heart-breaking volleys by firing squads; and Robert Graves, later poet, historian, and novelist, mentions his own experience when, named to a court-martial, he wangled his way out of the duty the morning he received secret instructions that he was to vote for the death penalty and nothing less, because a steadfast sergeant had finally broken and fled after posting a fine record in the ranks. Gibbs said cowardice was attributable to certain fetishes—a man might be brave against bayonets, and still quail under gas. Desmond Young, biographer of

Erwin Rommel after a later war, and a superior combat leader in the first one, gives eloquent testimony in his own autobiography of how combat officers hated these 1914-1918 executions conducted by staff officers after batmen brought them tea—his own Royal Rifle Regiment colonel going so far as to say he would execute no good British soldier for any kind of faintheartedness whatsoever, even saying decorations for valor would be in order only if God, in His Infinite Wisdom, headed the Board of Awards.

Among the Doughboy chronicles, only the activities of a Captain "Hard-Boiled" Smith in a detention barracks at Paris ever received attention during the Meuse-Argonne phase. In any organization of two million men there were bound to be some criminal elements, and when such deserted to crime in Paris, Smith dealt with them with his fists, much as did the American police of that day. It was inexcusable, but it was better than shooting them —which Pershing might have done had Secretary Baker sought Woodrow Wilson's permission for him to do so. But Doughboy executions in France added up to ten, these all for murder or rape, or both, in death on the gallows. No Doughboy was shot for military offenses.

As for the number of Doughboy stragglers and deserters, September 26 to November 11? "The wonder is," wrote General Alexander of his 77th Division, "considering the abundant opportunities for concealment in comparative safety, that so many reached the actual fighting front; it is cause for congratulation and pride." The candid Bullard, never one to gloss over faults, also remarked that when fighting progressed more fiercely, desertions grew fewer in percentage of men employed as loyalty to buddies held feeble spirits in line—even though the Military Police were always flushing skulkers out of barn lots and abandoned farmhouses after the brave battalions had passed. Somewhere deep in the Pentagon's bowels, where the "blind girl draws the numbers from the fishbowl," the figures on laggard legs might be obtained by S. L. A. Marshall—if Superman lent him the invisibility of that bat-winged cloak.

The White Lightnings and Gouraud's men were photographed on the road winding west from Grandpré to the Aisne November 5, the Bois de Bourgogne north of the road outflanked and empty, youths with scraggly beards waving their pie-plate hats beside French fathers with Smith Brothers beavers who held horizon-blue helmets aloft, a consummation devoutly wished since September 26. Gouraud could now cross the Aisne almost unmolested on *his* way to Sedan-Mézières. Time was when the New York mountain boys would have been left in the line, but now the affluent Liggett pulled them out at once, sending in the 42nd's Rainbows.

A later generation which followed the cloak-and-dagger activities of

Major General "Wild Bill" Donovan may be interested to know that he was now a chicken colonel commanding his regiment during recent bloody exercises, and somewhere along the mazes of the Rainbow's progress he had won the Medal of Honor by leading platoons, companies, and battalions in assaults before Marwitz's gunners got to him. Alexander Woollcott tells the tale of the spirited exchange between Donovan and Father Duffy when the colonel's stretcher reached a battalion dressing station, the dispute being over who would eventually bury whom. "Wild Bill" was a sobriquet any Bill Donovan of that day was given by neighborhood kids, thanks to the temperament of a baseball pitcher of that name. Actually, Donovan, with light-blue eyes and quiet manners, was a Columbia graduate, a lawyer, and the most gentle of men, a killer with the calm bearing of Princeton's Captain Wardlaw Miles. . . .

Meanwhile, the Rainbow's Major General Menoher was about to be given a corps in Bullard's Second Army as the old infantryman filched what he could to form a staff, and Brigadier General Douglas MacArthur, of whom Pershing expected great things, would be given interim and, eventually, permanent command. He had been first at the Culver Military Academy, first at West Point, and was first in his class to win two stars. (This officer seems to have been born with the number "1" tattooed on his right hand.)

In the center, last-ditch fighting grew so savage that crack outfits such as the 2nd's race horses were confined to limited gains for two days. Von der Marwitz now had no established lines, but he had gunners and machine gunners galore in almost unassailable hill pockets. And so the relentless Liggett, after the Doughboy-Marine team and the Middle Wests had broken the line along with the Confederate Army and were ready to wheel east to the Meuse crossings, sent in the Big Red One to expand his center. There was never confusion in the fighting, but each division was following Pershing's tactics of pushing on regardless of flank situations, and villages long since forgotten witnessed valorous scenes of individual enterprise and expediency as the veteran German, retiring skillfully, fought in island groups with all his furious sagacity. Transport was breaking down at bottlenecks, so many the new sedans at home, so few the trucks in France, that Pershing resorted in desperation to ordering ammunition trucks driven by night with lights on, and the drivers took their chances along with the rest of the Doughboys. Nevertheless, the weight of Doughboy idealism was irresistible. The 2nd and 89th broke through and were soon on the banks of the Meuse.

Perhaps the most brilliant feat of November's first week was that of Hanson E. Ely's handling of the 5th Division. He had crossed the Meuse on engineers' bridges and by rafts constructed on small tributaries and then, having floated to the broad river's confluence, he had outflanked Brieulles. Now he had Dun-sur-Meuse doomed on his left flank, in a maneuver that would have commanded the admiration of Julius Caesar, who wrote proudly of having bridged a stream in eleven days.

How well had Harbord and Pershing, from different camps, one an obscure ex-enlisted man and the other a two-star West Pointer, head to head across a table in Washington eighteen months before, chosen from the colonels the brightest of the toughest when they combed the Regulars' roster! Again it is worth a conjecture that Pershing, among other considerations, had chosen the Kansas State Aggies alumnus lest he be swayed by old loyalties, anguished entreaties. Even so, General Bliss, acting chief of staff at the time, refused him many he wanted, and wisely. There were going to be millions of trainees, and few competent to school them at division level. And how little Ely is remembered; though Bullard in retirement, seeing Ely when the latter had been given the honor of the sinecure at Governors Island in New York Harbor, said Ely was unchanged from the first day he ever saw him in Luzon; he was still ready to fight anyone, anywhere, anytime.

The Doughboys that November pushed on, guarding their own flanks, heedless of support from right or left. These were Pershing's tactics, and he had outlined them in a directive issued before Saint-Mihiel. It was a tactic that demanded individual initiative, quick decisions by the commander in the field, who would have no precise orders to follow as he improvised his advance. It was contrary to classical French military theory and to Foch's insistence on the advisability of writing everything down in detail. Foch himself on October 26 had issued a general order for all divisions everywhere to push on guarding their own flanks, a complete repudiation of Colonel de Grandmaison's doctrine, the latter, according to General Fuller, causing Napoleon to turn over in his tomb. (Fuller said Grandmaison's book should have been titled *The Quintessence of Defeat*.) Foch's order was a paraphrase of Pershing's Saint-Mihiel directive, and if Napoleon now ceased to turn over, Colonel de Grandmaison must have been revolving rapidly in his coffin. Gouraud's French were now too weary and warworn to move with anything like the vigor required of independent divisions pressing toward Sedan. But Pershing's concepts were vindicated. The first week of November saw everything come to pass that the American command had resolved to bring about the first week they had met with the Allies at the Crillon.

On November 7, a group of German civilians headed by Matthias Erzberger, leader of Roman Catholic Conservatives in the Reichstag, in dark sack suits that looked to have been slept in, reached Foch's railway car in the forest of Compiègne—not far from where an archer named Lionel in the Bastard of Wandomme's mercenaries pulled Joan of Arc captive from her horse, Wandomme selling her to still another bastard, Jean of Luxembourg, who in turn sold her to the legitimacy of the English, who in their turn outdid all the bastards in the chain of captivity. Captain Liddell Hart, who called Foch "The Man of Orleans" imbued with Joan's sacred fire, does not care to mention Joan's Compiègne or the "old undying sin we shared," as Rudyard Kipling wrote, "in Rouen marketplace." Jeanne d'Arc must have been graven on Foch's fiery heart the day Erzberger arrived. Foch immediately began sending telegrams to Haig, Pétain, and Pershing, urging them to increase pressure in savage fighting.

Chapter 22

ON TO SEDAN

"Bone Joor, M'Soor," she said, and just beamed.
Hell. You'd have thought I won the war.

Hunter Liggett could now turn his attention to the Borne de Cornouiller, where Doughboys and their French companions had made four miles in painful progression while the center fighting out of Montfaucon had gone twelve. Since September 26 the Borne had been menaced by Major General Claudel's French XVII Corps, the Frenchman briefed by Pershing to keep strong patrol pressure on barriers the Ice Age seemed to have erected on the heights of the Meuse northeast of Verdun for benefit of the Neanderthaler Hohenzollerns happening along about eighteen thousand years later. The Iron Commander had wanted to spare Claudel's attenuated battalions the earliest essays of his own first-arriving green troops, not then suitable for intermingling with the poilus—the latter now with habitual skill taking every care to stay alive.

By October 31, Claudel's corps, beefed up with such as the experienced 26th Division, was atop such main positions as Richène Hill of the Consenvoye Heights, now Franco-American. Poilus and Doughboys had hacked their progress in attrition warfare suggesting the blood-drenched tactics of the Allies in three fruitless years. . . . But Liggett knew that a frontal approach from that bitter platform to capture Verdun's four-year tormenter, the Borne de Cornouiller, would be re-enacting Joffre's earlier follies. He decided to explode a pinwheel around it, with pressure from the south, another column moving from the east, and the main body of French Colonials

356

scaling the Borne from the west. He had no fear of being outflanked in such maneuvers; the growling Ely to the north with his 5th Division, reinforced with an infantry regiment from the 32nd's *Gemütlichkeit* boys, would see to that.

After November's second day, Liggett needed no solitaire cards for this Borne battle. He had both the troops and the commanders to prove his dispositions. Claudel's XVII Corps, after a blood-drenched four years along every front, had now moved to Bullard's American Second Army wanting Metz and the Briey Fields, the poilus being replaced by the French II (Colonial) Corps.

How little of the Great War Liggett's Yank commanders had seen by comparison with the Frenchmen leading the divisions of the Colonials! . . . Let bugles sound a truce, and all Doughboys pause to contemplate the careers of such as Jean Baptiste Marchand, commanding the 10th Colonial Division, Marchand an old pro from Saint-Cyr.

All the world first heard of him in 1898 as Captain Marchand, where he stood entrenched six hundred miles south of Khartoum on the White Nile with about two hundred Senegalese beneath a *tricolore* bleaching in the equatorial sun. There he was confronted by Baron Kitchener of Khartoum, Sirdar of the Egyptian Army, with five gunboats. Kitchener had informed the captain—though not in so many words—that Egypt was now the property of London's stock syndicates and Manchester's textile mills. Marchand by his tact (and tactics) had averted a war that hot afternoon between two imperial gluttons, marching his slender force out the back way, through the murderous banditry of the Azebu Gallas of the Ethiopian Highlands and across the Danakil deserts where tribesmen were, congenitally, professional collectors of enemy genitalia—arriving finally at Djibouti, French Somaliland, cesspool of Western imperialism. Kitchener for his services in the Sudan had received thirty thousand pounds sterling in royal baksheesh, and a better seat, and richer ermine, in the House of Lords.

Marchand got a ribbon for his tact, and by 1914 this explorer who had discovered the source of the Niger River had made general of brigade in time for the Battle of France. He then made major general to command his 10th Colonial Division (which now faced the Borne de Cornouiller) when Joffre made his suicidal efforts in Champagne's 1915. He had fought in the 1916 Somme's murders; and then saw his division butchered into mutineers in Nivelle's 1917 April fiasco on the Chemin des Dames. He was back at it again in October, 1917, around Verdun, when Franchet d'Esperey gave the Germans a local beating and then complained to Pershing about the near beer in Iowa. Boehn drove him back across the wagon

bridge in Château-Thierry's disaster of May, 1918, but he was fighting
Boehn on the Vesle the following July, had been sent to the American First
Army in time for Saint-Mihiel, and was now preparing to fight again north
of Verdun on a line of battle drawn up by a round-bellied general he had
never heard of before the Second Battle of the Marne.

(Doughboys of the 7th Machine Gun Battalion at the Château-Thierry
wagon bridge remember him well. Marchand was the French general they
were massed to hear lecture on the sins of looting, when his Senegalese
meanwhile stole the dinner of every man in the battalion, and this after the
cooks had cooled pie crusts a Labrador retriever could trot across, with a
lemon-extract filling a man could get drunk on. All Yank officers who came
in contact with him admired his skill; his refusal to pull rank or length of
experience won admiration from all—except possibly the un-pied machine
gunners of the 7th Battalion.)

So much for one Frenchman's love of *la patrie;* there were scores like
him. *"Dulce et decorum"* and marble figures with wings were their rewards.

The Borne still commanded the Meuse, frowning a mile north of the
Franco-Doughboy team east of that river. The hussy of Brieulles on the west
bank was in a loop of the river about four miles north by west of the
Borne, the town fronted by Lémont Woods. Squirrel hunters of the Confederacy's last division had killed its advanced snipers early in the fighting,
but all III Corps efforts had made only five flat miles toward it since September 26. The Borne de Cornouiller was the German's last chance of
holding the east bank of the river; once it fell there would be no line of communications back to Sedan and thousands would be bagged in any *"Sauve
qui peut"* scrambling. Its garrisons also knew, whatever the Messianic pro-
nouncements of Mr. Wilson in Washington, those who fell captive to the
French II Colonial Corps would, at best, have much hard labor ahead of
them repairing their four-year destruction in France before seeing their
Fatherland again. At worst, as many a Doughboy who had fought alongside the Senegalese from Château-Thierry to the Meuse could recall, the
Germans knew that these assault troops often liked to return from a fight
with a pocketful of white men's ears.

And so the Germans on the Borne, beginning the night of November 3,
saw the pinwheel flare into brilliant artillery display. Ely's 5th Division
Regulars lit the first fuse. At the same time the 79th Division began its
attacks to reach the crown of Corned Willy Hill from the east, the French
Colonials began their climb from the banks of the Meuse, and the New
Englanders of the 26th Division held on the south and rested for a few
days. At the start the replenished 35th Division was a holding force beside
the 26th, but Foch was demanding greater pressure from Bullard's Second

Army astride the Moselle (he had tried to fragment Pershing's troops there), and the 35th Division was sent to him at the end of November's first week, the 81st Division replacing it for the final assault.

As the pinwheel began to spin for the last time, the Doughboys had to rely mainly upon Springfields and automatic rifles because the shortages of trucks for shells, and notably horses for the gun teams, were now so critical that little support could be given the Yanks moving up Corned Willy's cannoned slopes. The 15th French (Colonial) Division was in better shape and was given the harder progress. They *had* horses for their artillery as they left the banks of the Meuse, and gunners could give them fire curtains as they began the ascent. The Tidewater lads of the 79th Division, now an integral part of the French II (Colonial) Corps, had to pay with blood and bayonets for their resolve to meet their black brothers from an African promontory at the appointed places as they fought through the ridges and wooded traps that had punished such as the Ivy Leafs of the 4th Division for so many days. All had four days of furious assaults through patches of hilly bosks and thickets arranged around the Borne's whorl of guns like lozenges of melon around the tomato in the *printanier* of a garden salad before they killed the Germans on that last summit.

The Blue and the Grays of the 29th Division met the Colonials atop the hill November 7 after four days of furious fighting, when the New Englanders, rested three days, then took up the pursuit. The Borne de Cornouiller had cost the Americans fifteen thousand casualties, a pittance to what blundering Joffre had lost there over the tragic years. It was the last of a series of operations in coordinated strength ever conducted by the Doughboys; and it was accomplished by an army now of all-veteran caliber.

Among those standing in triumph on the fatal hill was Brigadier General Evan Malbone Johnson, USA, who had fought like a private soldier in the Argonne Forest thirty years after he had enlisted as one, and was now commanding a brigade in the 79th. Among those not witnessing the finale was Private Bailey's old Leatherneck who lived up to his sobriquet of "Hike 'em" Hiram Bearss. Colonel Bearss of the New Englanders was now in hospital. His legs had given out. Lads returning to the forty-eight states, when asked by their dads about the Argonne Forest, would say, "I was never in the joint. But if Mom will leave the room, I would like to say a few words about Corned Willy Hill. . . ." As the Borne fell, the 26th's New Englanders set out to show Ely's 5th what Yankees could do on *their* way to the Woëvre Plain.

As the divisions began their downhill swing, Bullard's newly created Second Army had been dispatched eastward to familiar ground, the truncated Saint-Mihiel salient, driving against Pershing's original target, the fortress of Metz, the Briey iron mines, and the Saar coal basin. Bullard had been given some good divisions—notably the 33rd Illini beefing up the French XVII Corps, the Truman Battery's replenished 35th Division backing it up—and some good commanders. The wistful Muir, who had played hooky to lead a platoon on the Vesle, now commanded the American IV Corps, composed of his old 28th Pennsylvanians with men cannibalized from many states, and the green 7th Division, Regulars fresh from the States. The battle-weary Ivy Leafs of the 4th Division, absorbing their replacements, were Muir's reserves. Menoher had turned his Argonne Rainbows over to Douglas MacArthur, and now commanded the American VI Corps. (The official date for Muir's promotion was November 10; but a two-star general did not go from one front to another, and collect a three-star staff in a single day.)

For his left front Muir had the rough customers of the 88th Division. On his right was a pioneer outfit, the 92nd (Negro) Division moving out from Pont-à-Mousson, the first of its kind in American history. Its formation had been regarded by the Army as political dynamite, antiadministration forces supposedly forcing Woodrow Wilson into a decision to defy nationwide social prejudices. Actually, it had been more the result of suggestions by philosophers and humanitarians, such as Joel Spingarn of Columbia University. Spingarn would have approved General George S. Patton, Jr.'s attitude in a later war. When Patton received his first Negro division, grapevine had it that General Eisenhower, a soldier faultless in his regard for minority groups, had sent an officer from his staff to brief Patton on the advisability of never referring to the racial background of his new regiments. The Green Hornet, who was a fighter incarnate, was said to have addressed his newcomers as follows: "Well, men, I am happy to have you here. I don't give a damn what color you are, just so you kill those sons-of-bitches in the green suits."

The 92nd's captains and lieutenants were Negroes from an Officer's Training Camp, a segregated one, at Des Moines, Iowa, which had had the largest gathering of highly educated Negroes in American history. Some of its National Guard colonels were from Negro regiments with Civil War records. Its major general, Charles C. Ballou, had been a West Point colonel at the War College when he was sent to Des Moines as its commanding white-man officer. One of its regiments had had initial success and then run into difficulty and confusion as liaison between Gouraud's poilus and the 77th Division on the Argonne's first day. When it was withdrawn and sent to the Saint-Mihiel sector, there had been recriminations by the French and investigations by the top brass, going all the way up to Wilson, the results of which ultimately were thrown out. The regiment had just been too green for such a tricky assignment. Bullard found the rank-and-file uniformly brave. He also found Ballou unchanged in his belief that his was a good division.

The division attacked and captured the Bois de Fréhaut the morning of November 10 in Bullard's first limited attack. It lost some ground in the night. The next day its Doughboys again attacked, this time capturing the Bois de la Voirotte, and were still at it when the signal came at eleven o'clock to cease firing. That second day all knew that stillness was a matter of hours, the war having lasted five hours, long enough to justify Ballou's faith. Even the brilliant 33rd Division had found the going tough for anyone threatening Metz, sustaining some repulses. The 92nd Division had suffered about a thousand casualties, their buddies still fighting across the Meuse.

Leo J. Bailey, now a corporal, his arm beginning to strengthen as he went about his duties in a prisoner-of-war company, soon learned that his old squad buddy, Louis Van Iersal of the 9th Infantry, was also a corporal, and had just been awarded the Medal of Honor, this Dutch-born, German-speaking, "half-American" of von Buy's classification having swum the Meuse. There was little obscurity about his feat, though it was an Intelligence mission accomplished in the dead of night. The enemy expected such solo performers to begin this work, and poured petrol on the river's surface, igniting it whenever a trigger snapped on pitfall footbridges and dumped such as Van Iersal into twenty feet of a chilling, rain-swollen stream. Expecting that any ordinary mortal would swim back to the west bank of the river, they searched there with machine-gun tracers. But Van Iersal was not an ordinary mortal. He swam *toward* the enemy's side, at Villers-devant-Mouzon, eavesdropped for a spell, and then breasted his way back home with professional knowledge of German dispositions. (In a later war, this paragon of the 2nd Division's 3rd Infantry Brigade astonished his old buddies by enlisting in the "goddam" Marines, who retired him as Sergeant Major Van Iersal after Hiroshima.)

There was sometimes tragedy in these crossings. A trio in the Leonard Wood Middle Wests, Sergeant Waldo Hatler, First Class Private Harold I. Johnson, and Buck Private David B. Barkeley, swam it successfully to look over the tactical situation around Pouilly, which was the 89th's target for November 10-11. It was a triple Medal of Honor performance, but Private Barkeley's decoration was sent to his mother; for the dark and bloody Meuse claimed him on the swim back.

Liggett's eager divisions began to vie with one another to cut von der Marwitz's escape route toward the Rhine. His machine gunners were playing on Sedan, and brigadiers such as Douglas MacArthur, and major generals like Robert Alexander, were understandably eager to lead their men first into the small city of Sedan, which lay like a checkered doormat beneath them where they stood on the heights of the Meuse.

It was then that a blue-sky order came from Pershing. He desired the honor of entering Sedan to go to the Doughboys of Dickman's I Corps— the draftees of the Bowery Backwoodsmen 77th, the National Guardsmen of the 42nd's Rainbows. He added, in a supplementary phrase, "assisted on the right by the V Corps." The Big Red One immediately interpreted this supplementary phrase—and there is an ambiguity in Pershing's directive—as giving them equal rights to join the land rush into the Cherokee Strip. The 1st Division was alongside its principal rival, the race horses of the 2nd Division, facing eastward to cross the Meuse five miles south of Sedan. Thousands of its Doughboys immediately did a left-face and set out for Sedan on the double, foot, horse, and gun, moving forty-eight hours mainly without food or water across the supply routes—the lifelines—of Dickman's I Corps.

The chain of command ran: Pershing, Liggett, Summerall, Parker (Frank Parker was now a brigadier commanding the 1st Division), down to such new colonels as Theodore Roosevelt, Jr., now commanding his regiment. Parker, as a colonel, had thrown a block for Ely at Cantigny, Roosevelt as a major doing the same thing. All in the 1st Division knew that Ely had crossed the Meuse with his 5th Division and was on his way to the Woëvre Plain; the Big Red One was not to be outdone by old grads such as Ely, Bamford, and Hines.

First knowledge of the lateral movement reached Alexander when his 77th Division was engaging the enemy. It was the most serious tactical offense in Alexander's knowledge of war. His captains and mess sergeants were sharing field rations with a horde of strangers crossing their lifelines, with infinite tact trying to straighten out exhausted men who nevertheless were swarming across their progress like Army ants. There was fellowship along the front lines, but none at raging Alexander's headquarters.

On they swept, poaching into MacArthur's preserves. That bandbox officer, moving about as usual near the front line, was wearing his floppy cap, his greenish blouse, walking in glittering boots. Some of the 1st Division thought him a German general, fired warning shots, and claimed him prisoner. When the general insisted that he was an American, he was told to "tell that to our Intelligence officer, Heinie." West Pointer MacArthur stood patiently until that functionary arrived to stand with egg on his face while the general told him what little intelligence he had. MacArthur, with the tact and esteem the French had spotted, then made room on his front by wedging farther westward, but the swarms came on.

Meanwhile, Marshal Foch, changing boundaries again—General de

Maistre had agreed with the Iron Commander that the first to reach Sedan deserved the honor of entering it—had de Maistre tell Pershing that the boundaries now would curve eastward so that the Yank western boundary would be well east of Sedan. General Gouraud had not yet come up with his main forces but would do so presently, and Foch desired that the great old battle-ax be given the honor. (Some of his forward patrols by-passing the fortress of Sedan on their right were menacing Mézières.)

These Frenchmen were still at it, the same soldiers who had survived the three-day stalemate at Blanc Mont the month before, when their dead comrades were described so vividly by Captain John W. Thomason, Jr., as all lying face toward the enemy, some still clutching fixed-bayonet Lebels in outstretched hands. They had been unable to seize the Mont, but theirs was a weariness of body and not of will. Since 1914's August, when so many brave brigades threw themselves away in incalculable bravery, many had broken, many had panicked at times, and some had mutinied due to faulty leadership. But, like Gouraud himself, they were still moving toward the enemy.

The Marshal had also telegraphed that he did not like the attitude of the German delegation, which had got off on the wrong foot by saying it had heard that Foch wished an armistice. The old professor promptly cut them off by saying he desired no armistice. Wherever had Germans got such a silly notion? Eventually the harassed German civilians admitted they desired one; whereupon the marshal said they must ask for one. Meanwhile, as before, he wanted the fiercest pressure put upon Germans wherever Allied troops faced them.

MacArthur, before Sedan, which could be his if he blew his whistle, virtually commanding the Rainbows now that Bullard was briefing Menoher on forming a new corps, gave the Big Red One a piece of his front; he was then knowingly edged into the new area Foch had decreed was French, a curve which needed a bureau of topographers to map. But the forward elements of the 1st Division, munching on scanty field rations and some drinking water shared by Alexander's Bowery boys, continued to swarm laterally across the front.

The front now had a patch of fighters walling off Gouraud's progress, whenever he managed to get up, well west of Sedan. Next to them were some of MacArthur's infantry—through no tactical fault of his own—also blocking Gouraud's access. Then came another patch of the Big Red One eastward, between the rest of the Rainbows and Alexander's 77th Division. (That latter officer had firmly closed the back door against the 1st Division's bloodthirsty mendicants.) Farther eastward, elements of the Big Red One were still in the positions first assigned to them in Summerall's V Corps, hard against the 2nd Division, which was on its fixed lines, its 2nd Engineers moving heaven and hell to bridge the Meuse ahead of the premier division's 1st Engineers, which they did. . . .

What a swelling progress these truant Doughboys had made—tactical atrocity or not—across that last line of battle! From 4:30 P.M. on the afternoon of November 5, when it first learned it could "assist" Dickman's Corps, the 16th Infantry, first of the Paris Paraders, covered fifty-four kilometers by 11:30 P.M., November 7, sponging handouts from buddies of divisions whose lifelines it was fouling. The 18th Infantry made fifty-three kilometers, the 28th Infantry of Cantigny's formal follies contributing fifty-two kilometers. But the palm went to the 26th Infantry, which Bullard had seen returning from Soissons led by a college boy. It progressed seventy-one kilometers westward, apparently intent upon seizing Sedan on its western flank before either the French or Dickman could reach it. No better incident can be cited to show that the Doughboy never lost his alacrity to get at the throat of the enemy.

Dickman, master of military punctilio, was choleric with rage, and sent his fine French liaison officer, Major Raoul Klein, over to the French corps commander on his left, offering his own corps' apologies for intruding upon that major general's boundaries. Klein came back with the word that the Frenchman refused to accept them, as Dickman had no cause to offer them. "He knows something," Klein said mysteriously.

Dickman said that the Iron Commander's remarks when he arrived were unprintable. Pershing said later that, had not the Armistice intervened, he would have taken some grave action. But everyone knew how he wore a Big Red One on his heart; and also knew that, whatever the foul-up, the action of these regiments, with armistice talk filling the air, was a man-to-man tribute to their virility, their never-satiated eagerness to get at the throat of the enemy. And so it ended with the prodigal not only forgiven, but sneakingly admired. . . .

The Germans would not feel the force of the Big Red One on the last day when the guns fell silent November 11 for another twenty-one years; it would encounter it in full-dress guts twenty-five years later in a Sicilian July, when Kesselring sent the Hermann Göring Panzer Division mauling down Etna's slopes with orders to break the beach junction between Montgomery's British and Bradley's Yanks. It was the Panzer's bad luck to run afoul the Big Red One at the junction—this time backed up by naval gunfire off the beaches, many in the division returning alumni from the old Doughboys, one of its outfits commanded by Brigadier General Theodore Roosevelt, Jr. It was a close-run fight, but the Hermann Göring Panzer Division eventually patched up its tanks and retired to lick its wounds.

It is said that Pershing, then in retirement at Walter Reid Hospital, broke into one of his wintry smiles "wide enough to eat a banana sideways" when General George C. Marshall, as Chief of Staff, Pentagon, entered The Presence to tell him of the feat. To Pershing it was still "the best damned division in *any* army," and an accolade he is reported to have said under his breath during a reunion of Cantigny veterans, and one which in the hindsight of two wars can be eternally argued. Undoubtedly the old General of the Armies extended his borrowed time until General of the Army Eisenhower sent him a cablegram saying he had fathered Franklin D. Roosevelt's victorious forces. He had lived on doggedly so that once again he might "walk the line" of the Big Red One; but creeping paralysis was on him. If he could not walk the line, he would never suffer himself to be carried along it in a jeep. That would not be up to the standard of the Corps of Cadets at West Point. . . . Years later, Douglas MacArthur, arriving back at the Philippines for a last sentimental visit, was presented with a jeep to inspect a guard of honor in the broiling tropic sun. But the octogenarian waved the jeep aside. "I will walk the line," he said, and did so. Douglas MacArthur was the last of the Doughboys to walk the line.

Woodrow Wilson had played a shrewd hand in the undermining of the German people's confidence in their wartime leaders, refusing to enter into the "long conversations" Foch had dreaded. Instead, he demanded that all terms of an armistice must be settled by Allied military leaders, in this case, actually, Marshal Foch. What Wilson neglected to include in his demands— in the light of history a grievous situation indeed—was the stipulation that defeated German generals meet with the Allied Commander November 8. As a consequence, a new government hastily formed with Prince Max of the Duchy of Baden as Liberal Chancellor of the crumbling German Empire sent only civilians to Foch's railway car on the gun spur in the forest of Compiègne. There was not a German military uniform in that railway car to admit leadership of a thoroughly beaten army, to proffer sword hilts, and to seek a peace. This proved to be one of the greatest assists Corporal Adolf Hitler, in uniform at the time, ever had. It was far from gallant Robert E. Lee's tragic cry upon learning U. S. Grant had bagged him: "Then I must go see General Grant, and I would rather die a thousand deaths." In a matter of twenty-two years, that same railway car would be filled with many German uniforms.

While the haggling continued, the Doughboys had two more days to fight their savage war. From Ostend to the Woëvre Plain the only positions the German could defend were southeast of Sedan, Corned Willy Hill no longer their left flank. The morning of November 10, elements of Doughboy divisions were crossing the river in force by many means, Foch asking all commanders to launch particularly brutal attacks that day. Engineers built seventy-five-man log rafts up the tributaries of the Meuse and then floated them across the swollen river, strung footbridges on pontoons. There were repulses at many points; the Germans were always professional when they were in strong positions; but Liggett had to keep driving in a war where all other parts of the Allied lines were mainly occupied with slow pursuit across fields and roads sown with mines. When the telegram came for firing to cease at the eleventh hour of the eleventh day of November, Doughboys had been shot off the pontoons of the Meuse within the preceding hour. Far away, Canadian platoons entered Mons after a sharp fight.

Where veterans in the Meuse line were halted in their tracks, forbidden to fraternize with the enemy, mainly they stretched upon the ground, thanked God they had stayed alive, and built their first campfires—feeling ill at ease because no guns were firing anywhere. A man could stand up. In the rear, Signal Corps units, the heavy gunners, the trains, could recollect villages they passed through, and some bolted back to them. Here and there units failed to get the word, and there were random killings.

"I didn't know the war was over until early that evening," said Corporal Sergeant Shaffer, sometime runner to the Truman Battery. "I only knew the 35th Division was going to fight on the fourteenth, and had spent the day taking down the antennae and lifting heavy things into trucks. We hadn't heard any firing, and it had come on to drizzle around dark. Then we heard a dispatch rider coming hell-bent down the road with his lights out, and we figured the war was still on. When he saw our trucks by the side of the narrow white road in the gloaming, he hit his brakes and the motor bike skidded one way and he slid the other. The engine was running mad, and we figured he'd been killed. But God looks after drunks. He jumped up, threw us a copy of the Paris *Herald* from his pouch, shouted, 'The damn war is over,' grabbed the bike, chased it to a leaping seat, and was gone. We knew where he was going to, and we took off for it. When we got there, the Frogs had come from the wooded patches and were stocked with beer, brandy, and those Van sisters, Rooje and Blank to sell. The street was already knee-deep in bottles, Frogs trading booze for coffee and real leather shoes, guys walking around in their sock feet begging other guys not to break any more bottles. I came to sleeping on some porch steps. An old farm wife in a starchy white hood was offering me a hot jug of our java. '*Bone Joor, M'Soor*,' she said, and just beamed. Hell. You'd have thought I won the war." Far on the left, Lieutenant Grantland Rice said that everyone in his division got drunk on Flemish hospitality.

In Italy, a token force, the Doughboys of the 332nd Infantry Regiment, U.S. 83rd Division, began their march into conquered Austria, above them an aviator eminently suited to von Buy's classification, Captain Fiorello La Guardia. Aviators in France outdid themselves in victory rolls, John Heisman's great Georgia Tech tackle, Lieutenant William Coleman, being killed in the midst of ecstasy. In Vladivostok, Doughboys filled the cafés. On the Swiss border, Lieutenant Thomas Hitchcock, Jr., seventeen years old now, had crossed Germany on foot after stepping from a prison train. He crawled beneath the wire, after studying the routine of German border patrols. Grinning Swiss informed him the war was just concluded. Sergeant York, in Nancy, said every drunken Doughboy there had a girl on his arm when he, after having a sandwich and a citronade, went to bed around sundown. Two thousand miles to the east of Sedan, Captain Robert Boyd of the 339th U.S. Infantry, with a force of three hundred Doughboys supported by a company of Royal Scots, a handful of Canadian gunners, was fighting for his life when the guns fell silent on the Meuse. He was at Toulgas, about 250 miles south of Archangel, trying to stave off annihilation by a force of one thousand Bolsheviks. About five thousand Doughboys would be fighting there for months after many Yanks had come home and staged their parades—Boyd a figure in perhaps the ugliest tale in American military history, victim of Woodrow Wilson's uncertain aims.

The farther away from Captain Boyd's firing line, the greater the rejoicing. Paris was wild, Pershing on the way to see Clemenceau the next day needing two hours for his car to cross the Place de la Concorde to the Hotel Crillon. London had its great show, and New York City went on a binge; but there was very little rejoicing in the small homes around Blackpool and Leeds, Marseille, the Shetland Islands, Melbourne, or Winnipeg.

The British Isles mourned three-quarters of a million dead, about 625,-000 of these killed in battle. More than a million uniformed French were in battlefield cemeteries. The Germans had seen about two million men killed between Vilna and the Marne, in Balkan mountains and sunny Palestine, in the four years it took for the rest of the world to whip them—their Austro-Hungarian Allies losing half that number. Italy counted her war dead at a half-million. Africa had seen more Negroes killed in the white man's war than in a hundred years of tribal warfare. India and other Asiatic possessions, along with African colonies, had about 2 million and a half killed. No one ever knew what Russian deaths totaled. It was anyone's guess; possibly three million were killed outright in the War to End War; this was augmented so hugely by German prison deaths, and by typhus and famine and the limitless savagery of the civil wars between Reds and Whites, that it would not be an exaggeration to estimate the Russians lost upwards of twenty million people. The Doughboys buried only eighty-three thousand casualties. . . .

There was no stillness on the Yank fighting lines, as at Appomattox. It was a matter of noisy laughter, of men too weary to shed tears. "I saw battle-corpses," Walt Whitman had written after another war,

... myriads of them, and the white skeletons of the young men, I saw them, I saw the debris and the debris of all the slain soldiers of the war, but I saw they were not as I had thought, they themselves were fully at rest, they suffered not, the living remained and suffered, the mother suffered, and the wife and the child and the musing comrade suffered, and the armies that remained suffered.

EPILOGUE

The 190,000 of us in hospitals were beginning to be moved home, now that ocean transport was safe for many men in heavy plaster; and our faraway buddies were beginning their march to the Rhine. We followed the usual route: Savenay near Saint-Nazaire for the plasterers, and thence mainly to Brest for the voyage home. The American boxcars that housed our tiers of stretchers, three deep on either side of the aisle, were shockingly clean; and the Army nurses detailed to attend us must have been chosen for beauty as well as skill, so pretty and sweet-scented were they in winter's blue capes. Case histories in swatches on cords around our necks always interested them. "Stallings? Any kin to Arnold Stallings?" Yes, he was a favorite cousin, a Latin instructor. "Well, the lieutenant will make it home to see his mother, but not much more after that." "Gas?" Well, it was all right just to make it home. . . .

The captive aviators returned to freedom on crutches, or stretcher-ridden, were still unchanged. "Watch out when you change Captain Reddison's bandages," I heard a railroad nurse whisper to a girl with a basin, gauzes, and Dakin solution. "He's a garter-popper. I'm black and blue."

Harbord was knocking his brains out getting us home. (How well he knew troops!) He was using a half-finished hospital on the heights above Brest at Kerhuuon for the overload, long wood sheds of board-and-batten topped with tar paper where the influenza patients had been removed from incoming transports to recover or die. Ward doctors were thinning out,

369

ours just off the boat, a devoted old boy from a village doing his bit, and now confronted with gunshot wounds beyond his imagination—as if all America had been placed upon his surgery couch after a riotous Fourth of July. He was assisted by a surgeon who had developed cancer after too many searchings for foreign bodies under a fluoroscope, the stump of his armpit smelling worse than we did as he worked with a remaining right arm. The third doctor of the team was a wounded veterinarian who told a hilarious tale of how he had delivered a breech-birth calf to save an old Frenchwoman's cow. (She did not think a man had any delicacy who would do such a thing in the presence of a lady, and had to be coaxed into holding a lamp, the veterinarian decked for the count when the calf finally arrived as if shot from a cannon.) The vet now wore an enlisted man's uniform.

There were two sleepless Army nurses of true beauty in Base 65, Miss Hilda Laconius, a brunette with sapphire eyes, and Miss Milly Warren, a brown-eyed honey-blonde. Someone in Tin Pan Alley had written a song about the Red Cross nurse being the "Rose of No-Man's Land" and back home people thought of Red Cross workers as being the sole custodians of the casualties. There were some in France, and devoted; but around-the-clock work was done by the U.S. Army nurse in her unsung thousands. Thanksgiving came around and the "house-organ" *Stars and Stripes* said all two million had been served a turkey dinner with the cranberry trimmings. Laconius and Warren managed us all exactly one baked potato each that day for our dinner; but no one cared; after hours, the wards were alive with dice games and fifths of Martinique rum.

We were soon visited there by an ambassador from the Lost Battalion. He had lain some days on Whittlesey's bench with two broken arms, two broken legs, shot-through jaws. Now his plastered arms were folded as in prayer, his legs in plaster, his jaws wired, with two front teeth extracted so that he could suck nourishment through a tube. He soon began to send many "to the cleaner's" in dice games. He could wiggle the toes on one foot, another lieutenant holding a mirror so that he might "read 'em and weep." The fiery *Rhum Negrito* was too painful for his mouth wounds; and so I extracted a rubber tube from the very fiber of my being, and someone flushed it with a rum calculated to kill *Staphylococcus aureus*—or leprosy, for that matter. Then someone filched a small funnel, and with the tube thrust through his nostrils well past the fractured area, a brother officer slowly pouring, he could get drunk along with the rest. He showed no emotion until the night a crap shooter mentioned that his toes were not giving enough rattle to the bones; then he wept because he was unable to get to his feet and fight the critic.

(In Coblenz, Lieutenant Fritz Prinz of the German Army, who had called upon Whittlesey to surrender and then tried to roast him alive, had waited in hopes of meeting him. Prinz's division had staged a rattling good parade in Coblenz, goose-stepped behind the band where the glockenspiels twirled their wolf tails in glory, and the German division which had been unable to conquer my friend with the wiggling toes let the German people know they had let their army down!)

Couriers, lightly injured, sometimes passed through us. We learned gradually of the occupation troops along the Rhine. Major General Dickman, commanding them, had once sent a platoon to a mountaintop *Schloss* to set up an outpost. The platoon leader had been greeted in the castle yard by a raging countess, who said that she had four young daughters, a well-stocked wine cellar, and would tolerate no American enlisted riffraff on her premises. The Doughboys, of the 4th Division, politely heard her out, pieces grounded and mittened hands holding Springfields between the bands as light snow powdered their faces. They simply stood there at ease, these lads who had seen the destruction between Soissons and the Meuse. Then the lieutenant posted his men. Not one Doughboy knocked her down. The lieutenant had not even kicked her teeth out. . . . None of us in the Laconius-Warren ward liked anything we heard about a beaten enemy not admitting it, and we were, like most men long bedridden, thoughtful—from our broken-legged West Point colonel to the dying boy who, wanting to reach home, would walk on his crutches nightly, up and down the aisle, until he died on his feet walking home, taking the high road.

Shortly before Christmas it began to look as if I might miss another boat or two. My fever was rising, and I could feel the pus beginning to boil up in my best hip. I had a sequestrum. I shook down the thermometer surreptitiously until the sapphire-eyed Miss Laconius caught me at it. That was enough. I was down for surgery the following afternoon. It was interesting on the way to the surgery, overseas cap on my head. A leaden sky, a light rain, and no duckboards; but it was outdoors. The bearers in hipboots were above their knees in mud, but I knew that, in Haig's Flanders, sometimes bearers were fifteen hours going fifteen hundred yards to a collecting station with Tommies bleeding to death. The bearers decided not to enter the antechamber to the surgery. They chose to go around by the morgue, step from their boots and put me down in their sock feet.

It was pleasant at first, the one-quarter grain of morphine hypo all such were given lest they show trepidation—as if any of us were now capable of showing any apprehension whatsoever—soon had me sleeping. I awakened chilled on the concrete floor around midnight, the two Doughboys against the wall still shrouded in their white sheets. I could not possibly have been left for dead, or died in surgery, else we would have been a deathless trio. Blankets were in short supply, and mine were still covering me. I had pinned three cigarettes and three kitchen matches into the surgical gown to save postanesthesia arguments between myself and Miss Laconius, with whom I had fallen in love—along with fifty-one others. I smoked them in miserly style and grew colder. I tried singing to summon warmth. Some snatches of

> Bang away at LooLoo,
> Bang away good and strong;
> Whadda you going to do for your banging,
> When LooLoo's dead and gone?

Then I tried some verses from my first innocent platoon's improvisations on "Mademoiselle from Armentières, the ones where the last stanza began: "The first three months and all was well, parley-voo."

Around three o'clock in the morning there was a flashlight's ray passing and flickering by the far window. I whistled shrilly. He was a big fellow, a first lieutenant, a wounded casual who had offered his services for guard duty. He stepped from his boots into the morgue. Had I risen from the dead? No; I was down for surgery the afternoon before. Did not know what had happened. "Marine," he said, "there wasn't anyone on duty here. They were all down seeing Woodrow Wilson land from the *George Washington*. I was there. Came on duty at midnight."

"How'd he look?" I asked.

"Just the way we did when we were rookies," said the officer of the guard. "And if he goes to sleep on the Paris train, he'd better tie his shoes to their laces around his neck like a hobo on a park bench or he'll leave the train at Paree in his sock feet. That's how he looked."

I felt beneath my bandages, for my hip was no longer pulsating, and my fingers came away with a smear of greasy pus and thin blood. "If you can find some bearers," I said, "I can go back to my bed. All I'll need now is a pair of tweezers to make the hole bigger. Maybe you can find some iodoform gauze wicks and rustle up the tweezers, and we can fix it right here."

After a few minutes the Doughboy lieutenant said, "We've got it oozing real good. If this keeps up, Marine, you'll make the next boat."

The next boat was the old French liner *France*. We boarded it at midnight. Topsides were jammed with home-going troops, and the passageways in steerage were too narrow for any but ambulatory immigrants the *France* had once shoveled ashore at Ellis Island like scoops of coal. French seamen placed us rump-side on tarpaulins and dragged us along the steel plates to portless iron cells in the bowels of the ship, many of us with no immediate foreign-born background marveling at the guts it must have needed for the backwash of Europe's slums to have made such a seemingly forlorn voyage.

We were eight to a cell, and the ambulatory brought news to the stretcher-ridden of topside doings, as well as rationing us, and helping the few sleepless nurses change bandages. (My only concern was a file of body lice which now decided that the better hunting was not in my head—even a louse would have shunned my armpits—but in my eyebrows.) Some said that among Chemical Warfare troops topside arriving too late to asphyxiate the Germans was a Captain Tyrus Raymond Cobb. "I wish the war had lasted long enough for old Ty to go into the Kaiser with his spikes high," the major above me said.

It was a timeless voyage; no day or night, just the single light bulb and the roar of the overhead blower. Messengers eventually brought word that the decks were filled with cheering men as we passed the Statue of Liberty. "I first saw her when I was four years old," said the lad across from me. "In a damned sight worse crate than this. The sea came in. Even if I can't see her now, it's good enough just to know the old girl is still there."

I was astonished to learn in 1923 that the General of the Armies was going to South America as a political emissary of Calvin Coolidge, heading a commission to adjudicate the border dispute between Peru and Chile. It was unlike the Iron Commander to confound politics with soldiering. He had refused the offer of the presidency on a platter when the G.O.P. asked him to sit on his sister's front porch in Laclede, Missouri, until the landslide votes were counted. "The President asked me to go," he explained to friends. It could have been any President of his United States, from Chester A. Arthur to Harry S. Truman.

The U.S. Navy prepared the cruiser U.S.S. *Rochester* to ferry the general there, and supplied a beefed-up Marine detachment, many bemedaled at the Iron Commander's hands, in honor of Harbord's great friend. Captain John W. Thomason, Jr., officer of the guard, asked me to lunch aboard the *Rochester* the noon before Pershing was to come aboard. The general had capacious admiral's quarters in what had once been the battleship *New York*—quarters paneled in mahogany suggesting the smoking room of a North German Lloyd steamer with the trim of an early Estey organ.

When I saw Thomason after the trip, he told me the General of the Armies of the United States liked to retire early to his mahogany quarters and shop-talk Doughboy campaigns there with the detachment commander, who wore the *fourragère* of the Croix de Guerre, the Navy Cross, and several other interesting ribbons—himself obviously from one of the many brilliant infantry brigades Pershing sent into battle.

"He loved stories of men under arms," Thomason said. "Troops were his whole life." He had been little in the society of his company officers. He enjoyed the detachment commander's account of the long-awaited football game between the 2nd Division's race-horse brigades at Coblenz. It was witnessed by many demobilized German officers who boasted small nicks of manliness on a swordsman's cheekbones from student fencing days. They were horrified when, on the opening kick-off, the Doughboy tailback returning the ball reached mid-field to be swallowed in a storm of Leatherneck tacklers. He came up with his eyebrow hanging down over his eye, his face blood-strewn. It was now time, according to German etiquette, to say "*Touché*" and put by the sword. Instead, the tailback ran to the sidelines as time was called. Surgeons put some sutures in the wound and taped it. The Doughboy then returned to the fray, called his own number, and bulled the line for eight yards. "*Schrecklich!*" screamed the German officers, many seeing Doughboys for the first time. The two old soldiers told many stories in the admiral's quarters of the *Rochester*.

The Iron Commander never referred to his mission to Chile and Peru. "He knew," Thomason told me on his return, "it would be rose petals one day, spitballs the next." He was more interested in the operation, which never came off, planned for November 14, 1918, and the subsequent march to Berlin in the spring of 1919.

"But, my General," said Thomason, "the Germans might have been very tough hombres once we neared the Rhine. They still had a lot of *bons soldats*. I know they weren't using blank ammunition the morning of the Armistice when I scampered across those fire-raked pontoons of the Meuse."

"Some might have fought after they surrendered," said the General of the Armies. "Until we came down the Linden as an army with banners."

"General, there would have been a lot of sniping from the rooftops of the Linden. I've seen some who would have mounted machine guns on the Brandenburger Tor."

"Yes," said the Iron Commander. "We would have flushed them out and hanged them to the lamp posts of the Linden to let the Germans know who won the war. The Germans are being told the people let the armies down."

It was a subject the General of the Armies never tired of discussing as the *Rochester* threaded its way through the canal, ceaseless in his resolve to found many schools to develop the multiple techniques of the next inevitable war with Germany. "He would bang on the table," Thomason told me in awe. The slackness Weygand saw in Souilly's bitter hours was no longer there. He was sixty-three years old, the blue returned to his eyes, his backbone in ramrod form, himself again capable of outbreaks of temper in brimstone language which many witnessed in the first French winter. "They never knew they were beaten in Berlin," he said. "It will all have to be done all over again."

APPENDIX

AMERICAN DIVISIONS SENT TO EUROPE

THEIR DATES OF ARRIVAL, CASUALTIES AND LOCALITIES
FROM WHICH ORIGINALLY RAISED

REGULAR ARMY DIVISIONS

Div.	Date Div. Hdqrs. arrived in France	Battle deaths and died of wounds	Wounded	Locality from which division was originally raised (Many divisions were reorganized prior to sailing for Europe)
1	June 26, 1917	4,996	17,324	At large.
2	. . . . .	1 5,155	2 18,080	At large. (Included one brigade of marines.) Division formed in France in 1917.
3	Apr. 4, 1918	3,401	12,000	At large.
4	May 17, 1918	2,903	9,917	Do.
5	May 1, 1918	2,120	6,996	Do.
6	July 22, 1918	68	318	Do.
7	Aug. 11, 1918	287	1,422	Do.
8	Nov. 9, 1918	. . . . .	. . . . .	At large. (Part arrived in France just prior to Armistice.)

NATIONAL GUARD DIVISIONS

Div.	Date Div. Hdqrs. arrived in France	Battle deaths and died of wounds	Wounded	Locality from which division was originally raised
26	Oct. 28, 1917	2,281	11,383	New England.
27	May 31, 1918	1,829	6,505	New York.
28	May 18, 1918	2,874	11,265	Pennsylvania
29	June 28, 1918	1,053	4,517	New Jersey, Virginia, Maryland, Delaware, District of Columbia.
30	May 24, 1918	1,641	6,774	Tennessee, North Carolina and South Carolina.
31	Oct. 15, 1918	. . . . .	. . . . .	Georgia, Alabama and Florida. (Became 7th Depot Division.)
32	Feb. 20, 1918	3,028	10,233	Michigan and Wisconsin.
33	May 24, 1918	993	5,871	Illinois.
34	Oct. 3, 1918	. . . . .	. . . . .	Nebraska, Iowa, North Dakota, South Dakota and Minnesota. (Personnel used as replacements.)
35	May 11, 1918	1,298	5,998	Missouri and Kansas.
36	July 30, 1918	591	1,993	Texas and Oklahoma.
37	June 23, 1918	1,066	4,321	Ohio.
38	Oct. 4, 1918	. . . . .	. . . . .	Indiana, Kentucky and West Virginia. (Personnel used as replacements.)
39	Aug. 27, 1918	. . . . .	. . . . .	Arkansas, Mississippi and Louisiana. (Became 5th Depot Division.)
40	Aug. 24, 1918	. . . . .	. . . . .	California, Colorado, Utah, Arizona and New Mexico. (Became 6th Depot Division.)
41	Dec. 31, 1917	93	315	Washington, Oregon, Montana, Idaho, Wyoming, Colorado, North Dakota, South Dakota, New Mexico and District of Columbia. (Became 1st Depot Division.)
42	Nov. 1, 1917	2,810	11,873	Composite division from 26 States and District of Columbia.

AMERICAN DIVISIONS SENT TO EUROPE

THEIR DATES OF ARRIVAL, CASUALITIES AND LOCALITIES
FROM WHICH ORIGINALLY RAISED

NATIONAL ARMY DIVISIONS

76	July 16, 1918	4	22	New England and New York. (Became 3d Depot Division.)
77	Apr. 13, 1918	2,110	8,084	New York City and vicinity.
78	June 8, 1918	1,530	5,614	New York, New Jersey and Delaware.
79	July 16, 1918	1,517	5,357	Pennsylvania, Maryland and District of Columbia.
80	May 30, 1918	1,241	4,788	Virginia, West Virginia and Pennsylvania.
81	Aug. 16, 1918	248	856	North Carolina, South Carolina and Florida.
82	May 13, 1918	1,413	6,664	Georgia, Alabama and Tennessee.
3 83	June 17, 1918	67	257	Ohio and Pennsylvania. (Became 2d Depot Division.)
84	Sept. 25, 1918	. . . . .	. . . . .	Kentucky, Indiana, Illinois. (Personnel used as replacements.)
4 85	Aug. 10, 1918	145	281	Michigan and Wisconsin. (Became 4th Depot Division.)
86	Sept. 23, 1918	. . . . .	. . . . .	Illinois and Wisconsin. (Personnel used as replacements.)
87	Sept. 9, 1918	. . . . .	. . . . .	Arkansas, Louisiana, Mississippi and Alabama.
88	Sept. 4, 1918	20	58	North Dakota, Minnesota, Iowa and Illinois.
89	June 21, 1918	1,466	5,625	Kansas, Missouri, South Dakota, Nebraska, Arizona, Colorado and New Mexico.
90	July 7, 1918	1,496	6,053	Texas and Oklahoma.
91	July 23, 1918	1,454	4,654	Montana, Nevada, Wyoming, Utah, Washington, Oregon, California and Idaho.
92	June 19, 1918	182	1,465	Colored troops (various states).
93	Mar. 5, 1918	591	2,943	Colored National Guard and other troops (various states) four infantry regiments only.
Other troops........		976	2,802	
		52,947	202,628	

1 Includes 2454 Marine Corps and 18 Navy serving with the Marine Corps.
2 Includes 8894 Marine Corps and 123 Navy serving with the Marine Corps.
3 332d Infantry of this division went to Italy in July 1918 and saw active service.
4 339th Infantry of this division served at Archangel, Russia, for a time.

AMERICAN DIVISIONS SENT TO EUROPE

THEIR POPULAR NICKNAMES, COMPOSITION, DAYS IN MAJOR OPERATIONS, DAYS IN SECTOR, MILES ADVANCED, PRISONERS CAPTURED, PRISONERS LOST AND REPLACEMENTS RECEIVED

Div.	Popular Nickname	Inf. Brigades	Inf. Regiments	F.A. Brig.	F.A. Regts.	Engr. Rgt.	M.G. Bns.	Training in Line	Sector	Battle	Total	Approx. Miles Advanced	Prisoners Captured	Prisoners Lost	Replacements Received	Div.
1	(Big Red One)[1]	1, 2	16, 18, 26, 28	1	5, 6, 7	1	1, 2, 3	47	148	28	223	32	6,469	152	30,206	1
2	(race-horse brigades)	3, **4**	9, 23, **5, 6**	2	12, 15, 17	2	4, 5, **6**	58	48	33	139	37	12,026	157	35,343	2
3	Marne	5, 6	4, 7, 30, 38	3	10, 18, 76	6	7, 8, 9	0	39	50	89	25	2,240	314	24,033	3
4	Ivy (Ivy Leafs)	7, 8	39, 47, 58, 59	4	13, 16, 77	4	10, 11, 12	0	11	36	47	15	2,756	72	19,559	4
5	Red Diamond	9, 10	60, 61, 6, 11	5	19, 20, 21	7	13, 14, 15	33	39	32	104	18	2,356	100	12,611	5
6	None	11, 12	51, 52, 53, 54	6	3, 11, 78	318	16, 17, 18	6	37	0	43	0				6
7	None	13, 14	55, 56, 34, 64	7	8, 79, 80	5	19, 20, 21	0	33	0	33	1	12	3	2,784	7
8	Pathfinder	15, 16	12, 62, 8, 13	8	2, 81, 83	319	22, 23, 24						69	20	4,112	8
26	Yankee	51, 52	101, 102, 103, 104	51	101, 102, 103	101	101, 102, 103	42	118	45	205	23	3,148	457	14,411	26
27	New York (Orions)	53, 54	105, 106, 107, 108	52	104, 105, 106	102	107, 108, 109	25	0	32	57	7	2,357	229	5,255	27
28	Keystone	55, 56	109, 110, 111, 112	53	107, 108, 109	103	104, 105, 106	14	44	44	102	6	921	732	21,717	28
29	Blue and Gray	57, 58	113, 114, 115, 116	54	110, 111, 112	104	110, 111, 112	13	46	23	82	4	2,187	68	4,977	29
30	Old Hickory	59, 60	117, 118, 119, 120	55	113, 114, 115	105	113, 114, 115	33	1	35	69	18	3,848	75	2,384	30
31	Dixie	61, 62	121, 122, 123, 124	56	116, 117, 118	106	116, 117, 118							2		31
32	Iron Jaws (Gemütlichkeit boys)	63, 64	125, 126, 127, 128	57	119, 120, 121	107	119, 120, 121	25	37	38	100	22	2,153	161	20,140	32
33	Prairie	65, 66	129, 130, 131, 132	58	122, 123, 124	108	122, 123, 124	27	33	38	98	22	3,987	127	5,415	33
34	Sandstorm	67, 68	133, 134, 135, 136	59	125, 126, 127	109	125, 126, 127									34
35	None	69, 70	137, 138, 139, 140	60	128, 129, 130	110	128, 129, 130	37	43	30	110	7	781	167	10,605	35
36	Lone Star	71, 72	141, 142, 143, 144	61	131, 132, 133	111	131, 132, 133	0	0	19	19	13	549	24	3,397	36
37	Buckeye	73, 74	145, 146, 147, 148	62	134, 135, 136	112	134, 135, 136	7	57	13	77	19	1,495	23	6,282	37
38	Cyclone	75, 76	149, 150, 151, 152	63	137, 138, 139	113	137, 138, 139							2		38
39	Delta	77, 78	153, 154, 155, 156	64	140, 141, 142	114	140, 141, 142							2		39
40	Sunshine	79, 80	157, 158, 159, 160	65	143, 144, 145	115	143, 144, 145									40
41	Sunset	81, 82	161, 162, 163, 164	66	146, 147, 148	116	146, 147, 148							4		41
42	Rainbow	83, 84	165, 166, 167, 168	67	149, 150, 151	117	149, 150, 151	31	100	45	176	34	1,317	112	17,253	42
76	None	151, 152	301, 302, 303, 304	151	301, 302, 303	301	301, 302, 303									76
77	Metropolitan	153, 154	305, 306, 307, 308	152	304, 305, 306	302	304, 305, 306	25	31	63	119	44	750	403	12,728	77
78	Lightning (White Lightnings)	155, 156	309, 310, 311, 312	153	307, 308, 309	303	307, 308, 309	0	18	22	40	13	432	123	3,190	78
79	Liberty	157, 158	313, 314, 315, 316	154	310, 311, 312	304	310, 311, 312	0	29	18	47	12	1,077	80	6,246	79
80	Blue Ridge	159, 160	317, 318, 319, 320	155	313, 314, 315	305	313, 314, 315	16	0	31	47	24	1,813	100	4,495	80
81	Stonewall	161, 162	321, 322, 323, 324	156	316, 317, 318	306	316, 317, 318	14	18	5	37	3	101	51	1,984	81
82	All American	163, 164	325, 326, 327, 328	157	319, 320, 321	307	319, 320, 321	17	58	30	105	11	845	240	8,402	82
83	Ohio	165, 166	329, 330, 331, 332	158	322, 323, 324	308	322, 323, 324									83
84	Lincoln	167, 168	333, 334, 335, 336	159	325, 326, 327	309	325, 326, 327							1		84
85	Custer	169, 170	337, 338, 339, 340	160	328, 329, 330	310	328, 329, 330									85
86	Black Hawk	171, 172	341, 342, 343, 344	161	331, 332, 333	311	331, 332, 333							18		86
87	Acorn	173, 174	345, 346, 347, 348	162	334, 335, 336	312	334, 335, 336									87
88	Cloverleaf	175, 176	349, 350, 351, 352	163	337, 338, 339	313	337, 338, 339	22	21	0	43				734	88
89	Middle West	177, 178	353, 354, 355, 356	164	340, 341, 342	314	340, 341, 342	0	54	28	82	30	5,061	9	7,669	89
90	Alamo	179, 180	357, 358, 359, 360	165	343, 344, 345	315	343, 344, 345	0	43	26	69	17	1,876	25	4,437	90
91	Wild West	181, 182	361, 362, 363, 364	166	346, 347, 348	316	346, 347, 348	0	6	17	23	21	2,412	81	12,530	91
92	Buffalo	183, 184	365, 366, 367, 368	167	349, 350, 351	317	349, 350, 351	7	56	0	63	5	38	28	2,920	92
93	None[2]	185,	369, 370, 371, 372													93

Marine units, all in 2nd Division, in bold face type.
[1] Unofficial nickname used in The Doughboy.
[2] Never operated as a division.

American Army Commanders[1]

Name of Army	Commander	Period (1918)
First	General John J. Pershing	Aug. 10– Oct. 16
	Maj. Gen. Hunter Liggett[2]	Oct. 16–Nov. 11
Second	Maj. Gen. Robert L. Bullard[2]	Oct. 12–Nov. 11

[1] From date of organization until the Armistice.
[2] Appointed Lieutenant General on Nov. 1, 1918.

———— ◆ ————

American Corps Commanders[1]

Name of Corps	Commander	Period (1918)
I	Ma. Gen. Hunter Liggett	Jan. 20–Oct. 12
	Maj. Gen. Joseph T. Dickman	Oct. 12–Nov. 11
II	Position vacant	Feb. 24–June 15
	Maj. Gen. George W. Read	June 15–Nov. 11
III	Position vacant	Mar. 30–June 17
	Maj. Gen. William M. Wright	June 17–July 12
	Maj. Gen. John E. McMahon[3]	July 12–July 14
	Maj. Gen. Robert L. Bullard	July 14–Oct. 12
	Maj. Gen. John L. Hines	Oct. 12–Nov. 11
IV	Position vacant	June 19–Aug. 18
	Maj. Gen. Joseph T. Dickman	Aug. 18–Oct. 12
	Maj Gen. Charles H. Muir	Oct. 12–Nov. 11
V	Maj. Gen. William M. Wright	July 12–Aug. 18
	Maj. Gen. George H. Cameron	Aug. 18–Oct. 12
	Maj. Gen. Charles P. Summerall	Oct. 12–Nov. 11
VI	Position vacant	Aug. 1–Aug. 26
	Maj. Gen. Omar Bundy	Aug. 26–Sept. 13
	Position vacant	Sept. 13–Oct. 23
	Maj. Gen. Charles C. Ballou	Oct. 23–Nov. 10
	Maj. Gen. Charles T. Menoher	Nov. 10–Nov. 11
VII	Maj. Gen. William M. Wright	Aug. 19–Sept. 6
	Position vacant	Sept. 6–Sept. 13
	Maj. Gen. Omar Bundy	Sept. 13–Oct. 25
	Position vacant	Oct. 25–Nov. 11

———— ◆ ————

American Division Commanders

Name of Div.	Division Commander	Period[1]
1	Maj. Gen. William L. Sibert	Oct. 23, 1917[2]– Dec. 14, 1917
	Maj. Gen. Robert L. Bullard	Dec. 14, 1917– Apr. 5, 1918
	Brig. Gen. Beaumont B. Buck[3]	Apr. 5–Apr. 13
	Maj. Gen. Robert L. Bullard	Apr. 13–July 15
	Maj. Gen. Charles P. Summerall	July 15–Oct. 12
	Brig. Gen. Frank E. Bamford[3]	Oct. 12–Oct. 18
	Brig. Gen. Frank Parker	Oct. 18–Nov. 11
2	Maj. Gen. Omar Bundy	Mar. 17–July 15
	Maj. Gen. James G. Harbord	July 15–July 26
	Brig. Gen. John A. Lejeune, USMC[3]	July 26–July 27
	Maj. Gen. James G. Harbord	July 27–July 28
	Brig. Gen. John A. Lejeune, USMC[4]	July 28–Nov. 11
3	Maj. Gen. Joseph T. Dickman	May 31–Aug. 18
	Brig. Gen. Fred W. Sladen[3]	Aug. 18–Aug. 27

	Maj. Gen. Beaumont B. Buck	Aug. 27–Oct. 18
	Brig. Gen. Preston Brown	Oct. 18–Nov. 11
4	Maj. Gen. George H. Cameron	July 18–Aug. 14
	Brig. Gen. Benjamin A. Poore[3]	Aug. 14–Aug. 27
	Maj. Gen. John L. Hines	Aug. 27–Oct. 11
	Maj. Gen. George H. Cameron	Oct. 11–Oct. 22
	Brig. Gen. Benjamin A. Poore[3]	Oct. 22–Oct. 31
	Maj. Gen. Mark L. Hersey	Oct. 31–Nov. 11
5	Maj. Gen. John E. McMahon	June 14[2]–Oct. 18
	Maj. Gen. Hanson E. Ely	Oct. 18–Nov. 11
6	Maj. Gen. Walter H. Gordon	Aug. 31–Nov. 11
7	Brig. Gen. Charles H. Barth	Oct. 10–Oct. 24
	Brig. Gen. Lutz Wahl[3]	Oct. 24–Oct. 28
	Maj. Gen. Edmund Wittenmyer	Oct. 28–Nov. 11
26	Maj. Gen. Clarence R. Edwards	Feb. 6–Oct. 25
	Brig. Gen. Frank E. Bamford	Oct. 25–Nov. 11
27	Maj. Gen. John F. O'Ryan	July 25–Nov. 11
28	Maj. Gen. Charles H. Muir	July 1–Oct. 23
	Brig. Gen. Frank H. Albright[3]	Oct. 23–Oct. 25
	Maj. Gen. William H. Hay	Oct. 25–Nov. 11
29	Maj. Gen. Charles G. Morton	July 27–Nov. 11
30	Brig. Gen. Samson L. Faison[3]	July 16–July 18
	Maj. Gen. Edward M. Lewis	July 18–Nov. 11
32	Maj. Gen. William G. Haan	May 20–Nov. 11
33	Maj. Gen. George Bell, Jr.	June 23–Nov. 11
35	Brig. Gen. Nathaniel F. McClure	June 20–July 20
	Maj. Gen. Peter E. Traub	July 20–Nov. 1
	Brig. Gen. Thomas B. Dugan[3]	Nov. 1–Nov. 2
	Maj. Gen. Peter E. Traub	Nov. 2–Nov. 11
36	Maj. Gen. William R. Smith	Oct. 10–Nov. 11
37	Maj. Gen. Charles S. Farnsworth	July 28–Nov. 11
42	Maj. Gen. Charles T. Menoher	Feb. 21–Nov. 10
	Brig. Gen. Douglas MacArthur	Nov. 10–Nov. 11
77	Maj. Gen. George B. Duncan	June 21–July 20
	Brig. Gen. Evan M. Johnson[3]	July 20–July 28
	Maj. Gen. George B. Duncan	July 28–Aug. 19
	Brig. Gen. Evan M. Johnson[3]	Aug. 19–Aug. 27
	Maj. Gen. Robert Alexander	Aug. 27–Nov. 11
78	Maj. Gen. James H. McRae	Sept. 16–Nov. 11
79	Maj. Gen. Joseph E. Kuhn	Sept. 16–Nov. 11
80	Maj. Gen. Adelbert Cronkhite	July 23–Nov. 11
81	Maj. Gen. Charles J. Bailey	Sept. 18–Nov. 11
82	Maj. Gen. William P. Burnham	June 25–Oct. 4
	Maj. Gen. George B. Duncan	Oct. 4–Nov. 11
88	Maj. Gen. William Weigel	Sept. 23–Nov. 11
89	Brig. Gen. Frank L. Winn	Aug. 10–Sept. 6
	Maj. Gen. William M. Wright	Sept. 6–Nov. 11
90	Maj. Gen. Henry T. Allen	Aug. 24–Nov. 11
91	Maj. Gen. William H. Johnston	Sept. 22–Nov. 11
92	Maj. Gen. Charles C. Ballou	Aug. 23–Nov. 11

[1] 1918 unless otherwise indicated. Other reference numerals used above are explained on the next page.
[2] The first date which appears opposite each division is that of its first entry into line. It is not the date the division commander was appointed.
[3] Temporarily in command.
[4] Promoted to Maj. Gen. on Aug. 1, 1918.

Commanders of the Services of Supply:

Colonel David S. Stanley (temporary), July 5, 1917–July 24, 1917.

Major General Richard M. Blatchford, July 25, 1917–November 1, 1917.

Brigadier General Mason M. Patrick (temporary) from November 1, 1917, to November 27, 1917.

Major General Francis J. Kernan, November 27, 1917–July 29, 1918.

Major General James G. Harbord, July 29, 1918–May 26, 1919.

Brigadier General William D. Connor, May 26, 1919–August 31, 1919.

———————◆———————

Miles of Western Front occupied by American and Allied forces in 1918

Date (1918)	American	British	French[1]	Belgian	Total
Jan. 31	6	116	323	23	468
Mar. 20	17	116	312	23	468
Mar. 30	19	92	353	23	487
Apr. 10	31	92	348	23	494
Apr. 30	34	83	358	23	498
May 30	23	83	393	23	522
June 10	36	83	389	23	531
June 20	65	83	360	23	531
July 10	62	92	354	23	531
July 20	55	92	362	23	532
July 30	68	92	318	23	501
Aug. 10	79	93	277	23	472
Aug. 20	85	93	276	23	477
Aug. 30	90	87	262	23	462
Sept. 10	98	87	241	23	449
Sept. 30	82	83	258	28	451
Oct. 10	101	83	244	15	443
Oct. 30	79	68	248	15	410
Nov. 11	83	70	214	25	392

[1] The sections of the front which were held by Italian and Portuguese divisions are included with French.

Maximum number of miles of front line held at one time by American units:

101 miles on October 10, 1918.

Total length of the Western Front:

Oct. 1914—468 miles.
July 17, 1918—532 miles.

Maximum number of American divisions that saw action during any one week:

29 during second week of October 1918.

Approximate average actual strength of the various combat divisions on the Western Front during the year 1918:

American 25,500
British 11,800
French 11,400
German 12,300

Greatest number of Americans that arrived in Europe during any single month:

313,410 during the month of July 1918.

Cumulative arrivals in Europe of American military personnel for the A.E.F.:

By May 31, 1917	1,308
By June 30, 1917	16,220
By July 31, 1917	20,120
By Aug. 31, 1917	39,383
By Sept. 30, 1917	61,927
By Oct. 31, 1917	92,265
By Nov. 30, 1917	129,623
By Dec. 31, 1917	183,896
By Jan. 31, 1918	224,655
By Feb. 28, 1918	254,378
By Mar. 31, 1918	329,005
By Apr. 30, 1918	434,081
By May 31, 1918	667,119
By June 30, 1918	897,293
By July 31, 1918	1,210,703
By Aug. 31, 1918	1,473,190
By Sept. 30, 1918	1,783,955
By Oct. 30, 1918	1,986,618
By Nov. 11, 1918	2,057,675

Actual combat strength of the A.E.F.:

Mar. 21, 1918	162,482
May 27, 1918	406,844
Aug. 10, 1918	822,358
Sept. 12, 1918	999,602
Oct. 12, 1918	1,078,190
Nov. 11, 1918	1,078,222

These figures include only combat troops and exclude the troops in the S. O. S., headquarters, schools, hospitals, liaison service and other special services.

Combat strength of A.E.F. by branch of service at the time of the Armistice:

Infantry and M. G. Battalions .	646,000
Engineers	81,600
Signal Corps	21,300
Air Service	34,800
Artillery	278,500
Tank Corps	10,200
Amm. Trains, Q. M., etc. . .	70,800
Medical Department	¹152,300
Cavalry	6,000
Ordnance	¹22,900

¹ Including those on duty in the Services of Supply.

Total strength of A.E.F. on Nov. 11:

Its total strength was 1,981,701, in which were included 32,385 marines.

Number of civilians employed by A.E.F.:

42,644 at the time of the Armistice.

Greatest number of American soldiers in hospitals in Europe at any one time:

190,564 men on November 7, 1918.

Percentage of total strength in various branches of the A.E.F., Nov. 1918:

	Officers; % of total	Enlisted Men; % of total
Infantry	23.83	32.40
Engineers	8.69	12.68
Field Artillery	10.91	11.18
Casuals (all branches) . .	3.39	10.81
Medical Dept. (Army) . .	18.46	7.26
Quartermaster Corps . .	6.33	7.16
Coast Artillery Corps . .	4.00	3.78
Air Service	7.30	3.11
Ammunition Trains . .	1.47	2.48
Signal Corps	1.63	1.83
Supply Trains	1.02	1.61
Ordnance Department . .	1.53	1.16
Marines	0.75	0.96
Headquarters Troops . .	0.21	0.78
Military Police	0.49	0.67
Hdqrs. Detachments . .	0.00	0.55
Tank Corps	0.91	0.50
Cavalry	0.25	0.29
Postal Express Service . .	0.15	0.15
Medical Dept. (Navy) . .	0.07	0.02
G.H.Q. and General Staff	8.49	0.00

Provisions for hospitalization in A.E.F.:

On November 11, 1918, there were 192,844 normal beds, which could have been increased in an emergency to 276,-547. There were 153 base hospitals, 66 camp hospitals, 12 convalescent camps, 21 hospital trains and 6,875 ambulances.

A READER'S GUIDE

As this book is, by intention, an informal narrative of the Doughboy War, it has not been adorned with the paraphernalia of the professional historian. However, while the reader has been spared the ordeal of footnotes, while the scholar will not find the less offensive and occasionally useful chapter notes in the back, and while I have chosen to eschew a formal bibliography, those readers who are interested in the subject of World War I deserve some explanation about my sources, and may even appreciate suggestions for further reading. In addition, there are some matters too minor in importance to include in the text on which I would like to comment.

Marksmanship

Some historians have not given full credit to the importance of the rifle in this war in which machine guns and artillery came into such prominence. Yet in 1918 it was the rifle on which Doughboy infantrymen, like Captain Reid's Sergeant Fisher in the stand on the Marne, and York and Woodfill in the Meuse-Argonne, placed their main reliance. In this connection it is worthwhile to note the marksmanship of the II Corps of England's Old Contemptibles at Le Cateau in 1914. There Major General Sir Horace Smith-Dorrien with three divisions of British Regulars fought a rear-guard action which so impressed the invaders that they reported they had encountered *machine-gun* companies, cadres unheard of at the time. The British infantry was armed only with the Enfield rifle, but, as the Bixsley tests will show, each man was capable of delivering fifteen well-aimed shots per minute at 1,000 yards. German uhlans made first contact with the Tommies. The former were soon unhorsed and advanced as dismounted fighters armed with short-barrel carbines effective only within 800 yards; few in the van survived to crawl within range. Let anyone who ever fired a high-powered rifle on a 1,000-yard range consider the accuracy of these British. At that distance, firing on a 36-inch target, the marksman can see the numbers on *all* targets and sometimes score a bull on No. 17 target instead of on his own No. 16, after "doping" the wind and setting the sight-leaf to allow for the bullet's sinking through cooling shadows as it describes the parabola of its trajectory. At Le Cateau it mattered little if a Tommy misread his target—except of course to the No. 17 uhlan. These British soldiers were more than craftsmen with a rifle; they were artists, and they were out of reach of everything but enemy artillery. In a defensive situation with adequate support they were well-nigh invincible, but Sir John French killed them off in hopeless frontal assaults in his follies of early 1915.

Casualty Figures

It must be pointed out that accuracy in counting casualties, difficult after any war and often subject to disagreement, probably has never been more so than after

383

World War I, with so many nations and men involved, records unreliable or lost, and so many soldiers unaccounted for. Russian losses, for example, will doubtless never be known. Hanson W. Baldwin, in *World War I: An Outline History*, estimates Russian military casualties at over six and a half million, and thinks Nikolai N. Golovin's much larger estimates in his *The Russian Army in the World War* are too high. I do not, mainly because of my conversations with Brigadier General Merian C. Cooper, USAFR (retired), whose knowledge of the Russian scene was gained at first-hand.

Accuracy in counting losses on the Western Front is also difficult. Estimates of the total casualties in the Battle of Verdun in 1916 range from a low 650,000 by Alistair Horne in *The Price of Glory*, to Baldwin's 760,000, to my own just under a million. The point to remember is that all such figures are estimates and that discrepancies are unavoidable. Fortunately for *The Doughboys*, the records for the A.E.F. are thorough and as reliable as any such records can be. These casualty figures and other data will be found in the Appendix, page 375.

Sources and Suggested Reading

For the average reader who does not care to make a detailed study of the First World War, the most confusing war ever fought, only four items are needed. These are:

TEXTS

The Great War, 1914-1918, by Captain Cyril Falls (New York: G. P. Putnam's Sons, 1959)

World War I: An Outline History, by Hanson W. Baldwin (New York: Harper & Row, 1962)

MAPS

The West Point Atlas of American Wars, Colonel Vincent J. Esposito, chief editor (New York: Frederick A. Praeger, 1959)

PICTURES

The First World War—A Photographic History, edited by Laurence Stallings (New York: Simon and Schuster, 1933. Reissue 1962)

Messrs. Falls, Baldwin, and Esposito are professionals of the first magnitude, whom I recommend without hesitation. However, for those who wish to go further into the subject, I list below a few of the thousands of writers who have provided me with information over the past forty-five years.

Background

The Guns of August, by Barbara W. Tuchman (New York: Macmillan, 1962). This work, beginning at the funeral bier of King Edward VII, and following through the failure of the Germans to capture Paris in 1914, is a marvelous feat of wit, military writing, and political philosophy, and it is invaluable as background to the four years of war that followed.

France

Foch, the Man of Orléans, by Captain B. H. Liddell Hart (Boston: Little, Brown, 1933).

Marshal Foch, by Captain Cyril Falls (London: Blackie, 1939).

Memoirs, by Marshal Ferdinand Foch, translated by Colonel T. Bentley Mott (New York: Doubleday, 1931).

Dare Call It Treason, by Richard M. Watt, with an introduction by Colonel John Elting, USA (New York: Simon and Schuster, 1963).

The Price of Glory: Verdun, 1916, by Alistair Horne (New York: St. Martin's Press, 1963).

Liddell Hart's book is one of the superior biographies in the English language, erudite and dexterous in its interweaving of military mass as the old marshal spends many posthumous hours on the analyst's couch. As usual, Captain Falls is warmer and more generous. Foch, as do all generals, gives himself the best of every argument. It is unnecessary to read more of French generals. Falls, Liddell Hart, Baldwin, and Mrs. Tuchman take care of them nicely, Liddell Hart particularly in his *A History of the World War, 1914-1918* (Boston: Little, Brown, 1935). Richard M. Watt's book is a must for all who wish to understand the crisis facing the Allies at the time Pershing and his staff were being briefed in the Crillon. It faithfully researches the thirty years of French corruption, military and civil, which led to the Nivelle mutiny. Alistair Horne's study of the horrors of the 1916 Battle of Verdun is a magnificent achievement of clarity amidst confusion, and a testament to human endurances in the face of hopelessness.

Germany

The German General Staff and Its Decisions, 1914-1916, by Erich von Falkenhayn (New York: Dodd, Mead, 1920).

Ludendorff's Own Story, by Erich Ludendorff (New York: Harper & Brothers, 1920).

The March on Paris and the Battle of the Marne, by Alexander von Kluck (London: Arnold, 1920).

The War of Lost Opportunities, by Max Hoffmann (New York: International, 1925).

Out of My Life, by Paul von Hindenburg (New York: Harper & Brothers, 1921).

Here are the workings of the General Staff mind at the highest levels. Falkenhayn later had his brilliant days, notably in the Balkans. Ludendorff's book was written before he began to lose his mind. Kluck was a better general than he is credited with being. When Moltke began to direct him by using a junior staff officer as Kluck's superior, the latter should have gone on the sick list and saved his reputation. However, Moltke himself beat him to the sick list. Hoffmann, who bluffed Leon Trotsky out of his shoes, and probably was the ablest of the lot, had a Satanic spirit. "Fortunately for the Allies," Colonel Esposito writes, "they left him on the Eastern Front in 1918." He was the cream of the Hindenburg-Ludendorff team on the Russian front. Hindenburg, as do all other generals, gives himself the best of it, but the book is a must for Monday morning quarterbacks interested in the Doughboy's War.

Great Britain

Liaison 1914: A Narrative of the Great Retreat, by Major General Edward L. Spears (New York: Doubleday Doran, 1931).

Private Papers, 1914-1919 of Sir Douglas Haig, edited by Robert Blake (London: Eyre & Spottiswoode, 1952).

The World Crisis, by Winston S. Churchill (New York: Scribner's, 1923 and 1931).

War Memoirs, by David Lloyd George (Boston: Little, Brown, 1933-1937).

Decisive Battles, by Major General J. F. C. Fuller, D.S.O., C.M.G. (New York: Scribner's, 1940).

General Spears was unsurpassed as a narrator in salon, saloon, or staff room. If he sometimes gives the British the best of it, this is hardly new. Haig, the soldier Pershing knew as indomitable in 1918, is revealed privately as a Scott Fitzgerald little rich boy biting the legs of royal lackeys. Sir Winston's work is, not surprisingly, of highest caliber, filled with trickeries at highest level. Lloyd George, wartime prime minister, who chivied Asquith out of his billet, had the military counsel of Captain Liddell Hart, and so naturally he digs up Sir Douglas Haig and beheads him. General Fuller is the most prolific of English historians, and greatly talented, though this true prophet sometimes "redoubles his effort after losing sight of his objective." In this particular work his critique of Churchill's Gallipoli campaign, probably the soundest strategic concept of the war and surely the most poorly implemented, deserves to be read for its superb staff style, though this campaign is not a part of the Doughboy War. (It should be read as a preliminary to Alan Moorehead's *Gallipoli*

[New York: Harper & Brothers, 1956], a romantic history of bravery that is my favorite book about men under fire.)

General Fuller also wrote an introduction to Leon Wolff's *In Flanders Fields* (New York: Viking, 1958), in which he, too, beheads Sir Douglas Haig and turns the body over to Mr. Wolff, who, in turn, "uses an axe and avoids the joints" in his study of the fighting around Ypres in 1917. This work is well-nigh magical in its ability to conjure the beauty of the human spirit out of the morass. The latest writer to behead Sir Douglas is Alan Clark, who, in writing of the murderous blunders of 1915 on the Western Front, lets his tactical cat out of the strategic bag by simply calling it *The Donkeys* (New York: William Morrow, 1962). How the "old school tie" subaltern of 1914 became a superior combat leader by 1918 is admirably recounted in *All The Best Years*, by Desmond Young (New York: Harper & Brothers, 1961), an autobiography that reads like a picaresque novel.

I have not mentioned the hardest-working, and possibly the ablest, of all historians, Brigadier General Sir James Edward Edmonds. His is the moving force back of forty-five volumes by His Majesty's Stationers Office for the Imperial General Staff. I have by no means read them all, but the maps are an education in themselves. If a reader will take Colonel Esposito's beautifully drawn maps in Volume II of the *West Point Atlas* as a pilot book, and then be prepared to disappear into the Library of Congress with Sir James's work for ten years, he will emerge an emaciated, but sadder and wiser, man. For an example of Sir James's strategy in marshaling his material, I cite *A Short History of World War I* (London: Oxford University Press, 1951).

Other Fronts

For the purposes of this narrative of the Doughboys in France and Belgium, one can ignore the fighting on other fronts, though it is axiomatic that every death in the Balkans, every wound in the Middle East, every prisoner taken in Russia, every ship sunk on the high seas influenced the outcome on the Western Front. There were Doughboys in Italy, though never in mass; there was a Doughboy contingent fighting under British command in North Russia long after November 11, 1918; and there were many Yanks at sea.

For those interested in going beyond the area of *The Doughboys*, Generals Count Luigi Cadorna, Armando Díaz, and many other Italian generals wrote their accounts of Italy in the First World War. However, for an over-all discussion of the Italian Front I recommend Captain Falls (*The Great War 1914-1918*). Falls is superb in his delineation of Ludendorff's tactical greed at Caporetto in his foolish rush to the Piave River, though personally I lean to Ernest Hemingway's *A Farewell to Arms* (New York: Scribner's, 1929) for a description of that Italian disaster. J. F. C. Fuller in *Decisive Battles* has a fine description of the final victory at Vittorio Veneto.

The best book on the Doughboys who perished in the Archangel expedition is *The Ignorant Armies*, by E. M. Halliday, with a righteously fierce foreword by Brigadier General S. L. A. Marshall (New York: Harper & Brothers, 1960). Other interesting books on the Eastern Front, in addition to Falls, Baldwin, and Tuchman, are: *A Soldier's Note-book*, by General A. A. Brusilov (New York: Macmillan, 1931); *With the Russian Army—1914-1917*, by Major General Sir Alfred Knox (London: Hutchinson & Co., 1921); and *The Russian Army in the World War*, by the refugee Lieutenant General Nikolai N. Golovin (New Haven: Yale University Press, 1932). Brusilov tells his story well and is the only officer who gave his name to a strategic innovation, the surprise attack without preliminary bombardment. Von Hutier, Ludendorff, and even Haig (at Amiens) profited by it. Knox was a gifted observer and gives a graphic, pathetic account of how Russian bravery had as much to do with keeping the Germans too busy to capture Paris as the mishmash of blunders on the Western Front; General Golovin's book is heavy going for all but professionals.

For the war at sea, in addition to accounts in Baldwin and Falls, I recommend *The Victory at Sea*, by Rear Admiral William S. Sims, USN (New York: Doubleday, Page, 1920), and *The Battle of Jutland*, by Commander Holloway H. Frost (Annapolis: U.S. Naval Institute, 1936).

America

The Road to War, by Walter Millis (Boston: Houghton Mifflin, 1939).
Mr. Wilson's War, by John Dos Passos (New York: Doubleday & Co., 1962).
The Millis book is a brutal but truthful one, written in the passion of the moment.
The Dos Passos work, by possibly the ablest of American documentarians, has
the reflection in tranquillity needed to contemplate the tragedy of Woodrow Wilson.
Mr. Dos Passos lends his beautifully documented work the finality of the Greek
dramatists. "It saddens my soul with its chill."

The A.E.F. in France

My Experiences in the World War, by John J. Pershing, 2 volumes (New York:
Frederick A. Stokes Co., 1931). This is an indispensable work and, as John Dos
Passos says, a fine one. The documentarian wonders if Pershing wrote it all by
himself. He did.

The Great Crusade, by Joseph T. Dickman (New York: Appleton, 1927). Dickman is frank in writing of how he was denied any bulletins of information whatsoever on the war he knew he would presently fight.

A.E.F.: Ten Years Ago in France (New York: Dodd, Mead, 1928) and *Commanding an American Army* (Boston: Houghton Mifflin, 1925). These two books
by the former Lieutenant General Hunter Liggett, whom a niggardly Congress
reduced to two-star rank, are all that is needed to perceive the complexity devolving
upon an officer who commands a million fighting men. Liggett says that all he knew
of the war during its first two years, when he was stationed in the Philippines, was
derived by following the battle maps in the seaborne copies of the London *Times*.

Personalities and Reminiscences of the War (New York: Doubleday & Co., 1925).
Fighting Generals (Ann Arbor, Michigan: Edwards, 1944). *American Soldiers Also
Fought* (New York: Longmans, Green, 1936). These three books by Robert Lee
Bullard, the third one in collaboration with Earl Reeves, are written with the candor
—and sometimes the anger—of the foot soldier, the infantryman. Captain Falls
regrets that Bullard, principal organizer of A.E.F. schools, did not see more of
British staff work. It is a good thing he did not see a British corps commander refuse
to be interrupted at his dinner when Desmond Young arrived from Bourlon Wood
as messenger from Brigadier General "Boy" Bradbury, aged twenty-three and a V.C.,
imploring for aid after the Cambrai smash.

The History of the A.E.F. (New York: Doran, 1920). The Lieutenant Shipley
Thomas who questioned Corporal Feltporch at Cantigny came home a captain and
wrote the pioneer work, with few resources available. It deserves the plaudits due
a pioneer.

And They Thought We Wouldn't Fight (New York: Doran, 1918). Floyd Gibbons,
erratic, brilliant, humorous, has no standing whatsoever with historians. He has with
me.

Frederick Palmer's four books, which historians also disregard, are most valuable.
His portrait of *Newton D. Baker*, 2 volumes (New York: Dodd, Mead, 1931), hit
off that fine man exactly. *John J. Pershing, General of the Armies* (Harrisburg:
Military Service Publishing Company, 1948) is the only intimate work on Pershing
I've ever discovered. *Bliss, Peacemaker; the Life and Letters of General Tasker
Howard Bliss* (New York: Dodd, Mead, 1934) is worth a dozen dryasdusts by the
Wilson idolaters.

The New Englanders at Seicheprey are well taken care of by three writers, all
of whom show great felicity toward Major General Clarence Edwards and none toward General Pershing: *With the Yankee Division in France*, by Frank P. Sibley
(Boston: Little, Brown, 1919); *New England in France, 1917-1918*, by Emerson
Gifford Taylor (Boston: Houghton Mifflin, 1920); *History of the Yankee Division*,
by Harry A. Benwell (Boston: Cornhill, 1919). There is much good Doughboy
material in all of these.

History of the First Division During the War 1917-19, by The Society of the
First Division (Philadelphia: John C. Winston, 1922). Here is a fine account of

the stylized attack at Cantigny, very poorly mapped. The division records in the Library of Congress fill twelve immense volumes. (I once rented a room to hold some of them.)

The story of the first Paris Paraders is told in *Story of the 16th Infantry in France,* by the regimental chaplain (Frankfurt-on-Main, Germany: Martin Flock, 1919), *History of the Third Division,* by the division historians (Germany: Andernach-on-Rhine, 1919), *The Second Division,* New York Historical Commission (Second Division Association, 1937). The charge at Belleau Wood produced a minor classic, Thomas Boyd's *Through the Wheat* (New York: Scribner's, 1927), a thinly disguised autobiography by a Marine private. The confusion of the Wood will be found in Volume 6 of *The United States Army in the World War, 1917-19,* by the Historical Division, Department of the Army (Government Printing Office, 1948). Colonel Esposito laments the skimpy cartography, but the work was finished under a Secretary of War who was even miserly with postage stamps.

The efforts of various elements, including several Presidents of the United States, to break up the Navy-Marine team are revealed in a book which eventually got Pentagon clearance: *Soldiers of the Sea,* a history of the U.S. Marine Corps, 1775-1962, by Colonel Robert Debs Heinel, Jr., USMC, with a foreword by Captain B. H. Liddell Hart (Annapolis: United States Naval Institute, 1962). This is a beautiful book.

McAlexander's stand on the Marne with the 38th Infantry is well done by Dickman, et al. The Wooldridge fight, which has been written down many times, is best told by himself in *The Giants of the Marne,* by Major J. W. Wooldridge, USA (Salt Lake City: The Sea Gull Press, 1923). The Soissons counterattack is graphic in a flamboyant piece of writing by the late Colonel John W. Thomason, USMC, in *Fix Bayonets!* (New York: Scribner's, 1926). Many old Doughboys did not like this book, because it dealt exclusively with the Marine brigade and the Moroccans. But it could apply to any of the Yank brigades there.

Americans All—The Rainbow at War, official history of the 42nd Division, by Henry J. Reilly (Columbus, Ohio: F. J. Heer, 1936). For a witty book on the 42nd's many characters, see *War Bugs,* by Charles MacArthur (New York: Doubleday, Doran, 1929). *California Rainbow Memories,* by E. J. Sadler (Los Angeles: privately printed, 1925), is an account of a Signal Corps Field Signal Battalion. *Diary of a Rainbow Veteran,* by Elmer W. Sherwood (Terre Haute: Moore-Langen, 1929), is valuable for its portrayal of the relation between supporting troops and infantry, and for its description of a mounted man's care of his horse. Also see *Chaplain Duffy of the Sixty-Ninth Regiment,* by Ella M. E. Flick (Philadelphia: Dolphin Press, 1935).

For the Pennsylvanians (28th Division), see *The Iron Division,* by H. G. Proctor (Philadelphia: John C. Winston, 1919).

The 4th and 32nd divisions are honored respectively in *The Fourth Division,* by Christian A. Bach, issued by the Division (Garden City, New York: Country Life Press, 1920), and *The 32nd Division in the World War,* by the Michigan and Wisconsin historians (Milwaukee: Wisconsin Printing Company, 1920). The latter was written when there was still bigotry against some in Lieutenant von Buy's classifications. It is a good one, filled with Doughboy lore such as "When a Boche meets a Boche," etc.

History of the Seventy-Seventh Division, by division historians. This work, well done, is largely by its chief editor, Major Julius Ochs Adler (New York: Winthrop, Hollenbeck & Crawford, 1919). I believe the account of fighting from the Second Marne through to Sedan is his, notably his account of the "Lost Battalion."

The Victorious 77th Division, by Lieutenant Arthur McKeogh (New York: John H. Eggers, 1919). This was the lieutenant who shot his way out of the German bivouac at Charlevaux Mill. He does not mention his feat. He was publisher's go-between for Pershing, and used to moan to me that the old General of the Armies would never get it finished. He suffered much from the antipreparedness idiocies of the Twenties, although not as much as I, who am officially listed in one Marine Corps history as "a leader" of the pacifist group. (I belonged to an American Legion Post at the time.) There are many accounts of the "Lost Battalion," the latest being a quotation from ex-Sergeant Walter Baldwin, by Richard Hanser and Hy

Stockton, in "Alamo of the Argonne," *True* magazine, December, 1960. The then Corporal Baldwin's account of its officers and men is the best I ever read.

The Saint-Mihiel attack is fully documented in regimental histories, and a study of Plate No. 68, *West Point Atlas*, shows its true lateral worth to Foch. For those who discount its importance, try Hindenburg's opinion of the defeat here in volume 8, *The United States Army in the World War*. Also see *The Reminiscences of a Marine*, by Major General John A. Lejeune (Philadelphia: Dorrance & Co., 1930).

The opening day, Argonne-Meuse, is fully documented by all elements taking part. Frederick Palmer, who spent six months walking the field, is best on matters attending September 26, 1918, in *Our Greatest Battle* (New York: Dodd, Mead, 1919). For desertions, see Pershing's diary, Bullard and Major General Robert Alexander, USA (ret.), *Memories of the World War 1917-1918* (New York: Macmillan, 1931). Alexander was the toughest-minded of all Pershing's generals. Contrast our secrecy with the eventual candor of Sir Philip Gibbs in *Now It Can Be Told* (New York: Harper & Brothers, 1920) and Robert Graves in his introduction to *The Enormous Room* in the unexpurgated English edition of e. e. cummings' pioneer work (London: Jonathan Cape, 1930). This book, dealing with French prisons for defeatists, traitors, and spies, is the work of an artist who suffered unjustly in several of them. It is a dark and sullen stream in human conduct, and greatly affecting.

The Blanc Mont attack is finely detailed in General Lejeune's book. Hanson E. Ely, to my great regret, wrote no account of it. For the Saint-Quentin Canal effort, four books are necessary. *The Story of the 27th Division*, by Major General John F. O'Ryan, 2 volumes (New York: Wynkoop, Hollenbeck & Crawford, 1921). This most elaborate of Doughboy division histories is probably the best. An accompanying volume of snapshots, *The Pictorial Record of the 27th Division*, edited by Alexander Starlight (New York: Harper & Brothers, 1919), could bear reissue, if only for the hirsute hilarity of the shots. For the 30th Division, see *The Thirtieth Division in the World War*, by Elmer A. Murphy and Robert S. Thomas (Leponto, Ark: Old Hickory Publishing Co., 1936). Colonel John H. Kerr has left his sheaf showing the proficiency of British-trained Yank staffs which is in the Hoover Library at Stanford University.

Sergeant York, His Own Life Story and War Diary, edited by Tom Skeyhill (New York: Doubleday, Doran, 1928). An amusing corollary is found in the late Brigadier General Theodore Roosevelt Jr.'s "The Sword of the Lord and of Gideon," in his much neglected *Rank and File: True Stories of the Great War* (New York: Scribner's, 1938). The Wilsonites gave this gallant soldier a bad time between wars, though it was his brigade which met the shock of the Hermann Goerings in Sicily, and he himself died of exhaustion shortly after Normandy's D-Day.

The latest account of the immortal ex-Sergeant Samuel G. Woodfill is well done by Avram Davidson in "Greatest Soldier in the AEF," *Cavalier* magazine (August, 1960). Lowell Thomas, who knew Woodfill intimately and wrote the original work on him, *Woodfill of the Regulars* (New York: Doubleday, Doran, 1929), adds a vivid description to close Mr. Davidson's fine article: "Tall, powerful, square-jawed, clear-eyed . . . He could start out across a wild country and come in at night with a mountain goat that he had followed over the ranges and brought down from a distance of a mile or so . . . as a fighting man, well, he looked like the sort who could handle any situation—do it alone."

The action of the two Yank divisions, the 37th and 91st, in crossing the Scheldt River has never been fully documented, although "they sure as hell crossed it."

The Negro troops, too, suffer from a lack of literary effort. Good books on them are: *From Harlem to the Rhine*, by Arthur W. Little (New York: Covici-Friede, 1936); *Negro Combat Troops in the World War*, by Chester D. Heywood (Worcester, Mass.: Commonwealth Press, 1929); and the Herculean labors of the Service of Supply are described by the man who cracked the whip in *The American Army in France*, by James G. Harbord (Boston: Little, Brown, 1936).

For the air-minded I recommend *Fighting the Flying Circus*, by Edward V. Rickenbacker (New York: Frederick A. Stokes Co., 1919). This little book is careless, candid, and charming. *Winged Defense*, by William E. Mitchell (New York: G. P. Putnam's Sons, 1925). Mitchell wrote well and profusely. At Cal Tech, Pasadena, there is a shelf of his publications, including one article in which Secretary of the

Navy Josephus Daniels offered to stand on the deck of a battleship while Mitchell tried to bomb it. To the delight of the Secretary's family, he did not stand on the deck of the German battleship *Ostfreisland*, off Hampton Roads, when Billy Mitchell sank it without a trace, twenty years before Pearl Harbor. I list these two books here, for our air fighting really began at the Second Battle of the Marne.

Miscellany

First Call, by Arthur Guy Empey (New York: G. P. Putnam's Sons, 1918). This was an instructional book by an American transfer who had stayed alive with the British. It excellently marks the contrast between enlisted men of the two English-speaking nations.

The Story of the First Gas Regiment, by James Thayer Addison (Boston: Houghton Mifflin, 1919).

In *Gas Warfare* (New York: Duell, Sloan and Pearce, 1942) Colonel Alden H. Waitt compares American and German gases used at the front.

Hugh Young, by Hugh Hampton Young (New York: Harcourt Brace, 1940).

Dr. Alice Gregory, one of America's first women to break the all-male barrier of the medical profession at the turn of the century, served as a surgeon with the French in forward dressing stations and hospitals. In an unpublished and untitled memoir she has an excellent description of the agonies of the Dakin-Carrel solution.

A fine account of the meetings between Kitchener and Marchand, amidst a week of hypocritical gallantries, is found in Alan Moorehead's *The Blue Nile* (New York: Harper & Row, 1962), a companion book to his equally brilliant *The White Nile* (Harper & Brothers, 1960).

Bruce Catton's description of U. S. Grant is taken from *Grant Moves South* (Boston: Little, Brown, 1960).

The Years of the Sky Kings, by Arch Whitehouse (New York: Doubleday & Co., 1959). This book, by an ex-enlisted man who rose to fame in the R.A.F. as a lieutenant, is the frankest, most iconoclastic of all books on the feats of the 1914-1918 pilots, giving them all their brave due, and relentless in its hard-hitting accounts. Quentin Reynolds is worth a salute for his *They Fought for the Sky* (New York: Rinehart, 1957), which is the other side of Arch Whitehead's medal.

The over-all reference to all Doughboy activities is the painstaking Library of Congress checklist on all Doughboy literature and other materials on the First World War: Code No. R 016. 9403. In addition, there is *Order of Battle of the United States Land Forces in the World War—AEF, Divisions* (Historical Section, Army War College, GPO, 1931).

INDEX